CORPORATE INFORMATION SYSTEMS MANAGEMENT
The Issues Facing Senior Executives

D0124535

CORPORATE INFORMATION SYSTEMS MANAGEMENT
The Issues Facing Senior Executives

Fourth Edition

Lynda M. Applegate

F. Warren McFarlan

James L. McKenney

All of the
Graduate School of Business Administration
Harvard University

IRWIN

Chicago • Bogotá • Boston • Buenos Aires • Caracas
London • Madrid • Mexico City • Sydney • Toronto

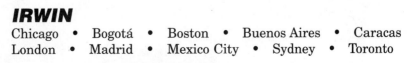

© Richard D. Irwin, a Times Mirror Higher Education Group, Inc. company, 1983, 1988, 1992, and 1996

Irwin Book Team

Publisher: *Tom Casson*
Senior sponsoring editor: *Rick Williamson*
Editorial assistant: *Carrie Berkshire*
Marketing manager: *Michelle Hudson*
Production supervisor: *Lara Feinberg*
Assistant manager, graphics: *Charlene R. Perez*
Project editor: *Paula M. Buschman*
Designer: *Matthew Baldwin*
Compositor: *Carlisle Communications, Ltd.*
Typeface: *10/12 Century School Book*
Printer: *R. R. Donnelley & Sons Company*

**Times Mirror
Books**

Library of Congress Cataloging-in-Publication Data

Applegate. Lynda M.
    Corporate information systems management : the issues facing
senior executives / Lynda M. Applegate, F. Warren McFarlan, James L.
McKenney. — 4th ed.
        p.   cm.
    Includes bibliographical references (p.   ) and indexes.
    ISBN 0-256-18213-2
    1. Management information systems.   I. McFarlan, F. Warren
(Franklin Warren)   II. McKenney, James L.   III. Corporate
information systems management. 1992.   IV. Title.
    T58.6.C674   1996
    658.4'038—dc20   95–39049

Printed in the United States of America
1 2 3 4 5 6 7 8 9 0 DO 2 1 0 9 8 7 6 5

To Karen, Mary, Paul, and Christopher

Preface

Corporate Information Systems Management: The Issues Facing Senior Executives, Fourth Edition, is written for students and managers who desire an overview of contemporary information systems technology (IT)—computer, telecommunications, and office systems—management. It explains the relevant issues of effective management of information services activities and highlights the areas of greatest potential application of the technology. No assumptions are made concerning the reader's experience with IT, but it is assumed that the reader has some course work or work experience in administration or management.

Our purpose is to provide perspective on the business management implications of the information explosion—as evidenced by the doubling of the number of volumes in the Library of Congress between 1933 and 1966, another doubling between 1967 and 1979, and yet another doubling by 1987. Huge leaps in the growth of scientific knowledge have stimulated a dramatic increase in the number of new products based on new information technologies that range from the sophisticated super computer to the humble, ubiquitous facsimile machine to the exploding presence of the Internet. These products have influenced the very heart of a corporation's strategy and operations, and they will continue to do so. In many cases, the firm's competitiveness and its very survival are at stake. The radical changes in IT are coupled with the increasingly global nature of business; this puts an enormous burden on individual managers to keep abreast of events and to make intelligent decisions and plans. The broad objective of this book is to help managers harness the power of new technologies to enable them to make better decisions and more effectively manage their firms, thereby enabling them to compete more effectively.

Since the first edition of this book appeared in 1983, IT and its applications have continued to evolve dramatically. This fourth edition addresses this evolution by emphasizing issues related to development of an IT-enabled strategy and organization design that permits a firm to simultaneously achieve the scale, scope, and efficiency that come from being large and the flexibility, speed, and responsiveness of being small. We highlight the special challenges related to electronic networking within and between organizations and pay particular attention to the key enabling technologies (e.g., client-server architecture, the Internet, groupware) required to implement the information infrastructure of the 1990s. Finally, we focus on a variety of options for managing the information resource—from "insourcing" to "outsourcing." This book will help present and future managers identify, implement, and deliver effective information services.

Corporate Information Systems Management, Fourth Edition, is organized around a management audit of the information services activity. This management audit details all the questions that should be asked in identifying whether a firm is appropriately using and controlling IT. The book's text, examples, tables, and figures convey and illustrate key conceptual frameworks. Chapter 1 presents an overview of the key questions to ask in assessing the effectiveness of an IT activity. Chapter 2 then presents frameworks we have found useful for analyzing and structuring problems in the field. Subsequent chapters show how IT can best be applied and how the IT activity can best be organized, planned, and controlled.

The material in this book is the outgrowth of directed field-based research we have conducted at the Harvard Business School since the early 1970s. We thank Dean John H. McArthur for making the time and resources available for this work.

We are particularly indebted to the many firms and government organizations that provided us with much time and insight during the course of our research. All of the examples and concepts in this book are based on observation of actual practice. Without the cooperation of these organizations, it would have been impossible to prepare this Fourth Edition.

We are especially grateful for the many valuable suggestions and insights provided us by our Harvard Business School colleagues Bill Bruns, Jim Cash, Peter Hagstrom, Richard Nolan, Donna Stoddard, John Sviokla, and Shoshana Zuboff as well as Professors Eric Clemons of the Wharton School, Janis Gogan of Bentley College, Benn Konsynski of Emory University, Charley Osborn of Babson College, and Keri Pearlson and Sirkka Jarvenpaa of the University of Texas/Austin. In addition, we acknowledge the valuable work of our doctoral students and research assistants Melinda Conrad, Kevin Davis, Carin Knoop, Chris Marshall, C. J. Meadows, Katherine Seger-Weber, and H. Jeff Smith. Lynn Salerno and Bernard Avishai, in their editorial capacity at the *Harvard Business Review,* and editors Barbara Feinberg and Paul McDonald provided valuable assistance. We would also like to express our appreciation to Maureen Donovan, Mary Kennedy, and Elayne Nascimento, who typed and edited numerous versions of the work.

Lynda M. Applegate, F. Warren McFarlan, James L. McKenney

Contents

11. A Portfolio Approach to Information Technology Development   264

12 Transnational IT Issues   280

The Challenge of Information Systems Technology

INTRODUCTION TO IT MANAGEMENT

The rapid evolution and spread of information systems technology (IT)[1] during the last 40 years is challenging both business and IT management to rethink the very nature of the business. New industry players are emerging (e.g., cable operators, systems integrators), and new internal organizational structures are being defined. Major investments in computer hardware and software are required to capture the benefits of powerful new technologies. Systems are being developed that profoundly affect how firms operate and compete; not only large corporations, but also mid-size and very small firms (that is, under $1 million in sales) are feeling the impact. IT's influence in large corporations is pervasive, affecting the smallest departments and managerial decision-making processes to an extent not even visualized 10 years ago.

Because many senior managers received their educations and early work experiences before the wide-scale introduction of computer technology, or in environments where the capabilities of IT were very different than those of today, they often fail to understand technology and lack sufficient grasp of the issues to provide appropriate managerial direction. In addition, many IT managers, given their early experiences with technologies so different from those of the 1990s, are also finding themselves unprepared to deal with current issues. (For example, understanding the programming challenges of

---

[1]In this book, IT refers to the technologies of computers and telecommunications (including data, voice, graphics, and full motion video).

mainframe-based COBOL—a systems development language that is still in common use within many organizations in the 1990s—does not prepare a person to deal with the challenge of implementing systems based on client-server architectures, object-oriented programming languages, and other key technologies for the 1990s.)

Over the past decade and a half, virtually all of the frameworks that guide IT management practice have been challenged. IT managers must continually struggle to address day-to-day operating problems, while assimilating new technologies and managerial approaches. IT managers who are not committed to continuing personal development quickly become obsolete; those who cannot similarly develop their employees find their businesses obsolete.

This book is aimed at two different audiences. The first is the general manager who is responsible for providing direction for all business activities. For this group we offer frameworks for evaluating IT activity in the firm. The book defines policies that must be executed and provides insights into the specific challenges of execution. Methods for integrating IT management with the overall activities of the firm are suggested.

For its second audience, senior IT management, this book provides an integrated view of IT management issues for the 1990s. Key frameworks for organizing and understanding a bewildering cluster of operational details are identified. The focus for IT senior managers is to move from analysis of the "bark composition of individual trees" to an overall perspective of the IT "forest" and its management challenge. The book thus integrates the needs of two quite different—though operationally interdependent—audiences and provides a common perspective and language for communication.

It would be a serious mistake to think of the problems of IT management as totally different from those found in other business areas. The issues of IT organization, for example, can be approached using general organization design theory.[2] Issues of IT strategy formulation are heavily influenced by theories of industry analysis[3] and business planning.[4] Notions of budgeting, performance measurement, transfer pricing, profit center management, and so forth, from the general field of management control are also relevant here.[5] In addition, the fields of operations and technology management

---

[2]For example, see P. Lawrence and J. Lorsch, *Organizations* (Boston, MA: Harvard Business School Press, 1986).

[3]For example, see M. Porter, *Competitive Advantage* (NY: Free Press, 1985) and A. Chandler, *Scale and Scope: The Dynamics of Industrial Capitalism* (Cambridge, MA: The Belknap Press of Harvard University Press, 1990).

[4]For example, see J. Bower, *Managing the Resource Allocation Process: A Study of Corporate Planning and Investment* (Boston, MA: Division of Research, Harvard Business School Classics, 1986) and J.B. Quinn, H. Mintzberg, and R. James, *The Strategy Process* (Englewood Cliffs, NJ: Prentice Hall, 1988).

[5]For example, see R. Anthony, *The Management Control Function* (Boston, MA: Harvard Business School Press, 1988) and K. Arrow, *"Control in Large Organizations,"* in *Behavioral Aspects of Accounting,* edited by M. Schiff and A. Lewin (Englewood Cliffs, NJ: Prentice Hall, 1974).

have aided our understanding of the management of IT operations (e.g., networks and data centers).[6] Insights from all of these disciplines are relevant for our understanding of IT management issues.

Concepts of IT Management

Integrating the IT "business" into the rest of the firm poses many organizational design and strategy formulation challenges. The following four concepts are essential for an understanding of the successful management of IT.

Strategic Relevance. The strategic impact of the IT activity varies among industries and firms and, over time, within an individual firm. Like the telephone, IT can be used in all firms to enhance operations; but, in a growing number of firms in the 1990s, it is also a core differentiator and strategy enabler. Further, IT may be more significant to some operating units and functions within a firm than to others. This notion of a variation in strategic relevance is critical for understanding the diversity of potential IT management and operational approaches.

Corporate Culture. The corporate culture—embodied by the organization's shared values and operationalized in its processes (e.g., the approach to corporate planning, philosophy of control, and speed of core product/technological change)—influences how the IT business should be managed. In addition, there are also generic tools that define the "state-of-the-art"; client-server IT architectures and graphical user interfaces are examples of generic IT tools for the mid-1990s. Combining these generic tools with the values, culture, and processes of a particular firm is the art of management. A combination that works in one corporate environment can fail abysmally in another.

Contingency. IT management is also influenced by the notion of contingency. Because IT management systems were often introduced during the 1960s and early 1970s to simplify information-intensive transaction processing, structured and mechanistic approaches resulted in great improvement. But as these new approaches and tools were assimilated into the firm, the initial surge of value from their introduction often gave way to frustration. In many cases, because of their inherent rigidity, these approaches answered some types of challenges very well and others not at all. For example, the emergence of PCs in the 1980s enabled end-user approaches to information processing, which, in turn, posed challenges to

---

[6]For example, see K. Clark and T. Fujimoto, *Product Development Performance* (Boston, MA: Harvard Business School Press, 1991) and J. Heskett, *Managing in the Service Economy* (Boston, MA: Harvard Business School Press, 1986).

prior mainframe-based systems and structures. More complex and flexible IT management approaches and tools were required to fit with the needs of a complex, changing business environment. As we face the challenge of managing the complex organizational designs of the 1990s, which are enabled by complex, distributed IT architectures, the notion of contingency will become even more important.

Technology Transfer.   The dramatic rate of IT evolution demands careful management attention. Failure to successfully manage the introduction and assimilation of emerging technologies results in a costly and ineffective collection of disjointed "islands of technology." Since changes in the IT infrastructure often directly affect organizational performance, implementation problems can also be catastrophic. Success can only come if people are able to change the way they act and the way they think. As a result, IT must be considered a tool to expand the "intelligence" of the people within the organization. Without a concomitant change at the individual level, technical success is likely to be accompanied by administrative failure.

CHALLENGES IN MANAGING IT ASSIMILATION

An understanding of the following factors that make the assimilation of IT a particularly challenging task is essential if a sensible IT management strategy is to be developed.

A Young Technology

At least in its modern form (with high-speed and high-performance computers and networks), IT has had a very short life.[7] As a result, the theory of IT management is still in its infancy; in contrast, management disciplines such as accounting, finance, and production have had thriving bodies of theory and practice in place since the turn of the century. Throughout the 1900s, significant changes in knowledge and theory have occurred in these established disciplines and have been assimilated into an organized field of thought. Evolution, not revolution, has been the challenge in these fields.

The challenge in IT, conversely, has been that of harnessing an exploding body of knowledge within a very short time frame. Not surprisingly, the half-life of administrative knowledge in this environment has been quite short. While building on past knowledge, most of the theories and frameworks discussed in this book have been developed within the past decade and a half. Indeed, this Fourth Edition differs markedly from its predeces-

---

[7]The computer was introduced in most large firms during the late 1950s and 1960s.

sor, which was published only three years earlier. We expect that this knowledge explosion will continue (and anticipate the need to significantly revise this book within the next few years).

Technological Growth

Another source of administrative challenge is the fact that the field has undergone sustained and dramatic growth in the cost performance of its technologies. Over a billion-fold improvement in processing and storage capacity has occurred since 1953, and the rate of change is expected to continue through the 1990s and early 21st century. (As with all technologies, a point of maturity will be reached, but we are not yet there.) Further complicating this, some core technologies—such as CPU size and speed— have grown explosively, while others, such as software development tools, have grown more slowly.

The technology explosion has enabled the development of new value-added applications, as well as improvements in old ones. One painful aspect of this has been that yesterday's strategic coup may be today's high-overhead, inefficient liability—outperformed by those "fast followers" that improved on the original design. The natural tendency to resist change has been exacerbated by the prevailing accounting practice of writing off software expense as it is incurred, rather than capitalizing it and amortizing it over a period of years. These practices conceal two facts: (1) that the organization has an information asset and (2) that it is aging and often very inefficient.

IT End-User Coordination

The complexities of developing IT systems have created departments filled with specialists who remain with the firm even though the reasons for their presence have disappeared. Today, new terminology, such as *data center consolidation, global development,* and *outsourcing,* dominates debate on the organization of IT resources.

Specialist departments with specialized vocabularies inherently have a more difficult time developing close relationships with the users of their services; this has been a significant problem for IT and business management for many years. While the proliferation of new technologies has changed the nature of the dialogue, the technocrat-versus-generalist problem remains.

Specialization is required to develop expertise and competence within a given discipline, but, in the process, specialists often develop their own language systems. To communicate with each other, they use words such as *bits, bytes, DOS, CICS,* and so on, none of which have any meaning to general managers. At the same time, general managers have a quite different language that includes such terms as *liquidity, margin,* and *asset valuation*—terms that may not have meaning to IT specialists. While it is clear that the continued penetration of IT to all parts of the organization has helped communication between IT specialists and end users, substantial problems remain. New approaches to integrating IT and business are still required to address this long-standing problem.

For numerous reasons, education only partially addresses this technical versus generalist gap. For many college and high school students, a course on IT literacy involves writing a single, simplistic computer program and learning to use PC-based word-processing and spreadsheet packages. While these experiences may help to demystify the technology and expand confidence, they do not help develop the skills necessary to actively participate in managing the information resource of a firm. Similarly, experience within the business environment in preparing spreadsheet programs as a staff analyst or working with a word-processing package does not provide the necessary perspective on the issues involved in defining and managing large-scale database management systems and global telecommunications that are vital to the firm's success. More importantly, these educational and work experiences can provide a false sense of confidence—a little knowledge can be very dangerous.

In the past, some general managers were better able to deal with IT issues than others. One of our colleagues describes the world as being divided equally into two classes of people—"poets" and "engineers." This split, of course, is also evident in the ranks of general management. Recently, however, graphical user interfaces (for example, the interface found on the Apple Macintosh and on computers running Microsoft Windows) have made technology easily accessible to virtually everyone. Both the poets and the engineers can now gain firsthand experience with IT.

Specialization

The increased complexity of contemporary technology has created a number of IT subspecialties in increasingly narrow areas of expertise. This explosion of new knowledge and skills poses new managerial challenge. As IT evolved, the number of experts required to manage the wide range of application development languages, data management approaches, telecommunications methodologies, and operating environments proliferated, which in turn increased the complexity of coordination and control. Today, many organizations have given up attempting to build and maintain all of this specialized expertise inside the firm and are turning to the outside. For many this involves outsourcing portions, or in some cases, all of the IT activities. This, of course, challenges the firm to shift from internal to external approaches to coordination and control.

Shift in Focus

A fifth challenge is the significant shift in the types of applications being developed. Early applications that automated clerical and operational control functions (e.g., inventory management, airline seat reservations, and credit extension) were heavily focused on highly structured problems, such as transaction processing for payroll and order processing. In these instances, the efficiency benefits of the automation could be precisely specified. (Note: In some cases [for example, the airline reservation systems of the late 1970s and early 1980s], automation also led to improved decision making and radical change in the basis of competition within the industry that could not be fully specified in advance.)

Increasingly, today's uses of IT are targeted toward less structured types of problems (for example, decision support, electronic commerce). As a result, structured, objective analysis of the advantages is extraordinarily difficult. Often, investment and decisions are based on management judgment that, while exceedingly important, is difficult to quantify in a meaningful way. Although these applications offer the potential to dramatically transform organizations and industries, the lack of clear specification makes implementation very difficult. The need to simultaneously manage organizational and technological change within this environment of uncertainty has resulted in failure rates that exceed 70 percent.

The design and implementation of applications that transform work, processes, organizations, and industries require a very different approach than would be used to design and implement systems that automate existing business systems and structures. The detailed systems study, with its documentation and controls prior to programming, is often too rigid and fails to build the end-user commitment necessary for success. Interactive "joint application design" and "rapid prototyping" are proving to be the best approach when the goal is to transform organizational processes. These approaches also appear to be required when building systems to support end-user decision making and intelligence. These new applications and application development methodologies are also forcing a shift in the way projects are evaluated. This is not an argument for a more permissive approach to system design and evaluation, but rather a cry to be more involved and creative while maintaining discipline.

In combination, these factors create a very complex and challenging managerial environment. They form the backdrop for the discussions of specific managerial approaches in the succeeding chapters.

QUESTIONS FROM SENIOR MANAGEMENT

In viewing the health of an organization's IT activity, our research has indicated that senior managers often ask questions in six critical areas.

Four of these areas are essentially diagnostic in nature, whereas the remaining two are clearly action oriented.

1. Is the firm being affected competitively either by failing to implement required IT applications or by faulty implementation of strategic applications? Is the firm missing opportunities that, if properly executed, would give it a competitive edge? How important is IT to success in the industry? Failure to do well in a competitively important area is a significant problem; failure to perform well in a nonstrategic area is often less critical to the overall health of the firm.

2. Is the firm targeting its IT application development efforts effectively? Is it spending the right amount of money, and is it focusing on the appropriate applications? At times, management asks this question for the wrong reasons. We are sure that many are familiar with the following scenario. An industry survey that compares IT expenditures for a firm's leading competitors is circulated among the senior management team. Immediately, attention is focused on those dimensions in which the firm is distinctly different from its competitors—most often attention is focused on those areas where the firm is spending a significant amount more than the competitors. This causes great excitement. After much investigation, it is often discovered that either the company uses a different accounting system for IT than its competitors and therefore the numbers are not directly comparable (e.g., they have excluded telecommunications expenses from their figures while the firm has included them), or the company has a different strategy, geographical location, and/or mix of management strengths and weaknesses than its competitors, and, therefore, what competitors are or are not doing with IT is not directly comparable.

Raising the question of effectiveness is appropriate, but attempting to answer it solely with industry surveys of competitors' expenditures is not. The IT management challenge is much too complex. Similarly, the rules of thumb on expenditure levels have become much less useful as the range of technologies and opportunities has increased. For example, a major catalog company that worked tirelessly to translate its catalog onto CD/ROM less than one year ago is now looking at distributing the catalog electronically via the Internet, a nonviable alternative as recently as two years ago.

3. Is the IT asset of a firm being managed efficiently? Sometimes a firm is spending appropriately, but is not getting the appropriate productivity out of its hardware and staff resources. This is a particularly relevant issue in the 1990s, a decade that will be dominated both by extreme shortages in qualified IT professionals and by intensified international competition. On the one hand, the international global highway allows the firm to access competent development staff around the world (for example, in India and the Philippines) at a fraction of European and U.S. costs. On the other hand, unless standards are rigorously enforced, the new distributed IT architectures can lead to an explosion of support costs. (One recently studied financial services firm estimated that as many as 2,000 people were needed to keep its 18 e-mail systems and 15,000 networked PCs running reliably.)

4. Is the firm's IT activity sufficiently insulated against the risks of a major operational disaster? The appropriate level of protection varies by organization, relative to the level of strategic and operational dependence on IT. In most instances, business managers underestimate the degree to which their firms are dependent on IT. Even small interruptions in service can cause massive customer defections or significant—and costly—operational disruption. For example, a 2-minute interruption of the air traffic control system over La Guardia airport resulted in a 40-minute delay to landing aircraft.

5. Are IT and business leaders capable of dealing with the IT-related management challenges? Historically, senior business leaders have been quick to replace the IT senior management team for performance problems. While often the quickest and most apparent solution to the problem, the high turnover can exacerbate the underlying cause of the problems. Failure to identify and address the underlying problems can spell disaster for the new team that is brought in to "clean up the mess," and the cycle of poor performance continues. This same cycle of failure can also be seen in outsourcing arrangements; business management often erroneously believes that it can solve IT performance problems by "throwing the problem over the wall" to be fixed by an IT vendor. Without commitment to actively participate in problem definition and solution, the outsourcing relationship may also be doomed to failure. Clearly, the skills and expertise required to manage the information resources of a firm tend to evolve over time with the evolution of the technology and its potential uses within the firm; the leadership skills and perspectives appropriate today may not have worked in the past and may not work in the future.[8] In many situations, the problem is also compounded by a lack of suitable explicit performance-measurement standards (metrics) and objective data for assessing performance. As will be discussed in subsequent chapters, we believe the development and installation of these metrics are absolutely vital.

6. Are the IT resources appropriately placed in the firm?[9] Organizational issues such as where the IT resource should report, how development and hardware resources should be distributed within the company, what activities, if any, should be outsourced, and the existence and potential role of an executive steering committee are examples of topics of intense interest to senior management.

These questions are intuitive from the viewpoint of general management and flow naturally from its perspective and experience in dealing with other areas of the firm. We have not found them as stated to be easily researchable

---

[8]See Chapter 2 for a more thorough coverage of this issue.
[9]Chapters 6 through 10 deal with issues raised by this question.

or answerable in specific situations and have consequently neither selected them as the basic framework of the book nor attempted to describe specifically how each can be answered. Rather, we have selected a complementary set of questions that not only form the outline of the book but whose answers will give solutions to the earlier questions.

The next section briefly summarizes these questions and relates them to the outline of this book.

ISSUES IN INFORMATION TECHNOLOGY

The IT Environment

Has the firm changed its management process to deal with the new role IT now plays? The answers to the senior management questions are made especially difficult by the changing role and applications of IT.

Chapters 2, 3, 4, 5, and *6* define a very different role for IT in the 1990s than in the 1970s. Figure 1–1 explores the changing role by focusing on three items: the administrative framework for facilitating and controlling the assimilation of information technology, the primary target of IT applications, and the way IT applications have been justified. (A more in-depth discussion of this framework is presented in Chapter 6.)

Era I.   From the 1950s to the early 1970s, the manager of data processing was the single source for providing information processing services and for

FIGURE 1–1   The IT Environment

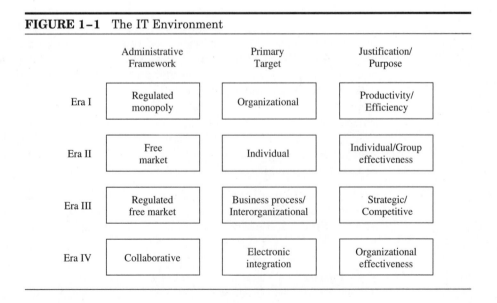

	Administrative Framework	Primary Target	Justification/ Purpose
Era I	Regulated monopoly	Organizational	Productivity/ Efficiency
Era II	Free market	Individual	Individual/Group effectiveness
Era III	Regulated free market	Business process/ Interorganizational	Strategic/ Competitive
Era IV	Collaborative	Electronic integration	Organizational effectiveness

managing technology expertise. To use an industrial analogy, IT operated as a "regulated monopoly." If someone wanted access to computing capabilities and technology expertise, there was no alternative but to go to the data processing manager. The primary focus of applications was organization-wide (payroll, accounting, production scheduling, and order entry). New applications were justified on either a cost-elimination or cost-displacement basis.

Era II.   Era II began with the introduction of minicomputers and time-sharing in the early 1970s. It was dramatically accelerated in the early 1980s by the personal computer, which introduced a wide range of new channels for users to acquire technology expertise and information processing capabilities. This led to a relatively "free market" for IT services—users no longer had to go to the IT manager to gain access to computer and communications technology. In Era II's free-market arena, the rigid top-down controls, developed and implemented in Era I, were no longer applicable. Individuals were the primary decision makers, and with sufficient discretionary resources to reinforce that independence, they could purchase computers that had 50 times the capability of earlier computers, at less than 1 percent of the price.

During this period, individual and work unit effectiveness became the key justification measure for project justification; but Era I applications and their administrative systems could not and did not disappear. Rather, the IT management environment was made more complex with the additional challenge of managing easily accessible, individually exploited technology concurrently with Era I technology.

Era III.   Era III is best distinguished by the justification/purpose column in Figure 1–1. A growing number of companies became aware of the opportunities to use IT to cause significant shifts in market share and competitive positioning and to produce organizational restructuring. These companies avoided choosing a specific side in the regulated versus free market debate. Rather, they attempted to create a "regulated free-market environment" where the primary objective was to exploit the awareness, knowledge, and expertise obtained during Era II in an effort to create dramatically different approaches to how business was conducted. Many times, these uses of technology transcended traditional company or industry boundaries. Other times, they enabled transformation of internal organizations and functions.

Era IV.   As discussed in Chapter 6, a new era, which we call the ubiquitous era of computing, is emerging in which the power of widely distributed, flexible information management systems and communication networks enables virtually instantaneous delivery of information and knowledge to the desktop (and laptop) of individuals located all over the globe. When combined with the seamless integration of data, voice, video, and graphics, managers will be able to communicate and share knowledge "any time, any place, and in any form." Today's explosive growth of the Internet suggests this is closer than had been anticipated.

IT Architecture and Organization

Is the firm's IT architecture and organization of IT resources evolving appropriately? Chapters 5, 6, 8, 10, and 12 are most closely aligned with senior managers' questions 5 and 6 listed earlier in the chapter. First and foremost, the "architecture" that defines the pattern of distribution of computer hardware, networks, software development resources, and databases within the corporation is examined in Chapter 6. These patterns of distribution have been well studied, and appropriate ways of thinking about them continue to be developed as new technological capabilities emerge.

Today, the technologies of computing and telecommunications are integrated with organizational design and industry issues. Resolving these architecture issues goes well beyond the technology itself and is heavily contingent on such influences as the corporate organization and culture, the leadership style of the chief executive officer (CEO), the importance of IT to achievement of corporate goals, and the current sophistication of IT management. Central administrative policies must ensure that a suitable, overall direction—the nature, intensity, and criticality of which vary widely among settings—is maintained.

Although the networked corporation is increasingly a reality, international coordination issues are more complicated than those in the domestic arena. Chapter 12 is devoted to discussing these international coordination issues, including staff availability, level of telecommunications sophistication, specific vendor support, geography and language, transborder data flows, national culture and sensitivity, and so forth. In particular, it focuses on new possibilities for getting work done via the international information highway.

Chapter 10 discusses the possibilities and risks of outsourcing portions or all of an organization's IT activity. In the 1970s, for medium-sized and large organizations, it was a matter of conventional wisdom and practice that a firm would have its own development staff and IT operations centers. In the 1990s, when only a small percentage of a firm's code is developed in-house and the IT development organization has become primarily an in-house systems integrator, these practices have undergone a sharp review and in many cases have changed.

Finally, there are issues of organization reporting chains, levels of reporting, IT leadership styles, and other coordinating processes, which we believe can be examined more thoroughly in the 1990s than a decade ago.

Although common questions and methods of analysis exist, very different answers will emerge in different organizational settings.

Appropriate controls over daily IT operations, as described in Chapter 8, ensure that both cost efficiency and operations reliability are achieved. IT operations activity represents a specialized form of manufacturing environment with unique problems. First, operations have moved from a primarily batch, job-shop style to a continuous-process manufacturing or utility style. Not only has this changed the way these tasks can best be organized, but it has dramatically altered the types of controls that are appropriate. Second, in a number of firms, the IT activity has embedded itself so deeply in the heart of the firm's operations that unevenness in its performance causes immediate operating problems. These firms need significantly greater controls and backup arrangements than firms with less dependence on IT.

The performance of operations can be measured on a number of dimensions: cost control, ability to meet batch report deadlines, peak-load, on-line response time, and speed of response to complaints or unexpected requests, and so forth. To optimize all of these simultaneously is impossible. Each firm needs to clearly identify its priorities before it can come up with a coherent operations strategy. Different firms will have quite different needs; hence, a search for a universal IT operations strategy and set of management tools represents a fruitless quest.

Management Processes

Are the firm's IT planning and control processes appropriate? The senior manager's questions of efficiency and, to a lesser degree effectiveness, are best addressed by ensuring that appropriate IT management processes, discussed in Chapter 9, are in place. The role of planning is to ensure that long-term direction is carefully delineated and that the hardware and staff resources necessary for implementation are obtained. Management control's role is to ensure that the appropriate short-term resource allocation decisions are made and that acquired resources are being utilized efficiently. The following issues are addressed:

1. The appropriate balance between user and IT responsibility for costs must be established. Decisions concerning whether IT will operate as a cost center, profit center, investment center, and so forth, are critical, as is the election of an appropriate IT transfer-pricing policy. Decisions change over time and are different for various organizations.

2. Firms must design and implement an appropriate IT budgeting policy. While many components of the IT budget are either fixed or transaction-driven in the short run, others are discretionary. These discretionary components need to be examined to ensure both that they are being allocated appropriately and that an appropriate balance is struck between the needs of many legitimate end users. This balance is necessary in a world where financial resources for projects are limited and project benefits in many cases are not easily quantifiable.

3. The appropriate level and frequency of IT performance monitoring must be established. Reporting should reflect performance against goals and also against objective standards wherever possible. Unfortunately, the move of IT operations from a primarily batch activity to an on-line or networked activity limits availability of well-defined, objective measures of performance and makes many traditional performance measurement approaches obsolete.

Project Management

Is the firm's project management process appropriate? The questions of efficiency and effectiveness are also addressed through analysis of the project management process in Chapter 11. The 1980s generated a plethora of so-called project management processes and methodologies, some of which have helped to rationalize a formerly very diverse area. The installation of these methodologies, while an obvious improvement, has created a new set of challenges.

The first challenge lies in the area of implementation risk. The advocates of these project management methodologies have implied that, by utilizing their approach, implementation risk will be eliminated. A careful examination of the long list of partial and major project fiascoes in the past decade suggests clearly that this is not the case. As described in Chapter 11, our contention is that project implementation risk not only exists, but also can be measured; a decision can be made about the acceptability of the venture long before the majority of funds must be committed to a project development effort. In the same vein, it is possible and appropriate to talk about the "aggregate implementation risk profile" of the portfolio of application development and maintenance projects. A common framework for defining and managing implementation risk can lead to a common language that can be used by business managers, users, and IT managers throughout the IT implementation process. It also provides a more structured and valid context for after-the-fact performance assessment.

The second challenge revolves around the fact that different types of projects are best attacked by quite different management methodologies. A single methodology can be a significant improvement over the anarchy and chaos that often preceded its introduction. Several years of its use, however, can create a straitjacket environment. A single approach may fit one kind of project very well and others considerably less well. Organization structure within a project team, types of user interfaces, leadership skill, and planning and control approaches legitimately differ by type of project. Today, it is clear that the most appropriate management approach for any project should flow out of the project's innate characteristics.

IT Strategy

Is the firm competitive and effectively focused on the right questions? We believe this question is best answered by looking carefully at the IT strategy formulation process covered in Chapter 3 and the planning process discussed in Chapter 9. The design and evolution of these processes turned out to be more complicated than anticipated in the early 1980s, when some fairly prescriptive ways of dealing with them were identified. Elements creating this complexity can be classified in three general categories.

1. The first is an increased recognition that IT plays very different strategic roles in different companies. These strategic roles significantly influence the planning systems and structures (who should be involved, the level of time and financial resources to be devoted to it, and so forth) and its interconnection to the corporate strategy and formulation processes. In firms where new IT developments are critical to the introduction of new products and the achievement of major operating efficiencies or accelerated competitive response times, senior management must spend more time overseeing IT strategy and operations than in firms where this is not the case. Additionally, the evolution towards a more ubiquitous networked world, discussed in Chapters 4 and 5, requires a solid set of standards and disciplines to ensure flexible, yet cost-effective, interconnectivity.

2. The second category of issues relates to IT and user familiarity with the nuances of the specific technologies being examined. The use of technologies with which both IT and user staffs have extensive experience can be planned in considerable detail and with great confidence. To IT and the users, newer technologies pose very different problems. Because in any given year a company will deal with a mix of older and newer technologies, the strategy formulation task is very complicated. For example, the introduction of laptop CD/ROM with full-motion satellite-linked video and interactive management support systems calls for exact timing to balance risk, cost, and market opportunity.

3. The third category of issues relates to the specific corporate culture. The nature of the corporate planning process—for example, the formality versus informality of organizational decision making and planning and the geographic and organizational distance of IT management from senior management—influence how IT planning can best be done. These issues suggest that IT planning, as important as it is, must be evolutionary and highly individualistic to fit different corporations.

The IT Business

Is the overall direction of the IT asset appropriately linked to general management and middle management needs and values? Chapter 13, the last chapter, integrates this discussion by considering the challenge of managing IT development and diffusion from the perspective of a business within a business; it emphasizes the present marketing posture of the IT business.

We see the early years of IT as unavoidably captured by the term *R&D:* "Can it work, and can we learn to make it work?" Subsequent years were characterized by start-up production: "Can large projects be managed in a way that will create useful, reliable services in a period of rapid growth when technology is new and changing?" During this period, IT managers learned to manage a service organization with a rapidly evolving technology, and the applications proliferated. Today's environment is characterized by focused marketing. The challenge is to carefully blend the new product opportunities posed by new technologies with the changing needs of customers.

CONCLUSION

This chapter has identified, from a managerial viewpoint, the key forces shaping the IT environment and senior management's most frequent questions in assessing the activity. In this final section, we would like to leave you with some questions we believe both IT management and general management should ask on a periodic basis—every six months or so. They are a distillation of the previous analysis and, we believe, a useful managerial shorthand.

1. Do the perspective and skills of the IT team, IT users, and general management team fit the firm's changing strategy and organization and the IT applications, operating environment, and management processes? There are no absolute final solutions—only transitional ones.
2. Is the firm organized to identify, evaluate, and assimilate new information technologies on a timely basis? In this fast-moving field, an internally focused, low-quality staff can generate severe problems. Unprofitable, unwitting obsolescence (from which it is hard to recover) is terribly easy here. There is no need for a firm to adopt leading-edge technology (indeed, many are ill equipped to do so), but it is inexcusable not to be aware of its possibilities.
3. Are the strategic planning, the management control, and the project management systems—the three main management systems for integrating the IT environment with the firm—defined and appropriately implemented and managed?
4. Are the security, priority-setting, and control systems for IT operations appropriate for the role it plays in the firm?
5. Are appropriate organizational structures and coordinating mechanisms in place to ensure IT is appropriately aligned to the needs of the firm?

To help answer these questions, this book presents a framework for analysis that encompasses four organizing concepts: *strategic relevance, corporate culture, contingent action planning,* and *managed IT technology transfer.* In each of the areas of IT—organization, strategic planning, management control, project management, and operations—we will examine the implications of these concepts. We realize that today's world is diverse—people with varied ideas, goals, skills, and backgrounds work within organizations with different strategies, organization designs, processes, and cultures; and they are supported by an ever-expanding set of increasingly powerful technologies. We have attempted to identify a sequence of frameworks that allows better analysis of the problems and issues facing organizations in relation to IT. In order to formulate realistic action plans, readers must apply this discussion to their own business situations.

Chapter

2

Manageable Trends

UNDERLYING THEMES

The preceding chapter identified key issues that make the assimilation of information technology (IT) challenging and discussed four implications of these issues for management practice. This book is designed to provide a comprehensive treatment of these key issues[1] by focusing on six themes that reflect current insight into management practice and guidance for administrative action. This chapter discusses the nature and implications of each theme. Because they represent what we believe to be the most useful ways to think about the forces driving how IT is being used and managed within firms in the 1990s, these themes also provide the organizational basis for the chapters that follow. Our expectation, as mentioned in Chapter 1, is that additional experience and research with existing technologies and the emergence of new technologies will inevitably produce new—as yet unimagined—uses of IT in subsequent years.

Six manageable trends will be discussed in this chapter:

1. *IT influences different industries, and the firms within them, in different ways.* The type of impact strongly influences which IT management tools and approaches are appropriate for a firm.
2. *Telecommunications, computing, and software technologies are evolving rapidly and will continue to evolve.* This evolution will continue to destabilize the economic viability of existing IT-based systems and offer new types of IT application opportunities.

---

[1]An analysis of these areas for a firm, complete with appropriate recommendations, is referred to as an IT management audit.

3. *The time required for successful organizational learning about IT limits the practical speed of change.* As the organization gains familiarity with a new technology, management's assimilation methods must change.

4. *External industry, internal organizational, and technological changes are pressuring firms to "buy" rather than "make" IT software and services.* This shift in the nature of the IT make-or-buy decision creates major IT management challenges.

5. *While all elements of the IT system life cycle remain, new technologies both enable and require dramatically different approaches to execution.* This significantly increases the complexity of the IT management challenge.

6. *Managing the long-term evolution of the partnership between general management, IT management, and user management is crucial for capturing the value of new IT-enabled business opportunities.*

THEME 1: STRATEGIC IMPACT

It is increasingly clear that different industries are affected in fundamentally different ways by IT. In many industries, IT has enabled massive transformation of the strategy of the firm and the "value chain" of activities through which it is executed. Technology is now a core component of many of the products that we use every day. For example, today's car now includes over 50 IT components, and over 800 programmers at a major defense contractor are required to develop software for the control panels of airplanes and submarines; in addition, IT has revolutionized our notion of service. Supported by IT, retailers like L.L. Bean now distribute catalogs of their products—previously available only in standard paper format, now in interactive, multimedia CD-ROM and over the Internet—directly to customers who can order products by telephone (or the Internet) and pay for them using secure financial credit networks. Within the firm, computer-aided design and manufacturing (CAD/CAM); factory automation and control systems; and IT-enabled purchasing, distribution, sales, and marketing systems have enabled firms to simultaneously compete on quality, speed, and cost. The ability to create new IT-based products and services and to streamline, integrate, and time-synchronize internal operating and management processes is transforming industries and the firms within them. As industry leaders "raise the bar," many firms are finding that in the 1990s IT has become a strategic necessity.

Table 2–1 presents a series of questions for managers as they contemplate IT marketing (customer focus) opportunities. If the answer to most of the questions is no, IT probably would play a rather limited role in transforming marketing. Conversely, if the answer is yes, technology has played or will play a major role. Table 2–2 provides a similar set of questions for managers contemplating IT opportunities in operations.

TABLE 2–1 Marketing (Customer Focus) Question for Managers

- Does the business require a large number of routine interactions each day with vendors for ordering or requesting information?
- Is product choice complex?
- Do customers need to compare competitors' product/service/price configurations simultaneously?
- Is a quick customer decision necessary?
- Is accurate, quick customer confirmation essential?
- Would an increase in multiple ordering or service sites provide value to the customer?
- Are consumer tastes potentially volatile?
- Do significant possibilities exist for product customization?
- Is pricing volatile (can/should salesperson set price at point of sale)?
- Is the business heavily regulated?
- Can the product be surrounded by value-added information to the customer?
- Is the real customer two or more levels removed from the manufacturer?

TABLE 2–2 Operations Questions for Managers

- Is there large geographic dispersion in sourcing?
- Is high technology embedded in the product?
- Does the product require a long, complex design process?
- Is the process of administering quality control standards complex?
- Is the design integration between customer and supplier across company boundaries complex?
- Are there large buffer inventories in the manufacturing process?
- Does the product require complex manufacturing schedule integration?
- Are time and cost savings possible?
- Is there potential for major inventory reductions?
- Are direct and indirect labor levels high?

Figure 2–1 shows different approaches to the use of IT by industry leaders in different industries. In the airline industry, for example, the reservation system, heavily used by travel agencies, has given its leading developers, American Airlines and United Airlines, major marketing (customer focus) and operational advantages. It has also enabled better aircraft utilization, new services such as "frequent flyer" programs, and the development of joint incentive programs with hotels and car rental agencies. In addition, the ongoing operations of seat allocation, crew scheduling, maintenance, and so on, have been profoundly influenced by IT. When an IT system fails, airline operations suffer immediately. As Figure 2–2 illustrates, some airlines invested less heavily in IT; some have paid a significant

---

FIGURE 2–1   IT Impact: Position of Industry Leaders

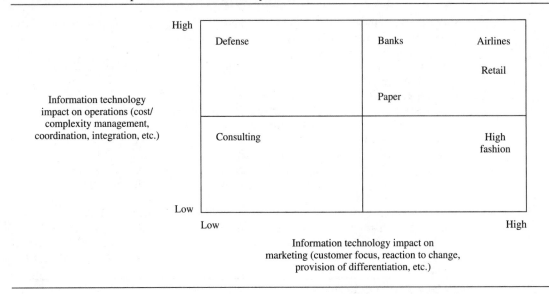

FIGURE 2–2   IT Impact: Position of Key Players in Airlines and Banks

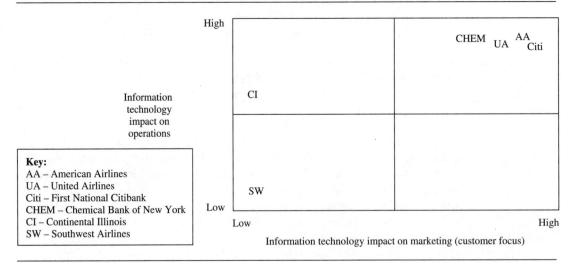

penalty in terms of their ability to differentiate their services in the eyes of the buying public and coordinate and cost-effectively deliver their services; in fact, failure to invest in IT has been cited as a leading cause for several airline failures.[2] Other airlines, such as Southwest, have pioneered radically different non-IT intensive ways of competing (frequent point-to-point flights, low labor costs, rock bottom prices, no food, no seat reservations, etc.).

In the banking industry, several banks (e.g., Bank One, Citibank, and Chemical Bank) have moved aggressively to distinguish their products and services through effective use of information technology. Other banks, however, have used it primarily to transform the back office (e.g., check processing). The prime reason Tom Theobold, CEO of Continental Bank, gave for outsourcing the IT function in 1991 was that over the past 20 years, he had been unable to find a bank that had developed and maintained sustainable competitive advantage through use of IT.[3] The problem of defining the competitive potential of IT is further complicated by the fact that while some firms fail to reap competitive benefits from their IT investments, others dramatically change the basis of competition. (Chapter 3 discusses these issues in greater detail.)

Figure 2–1 also shows the impact of IT on the leaders of several other industries. Defense, for example, with CAD/CAM, robotics, and embedded technology has been primarily affected on the operations side. The marketing impact on defense, however, has been considerably less significant, not only because of the much lower transaction rate, but also because the much higher transaction value introduces a different set of marketing forces that are less sensitive to technology's impact.

Conversely, retailing operations have been dramatically altered by bar coding and point-of-sale scanning technology that have enabled just-in-time ordering, massive cost-reduction programs, and major reductions in inventory levels. Quick response systems in retailing and efficient consumer response systems in grocery stores—which have been among the most exciting mid-1990s applications—have put great pressure on suppliers, distributors, and brokers to adapt their processes to survive. Similarly, display management, database marketing, and point-of-sale terminals that capture customer information at the time of a sale have made important marketing contributions. As mentioned earlier, the mid-1990s have seen the introduction of electronic-based catalogs through mediums such as CD-ROM and the Internet that have dramatically altered the concept of shopping. No longer must we go to a fixed location with fixed hours; today, shopping is done any time and any place.

---

[2]D. Copeland and J. McKenney, "Airline Reservations Systems: Lessons from History," *Management Information Systems Quarterly* 12, no. 2 (1988), p. 352.

[3]R. Huber, "How Continental Bank Outsourced Its 'Crown Jewels,'" *Harvard Business Review,* January–February 1993, p. 121–29.

Interestingly enough, as one player in an industry incorporates IT into its products and/or value chain, others within the industry are often forced to respond. For example, retailers like Wal-Mart—which uses IT extensively to coordinate and control operations—have put pressure on their suppliers to implement IT-based operations or risk losing valuable shelf space. The ability to ensure one-day inventory turnaround and computer-to-computer information sharing[4] has become the price for staying in business.

In the sawmill and cement industries, on the other hand, the operations and marketing impacts of the technology have been less dramatic. Although there was great technology-enabled change in production process control systems in the 1970s, the products remain commodities that are purchased primarily on cost and timely delivery. Further, core administrative processes have been automated to a point that overhead is an insignificant aspect of cost due to the establishment of electronic links to customers, automatic ordering, and sophisticated production control processes.

A Contingency Approach to IT Management

Figure 2–3 identifies the different competitive investment strategies facing industry players as they consider their relative position versus industry leaders and highlights the opportunities for using IT to transform marketing, operations, or both. Some firms have already used IT to transform marketing and production and the organization design and management processes required to support IT-enabled operations. Under the guidance of strong leadership, they have developed a defensible position relative to the competition. Within these firms, senior business leaders assume responsibility for planning and executing IT strategy for the firm. For example, the CEO of Bank One chairs the IT planning committee and considers himself ultimately responsible for IT direction and implementation; at H. E. Butt, the chief information officer (CIO) sits on the company's executive committee. For these firms, the challenge is to maintain advantage.

Other firms find themselves in a position where the opportunities for IT-enabled marketing are minimal, but significant opportunities exist to use IT to support manufacturing and logistics. For these firms, IT investments are often targeted towards streamlining, integrating, and coordinating production and distribution while controlling costs and improving product quality. Since these IT-enabled operating processes cut across many internal organizational boundaries, they require centralized oversight and an interfunctional, team-based approach to implementation and management. Strong relationships between IT and senior management must be in place to support the requirements for interfunctional integration.

---

[4]This capability—termed *electronic data interchange* (EDI)—is discussed in greater detail in Chapter 4.

FIGURE 2–3   Targeting IT-Based Investment (as Compared with Industry Leader)

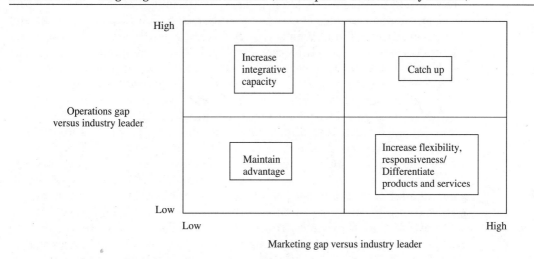

A third group of firms face the primary challenge of catching up with industry leaders by better differentiating their products and services to meet the needs of ever more-focused markets. Many of these firms face the need for IT investments in research and development as well as in the development of the marketing support systems and infrastructures needed to track industry trends and manage marketing strategy and execution. The ability to capture detailed data on individual buyer preferences and habits and competitor prices and product moves is key. Similarly, the capacity to leverage information and communication technologies to decentralize authority for product/market decisions, while simultaneously ensuring organizationwide integration and control, can dramatically increase customer satisfaction and speed of response. For example, one firm implemented handheld computers that fed information to a corporate data warehouse where it was integrated with competitor intelligence data, manufacturing/logistics data, and financial data, thereby enabling a much better understanding of market and business dynamics. By coupling this capability with sophisticated management and decision support systems, it was able to decentralize decision authority for product/market strategy and execution to 22 area business teams. As mentioned above, strong IT and general management links were needed to assure success.

Finally, some firms find themselves in a deep catch-up situation, having been outmaneuvered on both dimensions by strong industry leaders. Comprehensive, coordinated efforts are needed by both the CEO and IT management to enable the organization to achieve a defensible competitive position. The combination of being outmaneuvered by competitors, the long lead times required to develop a competitive response, and the high capital investment costs often create a situation so serious that the survival of the corporation is at stake. This is the situation in which People's Express and Frontier Airlines found themselves during the mid-1980s, as American and United Airlines used IT to redefine the basis of competition within the industry. The massive level of IT investment needed to maintain competitive position within the industry served to "weed out" competitors like Frontier and People's Express, which failed to recognize early the opportunities that IT would provide for integrating operations, identifying and meeting customer expectations, and differentiating products and services. By the late 1980s, both firms were out of business.

In summary, IT plays very different roles in different industry settings. (Figure 2–4 captures these differences.) Sometimes it has played a predominantly operational role, while at others its impact has been primarily on marketing. In many of these settings, industry leaders have been so aggressive that they have transformed the rules of competition, putting those who followed under great pressure. As the role of IT changes within the firm, leadership, organization design, and management processes also change.

Two aspects embedded in the previous discussion have profound importance to the management of IT in an individual firm. The first is that for some firms, the second-by-second, utterly reliable zero-defect quality of its IT operations is crucial to the survival of the firm. Even small interruptions in service or disruptions in quality may have profound impact. In other

FIGURE 2–4   Categories of Strategic Relevance and Impact

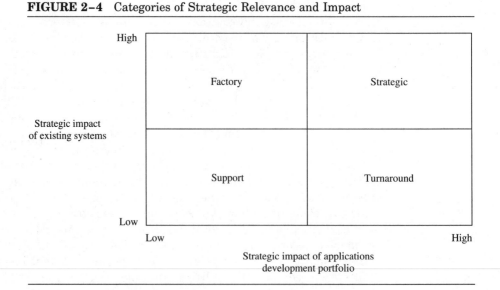

firms, it would take significant disturbances in IT operations over an extended period to have a major impact on the firm's overall operations.

The second aspect, discussed earlier, is that whereas new IT development initiatives are of great strategic importance for some firms, for other firms, IT is useful but not strategic.[5] Understanding an organization's position on these two aspects is critical for developing an appropriate IT management strategy. Four categories of IT are identified.

Strategic. For a growing number of firms, IT is essential for executing current strategies and operations; in addition, the applications under development are crucial to future competitive success. IT strategy, the backbone of such firms' competitive success, receives considerable attention. Banks, insurance companies, and major retail chains frequently fall into this category. Appropriately managed, these firms require considerable IT planning, and the organizational relationship between IT and senior management is very close; in fact, in some of these firms the head of the IT function, broadly defined, sits on the board of directors.

Turnaround. Some firms receive considerable IT support for operations, but are not absolutely dependent on the uninterrupted cost-effective functioning of IT to achieve operating objectives. The applications under development, however, are absolutely necessary to enable the firm to achieve its strategic objectives. A good example of this was a rapidly growing manufacturing firm. The IT used in its factories and accounting processes, though important, was not absolutely vital to its effectiveness. Nevertheless, the rapid growth in the number of products, number of sites, number of staff, and so forth, of the firm's domestic and international installations severely strained its operations, management control, and new product development processes. New IT applications were initiated to enable the company to define and implement new product initiatives, to streamline and integrate operations, and to restore management control. New IT leadership was sought and the position was redefined to encompass a more strategic role and to report to the CEO.

A second example of IT activity that can be classified as turnaround is found in a major pharmaceutical company. The firm recently implemented a major research computing center that provides sophisticated chemical modeling capabilities, which have facilitated several new major product discoveries, and it has streamlined the product-development process. But government regulations hamper the ability of the firm to take full advan-

---

[5]In the mid-1990s, few firms can be found for which IT is not strategic; however, the relative degree of strategic importance does continue to influence IT investment and management strategies.

tage of the potential improvements in product-development cycle times; it still takes almost a decade from the time of invention to get a product to market; needless to say, a three-day interruption in IT service is unlikely to be disastrous.

Another firm entered the turnaround category by systematically under-investing in IT development over a period of years until its existing systems were dangerously obsolete; in fact, it was running on unique hardware platforms that its vendor was about to discontinue. Application develop-ment projects, initiated to rebuild the systems, were considered to be a matter of high corporate priority. Again, unevenness in system operations was irritating, but not life threatening.

Factory. Some firms are heavily dependent on cost-effective, totally reliable IT operational support to enable internal operations. System downtime causes major organizational disruption that can cause customer defections or significant loss of money. The CEO of an investment bank became fully aware of the operational dependence of his firm on IT when a flood above the data center brought all securities trading to a halt. Failure to ensure an off-site redundant data center crippled the bank's trading operations and caused massive financial losses. Needless to say, the CEO has a new appreciation for the importance of IT in running critical areas of business operations; a redundant data center was implemented shortly after the incident.

Firms in the factory quadrant of Figure 2–4 are using IT, like the investment bank, to enable critical, time-dependent operations to function smoothly; but the IT applications under development, although profitable and important in their own right, are not fundamental to the firm's ability to compete. For the firms in this category, even a one-hour disruption in service has severe operational, competitive, and financial consequences. In the 1990s, mid-sized firms in this quadrant often turn to outsourcing to gain access to specialized expertise and costly security systems to help manage the risk.

Support. For certain firms—some of which have very large IT budgets—the strategic impact of IT on operations and future strategy is low. For example, a large professional services firm spends nearly $30 million per year on IT activities that support more than 2000 employees; all agree that the firm could continue to operate, albeit unevenly, in the event of major IT operational failure. And the strategic impact of the IT applications under development, viewed realistically, is quite limited. Appropriately, IT has a significantly lower organizational position in this firm than in those in other arenas, and the commitment to linking IT to business planning activities, particularly at the senior-management level, is essentially non-

TABLE 2–3 Senior Manager Perceptions of the Role of IT within Their Firm (N=160)

	1995	*2000*
Support	38%	7%
Factory	10	10
Turnaround	14	7
Strategic	38	76

existent. Until recently, although it keeps abreast of new technology, the firm, like its competitors, showed limited interest in the development and maintenance of a comprehensive IT strategy. Within the past two years, however, the firm spent a significant amount of money equipping 15,000 of its consulting professionals and field representatives with laptop computers, electronic mail, and a variety of specialized applications that allowed them to access and share information. Since the key to the firm's success lay in recruiting, developing, and retaining highly competent professionals with a broad range of skills and deep expertise within targeted areas, and in managing client relationships, this new IT initiative could shift the firm's focus toward the turnaround category. If successful, other firms within the industry may be forced to implement similar systems.

Surprisingly, we still find a large number of companies that senior management classifies as being in the support category. In spring 1995, 160 senior managers from firms located around the world were asked to classify their firms' approach to using IT—38 percent reported that their firm was positioned in the support quadrant; only 7 percent expected to be there five years in the future. (See Table 2–3.)

To diagnose how strategically important IT is for a firm or business unit, careful analysis of its impact on each part of the value chain is essential. A more in-depth discussion of this analysis is provided in Chapter 3. In addition, competitors' use of IT and new IT developments must be monitored on a regular basis to ensure that major opportunities have not been missed. For example, 15 years ago, the retailing industry was appropriately positioned within the support category. Within several years, the technology became available to allow a small player, Wal-Mart, to change the basis of competition; the past 10 years have been spent trying to catch up in an industry in which IT rapidly moved from support to strategic.[6]

---

[6]Subsequent chapters describe several widely used competitive analysis frameworks that suggest how managers can identify strategic IT applications.

THEME 2: INTEGRATING CHANGING TECHNOLOGY PLATFORMS

At the heart of the IT challenge lies the dramatic, sustained, long-term evolution of IT cost/performance and the merging of a variety of technology platforms. IT applications that were nonexistent in 1989 were state-of-the art by 1992 and by 1995 were routine; obsolescence is just a few years down the road.

The 1980s and 1990s saw the development of increasing communication and information storage capacities, which, in turn, supported an explosion of new types of software and IT applications. By the mid-1990s, many consider the useful life of a personal computer to be three years or less. The tremendous improvement in price/performance has enabled integration of video, voice, data, and graphics. This is radically changing the capabilities and potential uses of IT. For example, in 1995, full-motion digital video and voice annotations can be attached to documents, information reports, and spreadsheets.

But despite the integration in the classes of information, the separation of the management of computing, telecommunications, office automation, and broadcast technologies continues in many firms. The ability to capitalize on the real business opportunities afforded by the integration of these technologies can only come if we successfully merge the strategies, policies, and technology standards related to them. In this book, when we refer to IT departments, activities, or policies, we include all of these technologies. At present, many firms have begun the difficult process of coordinating these technologies; few have successfully integrated all of them.

There are three major reasons to manage these technologies—at least at a policy and standards level—as an integrated whole: (1) today's IT applications require an enormous number of physical interconnections among them (e.g., on-line information retrieval systems, electronic mail, and end-user programming require the physical integration of two or more of the technologies); (2) execution of IT application development projects utilizing technologies that are managed independently is exceedingly difficult;[7] and (3) efforts to identify potential business opportunities that take advantage of the emerging integration potential across these technologies are significantly hampered when the technology is managed separately.

The process of integrating technologies that were developed and managed separately is extremely complex. In many settings, integration will require a common operating and management process; some may choose to achieve integration at the senior management policy committee level, while requir-

---

[7]Projects that involve integration across technology platforms are usually large, high-risk, and costly; in addition, success often depends on substantial organizational and work-related change.

ing operating managers to work together as an interfunctional team. Failure to achieve management and operating integration can involve extraordinary expenses. This is especially true when integration involves PCs and local area networks (LANS). In fact, a recent study found that the cost of PC/LAN computing averaged $6,445 per user per year; this was 2.8 times higher than the $2,282 average cost per user per year of mainframe computing.[8]

Since 1980, the integration of technological platforms (except for broadcasting technologies) has advanced from a largely speculative idea to one that is overwhelmingly accepted in management practice. Chapters 6 and 8 discuss the technical issues that must be considered in cost-effectively integrating technology in a world of sustained, rapid technological change; Chapters 7, 9, and 10 discuss the leadership, management, and policy issues.

THEME 3: ASSIMILATING EMERGING TECHNOLOGIES

The task of implementing a portfolio of IT systems projects that are built around continually evolving technologies is an extraordinarily complex endeavor. Early involvement of end users whose daily activities will be influenced by the adoption of the technology has been shown to be a critical success factor. New IT innovations, however, are often complicated by the fact that user jobs may be eliminated by the new technologies that they are working so hard to help implement. Successful implementation of IT also often requires that users adopt new ways of performing intellectual tasks. To accomplish this, old procedures and attitudes must be abandoned, and new patterns must emerge and be accepted by individuals and work groups.

Since IT was first introduced in organizations, there has been an ongoing effort to understand the managerial issues associated with the evolution of IT and organization. Early work by Thomas Whisler and Harold Leavitt[9] on IT and the demise of middle management, by Dick Nolan on the evolution of IT and organization as a process of organizational learning,[10] and by Chris Argyris[11] on double-loop learning discusses approaches for dealing with individual acceptance and use of IT. Field research by Jim Cash and Poppy McLeod frames the issues within the context of the diffusion of technology

---

[8]International Technology Group, *Cost of Computing: Comparative Study of Mainframe and PC/LAN Installations* (Mountain View, CA, 1994).

[9]Thomas L. Whisler and Harold J. Leavitt, "Management in the 1980s," *Harvard Business Review,* November–December 1958, pp. 41–48.

[10]Richard L. Nolan, "Managing the Crisis in Data Processing," *Harvard Business Review,* March–April 1979, pp. 115–26.

[11]Chris Argyris, "Double-Loop Learning on Organizations," *Harvard Business Review,* September–October 1977, p. 115.

innovation.[12] Successful implementation of a technology often requires that individuals learn radically new ways of performing intellectual tasks, causing changes in information flows as well as in individual roles. Frequently, this requires more extensive organizational changes involving structures, operating processes, management processes, human resource management systems, culture, and incentives. We describe the technology innovation and diffusion process within four phases. These four phases are discussed in greater detail in Chapter 6.

Phase 1. Technology Identification and Investment

The first phase involves identifying a technology of potential interest to the company and funding a pilot project. An alternative approach is to use the business-planning process to identify promising IT applications that require technology innovation and fund investigation of their potential as part of the budgeting process. The first approach involves a "grass roots" effort that can be used to define potential benefits and risks and system implementation difficulties early in the process and to garner support by demonstrating the potential payoff. The latter approach requires the commitment of senior management to serve as product champions for systems innovations early in the process. Because it is inappropriate to demand objective payoffs at the pilot project stage, top-level management commitment is often difficult to secure.

Phase 2. Technological Learning and Adaptation

The objective during the second phase is to encourage user-oriented experimentation with the newly identified technology through a series of user-defined pilot projects. The primary purpose of the experimentation is to develop a broad base of user-oriented insights into how the new technology might be used to add value in the business and to make users aware of the existence of the technology. Frequently, the outcome of phase 2 provides a much different perspective on the technology than the one held by IT experts at the end of their phase 1 pilot.

The length of this phase varies with the type of technology, the characteristics of the users, the tasks for which the technology is used, and the organizational and environmental context.[13] For example, at one firm, a

---

[12]J. Cash and P. McLeod, "Managing the Introduction of Information Technology in Strategically Dependent Companies," *Journal of Management Information Systems* 1 (1985), pp. 5–23.

[13]L. Applegate, "Technology Support for Cooperative Work: A Framework for Introduction and Assimilation in Organizations," *Journal of Organizational Computing* 1, 1 (1991), pp. 11–39.

pilot project designed to test the use of handheld computers by the sales force was so successful that it progressed through phase 2 within several months and was fully deployed within 18 months. The technology, while new to the company, was not "new to the world"; the task that the technology would support was well defined, as was the influence of the technology on the task; careful attention was paid to involving and training both the users (and their bosses) from the start of the process, and incentives, compensation, and performance management systems were realigned to "fit" the new IT-enabled work process.

Phase 3. Rationalization/Management Control

By the time a technology has reached phase 3, it is reasonably well understood by both IT personnel and key users. The basic challenge in this phase is to develop appropriate systems and controls to ensure that the technologies are utilized efficiently as they diffuse throughout the organization. In earlier phases, basic concerns revolve around stimulating awareness and experimentation; in this phase, they center on developing standards and controls to ensure that the applications are done economically and can be maintained over a long period of time. Formal standards for development and documentation, cost-benefit studies, and user charge-out mechanisms are all appropriate for technologies in this phase. Failure to develop and maintain these standards can be extraordinarily expensive.

Phase 4. Maturity/Widespread Technology Transfer

By the time a technology enters the fourth phase, the required skills have been developed, users are aware of the benefits, and management controls are in place. A common pitfall in this phase is that enthusiasm for the technology dies while there is still opportunity to use it to add value. Lacking sufficient attention and resources, maintenance of existing applications may suffer and new value-creating uses may not be explored. Careful vigilance is also required in this phase to ensure that out-of-date technologies and applications are not extended beyond their useful life.

The four phases (innovation, learning, rationalization, and maturity), which are now clearly understood within most well-managed firms, provide a useful base around which to develop a strategic view of the diffusion of technology throughout the firm. As experiments with a specific technology spread, new innovations should be encouraged. Knowledgeable business managers have usually proven to be better sources of new application ideas than either technology experts or single-minded champions. As noted earlier, different technologies may pass through the phases in radically different ways. In addition, few firms progress through these phases in the orderly sequence of events that we describe here. Expect a certain amount of cycling back and leaping forward.

There are no hard and fast guidelines for deciding how much to allocate to exploiting technologies at different phases of evolution. Clearly, firms in the strategic category in Figure 2–4 can expect to spend more on phase 1 and 2 technology investments than those firmly positioned in the *support* category. But no matter what quadrant a firm is in at any point in time, it is important to remember that a new technology may offer a new business opportunity that can trigger a move from one quadrant to another.

In most firms, technologies in all four phases exist simultaneously in an organization at any point in time. The art of management in the 1990s is to simultaneously bring the appropriate management perspectives to bear on each technology. This calls for IT management and general management to be both subtle and flexible, qualities they often neither possess nor see as necessary. A "one-size-fits-all" approach to IT management simply will not do the job.[14]

THEME 4: SOURCING POLICIES FOR THE IT VALUE CHAIN

A significant issue in repositioning IT over the past decade has been an acceleration of the pressures that are pushing firms toward greater reliance on external sources for software and computing support. Many call this outsourcing, but, as we discuss in Chapter 10, there is a wide variation in the definition of that word within the industry. Escalating costs of large-scale system development projects, limited staff, availability of industry-standard databases and networks, availability of software packages, and a dramatic increase in the number of potential applications have been some of the factors driving the trend to use outside sources—a trend that we believe will continue to accelerate throughout the 1990s. The realization that they do not develop their own word-processing or spreadsheet software leads managers to ask: "Do I need to develop my order-processing system? If I can specify the process, can I hire someone to write the code?" Facing significant pressure to focus on core competencies and the rapidly increasing complexity of technology management, many have expanded their thinking: "Do I really need to run my large computing centers and corporate networks? Can I safely delegate the operation of the infrastructure to enable me to focus my energy and resources on creating value-added IT applications?" Factors to consider as firms struggle with the answers to these questions are summarized in Table 2–4. A detailed discussion of these issues is presented in Chapter 10.

---

[14]This will be discussed further in Chapters 6 and 7.

TABLE 2-4 IT Sourcing: Pressures to "Make/Own" versus "Buy"

Decision Criteria	Pressure to "Make/Own"	Pressure to "Buy"
Business strategy	IT application or infrastructure provides proprietary competitive advantage.	IT application or infrastructure supports strategy or operations, but is not considered strategic in its own right.
Core competencies	Business or IT knowledge/expertise required to develop or maintain an application is considered a core competency of the firm.	Business or IT knowledge/expertise required to build or maintain an IT application or infrastructure is not critical to the firm's success.
Information/process security and confidentiality	The information or processes contained within IT systems or databases are considered to be highly confidential.	Failure of routine security measures, while problematic, would not cause serious organizational dysfunction.
Availability of suitable partners	There are no reliable, competent, and/or motivated partners that could assume responsibility for the IT application or infrastructure. (Included are the financial viability of the partner, perceptions of quality of the partner's products and services, and perceptions of the ability to form a compatible working relationship over the life of the contract.)	Reliable, competent, and appropriately motivated vendors (or other partners) are available.
Availability of packaged software or solutions	The IT application or infrastructure required by the firm is unique.	Packaged software or solutions are available that would meet the majority of business requirements.
Cost/benefit analysis	The cost of purchasing the product or service and/or coordinating and controlling interorganizational relationships and operations is greater than the cost of performing the service in-house.	The cost of purchasing and managing the service is significantly less than the cost of performing the service in-house.
Time frame for implementation	There is sufficient time available to develop internal resources and skills to implement the IT application and/or to develop the IT infrastructure required by the firm.	The time required to develop internal resources and expertise and/or to implement the IT application or infrastructure project exceeds the organization's demand for the product or services.
Evolution and complexity of the technology	The firm is able to attract, retain, and develop the range of IT experts needed to implement IT applications and infrastructures at a reasonable cost.	The firm is unable to keep pace with the rapidly changing and increasingly complex technologies required by the firm.
Ease of implementation	Software development tools that provide rapid IT application development are available.	Tools to support rapid application development are not available or are viewed to be insufficient or ineffective.

The preference to buy rather than make has significantly influenced IT management practice as dissatisfaction with internally supplied services grows. The proliferation of end-user computing packages has resulted in the fact that in many firms in the mid-1990s less than 1 percent of all software has been developed by the IT group. The IT organization has increasingly turned into an in-house systems integration function, and, as discussed in Chapter 9, new management processes are required. For example, internal management control systems must be checked to ensure that they do not motivate inappropriate "make" versus "buy" decisions. When software development is being outsourced, clear interorganizational project management systems and audit procedures must be in place to ensure that both parties are able to deliver on their commitments. Implementation risk on a fixed-price contract is strongly related to vendor viability. A "good" price is not good if the supplier goes under before completing the project. Provisions for "death" and "divorce" become critical in situations where a firm is outsourcing operational IT components (e.g., data centers, networks) since the normal length of these contracts is approximately 10 years.

THEME 5: APPLICATIONS DEVELOPMENT PROCESS

Traditionally, the activities necessary to produce and deliver information service have been characterized as a series of steps:[15]

1. Design—definition of the functions and relevant technologies
2. Construct—detailed design, programming and testing (or buy)
3. Implement—gain ownership by users, redesign processes, reorganize
4. Operate—execute processes, continuous training to exploit system
5. Maintain—upgrade technology, adapt system to changing requirements

Since the First Edition of this book was published, very different types of technologies and projects have dramatically influenced the system development process. At one extreme are the traditional projects that were once the mainstay of the industry. These projects are noted for being large, requiring extensive development periods (often well in excess of 18 months) and significantly influencing the nature of work and organization across multiple areas of the business. These projects are inherently very complex. Often, the information required, how it will be processed, and the end results of the project are not clearly specified at the outset. In the 1990s, the

---

[15]It is worth noting that this list of responsibilities remains with the firm irrespective of whether all or a portion of the system development process and IT operations/management is outsourced. The job of IT and business management is to ensure that those tasks are performed in the most effective and efficient manner, irrespective of where or by whom they are performed.

traditional system life cycle continues to be appropriate for these projects, but the steps in the process are not performed in a highly structured and sequential fashion. There is a significant increase in the levels of interaction among a wide variety of IT and business professionals, each of whom brings different areas of expertise and management responsibilities; even vendors get in the act. This results in a much more interactive and iterative process; in addition, to manage complexity, these large projects are often subdivided into a number of smaller projects that may be managed in very different ways. For example, one team may use joint application development and rapid prototyping[16] to build the user interface for the system, while a second team conducts a pilot project of a portion of the system that will use a state-of-the-art technology that is new to the firm.

At the other extreme are more focused projects that may involve the construction of a decision support system (DSS) for a group of end users. This type of project may use rapid prototyping and joint application development methods from the outset. Alternatively, a team may be working on the introduction and assimilation of a new technology using the phased approach to organization learning discussed earlier in this chapter. Finally, some projects may involve the use of computer-aided software engineering (CASE) tools.[17] The key to understanding the complexity of the applications development challenge in the 1990s is to appropriately select and implement a system development methodology based on the nature of the project and the experience and expertise of both business and IT professionals. In addition, it is critical to remember that all projects require careful management by both business and IT professionals throughout all phases of the project.

The remainder of this section defines the components of the traditional system development life cycle and also identifies those aspects most likely to be mismanaged in the 1990s. (Chapter 10 discusses the overall project management process in greater detail.) While changing technology and improved managerial insights on the use of technology have significantly

---

[16]Joint application development is a system development methodology that involves both business users and IT professionals in all parts of the system design, development, and implementation process. Rapid prototyping refers to the process of building a smaller version of the system that has limited functionality; this allows IT professionals and business users to better define requirements and test key areas of functionality prior to full-scale system development.

[17]CASE tools are software programs that help system developers design and code business software. Some of the tools support designers in developing system specifications. Once those specifications are defined in the computer, the CASE tools automatically generate computer code—the instructions that tell a computer what to do—and then check the code for inconsistencies and redundancy. Others help developers, or even end users, design and implement information reporting or decision support systems. CASE tools often embody a specific approach to system development, which makes them more appropriate for some types of projects than for others.

altered the way each of these steps can be implemented, they continue to provide a useful framework with which to consider the range of system development activities; in fact, the increasing shift toward purchasing IT application development services increases the need for careful attention to IT project management. This is especially true in firms where the role of the IT manager is beginning to resemble that of an information broker.

Design

The objective of the design step is to produce a definition of the information service desired. This includes identification of the users, the initial tasks to be implemented, and the long-run service and support to be provided. Traditionally, the process is initiated by either a user request or a joint IT department-user proposal based on the IT plan. The design step is a critical activity that demands careful attention to short- and long-term information service requirements as well as reliable service delivery. Management of the design phase was traditionally done by the IT staff; in many organizations in the 1990s, the user is taking the lead.

Design normally begins with a feasibility analysis that provides a high-level picture of the potential costs and benefits of the proposed system and the technical/organizational feasibility of the project. If the results of the analysis are favorable, an explicit decision is made to proceed. This is followed by substantive collaborative work by a team of users, IT professionals, and experts to develop a working approach to, and set of specifications for, the system design. The design team should include key internal and external stakeholders who could either influence or be influenced by the new system. As a result, the team required to design interorganizational systems—those that enable on-line communication, information sharing, or management/execution of core operating processes—may require membership of key customers, suppliers, distributors, or other business partners. In other cases, vendors or consultants with specialized expertise may be included on the system design team. Depending on the systems scope, these design efforts may range from formal systematic analysis to informal discussion followed by rapid prototyping. The end product of design is a definition of the desired service accompanied by an identification of the means (including in-house or purchased services) for providing it.

Construction

A highly specialized activity that combines both art and logic, system construction involves selecting appropriate computer equipment and creating/or buying the specific computer programs that are needed to meet system requirements. Professional judgment is needed in the following areas:

1. Selection of computer equipment and software programming languages or packages. If the decision is made to outsource development, independent contractors or a specialized software development firm can be hired. Particular attention must be paid to long-term maintainability to avoid getting stranded in a "technological dead end."
2. Documentation of both the technical program structure and end-user operating instructions must be created. The importance of comprehensive, understandable documentation is often overlooked. Inadequate technical documentation can lead to excessive cost; inadequate user documentation can result in poor acceptance of the system.
3. Appropriate testing must be performed to ensure system robustness.

While this set of activities is primarily technical in nature, intense coordination and control are required to ensure that the project remains on track, within budget, and focused on user requirements. Even the best designs require numerous interdependent decisions. Large project teams must coordinate closely to ensure that the system components will work together flawlessly. Frequent interaction with end users is also required to ensure that the system requirements do not change. The decision to outsource portions of the project, or the entire project, markedly increases the coordination and control costs, and the technical decisions listed above must still be managed inside the firm.

Implementation

Implementation involves extensive user-IT coordination as the transition is made from the predominantly technical, IT-driven task of construction to user-driven management of the completed system. Whether the system is bought or made, the implementation phase is very much a joint effort. Extensive testing, which disrupts normal business operations, must be performed; training is required; work procedures and communication patterns are disrupted. Often, achievement of the benefits of the system is dependent on the ability of individuals and groups to learn to use the information from the system to make better decisions and add value to the business. It is essential to shape the organization's operational and management structure, processes, and incentives to exploit the potential of an IT system. At times, the impact of the system extends to groups and individuals outside the organization, which further complicates implementation. Perhaps most critical is the need to carefully define the activities that are required to ensure that the benefits of the project are achieved and documented.

Operation

In many settings, system operation receives little attention, as IT staff focuses its efforts on the enormous backlog of projects still waiting to be done. This can lead to intense frustration and conflict. Further, as systems migrate from the mainframe to the desktop, users become the system "operators" and are becoming all too aware of the complexity of the task. A significant amount of the difficulty can be traced to the faulty identification and communication of the system requirements. As systems become more complex, and as goals for the system become less certain, the difficulty of clearly specifying requirements up front becomes a major factor that complicates both implementation and operation.

In complex systems that will be operated by IT professionals, formal procedures are often in place that specify that operating personnel must "sign off" on a new system. The specific criteria for testing and approval are defined as part of the system design phase. This control mechanism distributes responsibility and authority for system development and serves as an important quality-control mechanism. This role separation is particularly important when the same department is responsible for both constructing and operating a system. These procedures and controls were developed to fit within a mainframe environment. The move toward a client-server architecture requires reevaluation of these traditional procedures and controls.

After the system is built and installed, measures must be developed to assess actual service delivery and its cost-effectiveness and quality. While many believe that "postimplementation audits" are inadequate for all system projects, increasing attention has been focused on the lack of control over end-user-developed systems. For example, a leading mutual fund received a great deal of attention recently when an error in a user-developed spreadsheet caused the firm to overstate earnings by several billion dollars. The error was not detected until after investors had been informed of their earnings. Customer dissatisfaction was high when they were later informed that the fund had actually suffered a loss for the year.

Maintenance

System maintenance refers to enhancements or changes in a system that has passed into the operation phase. It requires cycling back through the design, construction, and implementation activities. The need for system maintenance often arises from changes in the business or technical environment (e.g., changes in tax laws, organization changes such as new offices or mergers, business changes such as new product lines and acquisition of new technology).[18] It can be as simple as changing a number in a database

---

[18]The word *maintenance* is a complete misnomer because it implies an element of deferability that does not exist in many situations. *Modernization* is a better term.

of depreciation rates or as complex as rewriting the tax portion of the payroll. Effective maintenance faces two serious problems:

1. Most professionals consider it dull and uncreative because it involves working on systems created by someone else. Consequently, the work is often delegated to inexperienced employees or those who have shown less system development aptitude.
2. Maintenance can be very complex, particularly for older systems. It requires highly competent professionals to safely perform necessary changes in a way that does not bring the system (and the firm) to a crashing halt.

Several IT departments are developing IT quality procedures to help focus attention on "continuous improvement." Quality teams search out opportunities for enhancement and continuous improvement becomes everyone's job. This change in mind-set must be accompanied by a shift in emphasis from operating efficiency to customer satisfaction that is reflected in goals, performance measurement, and incentives. Newer IT system development tools provide support for continuous improvement by enabling end users to customize the system to meet the changing business need while effectively isolating the internal processing instructions from changes that could harm overall system operation. Managing the operations and enhancement of end-user-developed systems remains an area of particular concern for organizations that are becoming more dependent on locally developed information. The move to client-server computing, discussed in Chapter 6, is helping companies gain control of these applications.[19]

In summary, the complexity of the systems life cycle is evident from the above description. At any time, an organization may have hundreds of systems, each at a different position, within this life cycle. Traditionally, the IT department has been organized to support a phase of the system development life cycle (e.g., system analysis, programming, operations, etc.), rather than a specific application system. This inevitably creates friction because it forces the passing of responsibility for an application system from one IT unit to another as it passes through these steps. Until recently, the user was responsible for coordination of the system development process as responsibility was rotated among IT specialists. As mentioned earlier, the process was further complicated by the fact that the approach to system development varied widely from one type of application system to another.[20]

---

[19]Client-server computing allows end-user-developed systems to be transferred to a separate computer—designated as a "server"—for ongoing operation. The server, while it may be housed locally, is often controlled by a central computer/network operations center. With client-server computing, the operating responsibility can be shared between end users and IT professionals, and formal quality procedures can be implemented.

[20]In Chapter 8 we deal with the issues of operations management and the impact of buy decisions on the systems life cycle.

THEME 6: PARTNERSHIP OF THREE CONSTITUENCIES

Much of the complexity of IT management stems from managing the conflicting pressures of three different and vitally concerned constituencies: IT management, user management, and general management of the organization. The relationships between these groups vary over time as the organization's familiarity with different technologies evolves, as the strategic impact of IT shifts, and as the company's overall IT management skills grow.[21]

IT Management

A number of forces have driven the creation of an IT department and ensured its continued existence. The IT department provides a pool of technical skills that can be developed and deployed to resolve complex problems facing the firm. An important part of its mission is to scan leading-edge technologies and to ensure that potential users are both aware of their existence and of how they could be used to solve business problems. Because many systems are designed to interconnect different parts of the business, IT professionals have become key integrators who can help identify areas of potential interconnection between the needs of different user groups and thus facilitate the development of integrated business solutions. From their earliest roots, IT has involved process analysis and redesign. As a result, in many firms, IT professionals are becoming the "business process reengineering" specialists—a role of increasing importance within firms in the 1990s. In a world of changing technologies and changing business opportunities, this unit is under continuous pressure to remain relevant. As end users become more involved in system development activities, a new relationship must be forged to ensure that the unique skills and expertise of both groups are utilized to their fullest to solve business problems.

User Management

Specialization of the IT function has taken place at a cost. System design, construction, operation, and maintenance tasks have become the responsibility of the IT department, yet the user continues to assume responsibility for the business activities that the systems support. This is an obvious point of friction. Additionally, in the past, the "mysterious" requirements of the

---

[21]Chapters 7 through 12 are largely devoted to identifying the various aspects of managing this relationship.

technology alienated users from the system development and operations process, increasing the barriers to effective collaboration.

At times, vendors and consultants capitalize on this conflict by aggressively marketing their services directly to the users, who are then faced with the additional pressure of choosing among alternatives without fully understanding the criteria upon which to base their decision. Increasing user IT sophistication and experience, when coupled with the increasing availability of packaged, user-friendly software, has dramatically altered the conditions that initially led to IT specialization. In many firms, the boundaries are blurring as "hybrid" professionals with both business and technical expertise become more prevalent at both the user and IT specialist levels. But new state-of-the-art technologies continue to require specialized expertise. Appropriately, the relationship and apportionment of responsibilities between the IT specialist and user are being reappraised continuously. The management of these complex transitions is clearly general management's responsibility.

General Management

The broad task of general management is to ensure that appropriate structures, systems, and management processes are in place for ensuring that the overall needs of the organization are met. As IT assumes an increasingly visible role within an organization, executives' ability and interest in playing this role are a function of both their comfort with IT and their perception of its strategic importance to the firm as a whole. Since many have reached their positions with little exposure to IT issues or with exposure to radically different types of IT issues, they are often ill-equipped to assume this responsibility. It is important to note that much of this book is aimed at helping general managers assume a more active role in managing the information resource of the firm. As a new generation of managers with more experience and higher comfort levels with IT take on increasing responsibility, we expect more general managers will take a more active role.

In summary, as each group's perspective and attitudes evolve, some problems are solved while new ones arise. Managing the changing roles and relationships is one of the most complex issues facing all three groups as they attempt to harness the power of IT in the 1990s.

SUMMARY

In this chapter, we have identified the manageable trends that are relevant to all aspects of managing information services in the 1990s. Figure 2–5 maps the remaining chapters and identifies each chapter's emphasis in relation to our six organizing themes.

FIGURE 2–5   Map of Chapters and Themes

	Strategic Impact	Technology Integration	Managing Rapidly Evolving Technologies	IT Sourcing Policies	Application Development Process	Internal Roles for IT Success
Chapter 3 Effects of IT on Competition	•	•				
Chapter 4 Electronic Commerce	•	•				•
Chapter 5 Information, Organization, and Control	•	•				•
Chapter 6 IT Architectural Alternatives		•	•			•
Chapter 7 Organizing and Leading IT	•		•	•		•
Chapter 8 IT Operations	•			•	•	•
Chapter 9 IT Management Process	•		•	•		•
Chapter 10 Managing IT Resources through Strategic Partnerships	•			•		
Chapter 11 A Portfolio Approach to IT Development	•				•	•
Chapter 12 Transnational IT Issues		•				•
Chapter 13 The IT Business	•		•	•		•

Chapter 3 describes how IT is changing the way companies compete and provides five diagnostic questions for discovering the likely impact of IT in a firm. It then introduces the concept of value-chain analysis and shows how each element of the value chain is permeated by information opportunities in different settings.[22] The chapter concludes by identifying some strategic risks posed by this technology. Chapter 4 describes how traditional and emerging technologies (for example, interorganizational systems and the Internet) are presenting new opportunities for "electronic commerce" that have the potential to radically change our concept of organizations and markets. Chapter 5 identifies how these same technologies are changing organization structure, management controls, and other aspects of the firm's internal infrastructure.

Chapter 6 describes the issues involved in developing an information technology architecture and the challenges posed by the assimilation of new technologies. Chapter 7 discusses the special management issues posed by the rapid evolution in technology and the impact of this technology on IT organization structure and leadership. Chapter 8 covers the operational issues that ensure the delivery of reliable day-to-day service.

Chapter 9 explains the influence of corporate cultures on managerial roles and describes various IT management processes that can be used to integrate, coordinate, and control IT services within the firm. It also covers how planning is influenced by the strategic relevance of IT and its potential impact on the organization.

Chapter 10, which focuses on outsourcing IT services, identifies the main drivers for this important trend and the potential risks involved. It then provides a contingency approach for dealing with these issues and identifies the portions of management responsibility and oversight that we believe cannot be delegated.

Chapter 11 focuses on IT project management. It defines a contingency framework that can be used by IT professionals, business users, and general management to oversee different types of IT projects. The inherent risks and risk management strategies are also defined.

Chapter 12 extends our analysis of organizational culture to include the complexities and possibilities that arise as we move toward global IT management. Chapter 13 uses a framework for assessing an appropriate marketing mix to enable consideration of IT management as a "business."

---

[22]The value chain of a firm is the interconnected set of activities required to design, produce, and deliver products and services. The systems and structures required to manage these "primary value activities" are also considered. M. Porter, *Competitive Advantage* (NY: Free Press, 1985).

Effects of IT on Competition

To solve customer service problems, a major distributor developed an on-line order processing system and made it available for direct access by its key customers. The system was intended to cut order/entry costs, to speed processing time, and to provide more flexibility to customers. Although, initially, the company's expectations were modest, the system gave them significant competitive advantage; customer satisfaction increased, and the distributor also noted that revenues increased and market share improved. These benefits continued as long as the company continued to innovate. But five years later, in an attempt to control internal costs, the firm turned away from its commitment to customer service. Despite improved operating efficiency, profits and market share rapidly declined.

Elsewhere, a regional airline testifying before Congress claimed that the automated reservation system of a national carrier was "anticompetitive" and was forcing small airlines out of business. By locking in the travel agents to a common electronic distribution channel, the large firm was "locking out" competition. In addition, by providing access to information on the price of all flights on all carriers, the system allowed the large airline to systematically underprice the smaller firm. The airline ultimately went bankrupt.

Finally, a large aerospace company required major suppliers to acquire compatible computer-aided design (CAD) equipment to link directly to its design workstation or face being dropped as a supplier. The aerospace firm claimed that access to these direct computer-to-computer links dramatically reduced the total cost of, and time for, design changes and parts acquisition, while simultaneously improving quality. In addition, these on-line linkages enabled the firm to significantly reduce inventory levels, which further enhanced process efficiency; without these improvements in cost, quality, and cycle time, the aerospace firm would not have been able to respond to the demands of its customers.

These examples capture the changing nature of the role of IT within organizations and industries. Dramatic improvements in the price/ performance of information technology (IT) over the past three decades, when coupled with the increased penetration of IT within the firm and the learning that accompanies experimentation and use, have allowed computer systems to move out of the back office and to create significant competitive advantage. Particularly important are systems that electronically link customers and suppliers.[1] For many firms the evolution of IT-enabled strategy and organization design has been extraordinarily expensive and has extended over a number of years. The very competitive airline reservations systems, for example, evolved over 30 years and continue to evolve.[2]

Although such IT initiatives offer an opportunity for a competitive advantage, they also increase strategic vulnerability. In the case of the aerospace manufacturer, competitive position increased dramatically, but at the cost of independence. Once electronic linkages were in place and processes were redesigned to tightly integrate across organizational boundaries, it was much harder to change suppliers.

In some cases IT supported new business strategies that, if successfully executed, produced dramatic gains in market share. But, like any strategy, those gains were fleeting. As was the case for the distributor discussed at the beginning of the chapter, failure to continue to innovate resulted in loss of advantage. Opportunities for IT-enabled competitive advantage vary widely from one company to another, just as the intensity and the rules of competition vary widely from one industry to another. Similarly, a company's location, size, and basic product technology shape potential IT applications. These opportunities are not restricted to the large firms; they affect even the smallest companies as well as creating opportunities for new entrepreneurial ventures. In different situations, a company may appropriately attempt to be either a leader or an alert follower.

What is a strategic advantage for a first mover can become a strategic necessity for other firms in the industry as the rules of competition shift. Over the past decade, the stakes have become so high in many firms that attention to IT strategy has become a major responsibility of senior management.

ANALYZING IMPACT

The complexity of the IT management challenge increases considerably when IT penetrates to the heart of a firm's (or industry's) strategy. To facilitate planning, general managers need a comprehensive framework

---

[1]This issue is discussed at length in Chapter 4.

[2]James L. McKenney, *Waves of Change: Business Evolution through Information Technology* (Cambridge, MA: Harvard Business School Press, January 1995, pp. 16–38).

FIGURE 3-1 Competitive Forces

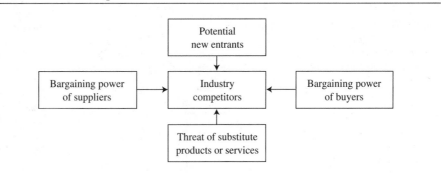

that views the use of IT from a strategic rather than a tactical perspective. Michael Porter's industry and competitive analysis (ICA) framework[3] has proven very effective in this respect.

Forces That Shape Strategy

Porter's work, directed at both strategic business planners and general managers, argues that many of the contemporary strategic planning frameworks view competition too narrowly and pessimistically because they were primarily based on projections of market share and market growth. He explains that the economic and competitive forces in an industry segment are the result of five basic forces: (1) bargaining power of suppliers, (2) bargaining power of buyers, (3) threat of new entrants into the industry segment, (4) threat of substitute products or services, and (5) positioning of traditional intraindustry rivals. Figure 3-1 presents these five competitive forces and Figure 3-2 provides a detailed description of the factors that determine the relative strength of each force.

Although Porter's initial work did not include IT as a component of the framework, it has proven extremely useful in this regard. Table 3-1 describes the impact of IT on the five competitive forces.

Column 1 lists the key competitive forces that shape competition in a given industry segment. In a specific industry, not all forces are of equal importance. Some industries are dominated by suppliers (for example, OPEC in the petroleum industry in the 1970s), while other industries are preoccupied with the threat of new entrants and/or substitute products (such as the banking and insurance industries).

---

[3]Michael E. Porter, *Competitive Strategy: Techniques for Analyzing Industries and Competitors* (New York: The Free Press, 1980).

FIGURE 3–2   Elements of Industry Structure

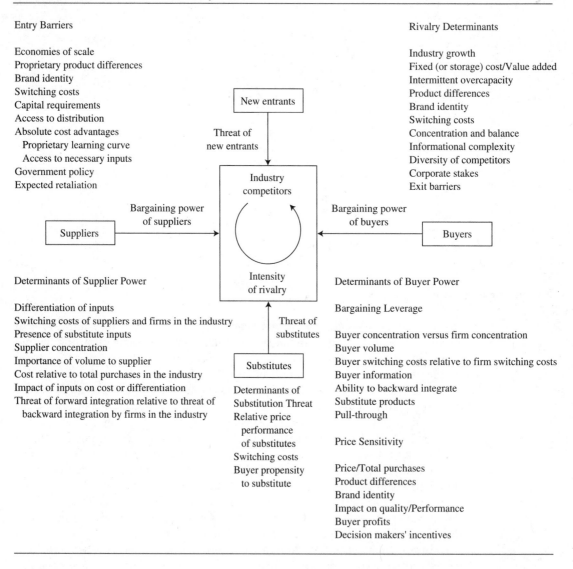

Entry Barriers

Economies of scale
Proprietary product differences
Brand identity
Switching costs
Capital requirements
Access to distribution
Absolute cost advantages
  Proprietary learning curve
  Access to necessary inputs
Government policy
Expected retaliation

Rivalry Determinants

Industry growth
Fixed (or storage) cost/Value added
Intermittent overcapacity
Product differences
Brand identity
Switching costs
Concentration and balance
Informational complexity
Diversity of competitors
Corporate stakes
Exit barriers

Threat of
new entrants

New entrants

Industry
competitors

Intensity
of rivalry

Bargaining power
of suppliers

Suppliers

Bargaining power
of buyers

Buyers

Threat of
substitutes

Substitutes

Determinants of Supplier Power

Differentiation of inputs
Switching costs of suppliers and firms in the industry
Presence of substitute inputs
Supplier concentration
Importance of volume to supplier
Cost relative to total purchases in the industry
Impact of inputs on cost or differentiation
Threat of forward integration relative to threat of
  backward integration by firms in the industry

Determinants of
Substitution Threat
Relative price
  performance
  of substitutes
Switching costs
Buyer propensity
  to substitute

Determinants of Buyer Power

Bargaining Leverage

Buyer concentration versus firm concentration
Buyer volume
Buyer switching costs relative to firm switching costs
Buyer information
Ability to backward integrate
Substitute products
Pull-through

Price Sensitivity

Price/Total purchases
Product differences
Brand identity
Impact on quality/Performance
Buyer profits
Decision makers' incentives

Column 2 of Table 3–1 lists key implications of each competitive force. For example, when new entrants move into an established industry segment, they generally introduce significant additional capacity because they frequently have allocated substantial resources to gain a foothold in the industry. Typically, new entrants cause a reduction in prices or an increase in costs.

TABLE 3-1 Impact of Competitive Forces

Force	Implication	Potential Uses of IT to Combat Force

Threat of new entrants	New capacity
	Substantial resources
	Reduced prices or inflation of incumbents' costs
		Provide entry barriers:
		  Economies of scale
		  Switching costs
		  Product differentiation
		  Access to distribution channels

Buyers' bargaining power	Prices forced down High quality More services Competition encouraged	Buyer selection Switching costs Differentiation Entry barriers
Suppliers' bargaining power	Prices raised Reduced quality and services (labor)	Selection Threat of backward integration
Threat of substitute products or services	Potential returns limited Ceiling on prices	Improve price/performance Redefine products and services

Traditional intraindustry rivals	Competition:
	  Price
	  Product
	  Distribution and service
		Cost-effectiveness
		Market access
		Differentiation:
		  Product
		  Services
		  Firm

Column 3 lists some examples of how IT can be used to change the balance of power among these five forces. For example, IT can raise barriers to entry by increasing economies of scale, increasing switching costs, differentiating a product or service, or limiting access to key markets or distribution channels.

Porter describes three *generic strategies* for achieving proprietary advantage within an industry: cost leadership, differentiation, and focus. (See Figure 3–3.) The latter strategy—focus—has two variants: cost and differentiation.

Each generic strategy involves two key choices: (1) the competitive mechanism—a firm can lower its cost or differentiate its products and services; and (2) the competitive scope—a firm can target a broad market or a narrow one. Cost leadership and differentiation strategies are targeted toward a broad market, while focused strategies seek to lower costs (cost focus) or differentiate products and services (differentiation focus) in a narrow industry segment. The specific actions required to implement each generic strategy vary widely from industry to industry, as do feasible

---

FIGURE 3–3   Three Generic Strategies Related to Competitive Advantage and Scope

---

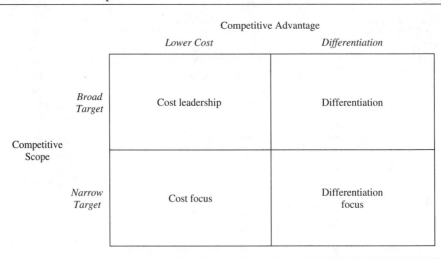

generic strategies in a particular industry. Selecting and implementing the appropriate generic strategy are thought to be central to achieving long-term competitive advantage in an industry.

At the core of the concept of generic strategies are two basic principles. First, competitive advantage is believed to be the goal of any strategy. Second, it is believed that a firm must define the type of competitive advantage it seeks to attain and the scope within which it will attain it. Porter believes that the decision to be "all things to all people" is a recipe for strategic mediocrity and below-average performance. More recently, attention has shifted from a focus on the specific strategy of a firm to a focus on core competencies.[4] This shifts the focus of attention from a specific strategy to the underlying organizational competencies that will enable (or prevent) a firm from reaching that strategy. Chapter 5 addresses this important issue in greater depth.

Search for Opportunity

Assessment of the impact of IT on strategy begins by addressing five questions. If the answer to one or more of these questions is yes, IT may be a strategic resource that requires attention at the highest level.

---

[4]G. Hamel and C.K. Prahalad, "Strategic Intent," *Harvard Business Review,* May-June, 1989.

Can IT Build Barriers to Entry?   A successful entry barrier offers not only a new service that appeals to customers but also features that keep the customers "hooked." The harder the service is to emulate, the higher the barrier to entry. A large financial service firm sought to build an effective barrier to entry when it launched a unique and highly attractive financial product, which depended on sophisticated software that was both costly and difficult to implement. The complexity of the IT-enabled product caught competitors off guard; it took several years for them to develop a similar product, which gave the initiating firm valuable time to establish a significant market position. During this time, the firm continued to innovate, enhancing the original product and adding value to the services. Competitors not only had to catch up, but had to catch a moving target.

The payoff from value-added features that increase both sales and market share is particularly strong in industries within which there are great economies of scale and where customers are extremely price sensitive. By being the first to move onto the learning curve, a company can gain a cost advantage that enables it to put great pressure on its competitors.

Electronic tools that increase the effectiveness of the sales force represent another kind of entry barrier—a knowledge barrier. For example, several large insurance companies have implemented sophisticated, customer-oriented financial-planning support packages that have greatly expanded the ability of their agents to deal with the rapidly changing and increasingly complex knowledge requirements within the industry. By increasing the capabilities of the sales force (a key strategic resource of the firm), these insurance companies have created significant barriers to entry that are exceedingly difficult to emulate. Many companies in the 1990s are finding that knowledge barriers are among the most potent of competitive forces.

Can IT Build in Switching Costs?   Are there ways to encourage reliance on IT-enabled products and services? Can industry participants be encouraged to embed these products and services into their operations in such a manner that the notion of switching to a competitor is extremely unattractive? Ideally, an IT system should be simple for the customer to adopt at the outset, but then through a series of increasingly complex— yet very valuable—enhancements, the IT system becomes tightly intertwined with the customer's daily routine. Proponents of electronic home banking hope to capitalize on the potential of increasing switching costs. Indeed, in France, a $3 billion "virtual" bank exists that has no branches; customers, who have tightly integrated their financial records into the bank's IT systems, conduct all transactions electronically.[5]

---

[5]Tawfik Jelassi, *European Casebook on Competing through Information Technology* Englewood Cliffs, N.J.: Prentice Hall, 1994).

A manufacturer of heavy machines provides another example of how IT can add value to and support a company's basic product line while also increasing switching costs. The company has embedded into its product software that enables remote monitoring and, in some cases, correction of problems. In case of mechanical failure, the diagnostic device calls a computer at corporate headquarters, where software analyzes and, if possible, solves the problem. If the problem cannot be solved remotely, the computer pages a mechanic and provides a complete record of the current problem and the maintenance history of the product. Availability of parts required to fix the problem is also noted, and technical documentation is provided. Now installed around the globe, the system has dramatically improved service quality and response time, significantly enhanced customer loyalty, and decreased the tendency of customers to buy service contracts elsewhere.

The joint marketing program of MCI, Citibank, and American Airlines, through which customers can earn American Airlines frequent flyer miles whenever they use the telephone or their credit cards, is another example of how IT can support value-added services that enhance customer loyalty and increase switching costs.

Can IT Change the Basis of Competition?   In some industries IT has enabled a firm to fundamentally alter the basis of competition within the industry. This occurs when a firm uses IT to radically change either its cost structure (cost advantage) or its product/service offerings (differentiation advantage).

For example, in the mid-1970s, a major distributor of magazines to newsstands and stores, a very cost-competitive industry segment, used IT to significantly lower its cost structure by developing cheaper methods of sorting and distributing magazines. By radically reducing both headcount and inventory, it was able to become the low-cost producer in the industry. Because buyers were extremely price sensitive, the distributor was able to quickly increase market share, but it didn't stop there. Having attained significant cost advantage, the distributor then built upon its IT platform to differentiate its products and services. Recognizing that its customers were small, unsophisticated, and unaware of their profit structures, the distributor used its internal records of weekly shipments and returns from each newsstand to create a new value-added product—a customized report that calculated profit per square foot for every magazine sold within each newsstand and then compared these data with aggregate information from other newsstands operating in similar neighborhoods. The distributor could thus tell each newsstand every month how it could improve its product mix. In addition to distributing magazines, the company used IT and the information it generated to offer a valuable inventory-management service. In this example, the distributor initially used IT to change its competitive position within an industry; it then used IT to fundamentally change the basis of competition.

Dramatic cost reduction can significantly alter the old ground rules of competition, enabling companies to find strategic opportunity in the new cost-competitive environment. For example, there may be an opportunity for sharp cost reduction through staff reduction or the ability to grow without hiring staff, improve material use, increase machine efficiency through better scheduling or more cost-effective maintenance, or inventory reduction. In the drug wholesale industry, from 1971 to 1991, the average operating cost/sales ratio of the major players dropped from 16 percent to 2 percent mostly through the use of IT, and a fragmented industry of 1,000 firms dropped to under 200, with the top five players controlling 75 percent of the market. Alternatively, there may be an opportunity to add value to existing products and services or to create new products and services that radically change customer buying patterns.

Understanding when to move on these issues is particularly difficult and troublesome. For example, few people doubt that videotext and cable services are becoming important as new retailing outlets. The exact timing of when they will be profitable and the exact nature of the products remain unclear. The situation confronting libraries is another excellent example of the uncertain nature of competitive decisions. Drawing on over 1,000 years of tradition in storing books made of parchment and paper, today's libraries are at a crossroads. Soaring materials costs, expansion of computer databases, CD-ROM technology, and electronic links between libraries promise to make the research facility of the year 2000 utterly unrecognizable from that of 1990. The period of transition will be relatively short, the investments high, and the discontinuity with the past dramatic.

As managers consider opportunities to use IT to radically alter the basis of competition, it is often difficult, especially in the early stages, to distinguish the intriguing (but ephemeral) from the important structural innovations. The consequences of action (or inaction) can be devastating if managers misread the cues.

Can IT Change the Balance of Power in Supplier Relationships?

The development of IT systems that link manufacturers and suppliers has been a powerful role for IT within the firm. For example, just-in-time inventory systems have dramatically reduced inventory costs and warehouse expenses, while also improving order fulfillment time. Traditionally, companies have used inventory to buffer uncertainty in their production processes. Large safety stocks of raw materials and supplies are kept on hand to allow operations to run smoothly. But inventory costs money; it ties up capital, it requires costly physical facilities for storage, and it must be managed by people. Increasingly, companies are using IT to link suppliers and manufacturers; by improving information flow, they are able to decrease uncertainty, and, in the process, reduce inventory, cut the number of warehouses, and decrease headcount while also streamlining the production process.

A large retailer capitalized on these advantages by electronically linking its materials-ordering system to its suppliers' order-fulfillment systems. Now, when 100 sofas are needed for a particular region, the retailer's computer automatically checks the inventory status of its primary sofa suppliers; the one with the fastest availability and lowest cost gets the order.

Equally important, the retailer's computer continually monitors its suppliers' finished-goods inventories, factory scheduling, and commitments against its schedule to make sure enough inventory will be available to meet unexpected demand. If a supplier's inventories are inadequate, the retailer alerts the supplier; and if a supplier is unwilling to go along with this system, it may find its share of business dropping until it is replaced by others. As a purely defensive investment, a major textile manufacturer recently undertook an $8 million new order-entry system simply to maintain its relationships with its top three customers because they had made it clear that anything short of full EDI inventory management would mean the end of the business relationship.

A major manufacturer proposed CAD to CAD links with a $100 million a year in sales pressed-powder metal parts manufacturer. Within 18 months, this system shortened the product design cycle from eight months to three.

Such interorganizational systems can redistribute power between buyer and supplier. In the case of the aerospace manufacturer, identified at the beginning of the chapter, the CAD to CAD systems increased dependence on an individual supplier, making it hard for the company to replace the supplier and leaving it vulnerable to major price increases. The retailer, on the other hand, was in a much stronger position to dictate the terms of its relationship with its suppliers (e.g., Wal-Mart with its steadily increasing demands, facilitated by its electronic linkages, is genuinely feared by many suppliers).

Can IT Technology Generate New Products?   As described earlier, IT can lead to products with higher quality, faster delivery, or less cost. Similarly, at little extra expense, existing products can be tailored to meet a customers' special needs. Some companies may be able to combine one or more of these advantages. In addition, at little additional cost, as in the case of the on-line diagnostic system for machine failure described earlier, electronic support services can increase the value of the total package in the consumer's eyes.

Indeed, mergers are currently being planned around those capabilities. A down-market catalogue company and a credit card company that specializes in the "unbanked market" (20 to 30 million U.S. wage earners) are focusing on combining their customer data files to facilitate cross-marketing and offer a new set of services.

In another example, credit card companies are voracious consumers of delinquent accounts receivable data from other firms; indeed, there is a whole industry dedicated to the collection and organization of these data.

Similarly, nonproprietary research data files often have significant value to third parties.

In some cases, a whole new industry has emerged (e.g., point-of-sale (POS) data in supermarkets). For example, a number of market research firms now purchase data from large supermarket chains, analyze it, and then sell it back to the supermarkets. The market research firm organizes these data by ZIP code into a research tool for retail chains, food suppliers, and others interested in consumer activity.

Finally, the information content of products has increased markedly. For example, today's upscale cars have more than 100 microcomputers in them controlling everything from antiskid braking to climate control. Sewing machines use microcomputers to control everything from stitching pattern to complex thread shifts. Fighter aircraft and submarines have highly sophisticated automated control systems.

ANALYZING THE VALUE CHAIN FOR IT OPPORTUNITIES

An effective way to search for potential IT opportunities is through a systematic analysis of a company's value chain—the series of interdependent activities that bring a product or service to the customer. Figure 3–4 shows a typical value chain[6] and briefly defines the meaning of each of the company's activities. In different settings, IT can profoundly affect one or more of these activities, sometimes simply by improving effectiveness, sometimes by fundamentally changing the activity, and sometimes by altering the relationship between activities. In addition, the actions of one firm can significantly affect the value chain of key customers and suppliers.

Inbound Logistics

As illustrated earlier, in many settings IT has expedited procurement of materials. One major distribution company, for example, installed hundreds of terminals on supplier premises to enable just-in-time, on-line ordering. The company required its suppliers to maintain adequate inventory and provide on-line access to stock levels.

This system has decreased the need for extensive warehousing of incoming materials and has reduced disruptions due to inventory shortfalls. The need to maintain inventory safety stocks and the associated holding costs has been passed along to the suppliers. The purchaser's computer, which can rapidly scan several suppliers' databases and order from the one offering the lowest price, has sharply eroded suppliers' margins. While the

---

[6]Michael E. Porter, *Competitive Strategy* (1980).

FIGURE 3–4 The Value Chain

Support activities	Corporate infrastructure						
	Human resource management						
	Technology development						
	Procurement						
		Inbound logistics	Operations	Outbound logistics	Marketing and sales	Service	
		Primary activities					Margin

Activity	Definition
Inbound logistics	Materials receiving, storing, and distribution to manufacturing premises.
Operations	Transforming inputs into finished products.
Outbound logistics	Storing and distributing products.
Marketing and sales	Promotion and sales force.
Service	Service to maintain or enhance product value.
Corporate infrastructure	Support of entire value chain, such as general management, planning, finance, accounting, legal services, government affairs, and quality management.
Human resource management	Recruiting, hiring, training, and development.
Technology development	Improving product and manufacturing process.
Procurement	Function or purchasing input.

Source: Michael E. Porter and Victor E. Millar, "How Information Gives You Competitive Advantage," *Harvard Business Review* July–August 1985, p. 151.

buyer has reaped many of the rewards, vendors have also benefited as changing suppliers has become more difficult.

A retail chain's direct linkage to its major textile suppliers not only improved delivery and enabled inventory reduction but also provided the flexibility to meet changing demand almost immediately. This, in turn, offset the impact of the lower price offered by foreign suppliers, thus enabling U.S. textile manufacturers to gain share in this cost-sensitive, highly competitive environment.

Operations and Product Definition

Information systems technologies can also influence a manufacturer's operations and product offerings. In 1989, a manufacturer of thin transparent film completed a $30 million investment in new computer-controlled manufacturing facilities for one of its major product lines. This change slashed order response time from 10 weeks to two days and improved quality levels significantly.

A financial services firm, having decided to go after more small private investors (with portfolios of about $25,000), introduced a flexible financial instrument that gave its investors immediate on-line ability to move their funds among stocks and other financial products, provided money market rates on idle funds, and offered the same liquidity as a checking account. The company, the first to introduce this service, captured a huge initial market share, which it has maintained over the years by continued product enhancement. In the first two years, the company achieved six times the volume of its nearest competitor. Five years later it still retained a 70 percent share of the market.

A videotext service company redefined its business as essentially a bit-moving operation—that is, getting data from one place to another. Under this broader concept, it offered a new line of financial services, for example, real-time financial information, such as up-to-the-second foreign exchange rates. The company made no important changes in its technology, but its sales and profits soared.

A major insurance company that defined its business as a provider of diversified financial services improved its services to policyholders by allowing immediate on-line checking of the status of claims and claims processing. The company also provided on-line access to new services and products, including modeling packages that enabled corporate benefits officers to tailor various benefit packages, balancing cost and employee service. In response to client demand, it also sold either software for claims processing or claims-processing services to corporate clients who elected to self-insure. The company credits these information technology-enabled product initiatives with keeping it firmly in place at the top of its industry despite tremendous competition from other diversified financial services companies.

Outbound Logistics

IT can also influence the way services and products are delivered to customers. As mentioned earlier, the reservation-system, provided chiefly by United Airlines and American Airlines, has profoundly affected smaller airlines that do not furnish this service. Indeed, in December 1984, the Civil

Aeronautics Board, believing that the systems strongly influenced purchasing behavior, issued a cease-and-desist order that required that all carriers' flights be fairly represented. Automatic teller machines, as well as theater-ticket and airline-ticket machines, allow cash and services to be rapidly and reliably delivered to customers where they work or shop.

Marketing and Sales

Marketing and sales, functional areas often neglected in the first three decades of IT, are now areas of high impact. In many firms, the sales force has been supplied with a wide array of handheld and laptop computers that enable firms to collect detailed customer and market data, which can then be packaged and delivered back to the sales force—and directly to customers.

A large pharmaceutical company offered on-line, order-entry for its products and those of its noncompetitors. This service increased its market share and revenues. The companies excluded from the system threatened legal action because of damage to their market position.

In the industrial air conditioning industry, a major corporation built a microcomputer-based modeling system to help architects model the heating and cooling system requirements for commercial properties. The system, which significantly reduced design time for the architects, led many of them to consider the company's products more favorably. A competing corporation subsequently made a similar computer model available via a communication network; in addition, it allowed the architects to access detailed information on cost and part availability. The new system neutralized the advantages gained by the competitor's earlier product.

An agricultural chemicals company developed a sophisticated on-line crop-planning service for its chief agricultural customers. From a personal computer, using a standard telephone connection, farmers can access agricultural databases containing prices of various crops, necessary growing conditions, and the costs of various chemicals to support different crops. They can then access various models and decision support systems, tailor them to their unique field requirements, and examine the implications of various crop rotations and timing for planting. The model also helps the farmers to select fertilizer and chemical applications and to group their purchases to achieve maximum discounts. Finally, with a few keystrokes, farmers can place orders for future delivery. Similar services have been offered by a major seed company in coordination with a state agricultural extension service. Firms from different industries are using this technology to reach the same customers.

Along a different vein, to strengthen its marketing of agricultural loans, a major bank has offered a similar crop-planning service. Two previously noncompeting companies are now competing in the same sales software arena.

Over the past five years, a major food company has assembled a national database that keeps track of daily sales of each of its products in each of the 500,000 stores it services. This database is now totally accessible through a wide-area network to market planners in their 22 regional districts. Combined with market and competitor data from market research companies, this information has significantly increased the precision and sophistication of market planning and execution.

After-Sales Service

IT is also revolutionizing after-sales service; for example, on its new line of elevators, an elevator company has installed on-line diagnostic measuring and reporting devices similar to those used by the airlines. These devices identify potential problems before the customer notices a difficulty and enable the service representative to fix the elevator before it breaks down, reducing repair costs and increasing customer satisfaction.

A large manufacturer of industrial machinery has installed an expert system on its home-office computer to support product maintenance. When a machine failure occurs on a customer's premises, the machine is connected over a telephone line to the manufacturer's computer, which performs an analysis of the problem and issues instructions to the machine operator. Service visits have decreased by 50 percent, while customer satisfaction has significantly improved.

Corporate Infrastructure

A large travel agency has electronically connected small outlying offices located near big corporate customers via satellite to enable access to the full support capabilities of the home office. These network capabilities have transformed the organizational structure from one large central corporate office to many small full-service offices, resulting in a 27 percent growth in sales.[7]

Management Control. A major financial services firm used to pay a sales commission on each product sold by its sales force; thus, the sales force had maximum incentive to make the initial sale and no incentive to ensure the customer continued to be satisfied with the services and thus kept doing business with the firm. Using its new integrated customer database, the company implemented a new commission structure that rewarded both the initial sale and customer retention and growth of the

---

[7]Chapter 5 will examine these organizational ramifications in far greater detail.

asset base. This approach, made possible by new technology, aligned the company strategy and its sales incentive system much more effectively.

In some instances, IT has dramatically enhanced coordination by providing greater access to a more widely connected network using fairly simple but powerful tools such as voice mail, electronic mail, groupware, and videoconferencing. New networked "workflow" systems are also enabling tighter coordination of operations. For example, due to high capital costs and operating expense, every major U.S. air carrier uses a network to monitor the precise location of all its aircraft. It knows each airplane's location, the passengers on-board, their planned connections, and the connection schedules. It can instantaneously make decisions about speeding up late flights or delaying connecting departures. The opportunities for controlling fuel costs and preventing revenue loss (because many passengers must continue on competitors' flights if they miss their connections) amount to tens of millions of dollars a year. Trucking companies and railroads use similar methods to track cargoes and optimize schedules.

Human Resources

Human resources management has also changed. For example, to facilitate important personnel decisions, an oil company has given personal computers to all its corporate management committee members, thus giving full on-line access to the detailed personnel files of the 400 most senior members in the corporation. These files contain data on five-year performance appraisals, photographs, and lists of positions for which each person is a backup candidate. The company believes this capability has facilitated its important personnel decisions. Additionally, special government compliance auditing, which used to take months to complete, can now be done in hours.

Technology Development

To guide its drilling decisions, a large oil company processes vast amounts of data gathered from an overhead satellite. The company uses this information to support oil field bidding and drilling decisions. Similarly, CAD/CAM (computer-aided design and manufacturing) technology has fundamentally changed the quality and speed with which the company can manufacture its drilling platforms.

A seed company considers its single most important technology expenditure to be computer support for research. Modern genetic planning involves managing a global database of millions of pieces of germ plasm. These database planning and molecular simulation models—the keys to their future—are not possible without large-scale computing capacity. Repeatedly, their detailed data files have allowed them to find a germ plasm thousands of miles away in Africa to solve a problem in an Iowa cornfield.

Procurement

Procurement activities are also being transformed. For example, with a series of on-line electronic bulletin boards that make the latest spot prices instantly available around the country, a manufacturing company directs its nationwide purchasing effort. The boards have led to a tremendous improvement in purchasing price effectiveness, both in discovering and implementing new quantity pricing discount data, as well as ensuring that the lowest prices are being achieved.

A retailer, by virtue of its large size, has succeeded in its demand for on-line access to the inventory files and production schedules of its suppliers. This access has permitted the company to manage its inventories more tightly and to exert pressure on suppliers to lower price and improve product availability.

New market opportunities abound. For example, an entrepreneurial start-up provides desktop software to allow traders and others with intense needs for fast-breaking information to pull relevant material from over 400 continuous news feeds (e.g., Reuters, Dow Jones),[8] analyze the information, and deliver it to end users. The firm's revenues—$20 million in 1995—are growing rapidly.

In summary, a systematic examination of a company's value chain is an effective way to search for profitable IT applications. This analysis requires keen administrative insight, awareness of industry structure, and familiarity with the rules of competition in the particular setting. Companies need to understand their own value chains as well as those of key customers and suppliers in order to uncover potential new service areas. Similarly, understanding competitors' value chains provides insight on potential competitive moves. Careful thought is needed to identify potential new entrants to an industry—those companies whose current business could be enhanced by an IT-enabled product or service.

THE RISKS OF INFORMATION SYSTEMS SUCCESS[9]

Problems and Evaluations

While previous sections of this chapter focus on opportunities, this section discusses the potential problems that can arise when a firm's efforts are "too successful." Management policies and procedures that help ensure that potentially high-risk projects are appropriately evaluated are also discussed.

---

[8]Since the news feeds have different data sources, key items picked up by one might be missed by several others.

[9]The material in this section has been adapted from Michael R. Vitale, "The Growing Risks of Information Systems Success," *Management Information Systems Quarterly,* December 1986.

The risks discussed in this chapter concern strategic vulnerabilities as opposed to the implementation risks discussed in Chapter 10.

Systems That Change the Basis of Competition to a Company's Disadvantage.   When information systems are used to gain competitive advantage in a given industry, there is often a requirement for continued enhancement to sustain competitive position. An organization that is not prepared to stay the course with continued investments in information systems may be better off not entering the race in the first place.

This lesson was learned, through experience, by a U.S. commercial appliances manufacturer, whose products were typically purchased and installed by building contractors who worked from a set of technical specifications for size, capacity, and so forth. Historically, the company had offered contractors a mail-in consulting service that could translate specifications into products and instructions for wiring, plumbing, and so forth.

Initially, the company developed mainframe software that captured this consulting expertise. Contractors continued to send specifications by mail; the company would feed the requirements through the mainframe and mail back a neatly printed list of products and instructions. (As would be expected, most of the recommended products were manufactured by the company itself.) Over time, the appliance market evolved and so did the microcomputer industry. The system was a huge success; the company significantly increased its market share, but development stopped there. A competitor—larger, older, and equipped with a more progressive information systems staff—developed a similar system that ran on the more powerful IBM personal computer. Software was provided to contractors at no charge, as were network connections to the company's mainframe. Analysis could be performed immediately, and the required products, made almost exclusively by that system's owner, could be ordered at the push of a key. As IBM began to dominate the business/personal microcomputer market, the second company recaptured its lost market share and more.

By introducing customers and competitors to the use of information systems but then failing to track or adapt to changes in the technology, the first company turned an initial IT success into a competitive failure.

Systems That Lower Entry Barriers.   As described earlier, IT has been used to either raise or maintain barriers to entry in many industries. In situations where extensive investment in hardware and software is obligatory for all participants, the investment required for entry is also increased. In other circumstances, information systems have been used to capture distribution channels, again increasing the cost and difficulty of entrance.

On the other hand, by making an industry more attractive, a company may in fact trigger action by other competitors that have greater IT resources to expend. A major seller of health and casualty insurance faced that dilemma. The firm did the majority of its business on a payroll-deduction basis with very small employers who did not offer insurance as a fringe benefit. Because many of its customers did their payrolls by hand, bookkeepers became a major target for the insurer's sales force. The primary competition was not so much from other insurers as from the bookkeepers' lack of time and willingness to handle additional deductions. To help overcome this obstacle, the insurer considered offering a computerized payroll preparation package for small companies. The development of such software was considered to be well within the capabilities of its IT group, and its sales force was already in contact with many potential customers for the new service. Pricing was designed to provide some profit, but the main intent was to create tighter links to small customers.

Before much work had been done on the new payroll system, the vice president for IT recognized a danger. Although it might well be possible to convince customers to do their payrolls by computer, he could see there was a risk that the business would go not to the insurer but to one of the large, experienced firms that dominated the payroll business and could offer a more sophisticated customized package. Any of these organizations could, if they chose, also offer health and casualty insurance through a relationship with another insurer. The link to customers might be tighter, but it was not clear whether his company would be at the other end! This strategic analysis led the company to drop the idea of offering payroll service because to continue the project would, in the company's opinion, have risked opening its primary line of business to new competitors.

Systems That Bring on Litigation or Regulation. In the category of things that work too well for their own good are systems that, after achieving their initial objectives, continue to grow in size and effectiveness and eventually give rise to claims of unfair competition and cries for government regulation. Possible outcomes are forced divestiture of the systems or an agreement to share them with competitors.

The airline reservations systems used by travel agents illustrate this danger. The United and American reservation systems control the offices of nearly 80 percent of U.S. travel agents. Some of their competitors have claimed that this level of penetration allows the two big airlines to effectively control the industry's channels of distribution. Examples of such alleged domination include biased display of data, close monitoring and control of travel agents, and inaccurate data on competitors' flights.

After a lengthy investigation of these claims, the Civil Aeronautics Board (CAB) ordered changes in the operation and pricing of computer reservations systems. Nevertheless, United and American were sued by 11 competitors, which demanded that the two carriers spin off their reservations systems into separate subsidiaries. United and American opposed the suit but did agree, along with TWA, to provide unbiased displays.

Although they deny unfair practices, United and American have never denied using their reservations systems to gain competitive advantage.

Indeed, the two airlines claim that the systems are not economically viable on the basis of usage fee income alone—they were intended to generate increased sales. (United and American may already have recovered their investments in the reservation systems by making these sales.) The precedent of government intervention suggests, however, that future developers of competitively effective systems may find their returns limited by law or regulation.

The central theme of this controversy is that there is such a thing as an unfair "information monopoly" and that control of electronic channels of distribution may be unacceptable to the public. The tussle between the U.S. Justice Department and Microsoft, which is alleged to excessively dominate certain segments of the software industry to the detriment of the public interest, is another example of these issues.

Systems That Increase Customers' or Suppliers' Power to the Detriment of the Innovator. Although IT can strengthen a company's relationships with its customers and suppliers, in some circumstances it also provides tools and expertise that enable the customers and suppliers to function on their own; in fact, this change may be an inevitable outcome of evolving IT penetration in an industry.

An overnight delivery company, for example, instituted very fast delivery of electronically transmitted messages between its offices. The original was picked up from the sender and put through a facsimile machine at a nearby office; the transmitted image was received at an office near the recipient and delivered by hand.

As fax technology grew, the delivery company announced that it would place facsimile machines on its customers' premises and act as a switch among the installed machines. Delivery promised to be even quicker, since there would be no need to take the original copy to the sending office or to deliver the received copy; but, the value the delivery company was able to add to off-the-shelf facsimile technology was questionable. Little existed to prevent its customers from installing similar equipment directly; indeed, the manufacturer of the facsimile machines advertised its products prominently as the ones supporting the delivery company's system. The firm soon abandoned this line of business.

Bad Timing. Determining the time to make a bold move requires a careful balancing of cost and culture. Get there too early with an expensive, clumsy technology in an unreceptive customer environment (e.g., home banking) and you have a real fiasco. Get there too late, as the regional airlines and hundreds of drug wholesalers did, and you also lose. Behind the technology issues lie very real marketing and business policy issues.

Investments That Turn Out to Be Indefensible and Fail to Produce Lasting Advantages. There are numerous reasons an investment can turn out to be indefensible. In general, interorganizational systems with high potential daily transaction rates are very successful; however, those with low daily transaction rates (one to two per day or less) can become strategic liabilities, as end users get lost in procedural details. In addition, features of great value to end users, but easily replicable by the firm's competitors, are less valuable than those that, because of size and/or peculiar reinforcing linkage with the firm's products, are hard to replicate. Similarly, systems that enable a firm to start simple and continue to add new features and services as technology and industry conditions change are more effective than one-time moves that stand as fixed targets for competitors.

Systems That Pose an Immediate Threat to Large, Established Competitors.   Several hotel chains felt vulnerable to the changing whims of airlines that provided hotel reservation services. They attempted to form an association, hoping to have sufficient market power and purchasing power to form their own system. But the association's efforts and results were disappointing—and the association ultimately failed.

Inadequate Understanding of Buying Dynamics across Market Segments.   It is very easy to inappropriately apply a set of concepts that works in one market niche but not in another. For example, airline reservations systems have been widely cited as an example of effective IT use. As noted earlier, however, over the past decade, one of the most successful airlines has been Southwest. Aiming at the very price-sensitive market, it has carved out a scheduling and service strategy in which reservation systems play a distinctly subordinate role. Different market niches may have very different dynamics, and ignoring these differences causes problems.

Cultural Lag and Perceived Transfer of Power.   Some systems go beyond the customers' technical comfort level—clearly the case with the previously mentioned electronic home banking failure. Interestingly, as noted earlier, home banking has worked in the very different French environment. A related issue is the concern by one party in an interorganization system that it will be manipulated by the other party and not be able to resist the pressure without losing the business relationship. Not all IT efforts are win-win situations.

These are hard but very important problems. Quite separate are the areas of technical project management addressed in Chapter 10.[10]

Assessing Competitor Risk

Understanding competitive risks is the first step in managing them. Understanding, in turn, is a two-phase process: (1) predicting in detail the industry-level changes that may be brought about by development and

---

[10]Chapter 10 focuses primarily on the real problems of implementation, while this chapter is focused on failures of conceptualization.

implementation of particular information technologies and (2) assessing the potential impact of these changes on the company. Such foresight, sadly, is very cloudy and the probabilities of success are rough estimates.

Increasing use of information systems is often naively viewed as inevitable. Certainly, situations occur where firms must invest in and adapt to IT in order to remain viable, even if the increase in technological intensity causes a complete reevaluation and reformulation of the firm's strategy. But some technological "advances" have remained in an embryonic stage for years. Electronic home banking and home shopping, as noted earlier, are two examples. Sometimes these developments are stalled because of cost, IT capability, or consumer acceptance; other times, they are held back by lack of support from established industry participants. Rather than uniformly criticizing "laggards" for technological backwardness, it is more appropriate to entertain the possibility that they understand the technology completely and are prepared to utilize it when it becomes necessary, but are unwilling to precipitate a potentially unfavorable change in their competitive environment.

An appropriate place to start in considering the potential impact of a new strategic use of IT is with the motivation for the new system. As noted earlier, potential justifications include raising entry barriers, increasing switching costs, reducing the power of buyers or suppliers, deterring substitute products, lowering costs, and increasing differentiation. Inevitably, if the initiative is successful, the outcome over time will be a change in the competitive forces affecting the industry. It is tempting, but dangerous and shortsighted, to consider these forces as affecting only current industry participants—suppliers, buyers, and competitors. As some of the examples indicate, because certain IT uses can open up an industry to new, threatening, and potentially dominant players, it is sometimes prudent to delay offensive moves.

When a firm considers new investments in strategic IT systems, it must candidly assess whether it will obtain any sustainable competitive advantage or whether it will maintain the current competitive situation at an increased level of cost. Additional caveats in this area include recognizing that IT software purchased from a nonexclusive source is unlikely to confer lasting advantage. Also, the movement of skilled IT personnel between firms often results in a rapid proliferation of key ideas, leaving the pioneering firm relatively no better off than before. In the absence of strong, first-mover advantages, some investments in information systems, regardless of their short-term glitz and appeal, may simply not pay off competitively over the long run.

As will be discussed later, the long-term commitment of top management is essential; the company must have a clear picture of its long-range strategy, how this move fits into it, and the resources and capabilities of competitors, both current and potential.

A crucial component of the assessment is analysis of the likely long-term consequences of a new system. Initial development cost and short-term benefits may not be an accurate indicator of its potential effects. To help this assessment, some organizations have found it useful to prepare an "impact statement" that lays out the competitive changes expected to result from a new information system, focusing on both the substantial benefits accruing from an improved competitive situation and the risks. Consideration of the positive impacts of the new system on competition forces broad thinking on potential negative impacts as well.

Over time, the key to managing these sorts of risks will be the organization's ability to learn from its experience so that it can continue to roll out strategic IT applications as and when appropriate. There must be a common understanding among general managers and senior IT executives about which pieces of the development effort should be considered "directional"—that is, likely to have a major effect on the organization's future competitive position. A thorough review of the potential impacts should be carried out before such systems are developed and again before they are implemented.

THE CHALLENGE

Achieving the advantages while avoiding the pitfalls requires IT management—and user management—plus imagination. The process is complicated by the fact that, while many IT products are strategic, the potential benefits are subjective and not easily verified. Often a strict return-on-investment (ROI) focus may turn attention towards narrow, well-defined targets rather than to broader, strategic opportunities that are harder to analyze.

Visualizing their systems in terms of the strategic grid (see Figure 2–4), managers in a number of organizations have concluded that their company or business unit is located in either the "support" or the "factory" quadrant and have set up staffing, organization, and planning activities accordingly. But, because of the sharp change in IT technology performance and the evolution of competitive conditions, this categorization may be wrong at some point in the future. For example, the competitor of the distributor described in this chapter's opening paragraph was complacent about its position and lost the advantages it initially gained. Ignoring new competitive conditions, the company did not realize what was happening until it was too late. Playing catchup can be difficult and expensive in the IT area.

A NEW POINT OF VIEW IS REQUIRED

To address the issues raised here, managers need to reevaluate their perspectives and biases.

Planning Issues

The CEO must insist that the end products of IT planning clearly communicate the true competitive impact of the expenditures involved. Figure 3–5 provides a framework that identifies priorities for the allocation of financial and staff resources.

FIGURE 3–5   Identifying Resource Allocation Priorities by Strategic Business Unit

Goal of IT expenditure	Growing, highly competitive industry	Relatively stable industry, known ground rules	Static or declining industry
Rehabilitate and maintain system	1	1	1
Experiment with new technology	2	3	3
Attain competitive advantage	2	2	3*
Maintain or regain competitive parity	2	3	4
Defined return on investment[†]	3	3	4

*Assuming the change is not so dramatic as to revolutionize the industry's overall performance.

[†]In an intensely cost-competitive environment, defined ROI is the same as gaining competitive advantage.

Note: Numbers indicate relative attractiveness or importance of the investment, with 1 denoting the highest priority.

In this connection, managers should realize that an extraordinarily large amount of the systems development effort is often devoted to the repair and maintenance of worn-out legacy systems[11] that fail to address current business conditions. Also, a vital but often unrecognized need exists for research and development to keep up with the technology and to ensure that the company knows the full range of possibilities.[12] Distinctly separate are the areas where a company spends money to obtain significant competitive advantage or to regain or maintain competitive parity. Finally, projects where the investment is defined for pure measurable return on investment (ROI) can be viewed quite differently.

The aim of the ranking process is to allocate resources to areas with the most growth potential. Each company should have an IT plan that vividly communicates to the CEO the data derived from Figure 3–5, explains why IT expenditures are allocated as they are, and enumerates explicitly the types of competitive benefits the company might expect from its IT expenditures.

Confidentiality and Competition

Until recently, it has been the industry norm for organizations to readily share data about IT systems and plans on the grounds that, since IT was primarily a tool for back-office support, collaboration would allow all firms to reduce administrative headaches. Managers today, however, must take appropriate steps to ensure the confidentiality of strategic IT plans and thinking. Great care should be taken in determining who will attend industry meetings, what they may talk about, and what information they may share with vendors and competitors.

Evaluating Expenditures

Executives should not permit use of simplistic rules to calculate desirable IT expense levels. For example, the common practice of comparing IT budgets using ratios such as percent of sales can be misleading. We have observed some companies spending 10 percent of their total sales on IT that are clearly underinvesting; we have seen others spending 1 percent that are overspending.

---

[11]"Legacy" refers to transaction processing systems that were originally designed to perform a specific task. Over time, these systems may not accurately reflect business needs. In addition, as hardware and software improvements occur in the information systems marketplace, older IS solutions tie an organization to an out-of-date platform that is unable to deliver value-creating applications and is costly to operate and maintain.

[12]This idea is developed in depth in Chapter 6.

The IT-Management Partnership

To make full use of the opportunities that IT presents, managers must work in close partnership with technical specialists. Bridging the gap between IT specialists, business management, and general management is, however, an enduring problem. Often uncomfortable with technology, many business managers are unaware of the new options IT provides and the ways in which it can support strategy. For their part, IT professionals are often not attuned to the complexities and subtleties of strategy formulation and execution. They are generally not part of the strategy development process.[13]

Partnership is necessary. IT experts understand the economies of the technology and know its limits and can also help move the organization towards the potential of tomorrow's technology. A change that is clumsy and inefficient in today's technology might eliminate the need for architecture redesign in the next generation. For example, very rich, interrelated databases today may be slow to access, presenting serious cost (and possibly response-time) problems. Tomorrow's faster computer and communications technology may eliminate these problems.

General managers and business managers bring insight to corporate and business priorities. They have detailed knowledge of the industry dynamics and the value chains for different areas of the business and can help identify the most appropriate path to follow for implementation. Synthesis of the two worlds is essential.

Opening Questions

Finally, as a way of starting the process, establishing a joint task force to address the following questions has proved valuable.

1. *What business are we really in?* What value do we provide to our customer? Can today's communications and computer technologies add value? Can IT help us redefine our business to higher value-added segments?
2. *Who are our biggest competitors today and in the future? Who else does, or could, provide the same products or services?*
3. *Can we use technology to integrate our own value chain activities to improve efficiency and effectiveness of operations?* Can we use technology to integrate our value chain with that of our customers, suppliers, distributors, and so forth? Can we introduce significant switching costs?
4. *Can we use IT to create entry and exit barriers?*

---

[13]This is discussed further in Chapter 7.

5. *Are any big changes in our industry looming on the horizon (e.g., deregulation, trade agreements)? Can technology help us compete in the new setting?*
6. *Will future changes in related industries influence the competitive situation? Can IT help us compete effectively in the new environment?*
7. *What are the risks involved in IT-enabled strategic initiatives? Can these risks be managed?*

These last two questions may be the most difficult of all. The answers require anticipating what is going to happen both in the marketplace and in relationships with clients, customers, competitors, and regulators. Also, the company must determine which innovations will provide sustainable advantage versus which competitors will be able to readily copy—adding to the costs of all industry participants and/or decreasing all margins.

A Final Thought

At resource allocation time, the difference between an effective strategic initiative and a harebrained scheme is razor-thin. Only after the passage of money and time is the outcome obvious.

Chapter

4

Electronic Commerce: From Interorganizational Systems to the Internet[1]

When Rutherford B. Hayes, the 19th President of the United States, was first introduced to the telephone in the early 1880s, he noted that it was a wonderful invention, an important one, but businessmen could never use it; in his experience, people had to meet face-to-face to conduct substantive affairs. Little did he realize how the telephone would transform business practices over the next half-century, opening innumerable commercial opportunities in the process.

Hayes was not alone in his assessment. Few businesspeople in the late 19th century could foresee the profound changes that a wide variety of technological innovations—going beyond the telephone to include production machinery, transportation, electricity, and communications—would bring; for although revolutionary in their ultimate effect, the changes evolved gradually. The shift from an agricultural to an industrial economy; the exodus of people from rural to urban areas; the shift from craft-based work to mass production; and the decline of the small, owner-operated firms in favor of large, vertically integrated multinationals were most clearly understood when viewed retrospectively. The transformation within business was accompanied by equally dramatic changes in society and world economics. The upheaval created both pain and prosperity.

---

[1] Portions of this chapter are adapted from L. Applegate, *Managing in an Information Age* (Boston: Harvard Business School Publishing, 1995).

Many believe we are in a similar period of upheaval as we shift from an industrial to an information economy.[2] Although information technology has evolved over a 30- to 40-year time span, we are now experiencing a period of radical change as the cumulative impact of the technological, social, and economic adaptations begins to coalesce, giving rise to a new business model. Many of these changes are occurring inside the bounds of the firm (see Chapter 5), but equally dramatic ones are also occurring across organizational boundaries as firms large and small struggle to rewrite the rules of competition and redefine the nature of commerce in a world in which information can cross the globe in seconds.

Over the past three decades, the speed and functionality of technology to support information management and communication have dramatically increased, causing us to rethink the business value of information. No longer a by-product of production, information has become a product in its own right, one that can be bought and sold in the marketplace. Information is now a critical ingredient in production and a prerequisite to the development, coordination, control, and allocation of other resources. In addition, as the economic value of information increases, the economic rewards accruing to those who can access it, transform it, and use it also increase.

Some properties of information that influence its potential commercial value include:

- It is reusable. Unlike physical products, information can be sold without transferring ownership. As one information provider observed, "I sell it, yet I still own it, and you also own it. Its value increases over time."
- It can be used as an efficient (and effective) substitute for labor. These substitution effects are most visible in information-intensive, complex, and time-dependent activities.
- The time value of information also increases as the speed of business increases. In the 1990s, the traditional approach of measuring economic value in terms of the "time value of money" is being replaced by measuring the "money value of time."

Recently, there has been a strong upsurge in interest in the use of IT as a tool to support electronic commerce.[3] Much of the interest in this type of IT application has been fueled by initiatives aimed at developing an information superhighway over which information can flow without obstruction.[4]

---

[2] See, for example, C. Hecksher and A. Donnellon, *The Post-Bureaucratic Organization* (Palo Alto: Sage Publications, 1994); C. Handy, T. Allen, and M.S. Morton, *Information Technology and the Corporation of the 1990s* (New York: Oxford University Press, 1994); *The Age of Unreason* (Boston: Harvard Business School Publishing, 1990) among others.

[3] Information systems that cross organizational borders are termed *interorganizational systems (IOS),* and the computer-to-computer sharing of information between firms has been termed *electronic data interchange (EDI).* More recently, the term *electronic commerce* has been used to describe a wide variety of IT-enabled market transactions.

[4] British Broadcasting Company, *The Intelligent Island,* Video.

But this upsurge in interest obscures the fact that the notion of electronic commerce is not new; much is to be learned by exploring early developments in the design and implementation of IT systems that enable communication and sharing of information across organizational boundaries.

THE EVOLUTION OF INTERORGANIZATIONAL SYSTEMS

In a 1966 *Harvard Business Review* article, Felix Kaufman implored general managers to think beyond their own organizational boundaries to the possibilities of interorganizational systems (IOS)—networked computers that enable companies to share information and information processing across organizational boundaries.[5] His was a visionary argument. But that vision was already becoming a reality. An entrepreneurial sales manager at American Hospital Supply Corporation (AHSC) had already created a system to enable the company to exchange order-processing information with its customers across telephone lines. Another enterprising manager— this one at American Airlines—had begun to offer computerized reservation terminals to large travel agencies to simplify the airline reservation process for key accounts. From these entrepreneurial actions grew two legendary strategic IT applications that changed the face of their respective industries. In doing so, they helped change the role of IT to become a tool to support commerce—the organizational strategies, structures, and systems through which an organization conducts business with buyers, sellers, and other industry participants.

Today, many of the most dramatic and potentially powerful uses of IT involve networks that transcend company boundaries. These IOS enable firms to incorporate buyers, suppliers, and partners in the redesign of their key business processes, thereby enhancing productivity, quality, speed, and flexibility. New distribution channels can be created, and new information-based products and services can be delivered. In addition, many IOS radically change the balance of power in buyer-supplier relationships, raise barriers to entry and exit, and, in many instances, shift the competitive position of industry participants. A review of the development of AHSC's and American Airlines' IOS highlights this point.

IOS Evolution at American Hospital Supply (AHSC)[6]

The AHSC system was conceived in 1964 by a California sales manager attempting to help a local hospital having problems with its inventory. The

---

[5] Felix Kaufman, "Data Systems That Cross Company Boundaries," *Harvard Business Review,* January–February 1966.

[6] See M. Vitale and B. Konsynski, *Baxter Healthcare Corporation* (Boston: Harvard Business School Publishing No. 188–080, 1988), and J. Sviokla, *Baxter International: On-Call as Soon as Possible?* (Boston: Harvard Business School Publishing No. 195–103, 1994) for a detailed discussion of the AHSC/Baxter Travenol story.

salesperson, having learned firsthand the benefits that AHSC had gained from its recently installed internal inventory system, gave the hospital a box of prepunched cards—one for each item purchased from AHSC—that were inserted between boxes of supplies at the point when the particular items should be reordered. These cards were collected and fed into a card reader that the AHSC salesperson provided to the customer. Order data were sent across standard phone lines to a card punch machine at AHSC, and the result of this electronic data interchange (EDI) was a duplicate set of cards at AHSC containing all the information needed to process the hospital's order. The cards were then fed into AHSC's computer billing machine and order processing continued as usual. This simple process redesign dramatically improved the efficiency and quality of the order fulfillment process for both AHSC and the hospital. Accuracy improved, delivery times decreased, and the hospital reduced its inventory. AHSC noted that the new process greatly decreased the clerical work and time required to take orders. Within one year, AHSC had offered the on-line order system to 200 customers, who gladly signed on.

Over the years, the AHSC IOS, which became known as ASAP, was continuously improved to take advantage of emerging new technologies. By 1985, many hospitals ordered their supplies through personal computers (PCs) or mainframes linked directly to AHSC's mainframes, thus distributing both information processing and order-process control between the customer and AHSC. In addition, AHSC had implemented VIP, a system linking the company to its suppliers—other manufacturers of hospital supplies that also served as AHSC competitors. ASAP generated over $11 million per year in order-processing productivity benefits and an additional $4 to $5 million in incremental revenues for AHSC.

In 1985, AHSC was purchased by Baxter Travenol, which in 1987 partnered with General Electric Information Services (GEIS) to create the next generation of ASAP—ASAP Express. This system integrated VIP and ASAP to create a hospital-supply marketplace, facilitated by GEIS—a third-party information provider. With each successive generation of the ASAP system, functionality of the system was enhanced and additional benefits were accrued by both customers and AHSC/Baxter. In addition, each generation of the system redistributed information processing and managerial control of the order-fulfillment process toward a more distributed model. In 1994, AHSC/Baxter abandoned ASAP and, in partnership with Bergen Burnsweig (a pharmaceutical distributor), Boise Cascade (a marketer of office products), Eastman Kodak (a supplier of imaging systems), and TSI International (a supplier of EDI software and services), created OnCall. This system provided end-to-end electronic commerce for the hospital industry that eliminated all paperwork; in addition, future plans called for distributing electronic catalogs on CD-ROM and enabling on-line electronic shopping. (Figure 4–1 summarizes the evolution of AHSC's ASAP interorganizational system.)

FIGURE 4–1 Evolution of American Hospital Supply's (AHSC) ASAP System

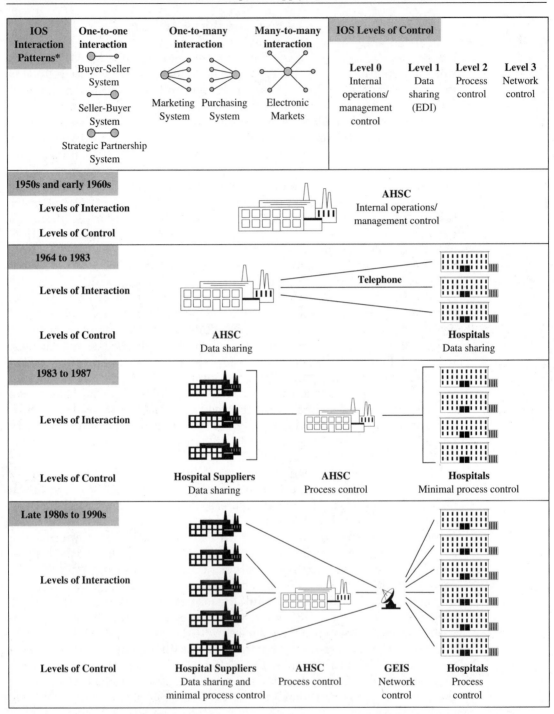

*See B. Konsynski, "Strategic Control in the Extended Enterprise," *IBM Systems Journal* 32, no. 1 (1993), pp. 112–30 for an expanded categorization of IOS Interaction patterns.

IOS Evolution at American Airlines[7]

American Airlines' IOS also began as an entrepreneurial venture that evolved through successive interorganizational and IT-enabled process redesign efforts to become a dominant platform for exchanging market information, products, and services in the airline/travel industry. The story began in 1967, when a marketing manager gave a computer terminal to several large travel agencies to enable them to directly connect to American's mainframe reservation system (SABRE) and thus simplify the process of booking a flight on American Airlines. Both American and the travel agents found that the new IT-enabled reservation process greatly increased efficiency and quality. However, in the regulated airline industry, with its simple, stable pricing and route structure, most customers booked their flights directly. Since travel agents played a minor role as intermediaries in the distribution channel, the importance of on-line linkages between travel agents and American was minimal.

This picture changed when the U.S. airline industry was deregulated in 1978. Airlines now had the freedom to change prices to respond to—and drive—market demand, and they could change routes in two weeks rather than two years. This opportunity greatly increased the complexity, uncertainty, and rate of change of market information, which, in turn, complicated customers' decision process as they attempted to book a seat. The importance of the travel agent as an intermediary linking consumers with the airlines increased significantly. American Airlines, capitalizing on lessons learned during its earlier experiments with connecting travel agents to its mainframe computer reservation system, was able to begin installing SABRE terminals within travel agent offices more than six months earlier than its main competitor, United Airlines.

The lead proved invaluable; it enabled American to lock in many key travel agencies before United was able to respond. Further, to achieve maximum penetration quickly, American did not charge travel agents for the terminals; but recognizing that United could quickly neutralize the lead by installing its own terminals for free, American created contracts with stiff penalties for any travel agent that used a competing system. The travel agents, struggling to adjust to much more complex and rapidly changing pricing and route structure as they served a rapidly increasing volume of clients, gladly accepted both the terminals and the contracts. In addition, since United and other airlines were not ready to roll out their own reservation terminals to travel agents, American was able to lure these businesses into participating in SABRE, thereby creating an

---

[7] See J. McKenney, *Waves of Change* (Boston: Harvard Business School Press, 1995) for an in-depth discussion of the evolution of interorganizational systems within the airline industry.

electronic market for reservation information—which American Airlines controlled.

Because of its size, United could respond quickly with a similar system and similar contracts; therefore, by the mid-1980s, American's SABRE system and United's APOLLO reservation systems had become the dominant platforms for booking airplane, hotel, and other travel reservations. Having lost control of both the distribution channel for their services and the information about those services to a competitor, other airlines filed complaints with the Civil Aeronautics Board (CAB), alleging that United and American were violating antitrust law by monitoring their pricing and reservation information, unfavorably displaying competitors' information (over 90 percent of all reservations were made off the first screen of information), broadcasting unfavorable messages to travel agents, and using the information to manage their own prices. Lawsuits inevitably followed. Since American- and United-owned reservation systems provided primary market access for almost two-thirds of the travelers making reservations through U.S. travel agents, which by the mid-1980s accounted for more than 80 percent of all reservations, this issue generated significant public interest.

Today, government sanctions, legal action, and industry consolidation have eroded the tight control that American and United previously exerted over both industry information and the distribution channel itself; yet ownership of these systems continues to provide proprietary advantages. Over the last five years, American Airlines, in an attempt to bypass the travel agent, has created electronic linkages directly to corporations and individual business travelers, allowing these end users to link directly to American Airlines' SABRE system to check availability and book reservations for flights, hotels, and car rentals. By tying into commercial credit card networks, travelers can purchase flight tickets on-line and have the tickets mailed directly to them or to a corporate travel unit. Most individual travelers access SABRE through on-line information services such as America Online, CompuServe, and Prodigy. Large corporations tie directly into SABRE using organizationwide area networks. (Later in the chapter, we will explore more fully the use of SABRE by end consumers.) Figure 4–2 summarizes the evolution of the American Airlines' reservation system.

The above discussion of AHSC's ASAP and American's SABRE illustrates how both systems evolved over time. Building on systems that supported internal operations, both ASAP and SABRE were initially designed to support simple buyer-seller transactions. Over time, both systems evolved to electronic market platforms that connected buyers, sellers, and channel intermediaries in a complex web of IT-enabled relationships. These examples also suggest shifts in patterns of power and control. These two evolutionary patterns are explored next.

FIGURE 4–2 Evolution of American Airlines' (AA) SABRE System

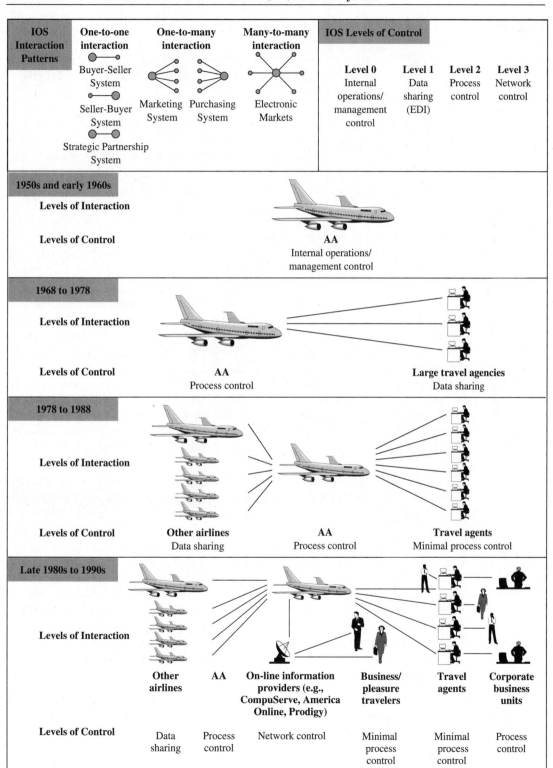

Patterns of Interaction among IOS Participants

The AHSC and American Airlines examples highlight varying patterns of interaction between firms as they use IOS to support business interaction. Three important patterns are noted:[8]

One-to-One. In its simplest form, an IOS can establish an electronic connection between two parties. For example, AHSC's ASAP system began as an electronic connection between AHSC and a key customer in California. Most commonly, one-to-one IOS are developed to support a relationship with a key supplier, customer, or vendor (i.e., buyer-seller IOS). IOS can also be used to establish linkages between strategic partners not involved in a buyer-seller exchange. As we saw at AHSC, buyer-seller IOS frequently evolve into more extensive systems supporting a number of key industry relationships; yet at other times, one-to-one IOS can be temporary systems designed to support a key project.

One-to-Many. IOS can be used to connect a number of upstream or downstream industry participants to a single central point. Marketing, sales, or distribution IOS may be developed to connect various customers and distribution channel intermediaries to a seller; supply management IOS are developed to connect suppliers and supply channel intermediaries to a producer. For example, American Airlines' SABRE system was initially used to connect travel agents (distribution channel intermediaries). Both AHSC's and American Airline's systems were designed to support complex, information-intensive, and high-frequency transactions (e.g., inventory status, pricing, etc.), and thus provided increased value to customers.

Many-to-Many. IOS can also be used to connect upstream and downstream industry participants, thereby creating an electronic marketplace for buying and selling services and sharing information. Both AHSC and American Airlines quickly recognized that the ability to link both upstream and downstream players to their respective IOS was key to sustaining competitive advantage. From their position at the center of market information transfer, they were able to exert significant control over market exchanges. Over the past decade, however, the number of electronic market platforms managed and controlled by a single industry participant has declined. Instead, coalitions of industry players or neutral third-party network facilitators have become increasingly important in developing and controlling industry and interindustry electronic market platforms. The beginning of a reliance on third-party information services providers is

---

[8] See B. Konsynski, "Strategic Control in the Extended Enterprise," *IBM Systems Journal* 32, no. 1 (1993), pp. 112–30, for an expanded categorization of IOS patterns of interaction.

evident at both AHSC and American Airlines. As will be discussed later, the Internet has recently emerged as a global, nonproprietary electronic platform that we believe will change the nature of electronic commerce in the coming years. By dramatically expanding global connectivity at a fraction of the price of today's proprietary systems, the Internet has the potential to dramatically increase interaction levels while further distributing control.

Levels of IOS Control

Examining the evolution of the AHSC and American Airlines IOS reveals three successive levels of IOS control. (In both instances, the IOS systems were built upon existing internal process and information control systems.)

Level 1. Data control

Level 2. Process control

Level 3. Network control

As the level of control increased, so did responsibility, cost, commitment, and organizational/technical complexity.

Data Control.   At the first level, an IOS participant performs no information processing and merely enters and/or receives data. This form of IOS is frequently referred to as electronic data interchange (EDI). While such simple systems may involve only one-way data transfer, most IOS in the 1990s allow two-way or even interactive data sharing. The information to be entered and the form in which to enter it are frequently specified through rigid protocols that are often embedded within the system. These protocols may be defined and controlled by one or more IOS participants. In the airline reservation system, for example, the travel agent was required to follow the policies and procedures embedded in the computer programs that American or United wrote and maintained.

At the data control level, user switching costs (for example, the costs of moving from one automated reservation system to another) are usually low. The limited functionality of the system discourages charging a high price for using the system, and the cost and effort required to learn to use technology are usually minimal. (As noted, the airlines needed to develop contracts specifying significant financial penalties to ensure that travel agents did not switch to another system.) Unless the IOS is tied to a more comprehensive strategy to ensure continuous value-added enhancements or to strong penalties for non-use, the ability to sustain proprietary advantage is low. As illustrated by AHSC's ASAP, sustained enhancements to the system enabled all participants to move to higher levels of control.

Process Control.   Companies participating at this second level of IOS control develop and maintain the software that controls the underlying interorganizational business processes and the information shared about them. One or more companies invest in the development to gain access to crucial market information and/or critical activities required to design, produce, distribute, and sell products or services. Investments and expenses associated with the development and operation of such a system can be truly extraordinary—hundreds of millions of dollars were spent by the airlines. American's SABRE system operated at the process control level at the time that it was first rolled out to travel agents; in the AHSC example, ASAP moved to the process control level when it switched from its card punch system to a mainframe computer. The hospitals began to participate in defining and implementing process controls through ASAP when they installed mainframes and/or PCs in the mid-1980s and began to integrate the supply management process across organizational boundaries. At this point, both AHSC and its customers began to share responsibility for process and information control, and the purpose of the IOS shifted from transaction processing to providing a platform for a strategic partnership that involved the exchange of a broad range of services (e.g., integrated inventory management, special discount pricing arrangements).

Along with the potential proprietary advantages that can be gained by process control come significant, ongoing coordination and control costs. Specialized units are usually needed to coordinate and control interorganizational processes and information. Extensive negotiation and time-consuming interorganizational project management are required to implement the initial system and the continuous stream of enhancements needed to keep pace with changes in the relationship. Interorganizational training and personnel development are also required.

Network Control.   At the network control level, one or more IOS participants own and/or manage the network and computer processing resources required by the IOS. (It is important to note that the participant who assumes responsibility for network control may or may not control interorganizational processes and/or data.) Traditionally, cost and complexity increase dramatically at this level. However, as we will see later in this chapter, the Internet could become a ubiquitous and low-cost global network platform that could dramatically alter network complexity and cost. Whether using proprietary networks or the Internet, IOS participants that assume control of the network must accept responsibility for both the security of the network and the integrity of the information exchanged over it. For example, the CIRRUS network, which permits automated teller machine (ATM) transactions nationwide, accepts a great deal of responsibility for the reliability, availability, integrity, security, and privacy of its system. Given the complexity, costs, and risks associated with network control, many firms "outsource" this activity to a specialized network provider—for example, common telecommunications carriers (e.g., AT&T,

MCI, Sprint), value-added network providers[9] (e.g., Tymnet, Telenet), information systems services companies (e.g., IBM Information Systems Services Company, General Electric Information Services), or an on-line information provider (e.g., American Online, CompuServe, Prodigy). In the AHSC example, ASAP initially used standard telephone lines, achieving very low levels of network control at a very low cost; subsequently, dedicated lines were leased from common carriers. AHSC paid these additional network costs to improve performance, control, and security as the nature of the information changed and the level of interaction increased. In the late 1980s, as AHSC expanded ASAP to a fully connected industry platform, they contracted with GE Information Services to control the network and ensure information integrity, security, and privacy. Similarly, in the late 1980s, American Airlines contracted with CompuServe to provide network control for Easy SABRE, which enabled business and pleasure travelers to bypass the travel agents and link directly to the SABRE system.

From Proprietary IOS to Ubiquitous Platforms for Electronic Commerce

The AHSC and American Airlines examples illustrate how firms have used IT to, in effect, vertically integrate without ownership—thereby gaining control over a channel intermediary or supplier. Both examples also illustrate how IT can be used to bypass channel intermediaries and link directly to end customers, simplifying product complexity, enhancing market penetration, and expanding opportunities to create IT-enabled buyer-seller partnerships. Over time, the pattern of interaction evolved from simple systems linking buyers and sellers to complex electronic markets integrating industry suppliers, producers, channel intermediaries, and customers through a web of electronic relationships. In both cases, visionary industry players with deep pockets invested early in the design of proprietary systems that permitted them to raise barriers to entry and exit and exert control over other industry participants. Eventually, industry adjustments led to a more distributed information and control system, the emergence of low-cost network providers increased participation, and the basis of service differentiation between industry players declined.

Today, countries around the world are launching initiatives designed to create national—and, in some instances, global— information superhighways that promise to provide a common information and communication

---

[9] A value-added network provider (VAN) provides standard communication services (e.g., end-to-end data communication between two computers), specialized network management and control services (e.g., routing, gateways, remote network monitoring, and error control), and user services (e.g., electronic mail, file transfer).

platform upon which business can be conducted. If successful, these initiatives could significantly alter the advantages gained from investments in proprietary IOS. With a common network platform and specialized IOS development tools, the cost and time required to build IOS would decrease dramatically. With a lowering of the level of proprietary investments, participation can be expected to increase. We can also expect a more rapid distribution of power and control, thereby neutralizing proprietary advantages much more quickly.

In the past, these information superhighway initiatives had limited impact on how business was conducted; in 1995, however, the vision of a ubiquitous, low-cost, global information platform for electronic commerce is rapidly becoming a reality. The reason can be summarized in a single word—*Internet*. Developed in the late 1960s by the Department of Defense as the ARPANET, this "network of networks" now links over 48,000 different networks that connect 35 million users in 160 countries. (By comparison, in March 1995, the "Big Three" for-profit on-line consumer information providers—American Online, CompuServe, and Prodigy—had only 5 million subscribers among them.[10]) By the year 2000, the number of users on the Internet is expected to surpass 100 million. (Figure 4–3 presents the global penetration of the Internet in 1995; Figure 4–4 summarizes key statistics concerning its evolution.)

Originally created to serve as a communication backbone in times of national (and later international) crisis and to support academic research on defense-related topics, the Internet has no central point of control, as its creators believed such control would pose an unacceptable risk of system failure in the event of hostile attack, natural disaster, or human error. As a result, the system grew as a truly distributed network, and network protocols were developed to create an "open system" environment, enabling the routing of messages and information across widely disparate network platforms.

In the mid-1980s, the ARPANET was segmented into Department of Defense (DOD)-related and non-DOD-related networks; the National Science Foundation assumed control of the civilian research network, which became the NSFnet and later the Internet. Initially, the Internet was restricted to research and educational uses; commercial uses were prohibited by the NSF Acceptable Use Policy. However, with political pressure mounting for creation of an information superhighway and the development of user-friendly tools for organizing and finding information, the rules mandating types of usage became difficult to enforce. By 1993 the Internet was open for business (see Figure 4–5).

Why the sudden interest in the Internet?[11] The information superhighway initiatives are only part of the story. More important are the radical

---

[10] P. Gralla, "On-Line Fever," *PC Computing,* September 1994, p. 140–54.

[11] A recent search of on-line news stories revealed over 25,000 stories in 1994 that contained the word *Internet;* by comparison, there were only 9,000 in 1993 and a handful in 1989.

FIGURE 4-3   Global Penetration of the Internet

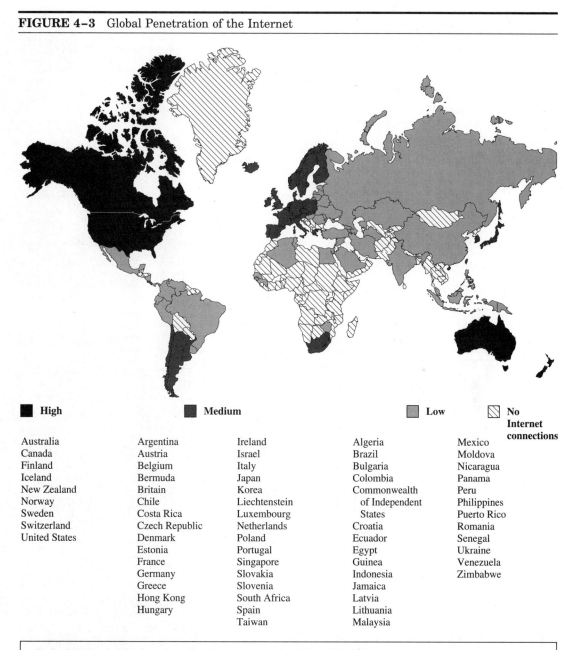

High	Medium		Low	
Australia	Argentina	Ireland	Algeria	Mexico
Canada	Austria	Israel	Brazil	Moldova
Finland	Belgium	Italy	Bulgaria	Nicaragua
Iceland	Bermuda	Japan	Colombia	Panama
New Zealand	Britain	Korea	Commonwealth	Peru
Norway	Chile	Liechtenstein	of Independent	Philippines
Sweden	Costa Rica	Luxembourg	States	Puerto Rico
Switzerland	Czech Republic	Netherlands	Croatia	Romania
United States	Denmark	Poland	Ecuador	Senegal
	Estonia	Portugal	Egypt	Ukraine
	France	Singapore	Guinea	Venezuela
	Germany	Slovakia	Indonesia	Zimbabwe
	Greece	Slovenia	Jamaica	
	Hong Kong	South Africa	Latvia	
	Hungary	Spain	Lithuania	
		Taiwan	Malaysia	

No Internet connections

Rating based on a ratio of people to direct Internet connections, from High (200 people or less to each connection) to Low (5,000 or more people to each connection).

Adapted from *Time* 145, no. 12 (Spring 1995), p. 81.

FIGURE 4-4   Time Line of Events

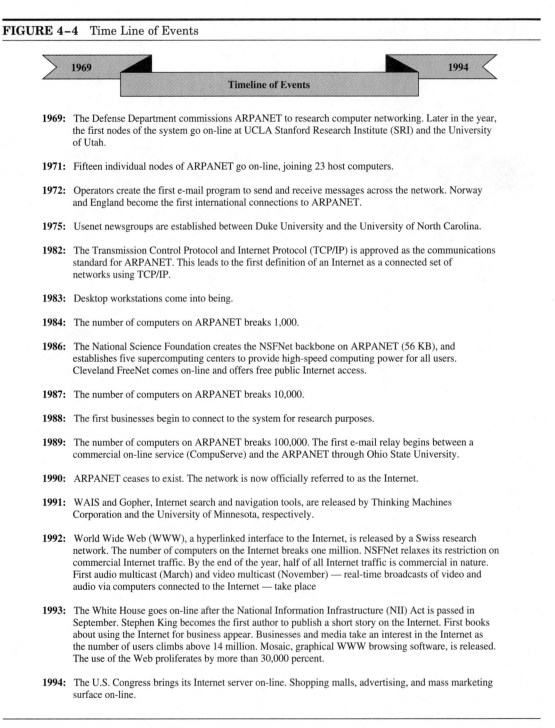

1969: The Defense Department commissions ARPANET to research computer networking. Later in the year, the first nodes of the system go on-line at UCLA Stanford Research Institute (SRI) and the University of Utah.

1971: Fifteen individual nodes of ARPANET go on-line, joining 23 host computers.

1972: Operators create the first e-mail program to send and receive messages across the network. Norway and England become the first international connections to ARPANET.

1975: Usenet newsgroups are established between Duke University and the University of North Carolina.

1982: The Transmission Control Protocol and Internet Protocol (TCP/IP) is approved as the communications standard for ARPANET. This leads to the first definition of an Internet as a connected set of networks using TCP/IP.

1983: Desktop workstations come into being.

1984: The number of computers on ARPANET breaks 1,000.

1986: The National Science Foundation creates the NSFNet backbone on ARPANET (56 KB), and establishes five supercomputing centers to provide high-speed computing power for all users. Cleveland FreeNet comes on-line and offers free public Internet access.

1987: The number of computers on ARPANET breaks 10,000.

1988: The first businesses begin to connect to the system for research purposes.

1989: The number of computers on ARPANET breaks 100,000. The first e-mail relay begins between a commercial on-line service (CompuServe) and the ARPANET through Ohio State University.

1990: ARPANET ceases to exist. The network is now officially referred to as the Internet.

1991: WAIS and Gopher, Internet search and navigation tools, are released by Thinking Machines Corporation and the University of Minnesota, respectively.

1992: World Wide Web (WWW), a hyperlinked interface to the Internet, is released by a Swiss research network. The number of computers on the Internet breaks one million. NSFNet relaxes its restriction on commercial Internet traffic. By the end of the year, half of all Internet traffic is commercial in nature. First audio multicast (March) and video multicast (November) — real-time broadcasts of video and audio via computers connected to the Internet — take place

1993: The White House goes on-line after the National Information Infrastructure (NII) Act is passed in September. Stephen King becomes the first author to publish a short story on the Internet. First books about using the Internet for business appear. Businesses and media take an interest in the Internet as the number of users climbs above 14 million. Mosaic, graphical WWW browsing software, is released. The use of the Web proliferates by more than 30,000 percent.

1994: The U.S. Congress brings its Internet server on-line. Shopping malls, advertising, and mass marketing surface on-line.

Adapted from *Internet Business Advantage* 2, no. 3 (April 1995), p. 14.

FIGURE 4–5   Growth of Commercial Use of the Internet

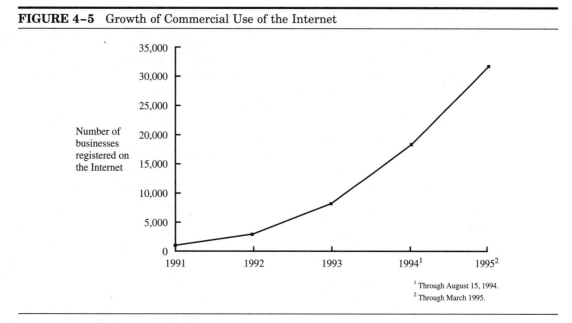

Number of businesses registered on the Internet

¹ Through August 15, 1994.
² Through March 1995.

Source: *Internet Letter* 2, no. 5 (February 1, 1995).

changes that occurred in the Internet's technical infrastructure over the past two years. To understand the potential impact of these technical changes, it is helpful to think back to the evolution of the personal computer as an important business tool.

Once in a while, a software application is created that enables a technology to become truly useful. Think back to the early 1980s, shortly after the introduction of the personal computer (PC). At first, the PC was considered a hobbyist's toy—useful only to "techies." Then the spreadsheet was developed and the personal computer became a serious business tool. This "killer application"—easy to use and targeted to meet a wide variety of recurring business activities—transformed the basic technology into a useful tool for the masses. On the heels of the spreadsheet came a host of other software products (e.g., user-friendly word processors) that expanded the uses of the technology and sped the diffusion of the PC to offices and homes throughout the world. By 1995, personal computers had become as commonplace in business as the telephone and were rapidly becoming household "appliances." In 1994 alone, U.S. households spent over $8 billion on personal computers—equivalent to what was spent on televisions.[12]

---

[12] S. Ratan, "A New Divide between the Haves and Have-Nots," *Time* 145, no. 12 (Spring 1995), p. 25.

In the same way, two powerful information management tools—the World Wide Web[13] and user-friendly information "browsers"[14] —have transformed the Internet from a tool for dedicated techies to a powerhouse of information and a vast network of communication for everyone. (Figure 4–6 summarizes basic elements of electronic commerce currently available over the Internet.) With such tools in place, the sites offering information over the Internet have grown explosively, along with the number of users—for example, between November 1994 and February 1995, the number of sites offering information grew from 7,000 to over 27,000.[15] In April 1994, the Clinton Administration approved a $6 million grant for the formation of CommerceNet—a consortium of high-technology firms, including Apple, Hewlett-Packard, IBM, and Intel—to exploit the commercial potential of the Internet, and Internet entrepreneurs were poised to assist companies wishing to buy and sell over this channel.

However, despite general excitement, many managers remain skeptical. No sooner have they finished reading an article proclaiming that the Internet is paved with gold, than they discover that everyone is browsing but no one is buying.[16] They read horror stories of security and performance problems and question—in the words of President Rutherford B. Hayes as he contemplated the telephone—whether "substantive business affairs" could ever be conducted in an environment, which, for many, has been compared to an on-line "red-light district."

As managers attempt to separate fact from fiction, it is important to step back and consider the general principles that govern traditional commercial transactions and the influence of proprietary IOS on the nature and structure of market exchanges. These principles can then be used to guide an evaluation of the opportunities and risks of electronic commerce.

MAKING SENSE OF MARKET RELATIONSHIPS

A market can be viewed as a web of transactions and relationships between buyers and sellers.[17] While only two basic roles are required in any exchange—producer and consumer— any number of facilitators can often

---

[13] World Wide Web (aka WWW or just "the Web") is a system for organizing information on the Internet. By pointing to a highlighted phrase and clicking, a user can effortlessly jump from one place to another place on the network (figuratively and physically).

[14] Browsers (Mosaic and Netscape) are Internet tools that allow people to navigate—or browse—the World Wide Web simply by pointing and clicking.

[15] *Internet Letter* 2, no. 5 (February 1, 1995).

[16] See D. Churbuck, "Where's the Money?" *Forbes,* January 30, 1995, and "Net Profits," *Economist,* 332, no. 7871 (July 9, 1994) pp. 83–85.

[17] T. Malone, J. Yates, and R. Benjamin, "Electronic Markets and Electronic Hierarchies," *Communications of the ACM,* June 1987, pp. 484–97.

FIGURE 4–6   Essential Elements of Electronic Commerce Available on the Internet in 1995

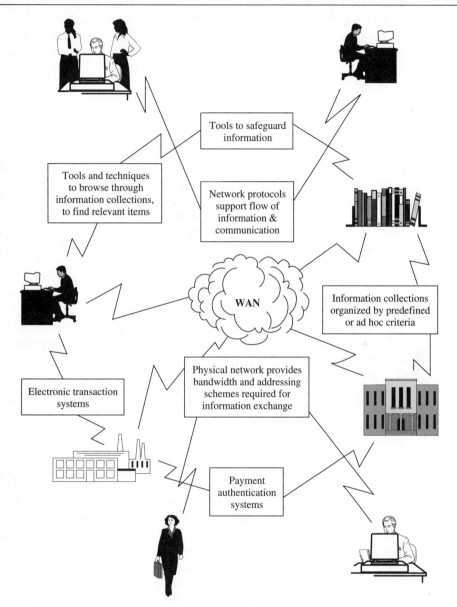

Adapted from: L. Applegate and J. Gogan, *Paving the Information Superhighway: Introduction to the Internet* (Boston: Harvard Business School Publishing, case 195–202, 1995).

act as intermediaries (e.g., advertisers, distributors, retailers, bankers, brokers). The participants within a market network work together to perform all the activities required to design, manufacture, distribute, market, sell, and maintain a product or service. In addition to these operational tasks, the "production network" must also carry out coordination, control, and resource management activities so that operations are performed effectively and efficiently.

IOS and Producer Relationships

The network of activities required to produce a product or service can be organized in three basic ways (see Figure 4–7). First, the activities can be incorporated within a single "vertically integrated" firm. Second, one or more selective activities can be outsourced to an external party. Finally, a "virtual corporation" can be created within which a firm retains the coordination, control, and resource management activities and contracts out all or most other activities.

Traditional economic theory suggests that managers choose to incorporate an activity within their organizational boundary (i.e., vertically integrate) when there is a significant risk involved in depending on "the market" for access to resources or services. These market risks increase when a firm must make a *significant investment in physical or human assets* to manage or carry out the market exchange;[18] or if the *resources or activities are critical* to the effective and efficient delivery of the firm's products and service; or if there is a *high degree of uncertainty* surrounding the ongoing nature of the relationship, which in turn makes it difficult to define both the interorganizational relationship in a comprehensive, structured contract and an efficient set of interorganizational governance mechanisms.

Eastman Kodak, for example, was highly vertically integrated even into the 1980s. Having been founded in the late 1800s on the principle of "commitment to quality," the firm established its own laundry to ensure that the cloth for wiping film was of the highest quality; it bought its own blacksmith and built its own foundry to make its machines; and it managed its own credit union to finance its products. For Kodak, the costs and risks associated with managing production outside the firm were deemed too great. General Motors followed a similar strategy until the 1970s. Many recall their familiar slogan—"Genuine GM Parts."

---

[18] Economic theory calls these asset specific investments. (See O. E. Williamson, and S. G. Winter, *The Nature of the Firm* (New York: Oxford Press, 1993) for an excellent summary of the economic theory of organizations.)

FIGURE 4–7 Patterns of Market Exchange

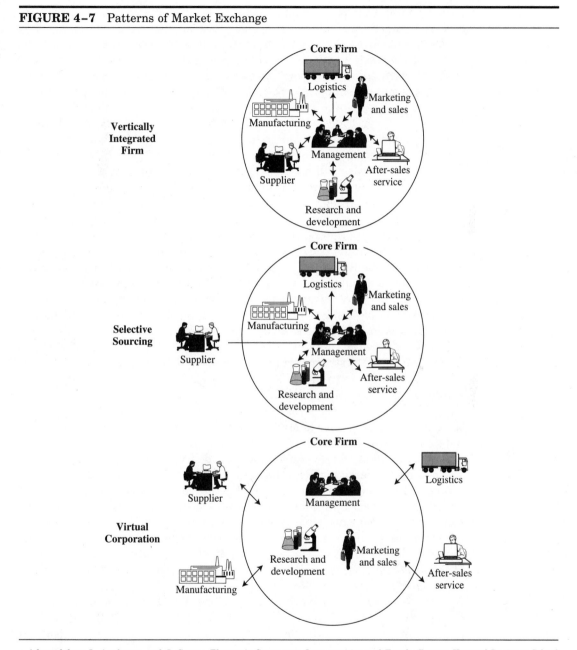

Adapted from L. Applegate and J. Gogan, *Electronic Commerce: Opportunities and Trends* (Boston: Harvard Business School Publishing, note 196–006, 1995).

However, if risks are low or if interorganizational governance structures and systems can be defined and efficiently implemented, managers may choose to outsource one or more of the production activities to capitalize on economies of scale. Traditionally, managers outsourced only those activities that represented a relatively low risk to the firm because the cost of coordinating and managing high-risk activities was simply too great. In the 1980s and 1990s, as managers struggled to respond to consumers' demands that they deliver their products more efficiently, effectively, and flexibly, more and more firms turned to outsourcing to enable them to reduce complexity, respond more quickly, and focus on core competencies.

As we discussed earlier, using IT to coordinate and control production activities across organizational boundaries has been a major factor in the shift from vertical integration to outsourcing as a dominant organizational model of the 1990s. Rather than simply outsource low-risk activities, however, a growing number of firms are using IT to coordinate and control activities traditionally considered high risk. Today's managers are choosing to outsource activities that require significant investments in proprietary assets; they outsource activities critical to the firm's success and that involve high levels of uncertainty about the ongoing nature of the relationship. For example (and as discussed in Chapter 10), in the late 1980s and 1990s, Eastman Kodak outsourced a significant portion of its IT platform.

Finally, a growing number of firms in the 1990s are defining IT-enabled interorganizational structures and systems that take the simple outsourcing model to the extreme: they are contracting out the majority of the activities of production, eliminating intermediaries in the distribution channel, and retaining within their organizational borders only a few selective core competencies and the management systems needed to coordinate and control the network of relationships.

Dell Computers, for example, was founded in 1984 by Michael Dell, a 19-year-old University of Texas (Austin) student who ran a simple mail order business from his dorm room.[19] IBM PCs, purchased at cost from the excess inventories of local computer dealers, were then sold directly to consumers through direct-response advertising. By eliminating the in-person sales force, relying on inexpensive advertising channels (initially, fliers on campus), and providing personal after-sales support (Michael Dell was a computer whiz), Dell was able to pass tremendous savings on to consumers, and the business grew rapidly. Indeed, by 1986, revenues had grown to $34 million.

At the same time, however, price-cutting by Campaq and other IBM clones seriously threatened Dell's position. In response, Dell shifted from ready-built IBM PCs to custom PCs, assembled from computer components purchased directly from a network of suppliers. This action dramatically

---

[19] P. Tufano, *Dell Computer Corporation* (Boston: Harvard Business School Publishing, case 294–051, 1994).

decreased the cost of the PC. A portion of the savings was passed on to the consumer, with the remainder directed toward creating telemarketing and after-sales support functions so the company could add value without relying on third-party distribution channels. *To coordinate and control the increasingly complex and uncertain business, Dell built proprietary IT systems that linked its vast supplier and customer network.* By 1988 revenues had soared to $160 million, and by 1992 net sales were in excess of $1.5 billion. In an industry not known for healthy margins, Dell's return on equity (ROE) in 1992 was 27.5 percent and its return on assets (ROA) was 11 percent. By comparison, IBM's, Apple's, and Compaq's 1992 ROEs/ROAs were −24.95/−7.9; 24.2/12.6; and 10.6/6.8, respectively.[20] Dell had stolen market share from the "Big Three" PC makers to become the fourth largest PC maker; at the same time, it had seriously eroded the profitability of channel intermediaries. "Dell's formula is elegantly direct: He has cut out the dealers and distributors . . . and runs a no-frills operation whose main focus is customer service," reported *Business Week.*[21]

In a similar way, Nike, Inc. has used IT to outsource its athletic footwear production to a network of suppliers and partners, focusing its attention and resources on product design and marketing.[22] Since its founding in the mid-1970s, Nike sourced its shoes from factories in Asia. Lacking IT to coordinate and control operations, Nike initially posted technicians at each factory to coordinate operations between corporate and local managers and to control product quality. "Our people living there and working with the factories as the product is going down the lines . . . is a lot different from accepting or rejecting the product at the end of the line— especially at the end of a three-month pipeline to the United States," a Nike manager explained, in the Harvard Business School case. *By the 1980s, these technicians had been replaced by a sophisticated IOS that linked designers in the United States with contractors in Asia, and later Indonesia, through a sophisticated CAD/CAM system; and interorganizational coordination and control systems monitored each phase of production process from product design through sales in the local retail channel.* By 1993, Nike earned $365 million on sales of $3.9 billion and boasted a return on equity of 24.5 percent.

These two firms developed sophisticated IOS to enable them to coordinate and control market exchanges and manage interorganizational resources. These IOS enabled Nike and Dell, and AHSC and American Airlines before them, to vertically integrate the activities of a web of independent companies to deliver high-quality products and services to customers.

---

[20] Standard & Poor's, Compustat.

[21] Anderson, et al., "The Education of Michael Dell," *Business Week,* March 22, 1993, p. 83.

[22] P. Rosenzweig, *International Sourcing in Athletic Footwear: Nike and Reebok* (Boston: Harvard Business School Publishing, case 394–189, 1994).

Such examples illustrate how IOS help companies rewrite the rules that have traditionally governed approaches to managing market exchanges. Advances in information and communication technologies and development of international standards governing communication and information exchange have enabled firms to create the technology platform required to *integrate, streamline, and manage interorganizational processes.* By building on the technology infrastructure used to automate hierarchical transactions, and coordinate and control internal processes, and by relying on low-cost, yet reliable, third-party network facilitators, they are able to *decrease the level of investment required to support interorganizational market exchanges, while dramatically improving coordination and control.* Finally, by monitoring real-time information on interorganizational process dynamics, they are able to *implement interorganizational partnerships despite high levels of environmental uncertainty and rapid rates of change.* Analysis of the evolution of IOS suggests that as the cost of IOS decrease and their flexibility and performance increase, and as global networks dramatically improve the ease of establishing interorganizational connectivity and control, the trend is to *move from vertical integration to outsourcing to virtual organizations.* In addition, there is evidence of *disintermediation of distribution and supply channels,* which allows producers and consumers to interact in a web of buyer-seller relationships reminiscent of the open markets of earlier days. Many believe that Internet use will speed up this economic transition.

IOS and the Changing Buyer-Seller Relationship

Traditionally, exchanges between buyers and sellers required significant face-to-face interaction. In the early days of town centers and open markets, these exchanges took place in a single location where people congregated to exchange goods and services.[23] The costs of doing business were small since the buyers and sellers lived close to the town center, knew and depended on one another for survival, and brought complementary products and skills to the relationship. Given the intense personal relationship among members, the small number of players, and their relative stability, information could be shared verbally at the time of the exchange, and credit could be extended through a personal handshake, even though most exchanges were completed immediately.

As transportation improved, local markets gave way to regional centers and later to port cities. But the slow pace of communication and transportation of goods limited the development of distant markets. While some merchants did attempt to sell products in distant markets, the lack of

---

[23] J. Beniger, *The Control Revolution* (Cambridge: Harvard University Press, 1986).

accurate and timely information on suppliers, products, and customers made it difficult to set prices and balance supply and demand. The inefficiency of the market was compounded by the time and cost of transporting goods over long distances. Those few who attempted to trade in distant locations depended on local merchants. To reduce the risk to the producer, the merchants bought the products directly or were paid on commission.

With the development of the railroads and communication technologies (e.g., the telegraph) in the late 1800s, the tools were in place to transfer goods and information about those goods much more rapidly. Markets grew quickly, and machine technologies that appeared around the same time allowed producers to meet those demands. Gradually, the *relationship selling* of the preindustrial era was replaced by *transaction selling*.[24] This latter form of market exchange reduced the buyer-seller interaction to a discrete transaction. The strategic relationship among members of a local community who depended on one another for survival gradually eroded. In transaction selling, the primary goal was to sell (or purchase) a product or service; it typically involved either a single transaction or a series of transactions through which a product or service moved from a seller to a buyer, and money (the most common type of payment) moved from a buyer to a seller. Large organizations created separate organizational units and management systems to carry out the activities for coordinating and controlling the physical distribution of products and services from seller to buyer, for securing distribution of the payment, and for overseeing the flow of information about the exchange.

While transaction selling is still widely used for all types of products—including those purchased infrequently (e.g., houses, cars) and those purchased on a routine basis (e.g., groceries, a cup of coffee on the way to work)—the 1980s and 1990s have seen a swing back to the relationship selling of the preindustrial era. In essence, when a buyer and seller develop a strategic relationship, the market exchange changes from one that is designed to promote the sale or purchase of a discrete product to one that is designed to enable both firms to meet their strategic goals. The exchange of products, services, and payments may still take place, but it is only one component of the interaction. At the heart of the relationship is mutual dependence, trust, and a commitment to supporting the well-being of the strategic partner.

Traditionally, relationship selling dramatically increased market exchange costs. It required significant investments in proprietary assets (for example, a dedicated sales force, specialized products and services, and specialized IT systems to enable customers to link directly to a buyer's

---

[24] See B. Shapiro, *Close Encounters of the Four Kinds* (Boston: Harvard Business School Publishing, case 589–015) for an excellent discussion of transaction and relationship selling.

internal information systems), and the market exchanges were often characterized by complexity and high levels of uncertainty. As a result, traditional business logic stated that strategic buyer-seller relationships should be reserved for a select number of key accounts.[25]

In the 1990s, however, IOS are creating a new business logic. Numerous examples of the use of IT for linking directly to end customers—often bypassing intermediaries in the distribution channel—can be found. As we have seen, American Airlines was a pioneer in the deployment of proprietary IOS to vertically integrate without ownership, connecting travel agents—a key intermediary in the distribution channel—to their internal computer reservation system. Today, they have extended that system, bypassing the travel agent to link directly to consumers. In the process, they are redefining market exchanges and the costs associated with them in terms of both transaction and relationship selling.

American Airline's decision in the late 1980s to offer access to SABRE through on-line information services (e.g., America Online, CompuServe, and Prodigy) allowed them to bypass travel agents and reach a vast market of individual travelers without having to incur the costs of hiring, training, and managing a specialized sales force. IOS dramatically reduced the complexity and cost of the market transaction for both American Airlines and the consumer. This, in turn, greatly expanded American's transaction-selling opportunities. Today, consumers can easily find the flight they want, book and pay for it, and receive the tickets through the mail. They can also guarantee a hotel room and reserve a car all at the touch of a button. This one-stop on-line travel agent, available as only one of many information services offered through low-cost, third-party information providers, has greatly decreased traditional transaction selling market exchange costs for both American and the consumer.

For key business accounts, American Airlines not only offers these basic transaction services, but it also provides IT-enabled special services designed to expand opportunities for relationship selling. With the goal of becoming a strategic partner to business customers, for instance, American Airlines identified an area of great concern—the rising cost of business travel in a time of increasing pressure to control costs. They then designed a package of specialized on-line services that could be customized to meet the needs of each key account.[26] A detailed travel record could be created for each employee, documenting how often the person travels and the destination. A comparison of the trip's cost with the cheapest rate available for each component (e.g., flight, hotel, car rental) could also be obtained. An on-line expense reporting system automatically created an expense report when

---

[25] B. Shapiro and J. Wyman, "New Ways to Reach Your Customers," *Harvard Business Review,* July–August 1981.

[26] The ability to use IT to share information and to interactively manage customer relationships does not replace the need for face-to-face selling, but does enable each salesperson to provide individualized service to a larger number of customers.

the reservations were made; the employee could update the report after the trip was completed and could submit it for payment with the touch of a key. Every month, a printed report was available for each employee, and customized reports could be created for managers at all levels to enable tighter control of travel expenses. A recently added feature allows frequent-flyer miles for business travel to accrue to the company rather than to the individual. These special features, customized for each key account, enhanced American's image as a travel consultant that could assist firms in managing a critical business cost.

As the functionality and availability of interorganizational market platforms increase, a growing number of firms discover that they can bypass channel intermediaries and exchange products and services directly with the consumers. IOS are being used to *reduce product and market complexity while simultaneously increasing market penetration.* By bundling traditional products and services with new value-added, customized information services, companies can *expand relationship-selling opportunities while decreasing the cost and complexity of offering customized services.* Telemarketing systems, when integrated with relational databases, have spurred the development of *database marketing. Electronic catalogs,* many of them delivered over CD-ROM or through on-line information providers, have expanded opportunities to reach distant markets with graphically rich product descriptions that can include video images. On-line *consultation and after-sales service* IOS, many of which integrate expert systems, enable 24-hour-per-day access to scarce product and technical knowledge and customized support. One value-added computer manufacturer estimated that it saved over $5 million per year by implementing an on-line PC-based/fax customer service center. *Interorganizational electronic mail* systems can be used to support national—or even international—account managers as they attempt to manage a larger, more diverse set of customers with a more customized set of services.

The Internet offers the potential of further enhancing both transaction-oriented and relationship selling. *Real-time customer interaction* can be integrated with database marketing to identify a specific product or set of products to meet both new and established customer's needs. The interactive nature of the Internet allows a seller to *embed a series of interactive queries within their marketing materials,* through which they can rapidly determine a new customer's salient characteristics and unique preferences and an existing customer's changing needs. The *hypertext*[27] *links enable sophisticated branching logic to help guide the buyer through complex product and service offerings* to find the specialized product or service to meet his or her needs. In addition, once the data are collected, they can be

---

[27] Hypertext is a link between one document and other related documents. By clicking on a word or phrase that has been highlighted on a computer screen, a user can skip directly to files related to that subject.

used to update customer and marketing databases to *continually refresh internal marketing, sales, and demand data.* The data can also be used to *continuously refine products and services* to meet a complex and ever-changing market.

Electronic catalogs are also being enhanced by the Internet's ability to enable *real-time, interactive selling.* For example, Digital Equipment allows potential customers not only to view but also "test drive" the Alpha computer.

Global penetration, low cost, and easy accessibility dramatically decrease the cost of communicating a message to a very large potential market. In addition, *electronic filters and Internet-ready direct marketing support systems* are becoming available to further support targeting marketing resources to a vast global market of consumers.

Marketers are also tapping into the naturally occurring *communities of interest* that spring up on the Internet to help reach potential customers. For example, Jim Beam Brands created a Virtual Bar where "patrons" can exchange whiskey recipes and scrawl virtual graffiti on virtual walls. Ziff Davis Expositions and Conferences developed a Virtual Trade Show, allowing manufacturers within an industry to display new products as they are introduced.

Of course, on-line shopping is available, but so too are *on-line shopping malls,* where a number of retailers can share the cost and expense of opening and managing their on-line stores. Third-party Internet providers—for example, Open Market[28] —serve as the development company, helping with the construction of the stores and then ensuring safe, reliable market transactions within them.

There is little doubt that the 1990s offer significant opportunities to dramatically alter the traditional rules of market exchange and, in so doing, to reap tremendous rewards. As managers evaluate the past and attempt to predict the future of electronic commerce, however, they must address several important issues.

MANAGING THE EVOLUTION OF TECHNOLOGY

In our judgment, in 1995, the role of the Internet as a tool to support electronic commerce is in its infancy; hence, while many are experimenting, there is little in the way of longitudinal case examples with demonstrable business results from which to define general principles. As a result, general managers interested in developing a prudent approach to experimentation must rely on a deep understanding of traditional market exchanges and more stable forms of proprietary IOS.

---

[28] See J. Gogan and L. Applegate, *Open Market, Inc.* (Boston: Harvard Business School Publishing, case 195–105, 1995).

As we discussed in Chapter 2, the assimilation of emerging technologies, like the Internet, is a process of organizational learning.[29] Individuals must learn new ways of working and new ways of interacting—and old approaches must be "unlearned." Success demands that users be heavily involved in defining and building the system, and development processes must be interactive. Since the learning curve for the technical aspects of the Internet is short and the cost of experimentation is relatively low, many firms are moving directly to phase 2 and have begun to identify several low-risk business applications for the technology. The most complex, high-risk, and potentially costly problem with Internet experimentation is the security risk, and companies must consider this issue carefully from the outset.

MAINTAINING A SECURE ENVIRONMENT FOR DOING BUSINESS

Maintaining security and integrity of information across interorganizational boundaries is always a challenge; on the Internet, however, it is a nightmare.[30] Recall that the Internet grew in an uncontrolled manner; anyone in almost any country can connect to the Internet with a PC, a modem, a network address, and a connection to an Internet server.[31] In 1995, connecting to the Internet cost approximately \$0.50 per month.[32] Roughly 25 percent of the 35 million Internet users in 1995 have the computing and communications capability necessary to roam freely through the World Wide Web using a Web browser (e.g., Mosaic or Netscape). Like the problem of figuring out how many locks to put on the door to your house, the level of security depends on how the system is used and whether there are any direct links between the Internet and your company's information system. (Note: these same security features can also be applied to any IOS.)

Managers who contemplate conducting electronic commerce across the Internet must assume that anybody in the world might come knocking at their door and plan accordingly. (Table 4–1 summarizes security features necessary for conducting electronic commerce.) They need to secure internal corporate networks from unwanted outsiders by using "firewalls"— electronic barriers created with dedicated hardware and software systems that screen network traffic and validate the flow of information between internal and external networks. Companies generally designate one or

---

[29] A more in-depth discussion of the technology assimilation process is provided in Chapter 6.

[30] See L. Applegate, and J. Gogan, *Paving the Information Superhighway: An Introduction to the Internet* (Boston: Harvard Business School Publishing, note 195–202, 1995).

[31] An Internet server is a specialized computer that manages network access to the Internet.

[32] "Doing Business on the Internet and Beyond," *PC Computing: Special Issue,* September 1994.

TABLE 4-1   IOS Security Issues

Problem	Business Concern	Solution
Authorization	Does a user have permission to access a specific computer or collection of information?	User name and password or other kind of access control mechanisms.
Authentication	Is the user truly who he or she purports to be?	Special-purpose hardware and software system generates random number, which the user then matches to authenticate identity.
Integrity	Did the person sending a message actually send it? Can the receiver be sure that the message has not been changed?	Digital signature.
Privacy	Is my conversation (or business transaction) private? Is anyone eavesdropping or spying?	Public/private key encryption algorithms.
Fraud/Theft	Is anyone stealing from me?	Log, audit, systems management policies and procedures.
Sabotage	Can someone enter my system and destroy or alter information?	Firewalls. Firebreaks.

Adapted from: L. Applegate and J. Gogan, *Paving the Information Superhighway: An Introduction to the Internet* (Boston: Harvard Business School Publishing, note 195–202, 1995).

more separate computers as Internet (or IOS) servers and carefully barricade their internal systems behind a firewall. In some instances, if high-level security is required, companies install "firebreaks"—physical barriers across which there are no electronic connections between the Internet server and internal company information systems.

In addition to firewalls and firebreaks, passwords can screen prospective users and ensure that only those on an approved list can enter. Of course, this requires additional administrative overhead and is somewhat antithetical to certain areas of electronic commerce. The benefits of opening an electronic store, for example, are greatly reduced if you must restrict access to those you already know. Instead, it may be more appropriate to "electronically tag" your merchandise so that a warning sounds if someone attempts to leave the "store" with merchandise that has not been purchased or is not for sale. Also, any authorization scheme is open to abuse. While passwords can be encrypted, they may still be easily intercepted in a networked computing environment populated with technologically sophisticated users.

In some situations, a company may wish to require individuals to validate that they are who they say they are. One approach to authenticating network users combines special hardware and software. Authorized users able to connect to a specific server (or to pass through a company firewall) receive a special handheld device about the size of a credit card. This device contains an encryption algorithm. When an authorized user tries to connect to another company's computer, he or she receives a five-digit (randomly generated) number as an authentication challenge. The user enters the number into the device, receives another five-digit number, and then replies with this number as the key to the challenge. If the remote system is satisfied with the response, the user can access the server.

Another thorny problem with electronic commerce is protecting the privacy of personal information. For example, one company created an internal Web application to enable information sharing among internal employees. Despite the fact that the server was behind a firewall and that password entry was required, the company found that an intruder had been able to "break in" and steal highly confidential information. Electronic financial transactions are also of great concern. Several companies, including Microsoft Corporation and Visa International, have announced partnerships to provide adequate security for on-line financial transactions.[33] Some are using digital signatures and encryption keys to authenticate financial transaction data; others require that credit card information be submitted via telephone, thus creating a firebreak. The search continues for a fool-proof form of "electronic currency" so that buyers and sellers can really begin to do business over the Internet.

The on-line world of electronic commerce also raises many new issues about information privacy. When we buy a published book, we assume that copyright protections and intellectual property rights have been addressed by the author and publisher. Each book is bound to ensure that all portions of the book are considered and protected as a whole. By contrast, in an on-line world, information is transmitted in small bits and pieces that can be reconstructed by many different users in different forms. Copyright laws have yet to be written to accommodate this, and maintaining intellectual property and privacy rights becomes a logistic nightmare. While digital signatures, firewalls, encryption algorithms, and passwords can help to protect our rights, they are not sufficient. Current security, privacy, and information integrity procedures and practices must be examined; and interorganizational information and communication policies must be established. Government regulations and legal issues must also be addressed.

---

[33] See "Microsoft, Visa in Pact for On-Line Bank Card Security," *The Reuters Business Report,* November 8, 1994.

DEVELOPING AND MAINTAINING INFORMATION PARTNERSHIPS[34]

As we discussed earlier, the trend in electronic commerce is shifting away from electronic vertical integration based on IT-enabled hierarchical control and toward the establishment of alliances and partnerships facilitated by distributed power and control and frequent interaction. In essence, IOS empower companies to compete, interestingly enough, by allowing them new ways to cooperate.

The Allegis Example

The notion of competition through cooperation is best illustrated by a notable failure. Allegis Corporation was the brainchild of United Airlines, which acquired Hertz Rent A Car and Westin Hotels in hopes of creating an integrated travel company with real synergies for the end customer. The venture was quickly torpedoed by skepticism on Wall Street, where great fear was expressed that the firm was getting involved in businesses whose operations they did not fully understand. Indeed, nobody speaks of the Allegis Corporation today without using the word *fiasco,* as the company was forced to divest itself of its pieces at great loss. However, in retrospect, it is hard to imagine a more prescient effort to form a market coalition exploiting the power of information technology.

The Allegis idea seemed to offer something for everyone. From United Airlines customers' view, by renting a Hertz car and staying in a Westin hotel, they could earn frequent-flyer miles on United. Hertz and Westin could benefit by sharing databases of customer information that were, in turn, linked to United's massive APOLLO system; and United could present itself to the customer as a single source of travel services. Eventually, perhaps, Allegis might have customized travel programs for a large number of regular customers.

Allegis's hard lesson—and also one highly instructive for many other firms—was that IT-enabled partnerships need not be based on ownership. Managers of companies in reciprocal industries can plan and coordinate common approaches to customers through shared information and frequent interaction without vertical integration. In retrospect, Wall Street quite rightly reckoned that although United's top managers could develop synergies in servicing customers, they were not likely to enjoy any operational advantages. Indeed, the real—and legitimate—fear was that management

---

[34] This section of the chapter was adapted from B. Konsynski and F. W. McFarlan, "Information Partnerships—Shared Data, Shared Scale," *Harvard Business Review,* September–October 1990.

time and attention would be drained by these diverse businesses with their specialized operating problems. Drawing on the experience of firms like Nike and Dell, ample evidence suggests that there is much to be gained by coordinating production activities through a network of IT-enabled relationships, while focusing efforts and resources on core competencies.

Benefits of Information Partnering

Through an information partnership, diverse companies can offer novel incentives and services or participate in joint-marketing programs. They can take advantage of new distribution channels and introduce operational efficiencies and revenue enhancements. Partnerships expand opportunities for scale and cross-selling. They can make small companies look, feel, and act big as they reach for customers once beyond their grasp; they can make big companies look small and close as they target and service custom markets. Information-enabled partnerships, in short, provide a new basis for differentiation. Many more of them will be appearing in the coming decade.

These new forms of market cooperation pass large volumes of electronic data precisely, instantaneously, and relatively cheaply. Greater computer speed and cheaper mass-storage devices mean that information can be archived, cross-correlated, and retrieved much faster and less expensively than before—and in ways that are customized for recipients. Additionally, the widespread emergence of fiber-optic networks has greatly improved cost-effective delivery of information to remote locations.

Also, managers are eager to lessen their financial and technical exposure. Partnerships allow them to share investments in hardware and software as well as the considerable expense of learning how to use both. The cost of developing certain software configurations is particularly great, posing huge problems for small and midsized companies competing against large companies. Software investments may reach hundreds of millions of dollars, which creates impenetrable entry barriers for smaller competitors— unless a number of them consolidate their purchasing power.

It is expected that consumers will continue to pressure firms to develop cooperative partnerships. Desktop clutter has led to a demand for simplification; people want simple, user-friendly interfaces that permit them to reach out to a variety of services both inside and outside the firm through a single device and with a minimum of confusing detail. This implies that users want companies to cooperate, at least on data-interface standards where possible; and, in fact, they have brought pressure to bear in this regard. Users also continue to demand higher service levels, including faster response time, broader access to data files, and increasingly customized service. Partnerships provide scale and clout for helping companies satisfy customers in these areas.

Types of Information Partnership

Four kinds of information partnerships have emerged: joint marketing partnerships, intraindustry partnerships, customer-supplier partnerships, and IT vendor partnerships.

Joint Marketing Partnerships.   Information technology offers companies an important new option—coordinating with rivals where there is an advantage in doing so and specializing where it continues to make sense. The IBM and Sears effort to market Prodigy is an example. At a cost of more than $500 million, these companies have assembled a package of over 400 electronic information services—home banking, stock market quotations, restaurant reservations, and so on—to be delivered across a standard telephone network to millions of American homes. Individually, these services would be used so infrequently—and would cost so much in both dollars and effort—that few customers would be likely to find any one of them practical; but these services have considerable appeal when bundled together and offered at a low cost. By selling advertising space around the edge of the screen, the partners are able to deliver the product to a home for only $130 per year, irrespective of usage.

In marketing partnerships, participant companies gain access to new customers and new territories; they gain economies of scale by sharing the cost of transacting, coordinating, and controlling market exchanges. Sharing allows the information provider to improve channel capacity utilization by selling excess capacity while dramatically lowering the level of asset-specific investments required to conduct business and dramatically increasing market penetration. For the consumer, life is simplified when a number of desired products arrive through a single channel.

Intraindustry Partnerships.   The most important and potentially difficult-to-manage information partnerships evolve not among companies offering complementary, yet noncompetitive services, but among competitors who see an opportunity or need to pool resources in order to stay in the game. A particularly interesting case is the alliance of 18 midsized paper companies that developed a global electronic information system to link them with hundreds of key customers and international sales offices. Costing $50 million to develop, the system was targeted at providing the speed and quality of response that were technically and financially unattainable by any participant individually. With combined sales of nearly $4 billion, these companies made this investment because they could see that to compete effectively in their service-oriented businesses, they must provide on-line, global information exchange with key customers on order entry, inventory status, and product specification. The alternative was to be excluded from important markets by large competitors able to provide these services on their own. This partnership was driven by survival.

Because of the inherent difficulty in creating and managing intraindustry partnerships among competitors, third-party network providers or industry associations often become involved. An example of one such coalition is the Insurance Value-Added Network Services (IVANS), which links hundreds of insurance companies' home offices and thousands of independent agents.[35] IVANS permits independent agents across the United States to access hundreds of property and casualty insurance companies for policy issuance, price quotation, and other policy-management services. It was initiated and created by the industry trade association, ACORD.

These small-to-midsized insurance companies were all concerned that several larger companies had invested in electronic channels of their own, thereby potentially monopolizing independent agents' business. The IVANS interface presents independent agents with a roster of smaller insurance companies and a level playing field—a distinct advantage for the agent, of course, who is concerned about maintaining a competitive environment. Understandably enough, ACORD's position as a trade organization allows it to be perceived as the fairest and, hence, most effective broker of a collaborative system among businesses. In a similar vein, MEMA/Transnet, which connects hundreds of manufacturers and thousands of retailers in the auto parts industry, resulted from actions by the Motor and Equipment Manufacturers Association (MEMA).

Some intraindustry partnerships are so important to a country or other political body that they are initiated and led by government. An example is Singapore's TradeNet system, which links the management and operations activities of the world's largest port.[36] The Singapore government spent approximately $20 million to develop a system for linking agents (e.g., freight forwarders, shipping companies, banks, and insurance companies) and government agencies (e.g., customs officials, immigration officials). Clearing the port used to take a vessel two to four days; now it takes as little as 10 minutes. It is hoped that this dramatic reduction in the time will help ensure that Singapore remains a port of choice in Asia, where the competition among ports is growing.

Buyer-Seller Partnerships. Some information partnerships are set up by sellers to service their customers. An example of this type involves a retail grocery chain that has negotiated its relationship with a supplier of disposable diapers, a very profitable, high-turnover item. Under the new partnership agreement, when a shipment of diapers leaves the retailer's warehouse, the manufacturer is notified; however, no order is transmitted and no delivery schedule is requested. The manufacturer, instead, is bound

---

[35] B. Konsynski, *IVANS* (Boston: Harvard Business School Publishing, case 187–188, 1987).

[36] B. S. Neo, L. Applegate, and J. King, *Singapore Unlimited: Building the National Information Infrastructure* (Boston: Harvard Business School Publishing, case 196–012, 1995).

by a performance contract to keep the warehouse sufficiently stocked, and the system provides the information to ensure this. The partnership is intended to reduce inventories in the retailer's warehouse and to facilitate full-scale coordination and mutual cost reduction—and it appears to be effective. Paperwork has been significantly reduced on both sides (orders, quotes, complicated billing, and so on), production schedules are now more responsive, and each company has trimmed its operations staff.

IT Vendor-Driven Partnerships. These partnerships allow a technology vendor to bring its technology to new markets and, in so doing, they provide a platform for industry participants to offer novel, technologically sophisticated customer services. General Electric Information Services and Automatic Data Processing are examples of firms successfully providing such data interchange platforms. Such information companies can become the strategic linchpin for an organization that wishes to pioneer such services.

A good example of this pioneering is ESAB, a large European welding-supplies and equipment company that tripled in size between 1973 and 1987—a period when sales fell off by half in the industry as a whole. A key to ESAB's growth was an alliance with a large independent network vendor. It used that third-party's information services to facilitate acquiring and rationalizing failing companies throughout Europe: closing their plants and moving production of what had been local brands to a central plant in Sweden, while providing the customers an on-line order-entry service. For its part, ESAB did not have the IT development resources in-house to build a European telecommunications system. From the customers' perspective, the old companies' local offices still provided goods and services. In fact, the information system governed the company's production schedule, manufacturing, and shipping so that customers received products, usually overnight, without realizing they were no longer dealing with a local manufacturer. Moreover, with this strategy ESAB slashed costs. The company has, in effect, replaced inventory and plants with information, using a technology platform that would have been extremely expensive to develop from scratch.

In another type of partnership, an information vendor formed an R&D alliance with a major customer. A common example is the establishment of a "beta site"—where an IT vendor tests a new technology product with selected clients to evaluate features, functionality, and performance, while also learning how companies will choose to use the technology to support individual productivity or business operations. Such partnerships provide advantages to both parties. The vendors gain valuable insight into the practical field problems associated with their technology, while the customer learns about, and participates in the development of, a new technology that may otherwise be beyond its skill and financial resources.

SUMMARY

Like the telephone before it, modern approaches to electronic commerce (IOS, EDI, and, more recently, the Internet) have become an integral part of the fabric of business. Consumers use IOS daily to obtain cash, transfer funds, make credit card purchases, manage their investments, get the latest news, and browse electronic catalogs. Businesses use IOS to streamline distribution channels, interact with customers, decrease internal operating costs, and outsource production activities. Information alliances are forming between the most unlikely partners. While the benefits of these IT-enabled processes and relationships are clearly evident, the risks must be managed to reap the rewards.

Managers must recognize that electronic commerce requires interorganizational business and management process redesign. Interorganizational structures and systems to coordinate and control the information-enabled relationships must be implemented, and interorganizational change processes must be managed. The dynamic and uncertain nature of the business and technology environments will make it impossible to create "iron-clad" contracts to define the relationship. Instead, information-enabled interorganizational authority and control systems need to be designed so that shared values are clearly articulated and interorganizational "boundary systems" are defined. (A more in-depth discussion of information-enabled authority and control systems is provided in Chapter 5.) Real-time shared information on interorganizational processes and frequent interaction—supported by IT, but not replacing face-to-face—are required to monitor interorganizational processes, enabling development of a more collaborative administrative structure.

In conclusion, we offer the following questions for the general manager:

1. Is your company capitalizing on the potential benefits of electronic commerce? Could actions by competitors or new entrants leave you fighting for survival? Are there actions you should take to preempt competitive actions by others?
2. Are you harnessing the power of the information embedded within your products and services to add value to customers? Are there potential new information-enabled products and services that could substitute for your current offerings?
3. Are you capturing the potential benefits of electronic channel integration? Can IOS be used to manage product and market complexity, thereby allowing you to eliminate channel intermediaries, simplify and streamline product/service delivery, and dramatically decrease costs?
4. Have you and your information partners jointly redesigned business processes and designed appropriate authority and control systems?
5. Have you selected your partners wisely? Do you have a shared vision and common purpose? Do you bring equal, and complementary, power and

resources to the relationship? Are you and your partners financially viable, and is the relationship financially and competitively sustainable?

6. Is the technical infrastructure you have in place the right one to effect and manage the types of electronic commerce you are considering? Are you maintaining the appropriate balance between experimenting with promising new technologies—like the Internet—while ensuring technical stability and performance? In approaching electronic commerce, many firms want to position themselves as "leading edge," but not "bleeding edge."

Chapter

5

Information, Organization, and Control

As companies use information technology (IT) to redefine the basis of competition within industries and the power relationships and organizational boundaries among industry players, they are also turning inward and reevaluating the role of IT within the firm. Imaginative companies are not just using the technology to support the existing organization design; they are creatively applying the speed, flexibility, and dramatically increased information processing capacity of 1990s information and communication systems to transform their organizations. To fully appreciate the potential for IT-enabled organization transformation, it is important to first understand the organization design challenge faced by managers in the 1990s.

THE ORGANIZATION DESIGN CHALLENGE OF THE 1990s[1]

From many quarters we hear that the hierarchical organization must wither away. In this view of the future, middle managers have the life expectancy of fruit flies. Those who survive will not be straw bosses but Dutch uncles dispensing resources and wisdom to an empowered labor force that designs its own jobs. Enabled, to use a trendy term, by information technology and propelled by the need to gain speed and shed unnecessary work, this flat, information-based organization won't look like the pharaonic pyramid of yore, but like—well, like what?[2]

---

[1] This section of the chapter is adapted from L. Applegate, *Managing in an Information Age* (Boston: Harvard Business School Publishing, 1995).

[2] T. Stewart, "The Search for the Organization of Tomorrow," *Fortune,* May 18, 1992.

Managers and academics spent the majority of this century building and perfecting the hierarchy; however, if we are to believe the press, they now appear to be engaged in destroying it. Networked, process-oriented, shamrock, learning, team-based, and fast-cycle are but a few of the organizational models that have been proposed. Despite the wide variety of names given to the "information age" organization, common themes have emerged. Most agree that the organization of the 1990s should be flat, fast, flexible, and focused on areas of core competency. Empowered, interfunctional teams of knowledge workers should design and manage streamlined, integrated product/service delivery processes to ensure zero-defect quality, continuous improvement, learning, customer satisfaction, and sustained profitability. Managers within these organizations must "think globally and act locally." Strategic alliances and partnerships should be used to expand organizational capabilities, scale, and scope and, at the extreme, support the development of "virtual corporations." Finally, a high-performance, widely distributed information and communication infrastructure must be implemented to enable flexible and timely information sharing both inside and outside the firm.

But all this recent attention ignores the fact that many of these proposed changes are not new; in fact, early descriptions of matrix and other hybrid organization models emerged in the late 1950s and 1960s.[3] Proponents of these models also called for flexible, adaptive, information-intensive, team-based, collaborative, and "empowered" designs. But in those days, most believed that these new "organic" organizations were only required for firms that operated in dynamic and uncertain environments or in emerging industries. Using this contingency approach, most organizations continued to be organized as traditional hierarchies; but, in the 1990s, hardly a firm can be found that is not operating in a dynamic and uncertain environment. In addition, hardly a firm can be found that is not in the process of implementing a major organizational change. Indeed, a survey of 12,000 managers in 25 different countries found that over 60 percent reported that their company was involved in a major restructuring effort between 1988 and 1990.[4]

All of the recent attention on new organizational models also ignores the fact that the hybrid designs of the 1960s and 1970s soon fell out of favor as managers found that the new structures and systems engendered conflict,

---

[3] T. Burns, and G. M. Stalker, *The Management of Innovation* (London: Tavistock, 1961); J. Woodward, *Industrial Organization, Theory, and Practice* (London: Oxford University Press, 1965); J. D. Thompson, *Organizations in Action* (NY: McGraw Hill, 1967); P. Lawrence and J. Lorsch, *Organization and Environment* (Boston: Harvard Business School Press, 1967, 1986); L. Greiner, "Evolution and Revolution as Organizations Grow," *Harvard Business Review* 50, no. 4 (1972), pp. 37–46; J. Galbraith, *Designing Complex Organizations* (Reading: Addison Wesley, 1973).

[4] R. Kanter, "Transcending Business Boundaries: 12,000 World Managers View Change," *Harvard Business Review,* May–June 1991.

confusion, information overload, and costly duplication of resources. The matrix organization was originally billed as the "obvious organizational solution" to the need to manage, rather than minimize, environmental complexity and speed of response. But Bartlett and Ghoshal[5] describe why many firms adopted the matrix, only to abandon it several years later:

> Top-level . . . managers . . . are losing control of their companies. The problem is not that they have misjudged the demands created by an increasingly complex environment and an accelerating rate of environmental change, nor that they have failed to develop strategies appropriate to the new challenges. The problem is that their companies are organizationally incapable of carrying out the sophisticated strategies they have developed. Over the past 20 years, strategic thinking has outdistanced organizational capabilities.

Why should we believe that today's managers can succeed in transforming their organizations when others failed?

Inability to cope with the increased information processing demands was a major cause of the failure of the matrix organization. In the 1960s, mainframe system architectures, with their centralized control of information processing, mirrored the centralized intelligence and control of the hierarchy.[6] The microcomputer revolution of the 1980s provided tools to decentralize information processing control that mirrored organizational attempts to decentralize decision authority and responsibility to small entrepreneurial units. While these decentralized IT resources helped improve local decision making, the debates and conflicts concerning whether to centralize or decentralize IT resource management reflected organizational arguments concerning the centralization or decentralization of organizational decision authority. However, the "network revolution" of the 1990s (e.g., client-server architectures, "information superhighway" initiatives) enables distributed information processing and intelligence that make the IT centralization/decentralization debates of the 1980s irrelevant.

General Electric CEO Jack Welch summed up the dilemma his company faced as it entered the 1990s.[7] "At the beginning of the decade," he wrote, "we saw two challenges ahead of us, one external and one internal. Externally, we faced a world economy that would be characterized by slower growth, with stronger global competitors going after a smaller piece of the pie. Internally, our challenge was even bigger. We had to find a way to combine the power, resources, and reach of a large company with the

---

[5] C. Bartlett and S. Ghoshal, *Managing across Borders* (Boston: Harvard Business School Press, 1989).

[6] See R. Nolan and D. Croson, *Creative Destruction* (Boston: Harvard Business School Press, 1995) for an in-depth discussion of the parallels between organization and information technology evolution.

[7] J. Welch, "Managing in the 90s," GE Report to Shareholders, 1988.

hunger, agility, spirit, and fire of a small one." As managers struggle to find a solution to the organizational design challenge, they must understand how emerging technology is enabling the handling of the increased information processing requirements of the new organizational models. (See Figure 5–1.)

Firms that can take advantage of the information revolution can now approach the task of creating an "information age" organization that is

FIGURE 5–1   The Organization and Information Technology Design Challenge of the 1990s

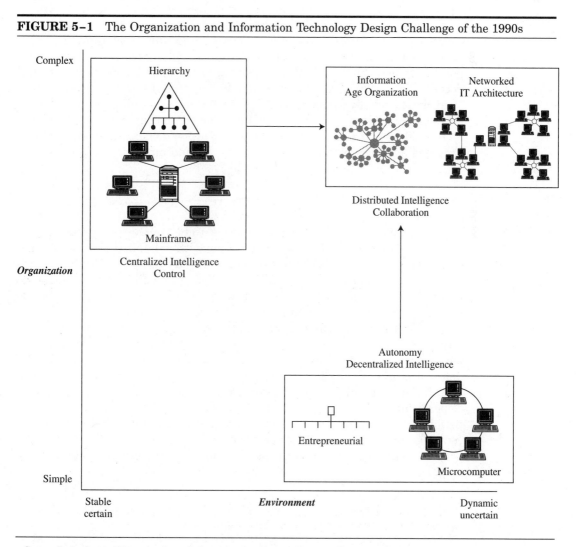

Source: L. Applegate, *Managing in an Information Age* (Boston: Harvard Business School Publishing, 1995).

capable of managing both speed and complexity simultaneously. Managers once stymied by the untimely, incomplete, and inaccurate flow of information from the workforce, customers, and suppliers can now access and communicate relevant and timely information across the world in seconds. This enables a shift in the nature of control from the rigid standards and supervision of the hierarchy to a "learning" model in which timely, flexible access to information enables development of a shared understanding of real-time business operations. Changes in authority are also possible. In some cases, decision making and authority can be moved from the field to corporate headquarters, thus achieving consistency, control, and efficiency. In others, decision making and authority can be decentralized to achieve local responsiveness, flexibility, and speed of response. More importantly, collaborative, "interactive" decision making and authority systems can be designed that enable both local and centralized control.[8] The important point is that technology neither encourages nor discourages centralized or decentralized structures and controls, but instead offers new possibilities. Traditional organizational models have been heavily influenced by "the art of the possible" in information handling. The technology of the 1990s allows us to readdress these long-dormant organization design issues by enabling fundamental change in the nature of control and authority structures.

From Control to Learning

A fundamental tenet of the hierarchy is tight control of operating processes.[9] Hierarchical process control begins with a detailed definition of the core operating processes of the firm—the primary activities through which an organization designs, produces, markets, delivers, and supports its products and services. To eliminate process complexity, the organization is broken down into distinct units of specialization, each responsible for a major operational task (e.g., R&D, manufacturing, marketing, sales). These units are then further subdivided into smaller and smaller units until the job of each individual in the organization is specified in detail. Equally detailed procedures, policies, and job descriptions are developed to govern how, and by whom, process activities are to be carried out and managed. Supervisors are inserted within the hierarchy to ensure that work is performed according to "standard operating procedures." These action controls are supplemented by personnel controls that ensure that the right people are hired for the jobs as specified and that the skills and knowledge

[8] Robert Simons, *Levers of Control: How Managers Use Innovative Control Systems to Drive Strategic Renewal* (Boston: Harvard Business School Press, 1995).

[9] R. N. Anthony, *The Management Control Function* (Boston: Harvard Business School Press, 1988); K. Merchant, *Rewarding Results* (Boston: Harvard Business School Press, 1989).

needed to perform the jobs are developed. Policies and procedures are communicated through orientation and training programs and written procedure manuals; compliance is measured and rewarded through periodic performance evaluations with supervisors. Because control demands a great deal of direct supervision, spans of control are limited and deep hierarchies are required. At upper levels of the hierarchy, the ability to standardize and control actions is more difficult. Where management judgment is required, where possible, action controls are replaced by results controls. Managers are evaluated in terms of their performance against specified targets (often financial), and no attempt is made to define the process through which those targets are reached. The success of this traditional control model is founded on a very important principle—the existence of a feedback loop that enables managers to understand the linkages among inputs, processes, and outputs.

Founded on the concept of simplification, routinization, and control, the hierarchy required ruthless elimination of uncertainty and a very stable environment to operate smoothly. Operations needed to be "sealed off" from all nonroutine events and conditions, so requests for changes in routine operating procedure to respond to a change in the local operating environment were pushed up the line for analysis and revision. Frequently, the only place that there was a complete picture of the entire operating process and its relation to end results was at the very top levels of the firm; and the picture from those lofty heights was often incomplete and out-of-date. As market dynamics heated up within industry after industry, traditional controls became less and less effective. (See Figure 5–2 for a comparison of hierarchical and information-enabled control systems.)

In the 1990s, networked, distributed information and communication systems allow rigid, costly hierarchical controls to be replaced by a new form of information age controls that promote flexibility, creativity, and learning while continuing to enable tight control of operating processes. Using this new model, processes are still defined in detail—often as part of a business process reengineering effort. However, rather than structure and standardize these processes, in effect casting them in concrete, IT can be used as a tool to streamline, integrate, and time-synchronize the processes. While automating for efficiency, these systems also siphon off detailed, timely information on end-to-end process performance, from the purchase of supplies to after-sales service. The data are fed into a flexible, shared "data warehouse" that integrates internal process performance data with data retrieved through interorganizational systems linked to external partners (e.g., suppliers, transportation) and customers. External scanning systems can be used to add critical competitive and market intelligence. This vast warehouse of internal and external data can also be married to data on financial and market performance to provide timely feedback on the links between actions and results. Early warning systems can be embedded into

FIGURE 5–2 The Interaction of Information and Control

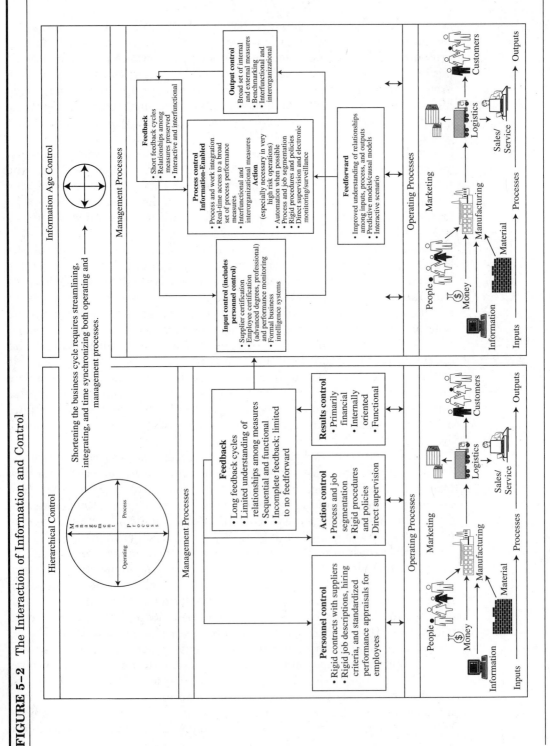

Source: L. Applegate, *Managing in an Information Age* (Boston: Harvard Business School Publishing, 1995).

the software to alert management to potential problems or impending disasters.[10]

Where hierarchical controls were primarily based on the monthly or quarterly flow of routine information, information age controls provide real-time and detailed understanding of the dynamics of the business, filtering out the routine data to be delivered in regular updates that are less time sensitive. As the information cycle time is shortened to match the faster pace of the business, the management control cycle time also decreases, enabling fast-cycled control in a dynamically changing environment. As managers learn to use the information to manage the business more effectively and efficiently, they not only create more focused and powerful feedback mechanisms, but also define *feedforward* systems that allow them to manage the business in a proactive way.

As they learn to manage at a much faster pace, leading companies are also learning to manage rather than minimize complexity. For example, the ability of some companies to use the technology to execute very complex micromarketing campaigns has created significant competitive advantage. A 1989 interview with the former chairman of People's Express Airlines illustrates this point. He noted that having adopted a low-cost strategy that stressed simplicity and no frills, his airline used a very limited amount of IT to support its operations or management. They limited complexity by assigning a single weekly fare for all seats on a given route. Time of day, day of week, and actual loading factors were not considered. In this CEO's judgment, the key date of the company's death was January 19, 1985, when American Airlines introduced its internal yield management system, which allowed it to set a different fare for each seat on every flight for every route—and it could change the entire fare schedule at a moment's notice. With that capability, on competitive routes, American assigned between 1 and 100 deep/deep/deep discount fares at $5 below People's Express' "everyday low price" discount. American then launched a national advertising campaign:

> Call your travel agent and find out who the real low-cost airline is. It is not People's Express. It is American Airlines.

Within 20 minutes of the time People's Express announced a fare change for a route, American adjusted its deep/deep/deep discount fare to $5 below the new People's Express fare and electronically communicated it to travel agents all over the United States and the world. Lacking equally responsive information management, control, and operating processes, People's Express found that it was impossible to compete against that level of managed complexity and responsiveness. In the 1990s, the ability to *manage complexity* has become a powerful source of competitive advantage.

---

[10] Taco Bell, Inc., calls these safety nets. See L. Schlesinger, *Taco Bell Corp.* (Boston: Harvard Business School Publishing, case 692–058, 1992).

From Autonomy to Collaboration

The close link between access to information and the delegation of authority has long been recognized.[11] In most hierarchically structured firms, detailed and timely information about competitors, customers, and internal organizational processes and capabilities resides largely at the bottom of the organization, where the action is. Lacking information on anything beyond their local view of the business, frontline employees often make decisions that are locally optimal. Conversely, access to information on corporatewide policies and perspective, strategic direction, and the dynamics of the business as a whole usually resides at the top of the firm. As a result, decisions made at the top of the firm often consider corporatewide initiatives and strategic direction but may not reflect an in-depth understanding of the business.

To minimize the problem of inadequate access to information, many large, complex organizations delegate decision-making responsibility to middle managers who are expected to have access to information on both the corporate perspective and local business dynamics. In reality, however, critical information from both the top and bottom of the organization is often lost. In addition, the time it takes to pass information through the middle management layers, and the filtering and reinterpretation of that information, seriously hampers the speed and effectiveness of organizational decision making.

As the pace of business increases and the environment becomes more complex and uncertain, many companies are recognizing that they can no longer afford slow-to-respond information and authority structures. The solution many have adopted is to "cut out the middle," forcing the top and bottom of the organization closer together. Line managers are empowered to make decisions, but often little thought has been given to the appropriate redistribution of information and authority and the changes in incentives, roles, and organizational values that must accompany it. To avoid organizational chaos, efforts to downsize, delayer, and empower must be accompanied by changes in information access, roles, and incentives. In addition, boundary and value systems must be implemented that define the shared vision and purpose that guides decision making and clearly delineates the limits of authority.[12] This does not mean that everyone in the organization

---

[11]M. Jensen and W. Meckling, "Theory of the Firm: Managerial Behavior, Agency Costs, and Ownership Structure," *Journal of Financial Economics* 3 (1973), pp. 305–60, E. Fama, "Agency Problems and the Theory of the Firm," *Journal of Political Economics* 80, no. 21 (1980) 288–307; G. Huber, "A Theory of the Effects of Advanced Information Technology on Organizational Design, Intelligence, and Decision Making," *Academy of Management Review* 15, no. 1 (1990) pp. 47–71; V. Gurbaxani and S. Whang, "The Impact of Information Systems on Organizations and Markets," *Communications of the ACM* 34, no. 1 (1991) pp. 59–73.

[12]See R. Simons, "Control in an Age of Empowerment," *Harvard Business Review* (March–April 1995) for an excellent discussion of boundary and value systems in the empowered organization.

must receive all information; that would result in information overload. Rather, it implies that decision makers at all levels must be able to directly access timely information that integrates a corporatewide perspective with knowledge of local business dynamics (see Figure 5–3).

By solving the problem of poor information access and communication, selecting where to locate accountability for key business decisions can be based on the nature of the business and the capabilities of the people, rather than on who has access to the appropriate information. For example, in dynamic and uncertain environments, where speed and in-depth understanding of local markets are critical, decision authority can be pushed

FIGURE 5–3 The Interaction of Information and Organization Design

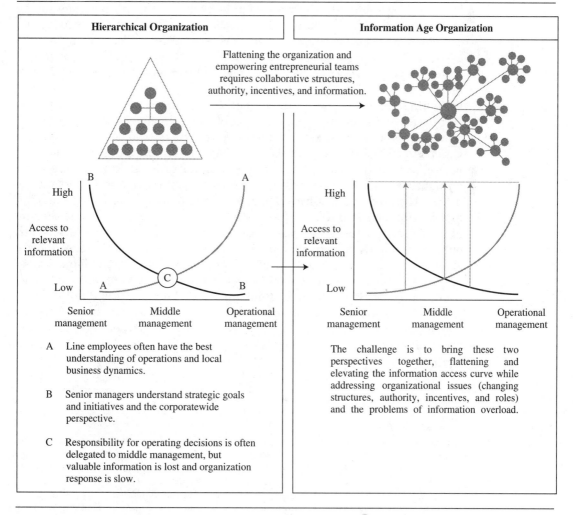

Source: L. Applegate, *Managing in an Information Age* (Boston: Harvard Business School Publishing, 1995).

down to frontline managers, along with the necessary corporatewide perspective to improve speed of response and customization of products and services to the changing needs of customers. By the same token, top management can develop a deeper understanding of local business dynamics and the changing nature of operations, thereby improving the quality of corporatewide strategic decision making and control.

While the above discussion emphasizes the importance of distributed information, new communication technologies are also enabling dramatic changes in organization design. For example, technologies such as video conferencing, electronic mail, and voice mail allow the top of the organization to appear psychologically closer to the middle and the bottom, and enable individuals and work teams to identify and work collaboratively with experts located in the most far-flung corners of the organization—and, in some cases, outside the organization.[13] Several years ago, one of the authors watched in fascination as a senior sales representative, reacting to a sudden market opportunity, used his firm's electronic mail system to assemble a 200-page proposal in 48 hours with the help of seven people across the globe whom he had never met. (The proposal was accepted.) The ability to collapse time and distance and to reach new sources of expertise made this capability a genuine competitive advantage.

Innovative companies that have implemented distributed information and communication systems in support of efforts to transform their organizations to meet the challenges of the 1990s are finding that the question of where to locate decision authority for key organizational decisions is seldom straightforward. As product/service delivery systems become increasingly more integrated and fast-cycled, managers are finding that decision making and control require intense collaboration, interaction, and real-time sharing of information across functional boundaries and organizational levels with outside suppliers, customers, and, occasionally, even competitors. Authority structures and incentives that vest all power in a single individual are no longer adequate; yet individuals must continue to accept individual accountability for their decisions. Boundary and value systems that prescribe the limits of authority and the ethical principles upon which decisions should be based become much more critical in an empowered organization in which major corporate decisions are being made in real time. Reports of the recent demise of Baring Bank highlight these potential risks.[14] The

---

[13] See L. Applegate, *IBM Computer Conferencing* (Boston: Harvard Business School Publishing, case 188–039, 1988); and L. Applegate and D. Stoddard, *Chemical Bank: Technology Support for Cooperative Work* (Boston: Harvard Business School Publishing, case 193-131, 1993) for examples of the influence of communication technologies on organizations.

[14] S. Lysin and G. B. Krecht, "How Many Other Barings Are There?" *The Wall Street Journal,* February 28, 1995; G. Millman, "Barings Collapses: Financial System Bears Up Well," *The Wall Street Journal,* February 28, 1995.

potential for abuse of power increased as the bank delegated authority for both trading and back-office transaction processing to an individual manager, and the lack of adequate "safety nets" failed to detect the problem in time to stem the losses.

Figure 5–4 and Table 5–1 summarize the role of a distributed information infrastructure in enabling managers to redefine organizational control and authority to meet the challenges of managing speed and complexity simultaneously. The following examples help to clarify the interaction between IT and organizations in the 1990s.

FIGURE 5–4   The Interaction of Information, Authority, and Control in the Information Age Organization

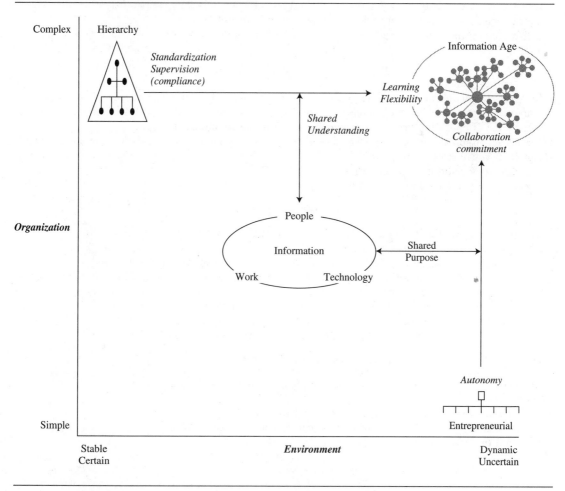

Source: L. Applegate, *Managing in an Information Age* (Boston: Harvard Business School Publishing, 1995).

TABLE 5-1 Characteristics of the Information Age Organization

Organization Structure

- Flat hierarchy with broader spans of control.
- Downsized corporate headquarters; staff reassigned to the field.
- Strategic partnerships and alliances enable focus on core competencies.
- Networked coordinating mechanisms (e.g., interfunctional teams and matrixed reporting structures) layered over hierarchical reporting structures.
- Functional units remain as center of expertise and career development.

Authority and Decision Making

- Shared authority and decision making replace clearly defined hierarchical authority.
- Senior management more involved in monitoring/understanding operations; responsible for defining, communicating, and consistently enforcing boundary and value systems.
- Interfunctional middle management operating units responsible for operating strategy development, strategy execution, network coordination, and innovation.
- Self-managing work teams responsible for defining and managing local operations and product quality.

Operating Processes

- Integrated, streamlined, and time-synchronized product/service delivery and new product development processes (includes customers, suppliers, channel distributors, strategic partners, etc.).
- Cycle time of operating processes matches cycle time in the environment.
- Increased complexity of operating processes matches the inherent complexity in the environment.
- Efficient, yet flexible, operations.
- Interfunctional and interorganizational.
- Focus on continuous improvement and innovation.

Management Processes

- Integrated, streamlined, and time-synchronized management processes (e.g., planning, resource allocation, performance management).
- Cycle time of management processes matches cycle time of operating processes.
- Increased complexity of management processes matches the increased complexity of operations.
- Efficient, yet flexible, management.
- Interfunctional and interorganizational.
- Increased vertical and lateral interaction.
- "Tight control" achieved through information versus structure and supervision.

Incentives and Rewards

- Shared incentive systems (e.g., team-based incentives) augment and enforce shared authority structures.
- Personal accountability and commitment maintained.
- "Stretch" targets motivate commitment to collaborate, maintain focus on organizational priorities, and intensify efforts to achieve organizational goals.

TABLE 5–1 Characteristics of the Information Age Organization (continued)

Roles / Skills and Expertise

- Roles evolve as individuals and teams struggle to redefine work within the new structure and incentive systems.
- Increased analytical/intellectual content of the work.
- People expected to have a broader skill base.
- Information competency at all levels.
- Increased emphasis on the development of leadership and change management skills.

Career Development

- Fewer opportunities for advancement available within the hierarchical reporting structure.
- Expanded jobs and increased lateral movement instead of hierarchical movement.

Source: L. Applegate, *Managing in an Information Age* (Boston: Harvard Business School Publishing, 1995).

INFORMATION, ORGANIZATION, AND CONTROL IN A RETAIL BANK

A prominent bank recently spent millions of dollars to create a centralized data warehouse that consolidated and reorganized its operating information by customer and by product. The implementation of state-of-the-art information packaging and delivery tools enabled the delivery of customized information to the desktops—and laptops—of employees and managers throughout the organization within a matter of seconds. The new system replaced a static set of individual data files that contained information by product. Previously, requests to obtain a customized report took many person-years of coding by IT professionals, and the time and expense prevented most requests from ever being filled. While the old system had meshed well with the company's long-standing structure and incentives, which focused on individual products, a change in strategy to "relationship banking" created chaos within the firm. Relationship managers had no easy way to identify the full set of relationships each customer had with the bank. Consequently, they were frequently embarrassed when making individual calls and tended to avoid cross-selling opportunities. They lacked a mechanism for regularly reviewing a customer's total investments with the bank and for defining an appropriate mix of products for the customer. Compounding the problem was the fact that a customer's name often appeared in several variations within isolated data files—sometimes two initials, sometimes the full name, and so on. Even if a salesperson had wanted to plow through mountains of product files for customer information, it is doubtful he or she could have caught all of the listings for every customer.

Use of the new system to access integrated information on every aspect of a customer's relationship with the bank enabled expansion of the role and authority of line employees while simultaneously enabling better control of the much more complex, dynamically changing business. The new system provided field sales with direct access to each customer's entire product portfolio. They could use this information to suggest that the customer give up outdated financial products and buy appropriate replacements. Information was also provided to senior and middle management, who monitored the success of the strategy and its execution across the bank, revising the corporate direction as appropriate. A new incentive system was instituted that paid commissions to relationship managers who developed comprehensive long-term relationships with customers, thereby aligning the employee's goals with company goals. Customer retention rose dramatically. Market share also rose as relationship managers used their improved understanding of the bank's customers to tailor products and services to the dynamically changing marketplace.

Many of the company's competitors scrambled to install similar systems but were faced with two or more years of costly systems programming to simply duplicate the flexible information management systems. Meanwhile, the bank had two years' lead time to learn more about customers and markets to enable it to push the bar ever higher. Stimulated by the improved performance of an industry leader, the ability to use information to learn more about the market, and to flexibly meet individual customer requirements while also tightly controlling the much more complex and dynamically changing operations has become a requirement for retail and wholesale banks that want to stay in business.

INFORMATION, ORGANIZATION, AND CONTROL IN THE SUPERMARKET

In the 1990s, many supermarket chains have applied the speed and flexibility of distributed information infrastructures to their decentralized inventory-monitoring systems. The old approach demanded that employees count stock. These numbers were sent to corporate headquarters, where they were translated into buying and merchandising plans that were then sent back to the stores months later. If sales of an item surged, store managers often learned about it too late to meet the demand. Furthermore, because suppliers had the only up-to-date facts on what was selling, they acted as "consultants" and sometimes pressured stores to overstock slow-moving products. The lack of accurate information at the store level also increased suppliers' bargaining power in setting prices.

Today, distributed information infrastructures have enabled a dramatic shift in the balance of power. Scanners at checkout counters log every item that leaves the store. The scanners post data to inventory records instantly and far more accurately than earlier methods. This information is available immediately at the store level and at corporate headquarters. As a result, authority for store-level inventory decisions has been pushed down to the local level. Purchasing contracts, however, are now managed and controlled at corporate headquarters, dramatically increasing the power that large chains have over suppliers and greatly decreasing inventory costs. Working off these corporatewide agreements, each store manager can change local inventory levels to meet the changing demands of customers—and they can do so at a moment's notice. Many stores now have electronic linkages with key suppliers that allow for on-line ordering and one-day delivery of products. For example, Frito-Lay can now replenish inventory at key supermarket accounts within one day; in 1990 it took over one week.

As a result of improved information and control of operating processes, information age supermarkets have dramatically lowered inventory levels, weeded out slow-moving items, boosted inventory turns, and matched product mix to their consumers' changing tastes. Advertisements, special promotions, and merchandising are targeted to deliver the highest potential revenues at the lowest possible costs; moreover, because they now possess the best information, the bargaining power with suppliers is greater. As we saw in the retail banking example, the new information-enabled operations and management processes coincided with changes in structure, authority, and incentives.

TARGETED OPPORTUNITIES

While the above discussion provides a more general framework for evaluating the influence of IT on organization design, there are many targeted opportunities that should also be considered.

Communicating Organizational Priorities

An organization has been defined as a social system that unites individuals and groups around a common purpose.[15] Traditional organizational and information systems often fall short of adequately communicating that purpose. Failure can often be blamed on one of three reasons: people do not understand the corporate goals, they understand them but lack the resources to meet them, or they simply are not motivated to fulfill them.

Sometimes people do not know what is expected of them because the corporate plan has changed and dissemination of the new message is lagging. For instance, a sudden cash flow crisis may cause the vice

---

[15] G. Morgan, *Images of Organization* (Beverly Hills: Sage Publishing, 1986).

president of finance to cut budgets. In a huge conglomerate that relies on old technology, it may take weeks to rework individual budgets and get new spending guidelines out to operating units. In the meantime, large amounts of cash may be drained away.

Even after a message has made the long trip from headquarters to widely dispersed units, the workforce may lack the information to act on it. For example, recall the bank that wanted to establish relationship banking. Without customer-oriented information, managers would not have been able to make decisions and take actions consistent with the company's goals.

When performance is not measured accurately or promptly, it is more difficult to maintain motivation, and ineffective work habits may take root. Sales representatives, whose bonuses are tallied only once a year, have no way of knowing where they stand one month, three months, or six months into a new year. They may not realize until too late that their sales techniques are not helping them meet organizational goals and personal performance targets. Appropriate incentives only work if the information needed to evaluate performance—and create the control feedback and feedforward loops—is provided in a timely enough manner to affect actions and decisions.

Meaningful Budgets

Budgets can be a powerful tool for communicating organizational priorities and expectations. In addition, when individuals and groups help to develop the budgets, they can become more committed to organizational goals. Each blank line on a budget form forces a manager to evaluate priorities and confront reality. With traditional approaches, the sheer time required to fill in the blanks prevented managers from trying out and prospectively evaluating alternative scenarios.

New analytical tools (e.g., customized spreadsheets) not only speed the budgeting process by allowing managers to "plug in" numbers faster, but also improve the quality of those budgets by allowing managers to try different "what if" scenarios and compare the outcomes. For example, if a manager is trying to project revenues, he or she can quickly run through several iterations based on possible changes in the market. The first analysis might assume a regulatory change that bolsters the sales of one product. Another might analyze revenues if the regulation is not passed. By using computer models to test various assumptions, managers can think more carefully about plans and the expenditures associated with them and then follow their evaluation through to its logical conclusion. In this way, the technology allows management to better anticipate and prepare for contingencies. Also, since individual unit budgets can be almost immediately consolidated into overall corporate financial plans, the process helps companies to coordinate diverse activities.

The new technology also lets managers continuously update operating plans and budgets based on actual performance. Organizations are no longer tied to plans that are out-of-date by the time they are approved. They can also use real-time information to better balance supply and demand. For example, Frito-Lay managers used the company's distributed information and communication infrastructure to enable them to change from an annual to a triennial planning cycle and to revise production schedules weekly rather than quarterly. Despite the increased complexity of the manufacturing process, savings of over $100 million per year in manufacturing and logistics costs were realized.

In short, the use of IT can help turn the budget process into a critical organizational communication process that helps focus attention on priorities and facilitates optimization of the company's performance under changing conditions. The controller of a large U.S. corporation claims that quickly consolidated on-line spreadsheets for each department and business unit have enabled a tenfold improvement in his company's ability to coordinate actions under various alternatives. Moreover, fewer staff are needed to implement the more complex process.

Effective Incentive Systems

Distributed information and communication infrastructures can also help managers create more effective incentive systems. Employees who are able to access timely and detailed performance reports that link their actions to accomplishment of organizational and personal goals are motivated to work harder (and smarter). A simple form of automated incentive system in one company continuously tallies sales commissions and provides salespeople with immediate access to their records. Additionally, incentive-based measurement systems can identify and track the contribution of a work unit, enabling the company to offer team-based incentives in addition to individual incentives. The automotive industry found this capability very attractive in providing appropriate incentives for their dealers. The first dealer a customer visits usually invests a great deal of time describing various car models and demonstrating their features, but the customer often buys the car from a different dealer who has done far less work. Knowing this pattern, the first dealer may do a hasty job of educating the customer and try to close the deal quickly. Although automakers may not like this situation, the industry's commission structure, which measures only sales, supports it. One manufacturer is now considering a customer-tracking system that would reward the salesperson who makes the initial presentation, even though another dealer makes the sale.

Some organizations use innovative systems to motivate distributors to sell their products. A contact lens company, for example, offered a consignment inventory to opticians who demonstrated that they could turn inventory at least 13 times a year. By selling from consignment, the optician was able to get paid immediately rather than over one week later; in addition, customers were impressed by the speed with which they were able to get their new lenses. Both the opticians and the lens manufacturer benefited from the simple, IT-enabled change. The IT system balanced the complex and fast-cycled inventory system. The system dramatically boosted the lens company's market share over a period of several years.

Solutions for Production

The increased power and versatility of today's information and communication systems can also help managers identify, and even correct, trouble spots in their production processes. One of the most common uses of IT is in production facilities, where digital monitoring and control systems can track efficiency and quality on a real-time basis, alert workers to product quality problems or equipment failures, measure and adjust machine speeds, and assess process productivity. Traditional factory systems force managers to rely on individual workers both to perform the production tasks and to spot problems in the process. Deviations from routine must be brought to the attention of the supervisor, who may, in turn, blame the employee for the problem. Once the problem is identified, the supervisor often must pass the information through the hierarchy until it reaches the plant manager or a higher-level manager for resolution. If resolution of the problem involves several different functional areas, the time required to solve it increases dramatically. In the 1990s, IT can be used to both automate operations—thereby eliminating much of the repetitive, manual, and error-prone work—and to expand the role and authority of interfunctional operating teams. Armed with real-time information, these teams are able to actively manage and continuously improve product/service quality and operating processes. Early detection of problems allows early correction, thereby improving the economics of manufacturing.

Examples of this type of application abound. One manufacturer installed an automated system that regularly pulled products off the line and put them through 20 tests, noting the smallest inconsistency in quality. A paper company uses a sophisticated monitoring device to detect variations in paper thickness or color that are invisible to the human eye. The ability of the machines to detect even the slightest flaws and to capture and store information on process performance allows workers to quickly adjust equipment and their actions as needed. It also allows management to develop a more timely and detailed understanding of process performance. As a refinement of an earlier version of this system, the machine operators and the system designers worked together to develop a set of dynamic graphs on display terminals showing paper thickness versus machine settings, which permitted even better understanding and control of operations through real-time learning rather than rigid action controls.

Facts to Make the Sale

Information technology can also help management align control and sales incentives with the realities of the market. Failure to achieve alignment can have embarrassing results. As noted earlier in our retail bank example, early attempts to switch from a transaction to a relationship sales model called for salespeople to contact upscale clients and attempt to sell them new financial products. Unfortunately, during these initial efforts, the bank—and therefore the salespeople—lacked information on each customer's total relationship with the bank. When the salespeople pushed products that were highly inappropriate for their clients, their image as financial counselors was quickly undermined. More importantly, however, the image of the bank as a secure partner in managing valuable financial assets was tarnished—for many customers, irreparably. Several key customers left the bank. Outmoded, static systems had thwarted efforts to better serve customer needs, and ultimately the bank had to cancel its well-conceived, but impossible-to-execute campaign until distributed information and control systems were implemented.

Adaptation to Change

More powerful and flexible information and communication infrastructures help companies adapt to regulatory or other environmental changes. When the 1986 tax law shifted the rules of the game for insurance companies, one company quickly capitalized on the change. Within weeks of the law's passage, the company launched a campaign to educate its agents and customers about the statute's ramifications and the desirability of repaying loans against insurance policies. How were they able to accomplish this? Several years earlier, well ahead of the need, this company invested in the implementation of a corporate data warehouse that allowed managers to view information by product, customer, geography, and so forth. Failing to recognize the potential value of flexible information management, the insurance company's competitors were unable to adapt to the change in the industry; inflexible, difficult to change, policy-oriented data systems could not provide the information required inside the company and by customers. In contrast, the forward-thinking insurance company was able to rapidly produce thousands of customized reports that explained in a few pages how the new rules would affect each of its policyholders.

Since loan interest was no longer tax-deductible and the cash-value buildup on a policy would continue to receive favorable tax treatment, the insurance company was able to persuade customers to pay back loans against their whole life policies. (Prior to that time, many customers were in the habit of borrowing against the cash value of their insurance policies at a low rate, deducting the interest on those loans, and pouring the money into high-yield financial products. The net effect was a huge drain on insurance company coffers.) Within weeks, the insurance company was able to convince customers to repay tens of millions of dollars on their loans and at the same time generate massive new sales of a single-premium life insurance product, which was both liquid and nontaxable under the new law. The ability to rapidly respond to environmental change paid a handsome dividend; of course, the flexibility built into the system was almost impossible to justify at the time the investment was made. However, afterwards, the firm wondered how it could have lived without it. (Chapter 6 provides a more in-depth discussion of IT investment strategies for the 1990s.)

SUMMARY

Because changes in organization and information infrastructure affect all areas of the corporation, they can be extraordinarily disruptive. Although the technical implementation and associated costs are clearly less of a challenge, managers should carefully study the issues and their many implications before going forward.

As noted earlier, the technology itself is organizationally neutral. It does not favor centralization over decentralization or one organizational design philosophy over another. However, the nature of the IT infrastructure can dramatically alter the choices available to management—the more flexible and distributed the IT architecture, the more organizational options available. These options must be weighed carefully to ensure appropriate alignment of structure, authority, and incentives, operating and management processes, and roles, skills, and career development. For example, redistribution of authority and decision-making power may demand new skills and the replacement of long-term employees, many of whom may take valuable organizational knowledge with them when they leave. The blurring of organizational boundaries may require redefinition of roles.

There is danger, too, in failing to adequately consider the value and strategic advantages that can be gained from implementation of an information age organization and its associated information infrastructure. Fragmented, static, and costly data-storage and limited data-retrieval systems are relics of the past. Like the traditional hierarchical organization upon which they were modeled, these traditional information infrastructures can only operate effectively in stable environments and structured organizations. The technology now exists to transform both the organization and information infrastructure to meet the challenges of operating in a dynamic, uncertain, and complex world; thus, in the 1990s, the question to ask as we ponder the potential of information and organization is not "What can the technology do?" but "What do we want it to do?"

IT Architecture: Evolution and Alternatives[1]

"This is the most turbulent market I have ever seen," a venture capitalist commented as he discussed a segment of the IT industry in 1994. As managers struggle with the potential and difficulties of assimilating and managing information technology (IT) in the 1990s, it is helpful to recall, as noted in Chapter 1, that computers were only introduced into organizations within the last 30 to 40 years. Those early computers filled a room and calculations could take several hours. By the mid-1990s, performance was measured in the billions of instructions per second and "palm-top" computers far exceeded the performance of the 1960s mainframes at a fraction of the price (see Figure 6–1). Consider this: in August 1993, Nintendo announced a video game computer that will cost $250 when it ships in 1995, yet will contain computing power that would have cost $14 million a decade earlier.[2] Wireless technology and the integration of data, voice, video, and graphics capabilities over blindingly fast, yet cost-effective, networks now allow "any time, any place, and any form" communication and information sharing. These dramatic improvements in IT price/performance enable equally dramatic changes in organizational strategy, structure, people, processes, distribution channels, and work. However, despite its potential, many managers remain ignorant of how to successfully tap the power of this valuable tool.

When companies first began to adopt information technology in the 1960s, Alvin Toffler predicted that the evolution of IT, in concert with changes in the nature of work and workers, would create a new world order,

---

[1] This chapter is adapted from L. Applegate, *Managing in an Information Age* (Boston: Harvard Business School Publishing, 1995).

[2] *Business Week,* March 6, 1995.

FIGURE 6–1   Evolution of Technology

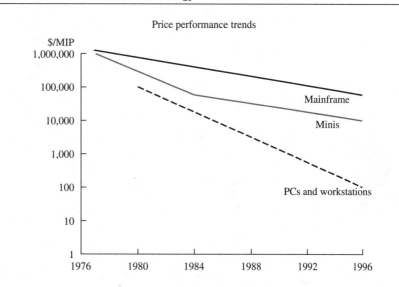

Adapted from J. McKenney, *Waves of Change* (Boston: Harvard Business School Publishing, 1995).

which he termed the Information Age.[3] From a technical perspective, the introduction of the Univac computer in the early 1950s, the installation of wideband transatlantic telephone cables in 1956, and, in 1957, the launching of the first satellite, Sputnik, laid the technological foundation for rapid, global information exchange.[4] While these technological changes made the news, an equally important event went almost unnoticed; in the mid-1950s the percentage of white-collar workers in the United States surpassed the percentage of blue-collar workers. Observed John Naisbitt in *Megatrends:* "For the first time in history, most of us worked with information rather than producing goods."[5] (see Figure 6–2).

The co-evolution of technology, work, and the workforce over the past 30 years has indeed dramatically influenced our concept of organizations and the industries within which they compete. As we have illustrated in earlier chapters, IT is no longer simply a tool to support "back-office" transactions; it has become a strategic business component, enabling the redefinition of markets and industries and the strategies and designs of firms competing

---

[3] A. Toffler, *Future Shock* (New York: Bantam Books, 1971).

[4] The Univac computer is widely regarded as the first commercial, digital computer. Development was completed in 1951; the Census Bureau, American Totalator (which sold systems to support horsetrack betting), A.C. Nielson, and the Prudential were among the first to adopt the Univac. By 1957, 46 had been sold.

[5] J. Naisbitt, *Megatrends* (New York: Warner Books, 1984).

FIGURE 6-2   Distribution of Workers

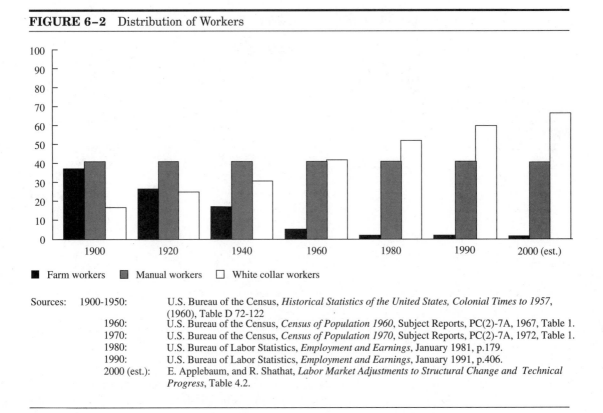

■ Farm workers   ■ Manual workers   □ White collar workers

Sources: 1900-1950:   U.S. Bureau of the Census, *Historical Statistics of the United States, Colonial Times to 1957*, (1960), Table D 72-122
           1960:   U.S. Bureau of the Census, *Census of Population 1960*, Subject Reports, PC(2)-7A, 1967, Table 1.
           1970:   U.S. Bureau of the Census, *Census of Population 1970*, Subject Reports, PC(2)-7A, 1972, Table 1.
           1980:   U.S. Bureau of Labor Statistics, *Employment and Earnings*, January 1981, p.179.
           1990:   U.S. Bureau of Labor Statistics, *Employment and Earnings*, January 1991, p.406.
           2000 (est.):   E. Applebaum, and R. Shathat, *Labor Market Adjustments to Structural Change and Technical Progress*, Table 4.2.

within them. Today's supersonic jets cross the Atlantic in three hours or less, and global communication networks carry information around the world in seconds. Distance and time have become much less significant determinants of market and organizational structures and processes.[6] Moreover, information has become a major economic good, frequently exchanged in concert with, or even in place of, tangible goods and services. As we saw in Chapter 4, the 1990s offer examples of "virtual" corporations—organizations comprising many small, independent agents (or firms) serving as nodes on an information network, thereby allowing small, entrepreneurial units to

---

[6] R. Miles and C. Snow, "Organizations: New Concepts for New Forms," *California Management Review,* 28-62073, 1986; T. Malone, J. Yates, and R. Benjamin, "Electronic Markets and Electronic Hierarchies: Effects of Information Technology on Market Structure and Corporate Strategies," *Communications of the ACM* 30, no. 6 (1987), pp. 484–97.; R. Johnston and P. Lawrence, "Beyond Vertical Integration—The Rise of the Value-Adding Partnership," *Harvard Business Review,* July–August 1988; W. Powell, "Neither Market nor Hierarchy: Network Forms of Organization," *Research on Organizational Behavior* 12 (1990), pp. 295–336.

achieve dramatic increases in scope and scale. Such arrangements challenge both our legal and social definitions of an organization.

Just as IT has radically altered how we view the relationships between firms, it also challenges our notion of relationships within them. As companies install sophisticated information and communication platforms with the potential to link everyone within the firm to a common source of organizational knowledge and a fully distributed network of relationships, the rigid walls around organizational layers and functions begin to deteriorate. In addition, personal portable technologies enable a new class of mobile worker, and a new class of work—"Telework."

These are but a few of the ways that IT is influencing industries, strategies, and organization designs in the 1990s. As it does so, IT plays a dual role: simultaneously helping to create the conditions that give rise to the need to change and providing the tools needed to support the change. But to achieve these information-age benefits, companies must adopt information-age technology architectures. Organizations must radically transform outdated IT architectures and the organizations required to support them. This technological transformation is every bit as daunting as the organizational transformation discussed in Chapter 5.

THE EVOLUTION OF IT ARCHITECTURE

The IT architecture of a firm is the blueprint that defines the technical computing, information management, and communications platform of the firm, the structures and controls that define how that platform can be used, and the categories of applications that can be created upon the platform (see Figure 6–3). The IT architecture provides an overall picture of the range of technical options available to a firm, and, as such, it also implies the range of business options.[7] It includes the hardware and software used to manage information and communication; the tools used to access, package, deliver, and communicate information; the standards, models, and control frameworks; and the overall configuration that integrates the various components. Decisions made in building the technical IT architecture must be closely linked to decisions made in designing the IT organization that will manage the architecture; together they must be linked to the strategy and organization design of the firm itself. For the purposes of this chapter, we will focus on the technical architecture. Future chapters will discuss IT leadership and organization design (Chapter 7), IT operations (Chapter 8), and IT management processes (Chapter 9) in greater detail.

Technology changes over the past 30 years have been marked by evolution and revolution. Periods of radical, discontinuous change were stimulated by

---

[7] See P. Keen, *Every Manager's Guide to Information Technology* (Boston: Harvard Publishing, 1991).

FIGURE 6-3 IT Architechture

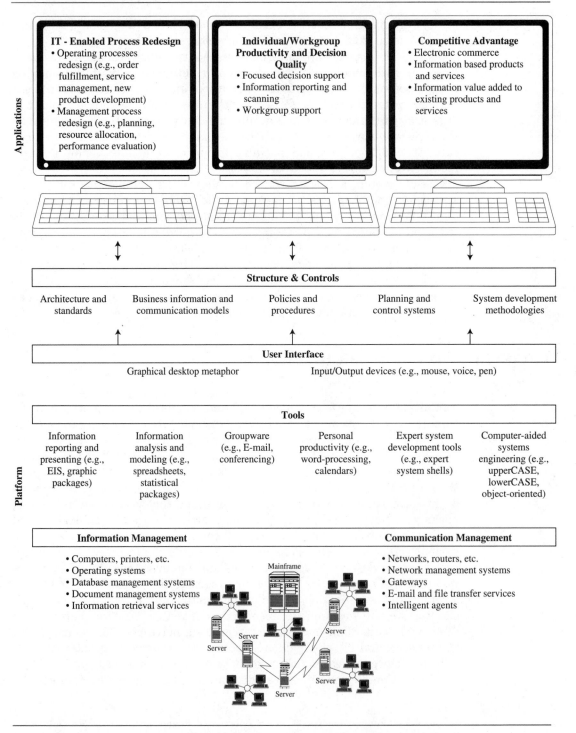

Applications

IT - Enabled Process Redesign
- Operating processes redesign (e.g., order fulfillment, service management, new product development)
- Management process redesign (e.g., planning, resource allocation, performance evaluation)

Individual/Workgroup Productivity and Decision Quality
- Focused decision support
- Information reporting and scanning
- Workgroup support

Competitive Advantage
- Electronic commerce
- Information based products and services
- Information value added to existing products and services

Structure & Controls

| Architecture and standards | Business information and communication models | Policies and procedures | Planning and control systems | System development methodologies |

User Interface

Graphical desktop metaphor   Input/Output devices (e.g., mouse, voice, pen)

Platform

Tools

| Information reporting and presenting (e.g., EIS, graphic packages) | Information analysis and modeling (e.g., spreadsheets, statistical packages) | Groupware (e.g., E-mail, conferencing) | Personal productivity (e.g., word-processing, calendars) | Expert system development tools (e.g., expert system shells) | Computer-aided systems engineering (e.g., upperCASE, lowerCASE, object-oriented) |

Information Management   **Communication Management**

- Computers, printers, etc.
- Operating systems
- Database management systems
- Document management systems
- Information retrieval services

- Networks, routers, etc.
- Network management systems
- Gateways
- E-mail and file transfer services
- Intelligent agents

Mainframe

Server Server Server Server Server

Source: L. Applegate, *Managing in an Information Age (Boston: Harvard Business School Publishing, 1995).*

periods of technological innovation that often began as a series of incremental changes in an earlier period. In the hands of innovative firms, these innovations coalesced into a new dominant IT design that radically altered the scope of IT use within organizations and industries.[8] As noted in Chapter 1, our distinct, yet overlapping, periods of innovation have been identified: the *Mainframe Era,* the *Microcomputer Era,* the *Distributed Era,* and the *Ubiquitous Era.* Table 6–1 summarizes the characteristics of the IT architecture during these four eras.

Era 1—The Mainframe (1950s to 1970s)

Few remember the drudgery associated with the manual, paper-based information systems of the early to mid-1900s. Mechanical technologies had automated factories, creating dramatic increases in efficiency of production; automobiles, roads, and railroads had enabled efficiency of distribution to distant markets; and radio and publishing had stimulated demand for low-cost mass-produced products. Those able to harness these new mechanical technologies were able to grow quickly, linking their dispersed organizations through rapidly improving telephone and telegraph communication systems; however, along with the growth came dramatic increases in complexity. While the hierarchy helped reduce the complexity through structure and systems, scores of middle managers and office clerks were required to process the information needed to do business. Supervisors walked the floors to directly monitor operations. When not walking the floor, they sat in glass-enclosed offices with a full view of clerical or factory operations. Clerks collected information through paper memos, reports, and word of mouth. This information was painstakingly recorded by hand on paper files and record cards stored in file cabinets. Product designs were drawn by hand, supported by slide rules to perform complex computations. In information-intensive industries (e.g., insurance and banking), punch card machines and mechanical calculators helped massive rooms filled with row after row of clerks process and analyze information. Middle management time was consumed in checking the accuracy of the data and creating reports for upper management to use in making decisions.

The introduction of the digital computer in the early 1950s served as the catalyst for radical change in organizational information processing. The early pioneers that defined the dominant IT architecture of the mainframe era were most often found in information-intensive firms (e.g., insurance, banking, airlines), and early uses of the technology were often targeted toward improving the efficiency of information-intensive, clerical tasks (e.g., accounting and personnel). Few attempts were made to "transform"

---

[8] J. McKenney, *Waves of Change* (Boston: Harvard Business School Press, 1995; R. Nolan and D. Croson, *Creative Destruction* (Boston: Harvard Business School Publishing, 1995).

TABLE 6–1 Evolution of IT and Architecture

	IT Paradigm			
	Mainframe Era (1950s to 1970s)	Microcomputer Era (1970s to 1980s)	Distributed Era (late 1980s to present)	Ubiquitous Era
Dominant technology	Mainframe/minicomputer: "centralized intelligence"	Microcomputer: "decentralized intelligence"	Client-server network: "distributed intelligence"	Unstructured network/personal portable technology: "integrated, mobile intelligence"
Organization metaphor	Hierarchy	Entrepreneurial	Transitional hybrids	Information age
Primary IT role	Automate existing processes	Increase individual/group effectiveness	Industry/organization transformation	Value creation
Typical user	IT specialists	IT-literate business analysts	IT-literate managers and field personnel	Everyone
Location of use	Computer room	Desktop	Expanded locations	Everywhere
Justification	ROI	Increased productivity and decision quality	Competitive position	Value creation
Information Management				
Information level	Data	Analytics	Information	Knowledge
Information model	Application specific	Data-driven	Business-driven	Knowledge-driven
Information storage	Application specific data files	Hierarchical DBMS ; early relational	Relational DBMS and document management systems	Hypertext and object-oriented knowledge management systems
Integration level (data, voice, video, graphics, text)	Computer support for data only	Beginning computer support for all information classes but limited integration	Beginning integration of voice, video, data, text, graphics	Sophisticated, integrated support for all information classes

TABLE 6–1 Evolution of IT and Architecture *(continued)*

	IT Paradigm			
	Mainframe Era (1950s to 1970s)	*Microcomputer Era (1970s to 1980s)*	*Distributed Era (late 1980s to present)*	*Ubiquitous Era*
Communication Management				
Connection media	Thick wire coaxial cable; air (microwave) and satellite	Twisted pair wire; thin wire coaxial cable	Cable, fiber, cellular, satellite; continued channel separation	Channel integration
Transmission protocols	Proprietary (WAN); packet switching, circuit switching	Proprietary (LAN); ethernet, token ring	Routers manage WAN & LAN integration: open standards	Merging of LAN/WAN technology; ATM, frame-relay
Maximum transmission rates	56 Kbps	1 Mbps	3-20 Mbps (1995)	10 gbps (or more???)
Tools				
Information reporting	Paper reports	Spreadsheets, modeling, word processing, paper reports	Beginning integration, structured query language	Ad hoc, integrated, associative, browsing, and linking; natural language queries
Information analysis	Batch transaction processing	Hierarchial information models	Relational information model and beginning object orientation	Unstructured, real-time business modeling and knowledge creation
Communication	Mainframe, e-mail	LAN, e-mail	Independent groupware products	Anytime/anyplace/any form
System development	Programming languages	End-user tools; 4th generation languages	Computer-aided software development environments	Object-oriented development environments

TABLE 6–1 Evolution of IT and Architecture *(concluded)*

	IT Paradigm			
	Mainframe Era (1950s to 1970s)	*Microcomputer Era (1970s to 1980s)*	*Distributed Era (late 1980s to present)*	*Ubiquitous Era*
	User Interfaces			
Input/output devices	Keyboard and monitor	Keyboard, mouse, and monitor	Keyboard, pen, mouse, and remote digital assistants	Natural interface on remote PDAs
Application interface	Command-driven text	Menu-driven	Icon-driven, windows, voice, and image	3-d graphical and virtual reality
	Structure and Controls			
Information management organization structure	Centralized	Islands of automation	Beginning distribution	Collaborative partnerships (includes outside vendors and industry participants)
Information management planning and control processes	Centralized control, timed to planning and budgetary cycle	Islands of control; ad hoc	Transition	Distributed/interactive management processes; Timed to business and information cycle
Information management operating processes	Single, structured model (e.g., system development life cycle)	Multiple models (e.g., system development life cycle, JAD, prototyping, end-user development)	Rapid prototyping; Multigenerational	Interactive; Process integration; Quality management; Continuous improvement
IT professionals	Technical specialists	Technical and end-user specialists	Hybrids • Process consultants • Information specialists	Domain specialists and Business/IT generalists

Source L. Applegate, *Managing in an Information Age* (Boston: Harvard Business School Publishing, 1995).

work; instead, each computer application was developed to replicate the tasks, thereby increasing overall efficiency and frequently replacing manual clerical work with computer data processing. Because existing processes were clerical and operational in nature, management found little need to become involved in designing or managing the technology. Furthermore, the IT architecture of the day—centralized mainframe computer systems and networks—was most appropriately managed and operated by the corporate management information systems (MIS) function; a single mainframe computer represented a sizable capital expense, required special facilities (e.g., climate control, special wiring, raised floors), and specialized expertise for system development, maintenance, and operation.

During the mainframe era, machine intelligence was centralized within the mainframe computer. Users "interacted" with the mainframe through a variety of data input/output devices that the mainframe controlled. While these devices contained a small amount of processing intelligence and memory needed to run the device itself, to the user they were essentially "dumb" terminals. They could collect data from the user and transfer them to the mainframe—called uploading—and they could transfer data processed on the mainframe back to the users—called downloading. However, they did not allow users to interact with the information unless they attached to the mainframe directly. Given the rudimentary communications technology of the 1960s and 1970s, extended work on the mainframe was essentially limited to those who resided in the same building in which the mainframe was housed. Access from remote sites was usually limited to very brief sessions in which a remote user would access a single record or piece of data.

Given such constrained local information processing capability and the limited direct interaction between users and the data, the mainframe era was characterized by a focus on data processing. Decision support systems (designed to convert raw data into useful information) and expert systems and other artificial intelligence applications (designed to convert data and information into knowledge) began during the mainframe era, but the limitations of the technology hampered widespread use until the microcomputer ushered in an era of rapidly increasing local information processing capacity.

Era 2—The Microcomputer (Late 1970s and 1980s)

Several factors combined to usher in the microcomputer era. With the introduction of the microprocessor in the late 1960s, technology became smaller and less expensive. Minicomputers, and later microcomputers, required less-specialized facilities; and the expertise required to develop, maintain, and operate local IT systems grew more prevalent. Finally, business managers began to recognize that the information generated by the IT applications was becoming crucial to effective decision making and work at the local level. They wanted to interact more directly with the data to create information. The ability to place computers within users' hands gave them the power to regain control over information.

Early data processing applications tightly coupled organizational data to the computer programs that processed them. This tended to lock the organization into the current way of doing business. If a manager or local decision maker wanted to view information differently or change the way it was processed to reflect changes in the business, costly and time-consuming revisions by systems development professionals were required. Gradually, centralized information processing and control no longer fit with the decentralized use of the business information.

During the 1980s, locally developed and locally managed IT applications, targeted at improving decision quality and individual/work unit productivity and effectiveness, proliferated in organizations. "Islands of automation" sprang up, initially in business units and later, with the advent of the microcomputer, on the desks of individuals throughout the organization. The decentralization of computing diffused awareness of IT throughout the organization and began to erode the dominance of the central mainframe computer (and the central IT function that managed it). Applications for the technology grew rapidly. Point-of-sale and automatic credit card scanners automated the sales process; digital machine control and CAD/CAM (computer-aided design and manufacturing) automated production systems; personal computers and spreadsheets automated planning, budgeting, and information reporting; personal/portable technologies (e.g., notebook computers, personal digital assistants, fax machines, cellular telephones) and associated software to support collaborative work collapsed the geographic and time barriers that defined workspace and worktime.

With the arrival of local information processing technologies and user-friendly application development packages, business users gained control of an ever-increasing portion of organizational information processing and management—but not all of it. Microcomputers did not replace mainframe systems. Instead, they were *added* to the existing centralized computing environment, and trade-offs concerning which technologies and applications would be managed centrally by the IT organization and which would be managed locally by the end users became a constant source of friction. The problems reached a peak as the strategic value of IT for many firms increased in the mid- to late-1980s.

Era 3—Distributed Information Systems (Late 1980s to the Present)

Fueled by the increased understanding that comes from hands-on experience in using IT at the local level, improved networks for sharing information inside and outside the firm, increased complexity and rate of change within the business environment, and the actions of a few visionary managers within information-intensive industries, business managers in a number of industries began to identify strategic opportunities for using IT to shift the balance of power and competitive position of their firm. Senior management took notice—and what they saw concerned them. While the strategic benefits of IT were clearly evident, the cost of IT had skyrocketed during the mid- to late-1980s,[9] and the need to share the information locked within decentralized IT systems had increased dramatically. These pressures to gain access to local information and control over locally managed IT resource spending coincided with (and spurred the continued development of) improved network capacity, performance, and management systems.

As we entered the 1990s, we entered the world of distributed information systems and *client-server computing*—a world in which users access and communicate information through a wide variety of powerful workstations and portable technologies *(clients)* that are linked to shared information and communication services *(servers)* through high-performance local and global networks.

In this view of the IT world, the centralized mainframe (often called the "enterprise computer") takes its place alongside a wide variety of desktop workstations and minicomputers as merely one more "server" on the network—albeit a powerful one. The servers are the specialists, in effect replacing many of the information management and control functions of centralized functional specialists and middle managers found in most traditional hierarchical organizations. For example, a company may create a customer database server that integrates, maintains, and controls access to corporatewide customer information; another server is created to integrate, manage, and control manufacturing production and performance data, while still other servers manage and control communication and information sharing inside and outside the firm. The clients are the generalists, providing access to a broad range of tools—for example, information reporting, spreadsheets, e-mail, and video conferencing—to help people inside and outside the firm get access to the information they need and communicate with the people they need to reach.

Client-server computing also invokes an "open system" view of the world. The ideal client-server architecture is independent of hardware and operating system software platforms, enabling tremendous flexibility in technology choices today and in the future. (It is important to note that, while many companies strive to achieve this type of flexibility in the *design* of their architecture, most voluntarily limit the actual choice of hardware and software in its *implementation* to decrease cost and complexity.)

---

[9] In *Waves of Change* (Boston: Harvard Business School Publishing, 1995), p. 25, McKenney reports that between 1982 and 1986 the use of personal computers quadrupled the total information processing power within organizations.

Finally, client-server computing fundamentally changes how people inter-act with each other and with the technology itself. The magnitude of the shift is comparable to the change in the nature of long-distance travel by rail or by car.[10] Consider a trip from Boston to Denver.

A journey by train takes place in a controlled and scheduled environment. You board the train at a specific station in Boston and anticipate arriving at a specific station in Denver at a specific time. You find a seat and relax as the train rolls down the tracks, making predictable stops along the way. If you get bored with the scenery on the trip, you can sleep but are limited to the accommodations provided for you in the sleeping car. If you get hungry, you can eat, but you are again limited to the food provided for you in the dining car. If you change your mind and wish to explore an interesting city en route, you must abandon your previous plan and get off the train. When you reach Denver, the train stops short of your final destination and provides little to no support for the remainder of the trip—you are on your own.

If you drive to Denver, you can leave when you want. Based on the purpose of your trip, you can choose among a wide variety of potential routes—each of which may have different points of interest along the way—and make any number of stops. If you get hungry, you can choose a restaurant that appeals to you. If you get tired, you can stop at a hotel of your choice. With all of this flexibility, however, you can't just relax and enjoy the scenery or read a book—unless someone else does the driving. You must stay actively involved, driving the car, making countless decisions, preventing accidents, and ensuring that you don't get lost. When you reach Denver, the car continues on to your final destination, dropping you off at the door.

The train trip offers a model of a centralized mainframe system. The train is managed and controlled from a central location by a group of highly trained (and highly paid) professionals whose major job is to get you to your final destination, providing a pleasant, worry-free trip along the way. Once on board, you can relax, but you have very few options and little control. If the train breaks down in Kansas, you must sit and wait till someone comes to fix it. If you change your mind about your final destination, you must start over, having already spent the money and time, but gaining little in the process.

The car trip offers a model of client-server computing. The supporting infrastructure is in place—the roads, support services along the way (e.g., gas stations, hotels), and the rules of the road (e.g., speed limits) that prevent chaos and ensure safety. But you may choose to drive a wide range of vehicles (as long as they are licensed, inspected, and insured). You can

---

[10] This analogy was originally developed by Geoff Bock. See G. Bock and L. Applegate, *Doing Business in a Distributed World: Clients, Servers, and the Stuff in Between* (Boston: Harvard Business School, note 195-211, 1995).

choose among a wide range of routes based on the purpose of your trip and can flexibly choose to visit any number of stops along the way. The car continues to support you throughout your journey to your final destination. As a driver, you are in control, designing a customized agenda to meet your needs and satisfy your curiosity. However, you must be actively involved and knowledgeable to get to your destination. While you may depend on professionals or knowledgeable "locals" to help you plan a trip to a new destination, ask directions if you get lost, or to fix your car if it breaks down on the road, you cannot abdicate your responsibility.

Managing the IT architecture of the distributed era presents the same organization design challenges that confront the information-age firm, discussed in Chapter 5. Rigid hierarchical controls and standardized operating procedures must give way to streamlined, integrated, and time-synchronized operations and controls. Centralized authority systems and functional hierarchical reporting and incentives must be replaced by more collaborative organization designs. With client-server computing, "just-in-time information" must be delivered to a myriad of users inside and outside the firm, who are attempting to manage in a "just-in-time organization." Traditional system development methodologies—lengthy, structured sequences of defining requirements, coding, testing, and implementation—do not always work. In client-server computing, the picture becomes much more complex. Development of the centralized platform often becomes much more structured and standardized, while end-user application development becomes much more interactive, iterative, and nonsequential. Interfunctional teams of business users and IT professionals—and, in some cases, customers, distributors, and suppliers—assume responsibility for defining, implementing, and managing information resources to add value to the business. Strategic partnerships with a myriad of vendors, systems integrators, outsourcers, and consultants are often required to manage the complexity and rapid evolution of the technology. Finally, leadership in defining the strategic direction and role of IT within the organization is a shared responsibility between IT and business management.

Era 4—Ubiquitous

While many companies struggle with the challenges of replacing outdated systems from the mainframe and microcomputer eras, distributed client-server computing is rapidly becoming the dominant IT architecture of the 1990s. A 1993 survey by Gartner Group found that 50 percent of the firms had implemented at least one client-server application, 33 percent were piloting one, and 14 percent were evaluating one.[11] Client-server

---

[11] Gartner Group, "A Guide for Estimating Client-Server Costs," *Gartner Group Strategic Analysis Report* (Stamford, CT: Gartner Group, April 18, 1994).

computing was also ranked number one in a 1994 survey of technologies of greatest interest in North America and Europe.[12] However, despite its infancy, evidence exists that a new IT architecture model may already be emerging. This new "peer-to-peer" architecture promises to deliver a truly ubiquitous IT platform upon which to conduct business, simplify our lives, and entertain and educate society. Forecasters predict that within the next few years, the hierarchically structured client-server networks of today will evolve to a flexible, unstructured information and communication network, over which data, video, voice, and graphics can be instantly delivered to personal, portable technologies of supercomputer strength. Gone will be the need for *computer-oriented humans as human-oriented computers* provide a totally natural means of interaction.[13]

Far fetched? Most say no. When will this era begin? Many who have "surfed the Internet" in the last six months believe that we are surprisingly close. (See Chapter 4 for a more in-depth discussion of the Internet.)

VALUE CREATION IN A DISTRIBUTED IT ENVIRONMENT

Just as the IT architecture and administrative framework within which it was managed have evolved over the past 30 years, so too have approaches for assessing the value of IT investments. In the 1960s, IT spending was viewed as a budgeted expense to be managed within the yearly budgeting cycle. The cost of developing new IT systems and maintaining and enhancing existing systems was justified on a project-by-project basis, and there were few attempts to track the value of the IT asset base and investments over time. Investments in infrastructure received little attention as managers concentrated on defining how computers and networks could be used to improve back-office efficiency. Since most applications were designed to automate existing information-intensive processes, it was often possible to predict efficiency savings in advance. As a result, standard measures of efficiency, such as return on investments (ROI), could be used for evaluation and budget justification.

With the introduction of microcomputers and the proliferation of end-user computing and decision-support applications in the early to mid-1980s, simple measures of organizational efficiency like ROI became less useful. Instead, measures of individual productivity (e.g., headcount reduction, sales per employee) and decision quality (e.g., customer satisfaction) were needed. With this class of IT application, recovery of the benefits was often

---

[12] CSC Consulting Group, "Critical Issues of Information Management," Seventh *Annual Survey of I/S Management Issues* (Cambridge: CSC Consulting, 1994).

[13] M. Bauer, et al., "A Distributed System Architecture for a Distributed Application Environment," *IBM Systems Journal* 33, no. 3 (1994), pp. 399–425; J. McKenney, *Waves of Change* (Boston: Harvard Business School Publishing, 1995).

tied not only to the application's successful technical implementation, but also to its use by individuals or groups to make better decisions or change personal work systems. Clearly, achieving these benefits was less directly under the control of the IT function, and the benefits themselves were much more difficult to predict with certainty before development and implementation of the application. In addition, there was a significant increase in the level of expenditures related to personal workstations and productivity software (e.g., word processing, spreadsheets) that could not be directly linked to benefits achieved through specific applications.

While all companies struggled to define a satisfactory methodology for controlling the rapid increase in decentralized information technology expenses and resources, some devised new metrics that shifted the burden of responsibility and accountability for decentralized IT expenditures to the local business units. Some companies required the units to pay up front for personal productivity applications and the technology required to support them. For example, at one firm the CEO required each individual sales district to commit to a 1 percent reduction in the cost of sales prior to rolling out handheld computers to the firm's 10,000-person sales force. Each district could choose how it wished to achieve this productivity target; some opted to increase sales while maintaining headcount; others opted to decrease headcount while maintaining sales; and still others attempted to decrease losses due to "stale product." (The first two benefits were achieved through improved personal productivity and efficiency, while the third resulted from improved decision quality.)

In the late 1980s, the increased emphasis on using IT to enable and support business strategy further complicated the task of assessing the value of IT investments. As managers attempted to justify strategic systems projects, they soon discovered that neither traditional financial nor individual productivity and decision quality measures were appropriate. Instead, justifying strategic IT applications required formal strategic and tactical planning, or, in the case of a new IT-enabled business venture, development of a formal business plan. As a key component of a strategic or business planning process, the cost of the technology development was viewed as a cost of implementing the strategy. As a result, the IT project was justified based on justifying the strategy itself.

In the 1990s, these three categories of IT application—process performance improvement; individual/work group productivity and decision quality improvements; and competitive advantage—continue to define key sources of IT value. (Note: Unlike the earlier eras, in the 1990s, all three categories of IT application can be considered *strategic*. In addition, new ways of defining and measuring value have replaced some of the traditional targets and measures). (See Table 6–2.) For example, the emphasis on "reengineering" organizational processes has shifted the focus of IT-enabled process improvement from merely automating existing back-office processes to transforming the core operating and management processes of the

TABLE 6–2 Valuing Information Technology Investments

	Value-Creating IT Applications				
Category I IT-Enabled Process Redesign		Category II Individual/Work Group Productivity and Decision Quality		Category III Competitive Advantage	
Representative Systems	Representative Value Measures	Representative Systems	Representative Value Measures	Representative Systems	Representative Value Measures
Operating Process Redesign Product/service delivery (e.g., order fulfillment, inventory management, supplier management, customer service, production scheduling) New product/service development (e.g., technology/market scanning, R&D project management, market testing) **Management Process Redesign** Planning, control, and incentive systems (e.g., business planning, resource allocation, performance monitoring, HRM)	Cycle time reductions Product/service quality improvements Operating process quality improvements Stakeholder satisfaction (e.g., customer, supplier, partner) Employee satisfaction Activity-based cost improvements Operating process improvements relative to industry/best-in-class benchmarks	**Targeted Decision Support Systems** (e.g., promotion planning, logistics planning, key account management) Individual/Workgroup Information Reporting (e.g., ad hoc information retrieval, business intelligence scanning) Workgroup Support Systems (e.g., collaborative writing, project management, workflow systems)	Improved decision quality Decreased time to decision Change in level of decision authority Improved individual/workgroup productivity Increased individual/workgroup satisfaction and morale Note: Some firms have used pilot studies to document benefits prior to widespread system implementation.	**Electronic commerce** (e.g., electronic data interchange, supplier management systems, electronic shopping) **Information-based products and services** (e.g., financial, market, and industry information services) **Information value added to existing products and services** (e.g., customer information kiosks, electronic catalogs)	Increased market share Increased price premium for products/services Improved operating margins relative to competitors New business revenues, market share and contribution to free cash flow Improvement in relative shareholder returns (ROE, stock price)

TABLE 6–2 Valuing Information Technology Investments (*concluded*)

IT Platform	
Representative Systems	*Representative Value Measures*
Corporate data and document management systems	**Direct benefits**
Local and wide area networks and network management systems	IT platform enhancements bundled with a value-creating application
Computer equipment and operating systems	**Secondary benefits**
Client/server systems and application development	*Options benefits*
Software development tools	• future value-creating applications that can be created using the platform
End-user system development tools	*Proprietary advantage*
Emerging technologies	• enhanced IT capabilities relative to best-of-class in the industry
	• lower IT operating and maintenance costs relative to best-of-class in the industry
	Strategic Necessity
	• respond to actions by competitor or new entrant
	• respond to demands by customers, suppliers, or other business partner

Source: L. Applegate, *Managing in an Information Age*, Boston: Harvard Business School Publishing, 1995

151

firm. With such a shift, a broader range of process performance improvement measures are sought, including time, quality, cost, and innovation potential. In addition, stakeholder (e.g., customer, supplier, and employee) satisfaction measures, when linked with process performance data, provide timely indicators of financial and market performance.[14]

Of equal importance with these direct measures of value, managers in the 1990s are finding it increasingly important to define measures of the value of investments in the IT *platform* itself. This demands a significant shift in perspective. While all IT costs were once considered a budgeted expense, in the 1990s, forward-thinking companies consider the firm's IT platform to be a sizable corporate asset that delivers value to the firm independent of the applications that run upon it. This latter view requires that IT platform costs be treated like a capital investment, not a period expense. Furthermore, the development of a distributed, information-rich, networked IT platform is rapidly becoming a strategic necessity for doing business in the 1990s. Consequently, firms must also assess the opportunity cost and relative competitive "disadvantage" of not maintaining a flexible and state-of-the-art IT platform. (Recall that Figure 6–3 defined the components of an IT platform as information management [e.g., computers, databases, printers], communication management [networks, network management systems, servers], tools [e.g., information access, analysis, packaging, and delivery applications such as spreadsheets, presentation graphics packages, query tools; communications tools such as e-mail, videoconferencing; and application development tools]; Table 6–2 suggests approaches to assessing the value of platform investments that are discussed in more detail below.)

But despite a strong belief that investments in IT infrastructure will pay off in the future, the ability to quantify the value of IT capital investments in infrastructure development and maintenance *a priori* has proven exceedingly difficult. A major problem is that any given IT investment is often merely a link in a long chain of other investment decisions—some prior and some yet to be made—which will be required to enable the investment's value to be fully realized. For example, many managers are surprised to learn that implementing a customer database by itself provides little *direct* value to the firm. A wide variety of application systems must also be developed to access the data and transform them into useful information. Each application must be analyzed separately to determine the potential value it may bring in terms of process performance improvement, individual/work group productivity and decision quality, and competitive advantage. The costs of achieving those benefits must also be analyzed.

In addition to the costs associated with application development, significant training costs will also be incurred. Individual managers and decision makers must have the skills, expertise, and motivation to use the informa-

---

[14] J. Heskett, E. Sasser, Jr., and C. Hart, *Service Breakthroughs: Changing the Rules of the Game* (New York: The Free Press, 1990).

tion to make better-quality decisions or improve customer service. Additional platform-related costs may also be necessary. New mainframe technology may be needed to run the customer database, network enhancements may be required to communicate information to individuals located throughout the firm, and personal workstations may be needed to access and process the information. In some cases, infrastructure costs may extend over more than one firm. Customers may need to develop specialized applications that allow them to directly update or draw information from a supplier's database. Distributors may need to access a manufacturer's database so they can ship products and track orders. Each additional application must be evaluated separately, yet each relies on a common infrastructure for development.

On top of the stream of investments needed to capture the value from investments in a firm's IT infrastructure, the early stages of project evaluation are frequently characterized by uncertainty about the nature and extent of potential opportunities and benefits and the full costs needed to achieve them. For example, one insurance company initially proposed developing a corporate customer database to improve service and decrease costs; it redesigned its customer service delivery process to implement a one-call, centralized customer service center. At a later date, the database also enabled a move to a case manager approach, which increased individual productivity and customer satisfaction. This resulted in lower service delivery costs and a simultaneous increase in customer retention rates. Still later, additional applications allowed customers to access and update data directly, leading to additional cost savings and improvements in customer satisfaction. Finally, applications allowing independent agents to evaluate and process claims in the field were implemented; these applications enabled the firm to process claims more quickly and at a lower cost, while simultaneously increasing quality and customer satisfaction.

When the centralized customer database was first proposed, managers were unaware of the full range of potential opportunities its implementation would foster. Though each opportunity required an additional outlay of funds, the implementation costs were significantly lower, and the time frame for implementation was much faster because of the earlier investment in developing the database. Moreover, the risk of subsequent investment decisions was also reduced because the availability of the customer database lowered the overall investment level and project complexity for subsequent applications. In essence, the earlier investment decreased the magnitude of downside risk for subsequent projects, while preserving the entire upside value to be gained.

In light of the above discussion, some have compared investments in the IT platform of a firm to investments in securities options.[15] Carl Kester, for

---

[15] S. Meyer, "Determinants of Corporate Borrowing," *Journal of Financial Economics* (1977); C. Kester, "Today's Options for Tomorrow's Growth," *Harvard Business Review,* March–April 1984.

instance, in a *Harvard Business Review* article, noted: "Thinking of investments as growth options challenges conventional wisdom about capital budgeting. For example, a company may be justified in accepting [some] projects with a negative NPV. [These projects] may initially drain cash flows. But, they may also create options for future growth . . . [which] more than offset [losses] from the project's cash flows." Kester continues: "A securities option gives the owner the *right* (as distinct from the *obligation*) to buy a security at a fixed, predetermined price (called the *exercise price*) on or before some fixed date (the *maturity date*)." In the case of a firm's investment in IT infrastructure, options theory would suggest that management has the option of building value-added applications that would use the infrastructure at a lower cost more quickly and with less inherent risk throughout the useful life of the technology. With this approach, assessing the options value of the IT platform is based on the nature of the benefits and the length of time over which the option will continue to deliver those benefits.

The nature of the benefit is based on four factors.

- Direct benefits accrue when value-added applications are "bundled" with the platform. These applications may be targeted at improving operating efficiencies, enhancing personal productivity and decision quality, or enabling and supporting the strategic initiatives of the firm.
- Second-order option benefits are obtained when the IT platform is used to support future applications that would not be possible if the platform were not in place.
- Proprietary benefits accrue when the availability of the IT platform provides the firm a distinct competitive advantage independent of the applications that may or may not be created upon it. These proprietary benefits are created when the IT platform itself provides capabilities, flexibility, speed of development, and inherent cost advantages not matched by other industry players.
- Strategic necessity benefits are derived when the availability of the IT infrastructure is required to maintain a favorable competitive position within an industry.

This approach to valuing IT investments recognizes that a variety of measures are available based on the nature of the IT system under consideration. The framework indicates distinct sources of value achievable through investments in a firm's IT platform that extend beyond the benefits obtained by deploying specific value-creating IT applications developed and delivered upon it. Three categories of value-creating application are defined—process performance improvement, individual productivity and decision quality improvements, and competitive advantage—that correspond to the evolution of IT impact within firms. While the framework provides a structured approach to assessing IT value, it is important to realize that the various sources of value are strongly linked and that specific IT projects often generate benefits across categories.

IT ARCHITECTURE IMPLEMENTATION ISSUES IN THE 1990s

The move to develop distributed—and ever more ubiquitous—IT platforms is a complex and difficult challenge. Localized "islands of automation" must be merged together, "legacy systems"[16] —many of which are critical for the successful operation of today's business—must be managed, new technologies must be evaluated and successfully introduced, and people must be trained. All this must be managed within the context of massive organizational upheaval and change. Many who are considering the task have compared it to changing the tires on a rapidly moving car; those who have been through it believe that they have totally redesigned and built a new car. The remainder of this chapter deals with the technology issues inherent in these management challenges.

Merging the Islands of Automation

As firms face the challenge of defining and implementing a distributed IT architecture, a variety of integration obstacles must be overcome. One of the most obvious involves the perennial problem of where to physically locate information and value-creating application systems. In the past, this decision was viewed as a linear trade-off. At one extreme were organizations that created a large, centralized hub connected by telecommunications links to remote computers in the field. At the other extreme were organizations with a small or nonexistent hub at the center, with most, or even all of its data and hardware, decentralized to the field. Between these two extremes lay a rich variety of intermediate alternatives.

Early solutions to this problem were heavily influenced by the technology architecture. The high cost of hardware and the significant economies of scale associated with mainframe computers made it necessary to consolidate processing power into large data centers. In contrast, the low-cost and off-the-shelf functionality of microcomputers permitted a more decentralized approach. In the 1990s, the availability of technology to implement a distributed architecture enables processing power and data to be located where it makes the most sense from a business perspective. In 1995, however, other factors continue to limit decision making.

The cost of implementing a truly distributed architecture is one significant limiting factor. A recent Gartner survey estimated that the move to client-server would cost a firm an additional $50,000 to $65,000 *per*

---

[16] *Legacy* refers to transaction processing systems that were originally designed to perform a specific task. Over time, these systems may not accurately reflect business needs. In addition, as hardware and software improvements occur in the information systems marketplace, older IS solutions tie an organization to an out-of-date platform that is unable to deliver value-creating applications and is costly to operate and maintain.

workstation over a five-year period.[17] This figure is a surprise to many companies that embark on client-server expecting to dramatically decrease the cost of delivering IT services. They underestimate the investment and time that will be needed to train end users and MIS support staff and to coordinate and manage the complex network and information management systems. They overlook the increased responsibility that end users must accept and the effort they must expend as they attempt to drive their IT systems rather than merely sit back and enjoy the ride. As firms merge the islands of automation, several trends are noted. (Table 6–3 summarizes decision criteria that can be used as management attempts to balance the distribution of IT resources.)

- There is a move to consolidate information processing and network management within a single location. Some large firms are creating a single "mega data center"—backed up by a fully staffed off-site redundant data center—to manage global information and communication. These centers house powerful mainframes and supercomputers that manage corporatewide data warehouses and massively parallel information processing. The increasing availability of powerful global networks and emerging global communication standards make this a feasible alternative—although the global telecommunications environment, which will be discussed later, still hampers full realization of the benefits.
- While the information and standards are moving to the center, processing of the information is moving to the field. Data replication technologies are the key to making this architecture work. These technologies create and maintain "shadow" databases that contain an up-to-date replica of the data required by local users on local servers.
- Where is the computer in a client-server architecture? It is not in a single place; it is the network. It has been estimated that up to 40 percent of the cost and effort of implementing a client-server architecture is due to network and distributed information management;[18] yet most IT professionals do not possess these skills. As a result, these valuable, scarce resources are often managed at the center.
- Successful implementation of a distributed client-server architecture is most often found in organizations—or portions of an organization—where there is significant pent-up demand for direct access to information. The ability to successfully satisfy this demand requires users who are (or are eager to become) both technically and informationally literate. This type of user is predominately found in organizations that are experiencing significant time-based competition and have begun to adopt the characteristics of the information age organization that were discussed in

---

[17] Gartner Group, "A Guide for Estimating Client-Server Costs," *Gartner Group Strategic Analysis Report* (Stamford, CT: Gartner Group, April 18, 1994).

[18] H. Ryan, *Preparing to Implement Client/Server Solutions* (Auerbach Publications, 1994).

TABLE 6-3 IT Resource Management

Pressure	Toward Centralization	Toward Decentralization	Toward Distribution
Management control	Hierarchical. Standardization. Efficiency. Organizational security, reliability.	Entrepreneurial. Local responsiveness. Effectiveness. Local security, reliability.	Information age. Learning. Efficiency and effectiveness. Global security, reliability.
Technology	Efficient use of resources. Specialized, costly equipment that is required by all. Requires specialized expertise to operate and manage.	Effective use of resources. Low-cost off-the-shelf equipment that is widely available. Expertise needed to operate and manage is widely available.	Effective and efficient use of resources. Mix of specialized and off-the-shelf. Mix of specialized and general expertise.
Data	Organizational data. Maintain data standards. Level of data sharing can be accommodated by network capacity and budget.	Local data. Maintain data relevance. Desire to optimize network capacity and minimize cost.	Increased need for vertical and lateral information sharing (including interorganizational). Desire to optimize information relevance and standards. High-capacity, low-cost networks are available and manageable.
IT professionals	Scarce resources with specialized knowledge and expertise. Minimize turnover risk/disruption. Richer career paths for IT professionals.	Widely available resources and generalized expertise. Turnover risk/disruption is minimal. Background enables lateral interfunctional career path.	Mix of scarce and generalized IT professional resources. Optimally manage turnover risk/disruption while providing expanded career paths.
End users	Low level of technical skill. Satisfied with routine information reporting. Lack of motivation to manage IT.	Technical sophistication. Desire flexible access to timely information. Motivated to manage IT.	High levels of technical and "information" literacy. High levels of commitment and motivation to become an active player in defining and managing information
Culture/ organizational fit	Organization is structured as a functional hierarchy. "Command and control" culture. IT function has always been centralized.	Organization is structured as decentralized profit centers. "Results" culture. Significant decentralization of IT resources and control.	Organization is structured as a matrix of autonomous, interfunctional teams. "Commitment, collaboration, and results" culture. Both centralized and decentralized IT resources and control.

157

Chapter 5. Management at all levels of the firm must be actively committed to transforming the organization; it makes little sense to embark on the difficult and costly task of transforming your IT architecture unless you also plan to transform the business processes it supports.

- The distributed IT architecture of the 1990s incorporates a range of technologies—including data, voice, video, digital production controls, and others—that must all operate in a coordinated and integrated manner. Developing and managing this coordination has not always been easy. In many organizations, these technologies evolved through separate streams of technical innovation that were introduced into organizations at different periods of time by different groups. Over the years, incompatible architectures have developed that are often managed by separate organizational units. In the 1990s, many firms continue to manage these technologies in separate units staffed with technology specialists who lack the necessary skills to create an integrated approach to information and communication management. These artificial walls must be broken down. The blurring of boundaries among the technologies and the expertise needed to deploy them are also being accompanied by a similar blurring of the boundaries within the industry; consolidation, partnerships, and strategic alliances have radically altered the global information industry.[19] This exerts further pressure on companies to consolidate management of the IT platform and the expertise needed to successfully deploy it.

Managing Global Telecommunications

Highly reliable, inexpensive digital telecommunications systems are central to the ability to successfully implement a distributed IT platform. The performance, cost, and reliability of telecommunications differ markedly in different parts of the world. In some developed countries, excessive tariffs and inordinate installation delays have significantly slowed the growth of telecommunications services. During the 1990s, privatization of government-owned systems and more cost-effective, time-responsive environments have begun to emerge. But significant management attention to the changing nature of telecommunications capabilities, reliability, and regulation is still required on a country-by-country basis.

In less-developed areas, the necessary communications platform to conduct even basic systems operations is often not in place. For example, because of an unacceptable level of communication failures (some more than 24 hours in duration), several forward-thinking companies that planned to do business in a less-developed area were forced to shut down a

---

[19] D. Yoffie, *Apple Computer 1992* (Boston: Harvard Business School Publishing, 1992).

sophisticated on-line system supporting multiple branches and to seek solutions that realistically addressed the unreliability of the infrastructure. In another situation, a company was able to achieve acceptable reliability only by gaining permission to construct and maintain its own network of microwave towers. While these problems seriously limit the ability of multinationals to develop a truly distributed IT architecture, advances in network capabilities and performance are helping to ameliorate the problem, paving the way for the much-touted global village. Managing the timing is the key challenge. This will be discussed further in Chapter 12.

Managing the IT Legacy

As discussed earlier, successful implementation and management of a distributed IT architecture demand an exceedingly high level of technological sophistication that is frequently unavailable within traditional IT departments. The technologies for successfully creating and delivering integrated systems and distributed information and communications management are only now beginning to emerge in a stable form. Standards remain in flux and professionals experienced in application development and delivery are in short supply. Such problems are exacerbated when companies grapple with the massive investment that has already been made in legacy systems that must either be abandoned or adapted to fit within a new distributed IT platform. Legitimate user demand for continued IT support exacerbates the problem. There is often a three- to four-year backlog of value-creating IT applications waiting to be implemented by a seriously overworked IT staff. This often leads to a perception of unsatisfactory support and to dissatisfaction with the IT function. Frustrated users have a tendency towards their own solutions, such as individual, stand-alone computers, which further complicates the overall IT management challenge. The following example illustrates the dilemma that many firms face.

In the late 1980s, senior management of a large insurance company asked a consultant, "Why does it take us so long to develop our strategic systems?" They went on to describe a strategic IT project believed to be absolutely critical to the success of their core business strategy. The project was three years late, significantly over budget, and a long way from completion. An in-depth analysis of the situation brought the following facts to light. The company had over 20 of IBM's largest mainframe computers— all running at peak capacity to supply the organization with the massive amounts of information needed to run the business. The software generating and managing this information had been developed in the 1960s in an out-of-date computer language that was difficult to maintain and almost impossible to update and change. A large percentage of the IT professionals and the budget was directed toward simply maintaining the status quo and supplying the information needed to keep the organization running. The few staff members who could be spared to work on the strategic systems project encountered numerous obstacles as they attempted to access information tightly embedded within these ancient systems.

In this example, senior management failed to recognize the real source of the problem. As a result, they were looking for the wrong solution. While they expected the consultant to suggest changes in IT leadership, what they really needed was a radical overhaul of their out-of-date and inflexible IT platform.

The insurance company is hardly alone; there are numerous examples of firms facing similar technological challenges as they attempt to develop and deliver IT systems for the 1990s on out-of-date technology platforms. Recognition of the true source of the problem and strong support from senior management are needed to break out of this downward spiral. Several forward-thinking firms have called a moratorium on IT spending and development to break the cycle and reevaluate the IT strategy, architecture, and priorities.

Given the magnitude and complexity of the task and the pace of technology evolution, many managers have sought partnerships with vendors who will assume responsibility for updating and maintaining the IT platform, thereby freeing up valuable resources so the firm can concentrate on defining and delivering value-added IT applications. The issues facing managers who are considering outsourcing all, or part, of their IT function are discussed in detail in Chapter 10.

While some turn to outsourcing, other firms address the problem of legacy systems while maintaining control of the IT platform within the firm. Time, expertise, commitment, and leadership are required. Management must firmly believe that the massive investment will provide the company with sustainable proprietary advantages. It must be confident that it will have ample time and skills to implement both the IT platform and the value-creating applications before a competitor can seriously erode those advantages. Many firms spend five years or more and hundreds of millions of dollars implementing a distributed IT architecture. New skills are needed by MIS professionals and end users. Vendors often play an important role in transferring into the firm both the new technologies and the skills needed to implement them; firms can use these vendor partnerships to build internal capabilities. The new architecture often evolves gradually and continues to evolve with changes in the business environment, organization, and technology.

Assimilating Emerging Information Technologies

As strategy, organization, and IT become inextricably intertwined, business managers must become active players in ensuring the successful identification and deployment of new technologies. This process requires an ongoing commitment to managing the IT assimilation process. While inherently complex, the task of managing the assimilation of emerging technologies required to implement the IT platform of a firm is especially difficult.

The process of assimilating a new technology has often been characterized as a series of tasks or stages through which a new technology is identified, assimilated, and institutionalized.[20] Although some have faulted these stage models for failing to depict the chaotic nature of true innovation,[21] the models have proven useful as long as sequential passage from stage to stage is not assumed. The IT assimilation model (described in outline form in Chapter 2 and presented in Figure 6–4) describes four stages: technology identification and investment, technological learning and adaptation, rationalization/management control, and maturity/widespread technology transfer.[22]

Phase 1: Technology Identification.   The first phase is initiated by a decision to invest in a new information processing technology. (Note: This technology may be an emerging technology that few firms have implemented, or it may be a more stable technology that is simply new to a given organization.) During the initiation phase, one or more complementary project-development efforts are undertaken. These projects are often characterized by uncertainty in the magnitude of the investments required and the benefits to be delivered. Pilot projects are often used to help reduce the uncertainty and to assess the degree of organizational change and skill development that will be required. These early prototypes, in retrospect, often seem quite clumsy; however, considerable learning takes place. An unsuccessful prototype can cause the firm to start over or to abandon the technology. For any number of reasons, a firm may delay future investment in the technology—"Stagnation Block A." The following example illustrates a firm in which organization learning was blocked in phase 1.

At the CEO's urging, an insurance company launched a major Executive Information System (EIS) project to put a workstation with access to internal and external information on every senior executive's desk. Eight months into the process, the CEO retired suddenly for health reasons. Without its key sponsor, the project died over the next six months. Three

---

[20] L. Applegate, "Technology Support for Cooperative Work: A Framework for Studying Introduction and Assimilation in Organizations," *Journal of Organizational Computing* 1 (1991) pp. 11–39; R. Walton, *Up and Running: Integrating Information Technology and the Organization* (Boston: Harvard Business School Press, 1989); R. Nolan and C. Gibson, "Managing the Crisis in Data Processing," *Harvard Business Review,* March–April 1979.

[21] J. Ettlie, "Organization Strategy and Structural Difference for Radical Versus Incremental Innovation, *Management Science,* 30 (1984), pp. 682–95; B. Quinn, "Innovation and Corporate Strategy: Managed Chaos," *Technology in the Modern Corporation,* M. Horwitch, ed. (New York: Pergamon Press, 1986).

[22] J. Cash and P. McLeod, "Managing the Introduction of Information Technology in Strategically Dependent Companies," *Journal of Management Information Systems* 1 (1985), pp. 5–23.

FIGURE 6–4   The Organization and Information Technology Design Challenge
of the 1990s

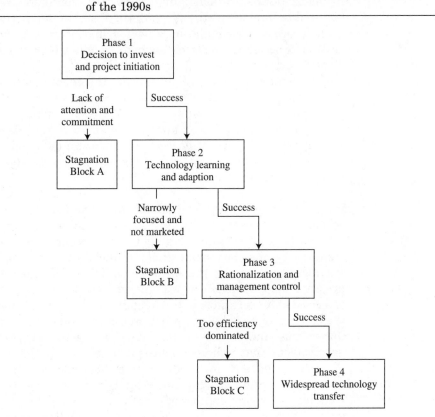

Adapted from Cash and McLeod, 1985.

years later, the problem is far enough in the past that the company is
willing to start over; in the meantime, the technology investment has
returned no value to the firm, and the technology itself has become
hopelessly outdated.

Phase 2: Technological Learning and Adaptation.   The second phase
involves learning how to adapt the new technology to particular tasks
beyond those identified in the initial projects. As new avenues are explored
and learning occurs, the benefits are often quite different from those
initially anticipated. Projects in this phase, while not as prone to technical
problems, are often still highly uncertain in their costs and benefits, which
leads to problems in planning and implementation. Evaluation of 37
different phase 2 technology projects showed that none were implemented

as initially planned. In each case, significant learning took place during implementation. Indeed, many of the competitive successes discussed in earlier chapters were phase 2 projects that evolved gradually through a series of successive refinements. Failure to effectively transfer the learning from phase 1 and 2 can lead to Stagnation Block B. An example of this type of block follows.

A large manufacturing company attempted to introduce computer-aided design and manufacturing (CAD/CAM) into its plants. The initial prototype was successfully tested in one plant. The MIS group then attempted to roll out the technology in several other plants. Prior to the phase 2 rollout, there was no attempt to document the problems faced by the initial plant and the factors that led to the system's eventual success, nor were users from the first plant involved in subsequent rollouts. Two of the subsequent plants were also successful in implementing the system, but three other plants revolted. The project was halted indefinitely as management attempted to understand the wide discrepancy in results.

Phase 3: Rationalization/Management Control. This phase typically involves a significant change in the organization's approach to the technology, continued evolution of the uses of technology, and, most importantly, development of management controls for guiding the design and implementation of systems that use these technologies. In this phase, system development methodologies become more structured, the roles and skills required of IT professionals and users become clearer, and the results more predictable. The most common problem in phase 3 is that in a search for efficiency, control stifles innovation—Stagnation Block C.

For example: A manufacturing company spent three years developing a state-of-the-art distribution center utilizing the most advanced client-server technologies. The technology was piloted in several smaller applications that were highly successful. The skills had been honed throughout the project. However, when the center opened, rigid control of information access and use was instituted. Because the cost of the new center had overrun the budget, management attempted to minimize additional investments in value-creating applications. In its single-minded effort to gain efficiency, the organization became so focused on standard procedures and cost elimination that enthusiasm for using the system to add value to the business was lost. Further, the rigorous protocols alienated users who then began to experiment with creating their own system within several branch offices. In this case, rigorous emphasis on control prevented logical growth.

Phase 4: Maturity/Widespread Technology Transfer. This final phase occurs when the technology is embraced throughout the organization. Efficiency is achieved, but not at the expense of effectiveness. Quite naturally, as time passes, new technologies continue to emerge that offer the firm the opportunity to either move into new application areas or to restructure old ones. A firm is thus confronted over time with waves of new technologies and at any one time is managing and assimilating a number of technologies, each in a different phase. In the 1990s, most companies are finding that the rapid pace of technological change is demanding that firms move through these phases in a much more timely manner. This increases the risk and the level of investment in organizational learning. As mentioned earlier, many firms seek partnerships to manage the successful assimilation of new technology.

SUMMARY

The challenge of managing the evolution of the IT architecture of the firm is daunting. While many firms in the 1990s are moving toward a more distributed IT architecture, the choices that are being made and the process through which the evolution takes place are often very different. Managers must consider the influence of legacy systems, organization culture and history, IT and business leadership, the capabilities of IT professionals and end users, and the demands of the business environment.

Continuous reexamination of the IT architecture and its relationship to strategy and organization must be a high priority. Radical change in the price/performance of technology can be expected to continue. The continued merging of core information technologies will alter the possibilities for organizations and players in the information industry. Managers can expect that both the risks and potential rewards involved in managing technology assimilation will continue to increase.

As IT becomes the major platform upon which a company is organized and business is conducted, senior management can no longer delegate responsibility for IT to operating managers and IT professionals. They must become active players. Strategies and policies that guide the development and deployment of IT within the firm must be defined, enforced, and continuously reviewed as part of an ongoing process of developing and monitoring business strategy. As part of this evaluation, it is important to recognize that uniformity in IT architecture and its use across the organization is not required. Different parts of the organization may legitimately require a different architecture model. This is particularly true in the case of a multinational firm. It is possible to have a common standard that supports flexibility.

Finally, a comprehensive approach to defining the IT architecture of a firm is necessary. The IT architecture is only one component of the information and communication infrastructure of the firm. Failure to recognize the complex interrelationships among the environment, organization structure, management controls, people, and processes can lead to the design of an elegant, but ineffective, IT platform.

Chapter

7

Organizing and Leading the Information Technology Function

The preceding chapter noted that the management structures needed for guiding new technologies into the organization are quite different from those for older, established technologies. The corporation must encourage information technology (IT) staff and users to innovate with the newer technologies, while focusing on control and efficiency in the more mature technologies. In this chapter, we will discuss two rapidly changing aspects of IT management: the range of organizational alternatives that have emerged for effectively assigning responsibility for IT development and the coordination and location of IT policy formulation among users, IT, and general management.

ORGANIZATION ISSUES IN IT DEVELOPMENT

Policies for guiding the deployment of IT development staff and activity in the future must deal with two sets of tensions. The first, as noted in the previous chapters, is the balance between innovation and control. The relative emphasis a firm should place on the aggressive innovation phase varies widely, depending on a broad assessment of the potential strategic impact of information technology on the firm, general corporate willingness to take risk, and so on. If IT is perceived to be of great impact in helping the firm reach its strategic objectives, significantly greater investment in innovation is called for than if IT is seen to be merely helpful.

165

The second set of tensions is between IT dominance and user dominance in the retention of development skills and in the active selection of priorities. The user tends toward short-term need fulfillment (at the expense of long-term architectural IT structure and orderly development), while IT can become preoccupied with the mastery of technology and an orderly development plan at the risk of slow response, or no response, to legitimate user needs. Balancing the roles of these two groups is a complex task that must be handled in the context of the corporate culture and IT's potential strategic role.

Table 7–1 reveals some consequences of excessive domination by IT and by users, clearly indicating that very different application portfolios and operating problems emerge in the two settings. Given the difficulty of

TABLE 7–1   Possible Implications of Excess IT and User Dominance

IT Dominance	*User Dominance*
Too much emphasis on database and system maintenance.	Too much emphasis on problem focus.
All new systems must fit the data structure of the existing system.	IT feels out of control.
All requests for service require system study with benefit identification.	Explosive growth in the number of new systems and supporting staff.
Standardization dominates with few exceptions.	Multiple suppliers deliver services. Frequent change in the supplier of a specific service.
IT designs/constructs everything.	Lack of standardization and control over data and systems.
Benefits of user control over development discussed but never implemented.	Hard evidence of benefits nonexistent.
Study always shows construction costs less than the outside purchase.	Soft evidence of benefits not organized.
Head count of distributed minis and development staff growing surreptitiously.	Few measurements/objectives for new system.
IT specializing in technical frontiers, not user-oriented markets.	Technical advice of IT not sought; if received, considered irrelevant.
IT spending 80 percent on maintenance, 20 percent on development.	User buying design, construction, maintenance, and operations services from outside.
IT thinks it is in control of all.	User building networks to own unique needs, not to corporate need.
Users express unhappiness.	Some users are growing rapidly in experience and use, while others feel nothing is relevant because they do not understand.
Portfolio of development opportunities firmly under IT control.	No coordinated effort between users for technology transfer or learning from experience.
No strong user group exists.	Growth in duplication of technical staffs.
General management not involved but concerned.	Dramatically rising communications costs because of redundancy.
	Duplication of effort and input everywhere because different data, hardware, and communications will not allow seamless movement.

anticipating the implications of introducing a new technology, this chapter will emphasize the need for experimentation, as illustrated by the following four cases.

Some Examples

Case 1: A Short-Term User-Need Situation, Strategically Important. The number one priority in a large machine-tool manufacturer's engineering department was computer-aided design (CAD). Given its early success, the effort was significantly expanded; the digital information design output was modified to enable department personnel to control computer-driven machine tools directly. This work was deliberately kept independent of their bill of materials/cost system, which was in a database format and maintained by the IT unit.

Short of staff to integrate the new system into the firm's Bill of Materials database structure, the user department decided to proceed—a decision that would result in major system integration problems in the future. The work was done over the objection of IT management, but the engineering department received full support from senior management because of the project's potential major and immediate impact on shortening the product development life cycle.

The engineers enthusiastically worked on the CAD project to make it work—the project slashed development time by half for new product designs—while the IT unit remained decidedly lukewarm. Although IT database integration issues still exist, realistically, the firm is no worse off in that regard than it was before the CAD project.

Case 2: User Control to Achieve Desktop Support. A division of a large consumer products manufacturer substantially invested in desktop support with modest up-front cost-benefit justification. IT encouraged managers and administrative support personnel to "use" the systems, with only cursory direction and some introductory training on the desktop units made available. After four months, three product managers had developed support for sales-force activities; two had developed a capability to use mainframe data spreadsheets, generating substantial savings; two others did little, but were encouraging their administrative support staff to try it out. The users were gaining confidence and pursuing new programs with enthusiasm.

Six months later, IT's challenge was to develop and evolve an efficient program with these seven "experienced" users; the IT manager estimated roughly two years would be needed to achieve this efficient integration. In retrospect, however, both he and divisional management felt that it would have been impossible to implement networked desktop support with a standard IT-dominated systems study and that the expense of the after-the-fact rationalization was an acceptable price for the benefits that accrued. The control over this first foray into desktop networks contrasted sharply with the strong central control IT was exerting over its mature data-processing technologies.

Case 3: Step-by-Step Innovation of a New Technology.   A large grocery chain acquired a system of point-of-sales terminals, which the retail division (with the support of the IT manager) had initially installed to assist store managers in controlling inventory. The terminals were to be used exclusively within individual stores to accumulate daily sales totals of individual items. These totals would permit the stores to trigger reorders in case lots at given times.

At the initiative of corporate management, these isolated systems evolved quickly into links to central headquarters. The links would feed data from the stores to new corporate computer programs that measured advertising effectiveness and the ability to manage warehouse stock levels chainwide. Because the communication protocols in the selected terminals were incompatible with those in the computer at headquarters, however, implementing this unplanned linkage was expensive.

Nonetheless, the possibilities and benefits of the resulting system would have been difficult to define in advance, since this eventual use was not considered important when the initial point-of-sale terminals were being installed. Further, in management's opinion, even if the organization had considered it, the ultimate costs of the resulting system would have been deemed prohibitive in relation to benefits (in retrospect, incorrectly prohibitive). In an uncertain world, there are limitations to planning; in this case, success of the first system laid the baseline for the next ones.

Case 4: User Innovation as a Source of Productivity.   A large bank introduced an electronic mail system and a word processor system to facilitate preparation of loan paperwork. The two systems soon evolved to link the bank's loan officers (initially not planned to be clients of either system) to a series of analytical programs—an evolution that developed out of conversations between a loan officer and a consultant. Bundled with the word processor loan system was a powerful analytical tool that officers could use to analyze loan performance. Because of the bank's electronic mail system, loan officers (at headquarters and in branches) could easily access the analytical tool.

Three months later, the bank faced a series of internal tensions as the costs of both systems unexpectedly rose due to this added use. In addition, there were no formal means of reviewing "experiments" or evaluating unanticipated uses of the systems by participants not initially involved. Eventually, a senior-management review committee supported the new use of the two systems, and it was permitted to continue. Substantial enhancements were added to the word processing software to make it even more useful to the loan officers.

Implications

Typical of emerging new services supporting professionals and managers in doing work, the above examples powerfully convey our conviction that it is impossible to foresee in advance the full range of consequences of introducing information technology systems. Excessive control and focus on quick results in the early stages can deflect important learning that could result in even more useful applications. In addition, because neither IT professionals nor users have outstanding records in anticipating how new technologies will impact organizations, a necessary general management role is to help facilitate this assimilation.

The material that follows is divided into three sections. The first discusses the pressures on users to gain control—not only over a system's development activities, but, when possible, over the resulting product so it can run on a stand-alone mini- or microsystem located in the department. The second section identifies the advantages of strong IT development coordination and the potential pitfalls of uncontrolled proliferation of user-developed systems. The third section identifies the core policies that must be implemented by IT management, user management, and general management, respectively, in order to ensure a good result. The general manager's role is particularly critical in creating an environment that facilitates technological change and organizational adaptation.

PRESSURES TOWARD USER DOMINANCE

A number of intense pressures encourage users to exercise stronger control over their systems development resources and acquisition of independent IT resources. These pressures can be clustered into five categories: pent-up user demand, the needs for staffing flexibility, competitive and service growth in the IT market, users' desire to control their destiny, and fit with the organization.

Pent-Up User Demand

The backlog of development work facing an IT systems development department is frequently very large in relation to its staff resources. The reasons for these staffing "crunches" are many. Existing systems, for example, require sustained maintenance to accommodate changing regulatory and other business requirements. As more systems are automated, maintenance needs continue to rise, forcing either increases in development staff or the postponement of new work. This problem intensified in the 1970s, when systems design philosophy shifted from one that incorporates data into programs to one that clearly separates database management from processing procedures. Effecting such a one-time conversion has been very expensive in terms of staff resources.

Further, the most challenging, high-status, high-paying jobs tend to be with computer vendors and software houses, which puts great pressure on an organization's IT department, whose most talented staff are tempted to move to these jobs; indeed, it is often easier for IT systems development to secure budget allocations than to find the staff resources to use them. The delays caused by these factors have led to enormous user frustration and a strong desire to take matters into their own hands.

Staff Flexibility and Growth. Because the central IT department appears to be unresponsive to users' demands, user-developed systems become attractive to users as a nonconfrontational way of getting work done. Deploying either their own staffs or outside software houses, users see that they are significantly speeding up the process of obtaining "needed" service.

Staff Professional Growth. An IT staff decentralized by both physical and organizational presence in the end-user department helps educate users to IT's legitimate potential; it also reduces communications problems between IT professionals and end users. Particularly important, it makes it easier to plan employee promotions that rotate IT staff to other (non-IT) jobs within the department, thus enhancing user-IT coordination. This also facilitates moving end users to IT positions.

Finally, from the viewpoint of a local department, the protocols of interfacing with the corporate network and of meeting corporate control standards can be very time-consuming and complex. A user-purchased stand-alone system independent of this corporate network may simplify the end-user's job in getting started and permit less-skilled staff resources to be utilized.

Competitive and Service Growth in the IT Market

Thousands of stand-alone software packages are available for specific applications, ranging from simple accounts-payable systems to complete desktop support products. These appear to provide beguilingly easy solutions to short-term problems. Marketed by hardware and software vendors to end-user managers, the systems' functional features are emphasized, and any technical and software problems are soft-pedaled.

Frequently, the local solution also appears to be more cost-effective than work done or purchased by a central IT development group. Not only is there no cumbersome project proposal to be written and defended in front of IT technicians who have their own special agendas, but often a simple up-front price is quoted. Developed under user control, the project is perceived to be both simple and relatively free of red tape.

User Control

The idea of regaining control over a part of their units' operations, particularly if information technology is critical, is very important to users. In many cases, this reverses a trend that began 20 years ago in a very different technology. Control in this context has at least two dimensions.

Development. Users can exercise direct control over systems development priorities. By using either their own staffs or self-selected software houses, which may offer highly specialized skills not present in the firm, users often hope to get a system functioning in less time than it would take to navigate the priority-setting process in the corporate IT department. A user systems staff is also seen as closer and more responsive to user needs because the local manager, rather than an outsider, sets priorities. Development mistakes made by a local group are more easily accepted than those made by a remote group, and they are rarely discussed; successes, by contrast, are often topics of conversation.

Maintenance. Users gain control over systems maintenance priorities, since the work will be done either by themselves or by software houses that are dependent upon them for income. Users often overlook the importance of this point initially: the assumption is that maintenance will be no problem or that it can be performed by a clerk following a manual—a rare occurrence! Needs and desires relentlessly change.

Fit with the Organization

As the company becomes more decentralized in structure and more geographically diverse, a distributed development function becomes a much better fit and avoids heavy marketing and coordination expenses. Among conglomerates, for example, only a few have tried to centralize development; most leave it with the original units. Heavily decentralized companies such as Providian Insurance have closed down their central IT development unit and placed the IT developers in key divisions. Finally, should the corporation decide to divest a unit, the process will be easier to implement if its IT activities are not integrated with the rest of the company.

User Learning

Predicting the full ramifications of introducing a new technology is very difficult. On one hand, enthusiastic user experimentation can stimulate creativity and produce new approaches to troublesome problems. Systems developed by a central IT unit, on the other hand, must overcome greater user resistance in adoption. This IT challenge simply reflects research in the fields of organization development and control, which has identified organization learning as a principal benefit of organizing in multiple profit centers, rather than by function. As noted earlier, this is increasingly evident in office support and new professional support such as CAD.

Summary

In aggregate, these five pressures represent a powerful argument for a strong user role in systems development and suggest when that role might be the dominant one. The pressures driving users toward purchase, development, and/or use of local systems and software can be summarized as short-term user control. Stand-alone desktop workstations and local development have been found to offer users more immediate solutions to the problems under their control and to do so in a climate they perceive as enjoyable. While particular benefits associated with phase 1 and phase 2 learning can be achieved by this approach, they may be gained with little regard for information hygiene and less regard for control, as discussed next.

PRESSURES TOWARD IT CONTROL

Countering the arguments of the previous section, pressures exist in many settings to consolidate a firm's IT development resource into a single unit or to at least keep it in two or more large clusters.

Staff Professionalism

As noted, a large central IT development staff enhances the organization's ability to recruit and retain (attract and keep challenged) specialized technical personnel. A central unit also provides useful support for a small division or unit that does not have its own IT staff and needs occasional access to information technology skills.

Additionally, it is easier to modernize a centralized unit than one in which the development staff is scattered throughout the firm. For example, as the average age of many IT development staffs continues to rise, more employees are becoming comfortable and set in their ways (the graying of IT). The central unit is a useful fulcrum to insert a limited number of high-energy people to aid in recharging older staff and redirecting them to today's radically different technologies. The importance of this new talent is intensified by the fact that existing staff's salary levels, individual interests, and perceived interpersonal relationships often make lateral movement out of the central IT system department undesirable. Many staff either must be retrained or let go. The inability of some firms to manage this is a key reason for the current popularity of outsourcing development to external vendors.

Developing and enforcing better standards of IT management practice is also easier in a large group. Documentation procedures, project management skills, and disciplined maintenance approaches are examples of critical infrastructure items in IT systems development departments. In 1988, a large chemicals organization faced with a deteriorating relationship between its central development department and key users was forced to distribute 80 percent of its development staff to four divisions, thereby changing both reporting responsibility and office location. Although the change has been generally successful in stimulating new ideas and better relationships with users (many development people better identified with users than with technical development issues), by 1993 the need for standards to control the costs of desktop proliferation became so intense that significantly tighter standards and management practices had to be instituted to bring order out of chaos. Many organizations have experienced such periodic swings of the centralize/decentralize pendulum because the benefits of a change, over time, give way to new problems that require redirection.

Central staff expertise is particularly important for supporting user-designed systems. Lacking practical systems design experience, the user often ignores normal data-control procedures, various corporate standards, and conventional costing practices. Consequently, purchasing from several suppliers or incrementally from one often results in a clumsy, hard-to-maintain system design.

For example, a large financial organization discovered that all the people involved in software design and purchase for three of the departmental systems used to process data on a daily basis had left the company. Further, no formal documentation or operating instructions had been prepared, and all source programs had been lost. What remained were disk files with object programs on them. The system ran, but why it ran no one knew; and even if the company's survival depended on it, changes would at best have been very difficult and time-consuming to execute.

A recent study of a financial services firm showed that an $8 million investment in networked personal computers had resulted in an average of $18,000 a year per machine to keep them up and running. Locally developed, rapidly evolving, and largely unmanaged, the distributed systems required more development money than the central development unit, which had extensive documentation and other controls. The situation was rectified before serious damage occurred.

Feasibility Study Concerns

A user-driven feasibility study may contain major technical mistakes that will result in the computer system's being either inadequate to handle growing processing requirements or not easily maintainable. Because of inexperienced staff, the feasibility study may repeatedly underestimate both the complexity of the software needed and the growth in the number of transactions to be handled by the system. (The risk increases if competent technical staff inputs to the feasibility study were limited and if the real business needs were not well understood.)

In addition, users often focus a feasibility study on a specific service without recognizing that successful first applications tend to generate unanticipated second applications, then third applications, and so forth. Each application appears to require only a modest incremental purchase price and, therefore, does not receive a comprehensive full-cost review. In consequence, fairly shortly, the hardware configuration or software approach selected cannot handle the necessary work. Unless the initial hardware selection and system design process has been carefully undertaken to allow for it, growth can lead to major business disruptions and very expensive software modifications.

User-driven feasibility studies are more susceptible to recommendations to acquire products from unstable vendors, given some unusually attractive product features. However, significant numbers of software vendors have failed, and a number of hardware manufacturers are in trouble. The same trends that hit the pocket calculator and digital watch industries in the late 1970s have recently affected this industry sector as it matures. Vendor stability is critical because many of these systems insinuate themselves into the heart of a department's operations. With software-intensive investments, failure of a special-features hardware vendor can mean both expensive disruption in the department's service and intensive, crisis-spending efforts to convert the software to another machine, unless an open systems approach has been established. In an open systems world, these concerns are particularly applicable to the packages and services provided by software suppliers. A single experience with a product from a failed software vendor provides painful learning.

Particular care must be taken on local development, since uncoordinated user groups tend to buy or develop systems tailored to very specific situations, creating long-term maintenance problems. In many environments characterized by such local development, there is also poor technology transfer between similar users and, thus, consequent lack of corporate leverage, an issue of low importance to the local unit.

A large forest products company, organized geographically, combined a system-minded regional manager with an aggressive growth-oriented IT manager who was promoted to responsibility for all administrative support in the region. Within three years, the region's IT budget was double that of a comparable region; moreover, although their applications were extraordinarily effective, only one was exported to another region. Subsequent review indicated that nearly half of the systems developed were focused on problems of potentially general interest and could have been exported to other parts of the company.

Corporate Database System

A corporate database strategy involves both collecting data files at a central location for reference by multiple users and developing client-server networks and procedures that allow users, regardless of physical location, to access data files easily. A central staff provides a focal point for both conceptualizing and developing the architecture of these systems to serve multiple users across the firm. The need for database sharing varies widely with the nature of the corporation's activities, of course. A conglomerate usually has much less need for data sharing across the firm than does a functionally organized, one-product company. However, electronic mail, videoconferencing, and shared financial performance information have become legitimate needs in many organizations, and a central department is better able to develop and distribute such systems to users or to coordinate a process whereby key parts of the system development efforts are outsourced to local development units.

Inevitably, when the issue of distributed development and hardware in several business units is raised, the first concern is that the company will lose the ability to manage and control its data flows. There is fear that data of significance to many people beyond those in the originating unit will be locked up in a nonstandardized format in inaccessible locations. While this is a valid concern in many settings, we should also examine these objections in light of several mitigating factors.

Timing. One mitigating factor is timing. In many cases, the argument raised against a stand-alone system is the erosion of data as a corporate resource. Allegedly, in order to preserve flexibility for future database design, the stand-alone computer should not be acquired. Often, however, such flexibility is not needed, as adaptive communication systems can provide control as well as access to distant users. In that context, a well-designed stand-alone system may be an equally good (if not better) starting point for these long-term systems as jumping directly from the present set of manual procedures. This possibility must be pragmatically assessed.

Abstraction of Data.   Another mitigating factor, often overlooked, is the capability for abstracting data, if necessary, from a locally managed system at planned frequent intervals and sending it directly to a central computer. Ordinarily not all information in a stand-alone file is relevant to or needed by other users. Indeed, often only a small percentage is widely relevant.

On the other hand, because locally designed data-handling systems can prove expensive to maintain and to link with each other, the firm must identify in operational terms the data requirements of the central files and provide guidelines for what can be stored locally and how accessible it should be to others. The problem is exemplified by the branch-office support systems that generate voluminous records in electronic format. Unless well designed, these files can be bulky, lock up key data from potential users, and pose potential security problems. For instance, a mail-order house recently discovered that each customer representative was using more than 200 disks per day and storing them in boxes by date of order receipt, making aggregate customer information impossible to obtain in a timely manner.

Organizing and accessing electronic files may require central storage to ensure appropriate security. Managing effective security—a topic of intense interest in a world of "hackers"—is usually easier when all files are in a single location rather than dispersed. Realistically, however, some data are so sensitive that they are best kept off the network—the only way to ensure real security.

Fit with the Corporate Structure and Strategy

Centralized IT development's role is clearest in organizations characterized by centrally managed planning and operational control. A large farm-equipment manufacturer with a tradition of central functional control from corporate headquarters successfully implemented a program wherein the corporate systems group developed all software for factories and distribution units worldwide. As the company grew in size, however, its structure became more decentralized; in turn, the cost of effective central systems development was escalating. The firm had to implement a marketing function to educate users on the virtues of central services and to decentralize some development functions. It is becoming increasingly common for centralized development groups to have an explicitly defined and staffed internal marketing activity.

Cost Analysis

Given its practical experience in other systems efforts, a centralized IT development group can produce a realistic software development estimate (subject to the problems discussed in Chapter 10) that takes into account the company's overall interests. Software development estimates are problematic in user feasibility studies for two key reasons. Most new systems are more software-intensive than hardware-intensive; software costs are typically 75 to 85 percent of the total cost for a customized system. Few users have had experience in estimating software development costs, and an order-of-magnitude mistake in a feasibility study—particularly if it is an individually developed system and not a "turnkey" (i.e., general-purpose) package—is not unknown.

Users also lack understanding of the true costs of an existing service, particularly given complicated corporate IT charge-out systems, many of which present calculations in terms of utilization of computer resource units that are completely unfathomable to the user; hence, each month or quarter, an unintelligible bill arrives, the amount of which is unpredictable. (In management control environments where the user is held closely responsible for variance from budget, this legitimately causes intense frustration.) For the user, a locally developed system, especially if it is for a stand-alone desktop device, is seen as producing both understandable and predictable costs. Further, since many corporate charge-out systems are designed on a full-cost basis, their charges to the end user seem high and thus offer great inducements to purchase locally.

Since much of corporate IT is fixed cost in the short run, many of these savings are false. However, because there are significant fixed-cost elements to a corporate information systems center, particularly in the short run, what appears to the individual user to be an opportunity to reduce costs may be a cost increase for the company—more hardware/software acquired locally and no possible savings at the corporate IT facility. Policies for ensuring that appropriate cost analyses are prepared must be established.

Summary

The pressures toward centralized IT control can be summarized as long-term information architecture. Inexorably, over the long run, most (but not all) stand-alone units will become part of a network and need to both receive and share data with other users and systems. In many respects, these pressures are not immediately evident when the system is installed but tend to grow in importance with the passage of time. Policies for managing the trade-offs between the obvious short-term benefits and long-term risks are delicate to administer, but necessary.

COORDINATION AND LOCATION OF IT POLICY

The tension between IT and users can be effectively managed by establishing clear policies that specify the user domain, the IT domain, and senior management's role. Senior management must play a significant part in ensuring that these policies are developed and that they evolve appropriately over time. Both IT and users must understand the implications of their roles and possible conflicts.

IT Responsibilities

The following tasks constitute the central core of IT responsibilities—the minimum for managing the long-term information hygiene needs of an organization:

1. Develop and manage the evolution of a long-term architectural plan and ensure that new projects fit into its evolution as much as possible.
2. Establish procedures to ensure that, for potential IT projects of any size, internal development versus purchase is compared. If projects are implemented outside the firm or by the user, establish the appropriate professional standards for project control and documentation. These standards must be flexible since user-developed systems for desktop units pose demands quite different from systems to be run on large mainframe computers. Further, define a process for forcing adherence to the selected standards.
3. Maintain an inventory of installed or planned-to-be-installed information services.
4. Create and maintain a set of standards that establishes:
   a. Mandatory telecommunication standards.
   b. Standard languages for classes of acquired equipment.
   c. Documentation procedures for different types of systems.
   d. A corporate data dictionary with clear definitions of which elements must be included.
   e. Identification of file maintenance standards and procedures.
   f. Examination procedures for systems developed in local units to ensure that they do not conflict with corporate needs and that any necessary interfaces are constructed.
5. Identify and provide appropriate IT development staff career paths throughout the organization. These include lateral transfers within and between IT units, upward movement within IT, and appropriate outward movement from IT to other functional units. (Although this is more difficult in distributed units, it is still possible.)
6. Establish appropriate internal marketing efforts for IT support. These should exert catch-up pressure and coaching for units that are lagging and slow down units pushing too fast into leading-edge technologies they do not understand.
7. Prepare a detailed checklist of questions to be answered in any hardware/software acquisition to ensure that relevant technical and managerial issues are raised. These questions should ask:

    a. Does the proposed system meet corporate communication standards?

    b. For desktop systems, has upward growth potential been addressed, and are adequate communication capabilities in place so that local files can be reached from other locations, if appropriate?

    c. Are languages being used appropriately and can they be maintained over the long term?

8. Identify and maintain relationships with preferred systems suppliers. Before entering a relationship with a vendor, the conditions for entertaining exceptions to established standards must be agreed on. For example, size, number of systems in place, and financial structure requirements should be clearly spelled out.

9. Establish education programs for potential users that communicate both the benefits and the pitfalls of a new technology and that define users' roles in ensuring its successful introduction in their departments.

10. Set up an ongoing review of systems for determining which ones have become obsolete and should be redesigned.

These issues apply with particular force to the design of systems that become embedded in the company's daily operations. Decision support systems do not pose quite the same problems, although the need to obtain data from the rest of the organization is rapidly putting them in the same situation.

These core responsibilities, of course, can be significantly expanded to impose much tighter and more formal controls if the situation warrants.

User Responsibilities

To assist in the orderly identification of opportunities and implementation of new IT services and to grow in an understanding of their use, cost, and impact on the organization, the following responsibilities should be fulfilled by the user of IT service:

1. Clearly understand the scope of all IT activities supporting the user. Increasingly, more experienced organizations have installed a user-understandable IT charge-out system to facilitate this.

2. To ensure satisfactory service, realistically appraise the amount of user personnel investment required for each new project, both to develop and to operate the system. These costs are often much higher than planned and are frequently ignored.

3. Ensure comprehensive user input for all IT projects that will support vital aspects of the unit's operations. This might include the nature of service, process of introduction, and level of user training for both staff and managers.

4. Realistically ensure that the IT-user interface is consistent with IT's strategic relevance to the business unit. If it is very important, the interface must be very close. If it is less important, more distance between the parties and more friction can be tolerated.
5. Periodically audit the adequacy of system reliability standards, performance of communications services, and adequacy of security procedures.
6. Participate in the development and maintenance of an IT plan that sets new technology priorities, schedules the transfer of IT among groups, and evaluates a portfolio of projects in light of the company strategy.

These represent the very minimum policies that the users should develop and manage. Depending on the firm's geography, corporate management style, stage of IT development, and mix of technology development phases, expanded levels of user involvement may be appropriate, including full-time assignment of their own staff. As these facets evolve, so will the appropriateness of certain policies.

General Management Support and Policy Overview

Distinct from the issues involved in the distribution of IT services is a cluster of broad policy and direction activities requiring senior management perspective. In the past, these activities were built into the structure of a central IT organization. Now, given the need to link IT to business, IT operations are frequently separated from IT planning. A chemical company, for example, reorganized in 1990 to establish a 500-person systems and operations department reporting directly to the head of administrative services, which works on corporate applications. (An additional 400 analysts and programmers are employed in the major divisional staffs.) This department does the company's implementation and operational IT work on a month-to-month, year-to-year basis. At the same time, a 25- to 30-person IT policy group reporting directly to the head of research works on overall IT policy and long-range IT strategy formulation for the firm. In a similar vein, a major conglomerate whose development staff and hardware are distributed to key users has a three- to four-person group at headquarters level. Firms that outsource most or all of their IT operations, development, and maintenance activities still need this policy group.

Key responsibilities of a corporate IT policy group should include:

1. Ensure that an appropriate balance exists between IT and user inputs across the different technologies and that one side is not dominating the other inappropriately. Initiate appropriate personnel and organizational transfers if the situation is out of balance. Establishing an executive steering committee, for example, is a common response to inadequate user input.
2. Ensure that a comprehensive corporate IT strategy is developed. A comprehensive overview of technology trends, current corporate use of

information technology, and linkage between IT initiatives and overall corporate goals is particularly important in organizations where resources are widely distributed. The resources to be devoted to this effort vary widely from organization to organization as IT's perceived contribution to corporate strategy, among other things, changes.

3. Manage the inventory of hardware and software resources, and assure that the corporate view extends to purchasing relationships and contracts. In most settings, the corporate group is the appropriate place to identify and manage standard policies for relationships with vendors.

4. Facilitate the creation and evolution of standards for development and operations activities, and ensure that the standards are applied appropriately. In this regard, the corporate policy group plays the combined role of consultant on the one hand and auditor (particularly if there is a weak or nonexistent IT auditing function) on the other. This role requires technically competent and interpersonally sensitive staff.

5. Facilitate the transfer of technology from one unit to another. This occurs through recognizing the unit's common systems needs as well as stimulating joint projects. Actual transfer requires regular visits to the different operating units, organization of periodic corporate MIS conferences, development of a corporate information systems newsletter, and other means.

6. Actively encourage technical experimentation. A limited program of research is a very appropriate part of the IT function; an important role of the corporate policy group is to ensure that research and scanning does not get swept away in the press of urgent operational issues. Further, the corporate policy group is in a position to encourage patterns of experimentation that smaller units might feel pose undue risk if they are the sole beneficiary.

7. Assume responsibility for developing an appropriate planning and control system to link IT firmly to the company's goals. Planning, system appraisal, charge-out, and project management processes should be monitored and (if necessary) encouraged to develop by the policy group. In this context, the group should work closely with the corporate steering committee.

As these responsibilities imply, the corporate IT policy group needs to be staffed with individuals who, in aggregate, have broad technical backgrounds and extensive practical IT administrative experience. Except in very limited numbers, it is not an appropriate department for entry-level staff members.

SUMMARY

This chapter has focused on the key issues surrounding the organization of information technology for the next decade. A significant revolution has occurred in what is regarded as good managerial practice in this field.

Important contributors to this change have been the development of new hardware and software technologies and managerial experience with IT. These technologies not only permit quite different types of services to be delivered, but also offer the potential for quite different ways of delivering these services. Consequently, what constitutes best practice has changed considerably, and the evolution seems likely to continue; many IT organization structures that were effectively put together in the 1970s have been found inappropriate for the 1990s.

Determining the appropriate pattern of distribution of IT resources within the organization is a complex and multifaceted subject. The general manager should develop a program that will encourage appropriate innovation on the one hand while maintaining overall control on the other. How these organization and planning issues are resolved is inextricably tied to non-IT-oriented aspects of the corporate environment. The leadership style of the person at the top of the organization and that person's view of the future provide one important thrust for redirection. A vision of tight central control presents a different context for these decisions than does a vision emphasizing the autonomy of operating units. Closely associated and linked to this is the corporate organizational structure and culture and the trends occurring within it. Also, the realities of geographical spread of the business units heavily impact IT organizational and planning possibilities; the corporate headquarters of a large insurance company, for example, poses different constraints than do the multiple international plants and markets of an automobile manufacturer.

On a less global scale are the present realities of quality and location of existing IT resources (organizationally and physically), which provide the base from which change must be made. Equally important is how responsive and competent current users perceive these resources to be. The unit that is seen (no matter how unfairly or inaccurately) as unresponsive has different organizational challenges than the well-regarded unit. Similarly, the existing and the perceived-appropriate strategic roles of IT on the dimensions of the firm's applications portfolio and operations have important organizational implications. If the firm is in the "support" quadrant, for example, the IT policy unit must realistically be placed lower in the organization structure in order to deal with its perceived lack of burning relevance to corporate strategy.

In dealing with these forces, one is seeking an appropriate balance between innovation and control and between the inputs of the IT specialist and the user. Not only do appropriate answers to these questions vary among companies, but different answers and structures are often appropriate for individual units within an organization. In short, there is a series of right questions to ask, and there is an identifiable but very complex series of forces that, appropriately analyzed, determine for each organizational unit the direction in which the correct answer lies—for now.

Chapter

8

Information Technology Operations

A major investment banking firm operated all of its foreign exchange trading and other trading activities out of a large computing center containing $15 million worth of hardware, totally without backup. One Friday afternoon, the water main running vertically through the building burst on the floor directly above the computing center. In a half-hour, the computing-center floor was covered with three feet of water and all the equipment was destroyed. The company went into the weekend with many of its key trading positions uncovered—indeed, not even knowing what those positions were. Truly extraordinary efforts were made to replace all of the equipment in a 48-hour period in order to prevent massive balance-sheet erosion. Multiple sites, much tighter environmental measures, better controls, and new management were all parts of the solution.

As a result of software glitches in a new installation in January 1990, AT&T's long-distance phone system went down for 14 hours. One insurance company had to send home 500 people who were working on telephone follow-ups to direct mailings, losing a day's sales. The insurer now spreads its business over several carriers to avoid such vulnerability in the future.

The chief executive officer of an industrial products firm discovered that the delay in year-end financial closing was not due to reduced emphasis on close control of financial accounting, but to unexpected work and personnel difficulties in the IT department. Increased use (and associated problems) of an on-line query system to provide salespeople and customers with detailed delivery and cost information had absorbed all available system support personnel. Consequently, no time was left for revising the accounting system for mandatory changes in tax laws before year-end closing.

The IT director of a large aerospace firm pondered whether to totally reorganize and consolidate 18 operations centers in order to save more than $50 million. Each center was configured to provide total support to a business unit; workloads were erratic, long response-time delays existed on some on-line systems, and the costs were high. In fact, the consolidated center produced annual savings in excess of $100 million.

Unusual problems? Hardly! Historically, the "glamorous" part of the IT function has been the technology-oriented new systems development activity. Systems maintenance and day-to-day operations and delivery of service have been distinctly secondary. Failures in the operations function, however, increasingly jeopardize entire organizations. In this chapter, the term *operations* is defined as the running of IT hardware and data input devices, equipment scheduling, and workforces associated with these activities. The chapter also deals with the special challenges of security and privacy.

CHANGING OPERATIONS ENVIRONMENT

Both the management resources devoted to operations activities and the sophistication of management practices within the operations center have often been inadequate for the growth and change companies have experienced in this area. Evolving technology is now triggering major changes in the way these activities are managed.

Move to On-Line Systems and Networks. In the past decade, a significant increase in on-line technology applications and growing sophistication in operating systems have transformed a batch, job-shop environment with heavy human control into, first, a process-manufacturing shop and then a largely self-scheduled and -monitored 24-hour-a-day utility with networked servers and clients scattered across the firm. This change in work flow has precipitated a total rethinking of what appropriate scheduling is and how adequate service levels are defined. These systems support thousands of internal devices and in many cases must provide "seamless" 24-hour-a-day service links to customers and suppliers around the globe. Any problems in this area immediately reflect unfavorably on the firm as a whole.

Diversity of Performance Measures. There is no such thing as an ideal standard IT operations management control system or an ideal measure of performance. How to balance the quality of service, the response time of on-line systems, the ability to handle unexpected jobs and costs easily, the installation of maintenance patches, and the ability to meet schedules on batch systems varies from one organization to another.

Efficiency-Effectiveness Balance. Different IT operations environments must strike different balances between efficiency (low-cost production) and effectiveness in responding to unplanned, uneven flows of requests. IT operations cannot be all things simultaneously to all people, but must instead operate with the priorities of trade-offs established by corporate strategy. To implement these priorities, some large IT operations have reorganized into series of focused, single-service groups, each of which can be managed to serve quite different user service objectives.

Changes in Staffing Needs.   Many formerly valuable employees are unsuited for new tasks, and their relatively simple jobs have been "automated away." Complicating this dilemma is the fact that in many parts of the world, this function is unionized. In settings where operations centers are becoming "lights-out factories," however, the problem is relatively transitory.

Continued Change in Technology.   Evolving technology, while offering potential benefits of lower cost and new capabilities, poses significant problems of change and introducing new operating procedures. It is an unusual IT operations center that has the same hardware/software configuration from one month to the next.

These issues are similar to those involved in running a manufacturing facility characterized as utilizing highly volatile technology and specialized labor, serving dynamic markets, and operating within a changing industry structure. Consequently, much of the analysis in this chapter draws on work done in manufacturing management, particularly as it relates to efficiency-effectiveness trade-offs.

A Focused Service Organization Alternative—An Example

A key question stemming from the manufacturing analogy is how focused the department should be. Should it subdivide itself into sets of stand-alone services networked together as needed or be organized as a general-purpose IT service? The problem faced by the company mentioned at the outset of this chapter—of either closing its books late or providing continuous on-line service for queries from the sales force—stimulated a review of how responsive its operations were to the demands of new services. It was impossible, they realized, for that monolithic unit to respond adequately to such very different user needs.

To address the problem, the IT development and maintenance group was reorganized into four independent systems groups, each operating independently of the others and reporting to the IT manager. One group supported the on-line query systems, with its goals being to provide 10-second response, one-day change implementation, and hourly refreshment of all data. This query system was moved to a stand-alone server in the corporate data center to keep its volatility of demand from disturbing the rest of the company's operations.

The second group was devoted to the general ledger accounting system. Their goals were to keep the software up-to-date for month-end closing, to schedule work so as not to interfere with other systems, to ensure the quality and reliability of accounting data, and to close the books five days after the last working day of the month. This system ran on the data center's large mainframe computer. The third group was responsible for all material-management systems. Their objectives were to ensure that all desired changes to the system were made and that all production control persons were well trained in use of the system so as to reduce rerun time dramatically.

The fourth group worked with the systems that supported new-product development. They were responsible for identifying system requirements of new products, maintaining the capacity simulator used in planning new-product development, establishing the data standards used to describe new products, and developing and performing analyses on new products as directed by the vice president of product development. Their systems also ran on the mainframe computer.

Each focused group included at least one user and two to three systems professionals, with the query group having its own server as well. All worked full time on their respective services with the exception of the new-product group, which had spurts of work as new products hit the market and lulls after the market settled down. This structure has produced happier customers, significantly better perceptions of service, and increased employee morale.

Alternative Organizations

Historically, IT systems were developed to be run out of an integrated IT operations unit. As we have noted, some firms have reorganized IT development and operations in order to be more responsive to user needs. For example, many organizations have not only shifted application programmers to users, but have also allowed maintenance and operations to be decentralized around local systems. As IT's monopoly of system construction and make-or-buy decisions erodes and user control increases, IT operations become fragmented into a series of focused services (for example, using a standard word processing system for customer mailings). For some users and applications, this may be very effective. The services for other users, however, may be dependent upon an integrated set of data and a network, in which case severe coordination problems are created by a focused factory concept. The challenge is to identify where focus in operations (either within the central unit or distributed to the user) is appropriate and where it is not. Implementation of this is discussed in the section on production planning and control later in the chapter.

Intensifying this challenge is the fact that in all but the most decentralized corporations, central telecommunications networks have been developed for binding corporations' activities together. These include the capacity for electronic mail, document transfer, data file transfers, and so on. Including everything from local area networks to satellite links, many of the networks are both very large and highly sophisticated as they evolve links between fragmented services. For example, a large aerospace company initiated a total rearchitecturing of its network after a confidential e-mail message from the president to the financial vice president wound up on the desk of a production planner in another country.

To build on the manufacturing strategy theme and develop an appropriate range of make-or-buy plans, the operations management discussion in this chapter is organized around these topics:

- Developing an operations strategy.
- Technology planning.
- Measuring and managing capacity.
- Managing the IT operations workforce.
- Production planning and control.
- Security.
- Privacy.

DEVELOPING AN OPERATIONS STRATEGY

The management team of an IT operations activity is trying to stay on top of a utility that is radically changing its production system, customer base, and role within the company. Twenty years ago, the manager and his staff could be described as monopolists running a job shop, where the key issues were scheduling (with substantial human inputs), ensuring that telecommunications were adequate, managing a large blue-collar staff, and planning capacity and staffing levels for future workloads of similar characteristics. Today, by comparison, they (1) operate an information utility that provides a 24-hour, seven-day-a-week service in support of thousands of terminals and PCs—perhaps located around the world—that must cope cost-effectively with uncertain short-term and long-term user demand; (2) manage a workforce far more highly skilled, more professional, and much smaller in numbers; and (3) evaluate external competing services that in many cases offer the potential to solve problems more economically and more comprehensively. Thus, while key issues for the IT operations manager continue to include staff, capacity, and telecommunications, they also entail appropriate assessment, assimilation, and integration of software and services emanating from outside the corporation.

Senior management must assess the quality of IT operations and—depending on how critical it is to the overall strategic mission of the corporation—must be involved in determining its structure and the standards for its quality of service. The central question for both senior management and IT management is whether the current IT operations organization effectively supports the firm.

In this context, an operations strategy must address four key issues:

1. Ensure that an architecture has been conceived and is being implemented.
2. Ensure that new systems are developed in ways that appropriately address their long-term maintainability.
3. Ensure that internal/external sourcing decisions are carefully considered (see Chapter 10).
4. Determine the extent to which IT operations should be managed as a single entity or be broken into a series of perhaps more costly but more focused subunits that provide more customized user service than is possible with a single facility. (This topic is discussed in the Production Planning and Control section.)

Effective IT operations hinge heavily on ensuring that the first step of the systems life cycle, the design phase, is well executed. The critical operations discussions for a system often occur early in the design phase. Both user and IT operational personnel should be intimately involved in the early design of significant processing systems. Strong IT operational input ensures that operational feasibility issues are given high priority from the beginning. It is easy for a development group to overlook such issues as appropriate restart points in case of hardware failures, adequate documentation and support for operational personnel when a program abnormally ends, and so on. They further need to ensure that inappropriate shortcuts are not taken during development and that the details of the conversion from the old to the new system have been conceived appropriately. These issues are particularly complex if an external package is sourced.

TECHNOLOGY PLANNING

Technology planning for operations is a process whereby potential obsolescence and opportunities are continually reviewed. The scope and effort of this review should be determined by the nature of the business and the state of IT: for a bank it should be across many technologies and be very extensive; a mail-order business may concentrate on office support technology; a wholesale distributor may primarily focus on computing and telecommunications technologies. To be effective, the review must involve high-caliber, imaginative staff. (The role of the emerging technologies department is discussed later.) It should regard today's IT possibilities in the context of the potential available two or three years in the future. This potential must be based on technological forecasting.

If a company is trying to distinguish itself from the competition through its application of information technologies, the resources dedicated to technological planning should be quite extensive. If a firm is trying to just stay even with competitors and sees its IT activity primarily as "support," simple comparison with the operations of competitors or leaders in particular fields may be sufficient. Some firms periodically solicit bids from different vendors to help ensure that their IT department is fully up-to-date. For example, a large insurance company whose IT department is dominated by the technology of one vendor has annually asked a competitor of the vendor to bid an alternative system, even though they have not perceived a need for change. As a result of these bids, however, they recently switched to another vendor's PCs, and on another occasion they installed a large machine purchased from a different vendor. These moves have kept the annual bidding process honest.

The objective of the review is to determine—relative to available and announced systems—how cost effective and adequate for growth the existing installed technologies are. The review should generate an updated priority list of technologies to be considered as replacements. Such lead time is critical; technology replacements or additions planned two years in advance cause a small fraction of the disruption that those planned only six months in advance do. (Realistically, of course, breakthrough announcements limit the precision of advance planning.) In order to better define the architecture of the future information service, the planning activity should include field trips to vendors, education sessions, and pilot studies as vehicles for obtaining an understanding of emerging technologies.

A useful approach to a technology review is categorizing the applications portfolio of operations systems by length of time since development or last total rewrite of each system. Discovering that a significant percentage of IT systems were designed a decade or more ago often indicates that a major redesign and rewrite will offer great opportunities for reduced maintenance and improved operational efficiency.[1] When a large international bank recently performed such a review, it discovered that 60 percent of its CPU utilization and 50 percent of its systems effort were devoted to maintaining and running transaction processing systems constructed in the second era (see Figure 8–1).

If a new technology involves hardware replacement, or the new systems use existing hardware more effectively, implementation may be transparent to the user. Other replacement technology, however, affects users consciously by providing different or improved service—as do report writers for databases or new terminals. These technologies basically support users rather than change their operations style. Still other replacement technologies

---

[1] Martin Buss, "Penny-Wise Approach to Data Processing," *Harvard Business Review,* July–August 1981.

impact user habits so dramatically that user leadership must drive the implementation effort if it is to succeed. Each implementation situation requires careful planning to ensure that service is not interrupted and that the affected individuals understand how to operate with the new service. Figure 8–1 summarizes the tensions and forces that must be managed in IT innovation.

Good technology planning includes an ongoing appraisal of user readiness, an inventory of how existing technology is used, an awareness of where technology is going, and a program of appropriate pilot technology projects. A large consumer products company, for example, has an IT unit with a very strong emerging-technology group; for each division and function, it maintains an updated log of services in use and an assessment of current problems. They are currently introducing a program of office support that includes a large portfolio of applications in a pilot division. Scheduled over 24 months, the detailed program for this division includes benchmarks and reviews for evaluating benefits, operating problems, and progress. Such pilot testing stimulates broader organizational awareness of the opportunities and operational issues associated with new technology and permits better planning for full-scale implementation in the other divisions.

As the above example suggests, a new, explicitly separate organization unit to address innovation-phase technology exploitation and management appears to be a promising approach. Called the "emerging-technology (ET) group," it often resides initially in the IT organization on a level equal with applications development and operations departments. A historical analysis of 12 firms found that the key difference between leading and lagging financial institutions, airlines, and manufacturers was the early formation of an ET group. In some large, strategic IT organizations, the ET unit has been placed outside the IT department to avoid its being swamped by the IT control philosophy.

FIGURE 8–1 Forces to Be Managed in IT Innovation

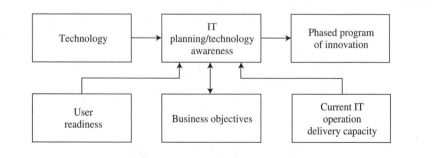

Source: Martin Buss, "Penny-Wise Approach to Data Processing," *Harvard Business Review,* July–August 1981.

TABLE 8-1 Characteristics of Effective Management of Emerging-Technology (ET) Groups by Phase

	Characteristic	
Management Issue	*Innovation-Phase Effectiveness*	*Control-Phase Efficiency*
Organization	Organic (ET)	Mechanistic (traditional IT)
Management control	Loose, informal	Tight
Leadership	Participating	Directive (telling, delegating)

Three issues must be dealt with by general management in structuring the ET group: organization, management control, and leadership. (See Table 8-1.) The following paragraphs address these three issues in relation to the innovation and control phases. Because the innovation phase is more troublesome for most organizations, it is discussed in more detail.

Innovation Phase.   The ET group might explore such current technologies as interorganizational image processing and small-scale expert systems. The atmosphere within the ET group is experimental; the organizational structures and management controls are loose and informal. Cost accounting and reporting are flexible (though accuracy is essential), and little or no requirement exists for pro forma project cost-benefit analysis. The leadership style resembles what Hersey and others[2] refer to as participating; that is, the distinctions between leaders and subordinates are somewhat clouded, and the lines of communication are shortened. The level of attention to relationships is high compared to that of task orientation. This informality is key to innovation and organizational learning.

A study of the tobacco industry[3] referred to such informality as organizational slack and stated that "the creation or utilization of slack normally requires the temporary relaxation of performance standards." In the effective companies, standards of efficiency were greatly reduced during the early testing phases of a new IT innovation. Organizations strategically dependent on IT should view innovation-phase activities as an integral part of their ongoing response to pressures to adapt to changing environments, and should fund them appropriately.

The dramatic growth of "information centers" in response to end-use computing illustrates the pressure and responses that lead to establishment of a separate department. These facilities are generally staffed with nontraditional data-processing professionals and have very different ac-

---

[2] P. Hersey and K. H. Blanchard, *Management of Organizational Behavior,* 3rd ed. (Englewood Cliffs, NJ: Prentice Hall, 1977).

[3] R. Miles, *Coffin Nails and Corporate Strategies* (Englewood Cliffs, NJ: Prentice Hall, 1982).

counting, justification, and cost-benefit systems. Firms strategically dependent on IT cannot afford to establish such centers reactively; they must productively forecast, assess, and test appropriate technology to introduce it at an early stage. These activities are unlikely to occur without specific responsibility being assigned to a person or an organizational unit whose role is somewhat analogous to that of a corporate R&D department. However, unlike a traditional R&D model, the manager of ET and the department staff serve primarily as facilitators, as opposed to gurus. Thus, ET might partially fund the use of professionals outside its organization to forecast, track, and test new database management system products.

In addition, ET contributes to the broad-based learning of a company by being responsible for "interorganizational technology transfer." This refers to designing and managing the phase 2 introduction and diffusion of the targeted technology throughout the firm. ET must first facilitate the development of user-oriented, creative pilot applications of the new technology; it then participates in discussions about how the new applications can best be developed and implemented, about the education and training needs of users and IT professionals for using the new technology, and the changes in strategy or structure that may result from implementing the new technology and associated applications.

After the ET group develops the ability to support the new technology, general management then decides whether to provide additional resources to continue the diffusion of the technology (phase 2). With requisite support of senior management, the ET group begins to teach others throughout the organization how to utilize it and encourages experimentation. A chief concern of the ET manager at this point becomes how to market it effectively. (In some organizations, the job of selling the new technology is easy because the organizational culture encourages innovation and experimentation.) In the words of March and Simon, innovation in such companies is "institutionalized."[4]

Again, the cultural differences between laboratory and operations are important. Part of the task of successfully selling this technology to other parts of the organization is finding a way to translate the unique language associated with the technology into a language compatible with the larger organizational culture. A study of the electronic industry suggested that these cultural differences exist more in the minds of the organizational participants than in any objective reality. The artifacts identified in the study resulted from the natural tendency of people "when faced with problems in human organizations of an intractable nature, to find relief in attributing the difficulties to the wrong-headedness, stupidity, or delinquency of the other with whom they had to deal."[5]

---

[4] J. March and H. Simon, *Organizations* (New York: John Wiley & Sons, 1958).
[5] T. Burns and G. Stalker, *Management of Innovation* (London: Tavistock Publishing, 1979).

The issue is not, however, whether the cultural differences exist only in people's minds but, rather, given that they do exist somewhere, what can be done about them. The study identified two useful solutions employed by the sample companies. One was assigning members of the design department to supervise production activity and production personnel to supervise the design activity. For IT, this means assigning responsibility for user implementation work to ET staff, as well as putting the user in charge of ET group projects. To be effective, this solution must be implemented with consideration for the wide gaps in technical expertise between subordinates and their managers. (That is, subordinates usually know more about the technology or business process than the manager does.) However, this has proven to be a viable approach when the key individuals are chosen carefully.

A second solution was effective in other settings: creating special intermediaries to serve as liaison between the design department and production shops. IT steering committees and user department analysts are examples of these intermediaries that have worked effectively in the IT environment. This strategy unfortunately tends to increase bureaucracy, but, for many organizations, it has proven to be a very effective way of improving communication.

ET managers must analyze existing or potential resistance to the changes the new technology elicits. Resistance to change often stems from the reluctance of organization members to disturb delicately balanced power and status structures. ET managers need to adopt a "selling" leadership style characterized by high task orientation and high levels of interpersonal interaction. Major organizational change threatens long-established power positions and opens up opportunities for new ones to develop. The new technology advocate who is insensitive to the political ramifications of the new system will face unpleasant, unanticipated consequences.

Once the range of potential uses has been ascertained and appropriate users are acquainted with the new technology, management must decide whether to put the technology permanently into place. At this juncture, the assimilation project moves from the innovative phases to the control phases.

Control Phase. The focus of the control phase is to develop and install controls for the new technology. Whereas the main concern during the innovation phase was effectiveness of the technology, control-phase management is concerned with efficiency. In installing the necessary controls, management's task is to define the goals and criteria for technology utilization. The most effective leadership style here is one of "informing," with lower interpersonal involvement relative to task orientation. During this phase, the organizational users (non-IT staff) are better able to judge the appropriateness and feasibility of the new technology to their tasks than they were during the innovation phase. The traditional IT organization and associated administrative systems are generally appropriate for this task.

For technologies in the later aspect of the control phase, IT managers typically exhibit a "delegating" leadership style. Interpersonal involvement and task orientation are low. With operation procedures now well understood and awareness high, effective managers let subordinates "run the show."

MEASURING AND MANAGING CAPACITY

The less one knows about computer hardware/software/networking technology, the more certain one tends to be in matters of capacity. In reality, the various hardware/software/network elements tend to interact in such a complex way that diagnosing bottlenecks and planning long-term capacity require a high degree of skill. To understand capacity and its key changeability, we must consider these factors:

1. Capacity comes in much smaller, less-expensive increments than it did a decade ago. In many organizations, this has created an "asymmetric reward structure" for capacity excesses versus shortages; that is, a shortage of capacity in critical operating periods is very expensive, while the cost of extra capacity is very low. For these organizations, a decision to carry excess capacity is sound.

2. A capacity "crunch" develops with devastating suddenness. During one six-month period, for example, a mid-sized sign manufacturer operated with few difficulties with a 77 percent load on the central processing unit (CPU) during peak demand. Senior management refused to listen to IT management's warning that they were on the edge of a crisis and would not permit ordering additional equipment. During the next six months, the introduction of two new minor systems and the acquisition of a major contract brought the CPU load during the first shift to 85 percent. This created a dramatic erosion in on-line systems response time and a steady stream of missed schedules on the batch systems. Working through weekends and holidays failed to alleviate the situation. To the untutored eye, the transition from a satisfactory to a thoroughly unsatisfactory situation occurs suddenly and dramatically.

3. There has been an explosion of diagnostic tools, such as software monitors and simulation packages, that assist in identifying systems' capacity problems. These tools are analytical devices and thus are no better than the ability of the analyst using them and the quality of the forecasts of future demands to be placed on the systems. In firms where operations play a vital role, these tools and their contributions have led to significant growth in both the number and quality of technical analysts in the IT operations group.

4. A dramatic increase has occurred in the number of suppliers of computer peripherals, as well as an explosion of open systems architectures. This has sharply reduced the number of firms that are totally committed to a single vendor's equipment. Additional features, coupled with attractive prices of specialist manufacturers, have pushed many firms in the direction of IT vendor proliferation. Combined with the integration of telecommunications and office support, this phenomenon makes the task of capacity planning more complex and increases the need to referee vendor disputes when the firm's network fails.

5. Complex trade-offs must be made between innovation and conservatism. Companies in which IT offers significant (in terms of overall company profitability) cost reductions or the possibility of significant strategic competitive advantage should push innovation much harder than other firms. Similarly, firms very dependent on smooth minute-to-minute operation of existing systems must be more careful about introducing new technology into their networks than other firms. Unanticipated interaction with existing systems could jeopardize reliable operation of key parts of the organization. (That was at the root of the AT&T network collapse noted at the beginning of the chapter. Inadequately tested switching software at one AT&T node interacted in an unexpected way with the rest of the network's software.)

6. The cost and disruption caused by change may outweigh the specific advantages associated with a particular technology. Therefore, skipping a generation of change is desirable in some circumstances, although this must be examined carefully from two perspectives:

    a. The system design practices of the 1960s and early 1970s were quite different from those of today. Some firms, eager to postpone investment, have stayed too long with the older systems and have exposed themselves to great operational risk when they have tried to implement massive change in impossibly short periods of time. In many cases, the results have been disastrous. (These time pressures were triggered either by external vendor decommitment of key components of an operating hardware/software configuration or an urgent need to modify software drastically to meet new competitive needs.) Software, like a building, depreciates. Because industry accounting practices, except for those of software companies, do not recognize this, it is very easy for general managers to overlook the problems of this aging asset. Fundamentally, too many operating managers mistakenly think of IT development as an annual operating expense as opposed to a capital investment or asset maintenance activity.

    b. Certain changes in the hardware/software configuration are critical if the firm is to be competitive; other changes cannot legitimately be considered essential. Investments in this latter category clearly can be postponed.

7. As investments in the products of small software and hardware vendors increase, the issues of vendor viability and product maintainability become important. The mortality rate among these small suppliers has been high since the early 1970s. When evaluating hardware vendors, the questions to consider are: If they go under, is there an acceptable, easily convertible alternative? Is it easy to keep existing systems going in both the short term and the long term? and What are the likely costs of these alternatives? In evaluating software vendors, the question is: Does the contract provide for access to source programs and documentation if the vendor goes out of business? An additional area of complexity is the vendor's posture toward program maintenance. This includes error correction and systems enhancements. How will these changes be charged? As noted earlier, experienced IT operations thinking is critical in these negotiations. When either the user or the systems and programming department purchased software without understanding the long-term operating implications, all too often the results have been very unhappy.

8. Finally, a hidden set of capacity decisions focuses on appropriate infrastructure backup—such as power, height above the flood plain, and adequate building strength for the weight of the equipment. The importance of the reliability of these items is often underassessed. For example, the temperature in a large metropolitan data center rose from 78 degrees to 90 degrees in a two-hour period, shutting down the entire operation. A frantic investigation finally found that, three floors down, a plumber had mistakenly cut off a valve essential to the cooling system room.

All the above points clearly show that capacity planning is a very complex subject requiring as much administrative thinking as technical thinking. Few organizations in the 1990s are building a new "factory"; rather, they are implementing a continuous program of renovation and modernization of their operations. This is a formidable and, unfortunately, often seriously underestimated task.

MANAGING THE IT OPERATIONS WORKFORCE

Personnel issues in the operations function have changed significantly in the past few years. Most dramatic has been the major reduction, and in *most* cases elimination, of the data input and preparation departments. The introduction of on-line data entry has not only changed the type of tasks to be done (keypunching, key verification, job-logging procedures, etc.), but has permitted much of this work to be transferred to the department that originates the transaction. Indeed, the work is often transferred to the *person* who initiates the transaction or it is a by-product of another activity (such as cash register sales of bar-coded items). This trend is desirable because it locates control firmly with the person most directly involved and it reduces costs. In some settings, however, it has been exceptionally difficult to implement, with users proving less enthusiastic than anticipated about taking over such accountability. Nevertheless, the large centralized data-entry departments have faded into history.

At the same time, jobs in the computer operations section are being altered significantly. For example,

1. Database-handling jobs are steadily being automated. The mounting of tapes and disks is automated and reduced. Many firms have successfully automated the entire tape library function.
2. The formerly manual functions of expediting and scheduling have been built into the computer's basic operating system, eliminating a class of jobs.
3. Consolidation of data centers allows significant staff reductions as well as reductions in software site rentals. In one company, a recent consolidation of 10 large data centers reduced staff from 720 to 380.
4. Establishing work-performance standards in this environment has become less feasible and less useful. As the data input function disappears and the machine schedules itself rather than being paced by the operator's performance, the time-and-motion performance standards of the 1960s and 1970s have become largely irrelevant. Inevitably, evaluating the performance of the remaining highly technical individuals has become more subjective. These people are either trouble-shooting problems or executing complex operating systems and facilities changes.

As these factors imply, the composition of the operations workforce has changed dramatically. The formerly large, blue-collar component has been virtually eliminated, while the technical and professional components have been increased significantly. In an environment of continuous technological change, the skills of these staff must continually be upgraded if they are to remain relevant.

Career Paths.   In this environment, career-path planning is a particular challenge. At present, three major avenues are available for professionals. Those with technical aptitude tend to move to positions in either technical support or systems development. A common exit point for console operators is as maintenance programmers. As a result of operations experience, they have developed a keen sensitivity to the need for thorough testing of systems changes. The second avenue is a position as a manager in operations, particularly in large organizations where management positions ranging from shift supervisors to operations managers are filled mostly through internal promotions. (The number of these jobs, however, is steadily decreasing.) Finally, in banks and insurance companies, in particular, there have been a number of promotions out of IT operations into other user positions in the firm. In the manufacturing sector, this avenue of opportunity has been rare. Any of these promotion paths, if given the proper attention, can make the operations environment an attractive, dynamic place to work.

Unionization. Although the trade union movement has been relatively inactive in the U.S. IT environment, it has been quite active in Europe and portions of western Canada. Organizing this department gives the union great leverage in many settings, because a strike by a small number of individuals can virtually paralyze an organization. For example, strikes by small numbers of computer operations staff in the United Kingdom's Inland Revenue Service have caused enormous disruptions in its day-to-day operations in the past. Changes in the skill mix that favor highly professional and technical staff suggest that this concern will be less important in the future.

In thinking about the potential impact of unionization, these points are important:

1. The number of blue-collar jobs susceptible to unionization has dropped dramatically. In the technology of the past generation, IT shops were more vulnerable to being organized than in the current or future generations.
2. The creation of multiple data centers in diverse locations tends to reduce a firm's vulnerability to a strike in one location. The networks of the future will reduce the risk even further. This has been a factor, although generally not the dominant one, in some moves toward distributed processing.
3. The inflexibilities that accompany unionization can pose enormous problems in this type of organization, given the frequency and unpredictability of operating problems and the need for high-technology skills. Further, the dynamics of technical change continuously transform IT operating functions and jobs. If the technology were ever to stabilize, the inflexibilities presented by organized labor would be of less concern.

Selection Factors for Operations Manager and Staff

Selecting the appropriate IT operations manager and key staff is crucial. Several factors generate the need for particular skills in different environments.

Scope of Activities. As scope widens from on-line satellite to knowledge-based systems, the IT activity demands greater diversity of staff, and the complexity of management increases dramatically. Significantly more sophisticated managerial skills are required.

Criticality of IT Operations Unit.   Firms that are heavily dependent on IT operations (factory and strategic) are forced to devote higher-caliber professional staff resources to this area. Uneven quality of support is very expensive for such companies.

Technical Sophistication of the Shop.   A shop heavily devoted to batch-type operations (there are still some around) with a relatively predictable workload and a nondynamic hardware/software configuration requires less investment in leading-edge management than does a shop with a rapidly changing workload in a volatile technical environment. The latter type of shop requires staff who can effectively lead such efforts as upgrading operating systems.

These factors suggest the impossibility of describing a general-purpose IT operations manager. Not only do different environments require different skills, but over time the requirements within an individual unit shift. The overall trend of the last decade is toward demand for an even higher quality of manager. The tape handler or console operator of the early 1970s has often proven inadequate for the job.

Human Issues in Managing the Workforce

A series of long-term human issues must be dealt with in managing the workforce effectively.

1. The problem of staff availability and quality is a long-term challenge for IT operations. In an environment demanding small numbers of highly skilled workers, intensified efforts are needed to attract quality individuals to the IT operations group. Career paths and salary levels require continuous reappraisal. In factory and strategic companies, IT operations must not be treated as an unwanted stepchild of the development group.
2. IT operations must develop appropriate links to both the users and the development group. The linkage to development is needed for ensuring that standards are in place so that both new systems and enhancements to existing ones are operable (without the development staff being present or on call every time the system is run) and that no unintended interactions with other programs and data files occur. Establishing a formal IT operations quality-assurance function is a common way to deal with this. No system is allowed to run on the network until it has been certified by the IT operations unit as meeting the company's standards. The user linkage is critical for ensuring that when an operating problem occurs, the user knows who in the IT operations unit can solve it—and for avoiding endless rounds of finger-pointing.
3. A long-term IT operations staff development plan that includes specific attention to training should be generated.

4. Issues concerning the quality of work life must be addressed continuously. These include such items as flexible time, three- or four-day workweeks, shift rotation, and so on.

No single ideal policy or procedure can address these issues. Rather, a continuous reassessment must occur to ensure that the best of current practice is being examined and that the unit does not inadvertently become frozen in obsolete work practices.

PRODUCTION PLANNING AND CONTROL

Setting Goals

Operations production planning is complicated by the multitude of goals an IT operations function may have. Among the most common goals are these:

- To ensure a high-quality, zero-defect operation. All transactions will be handled correctly, no reports will be lost or missent, and so forth.
- To meet all long-term job schedules (or to meet them within some standard).
- To be able to handle unanticipated, unscheduled jobs, processing them within x minutes or hours of receipt provided they do not consume more than 1 percent of the CPU resource.
- To provide an average response time on terminals for key applications during the first shift of x seconds. No more than 1 percent of transactions will require more than y seconds.
- To limit day-to-day operating costs to specified given levels. Capital expenditure for IT equipment will not exceed the budgeted levels.

Establishing Priorities

By and large, IT operations goals are mutually conflicting: all of them cannot be optimized simultaneously. Where IT operations support is critical to achieving corporate missions (factory and strategic), establishing priorities requires senior management guidance. In environments where it is less critical, these goals can be prioritized at a lower level. Failure to set priorities in a manner that makes for widespread concurrence and understanding of the trade-offs to be made has been a primary cause of the poor regard in which some operations units have been held. When their goals were not prioritized, their task has been impossible.

A firm's priorities give insight into how it should address two other items: organization of the capacity and ensuring consistent operating policies.

Organization of Capacity.   Whether to have a single, integrated computer configuration or a series of modular units, either within a single data

center or in multiple data centers, is an important strategic decision—
assuming the nature of the workload allows a choice. Setting up modular
units ("plants within a plant") allows specialized delivery of service for
different applications and users. These multiple factories also allow for
simpler operating systems and for quite different types of performance
measures and management styles to be implemented for each. This focused
factory concept has been too often overlooked in IT operations.

Consistent Operating Policies.　Uncoordinated management specialists, each trying to optimize his or her own function, may create a
thoroughly inconsistent and ineffective environment. For example, in a
large insurance company, the following policies were simultaneously operational:

- An operator wage and incentive system based on meeting all long-term
  schedules and minimizing job setup time.
- A production control system that gave priority to quick-turnaround,
  small-batch jobs meeting certain technical characteristics.
- A quality-control system that focused on zero defects, ensuring that no
  reruns would have to take place.
- A management control system that rewarded both low operating budgets
  and low variances from the operating budgets. Among other things, this
  control incentive had pushed the company toward a very constrained
  facilities layout as a means of minimizing costs.

While each policy might make sense individually, collectively they were
totally inconsistent and created tension and friction within the IT operations group. Not surprisingly, the key users' perceptions of service varied
widely.

Strategic Impact of IT Operations

The management focus brought to IT operations depends on the IT function's role in the firm. IT operations in the "support" and "turnaround"
categories can appropriately be oriented toward cost efficiency. Deadlines,
while important to meet, are not absolutely critical to these organizations'
success. Quality control, while important on the error dimension, can be
dealt with in a more relaxed way. It is appropriate to take more risks on the
capacity dimension for both job-shop and process-type IT operations in
order to reduce the firm's financial investment. Less formal, less expensive
backup arrangements are also appropriate. Finally, corners can safely be
cut in user-complaint response mechanisms.

The factory type of operation poses very different challenges, because IT
is integrally woven into the ongoing fabric of the company's operations.
Zero-defect accuracy, fast response time, and prompt schedule-meeting are
absolutely critical. Capacity to meet various contingencies is also critical,

because severe competitive damage may occur otherwise. Consequently, the issue of capacity needs to be managed more carefully, and more reserve capacity for contingencies usually needs to be acquired. New operating systems and hardware enhancements must be very carefully evaluated and managed to avoid the danger and financial damage of downtime. These factors cause a company to make any necessary cost-reduction decisions more carefully than in organizations less dependent on IT service.

The strategic operation faces all the issues of the factory operation, plus several others. Capacity planning is more complicated because it involves major new services, not simply extrapolating figures for old services with new volume forecasts. A stronger liaison must be maintained with users in order to deal with the potential service disruptions associated with adding new technology and new families of applications. These factors suggest the need for more slack in both capacity and budget to protect vital corporate interests.

Implementing Production Control and Measurement

The issues raised in the previous section show why only an evolutionary, adaptive control and reporting structure will work. The indexes, standards, and controls that fit one organization at a particular time will not meet their own or other organizations' needs over an extended period of time as both the technology and the organization evolve more toward on-line systems.

Within the appropriate goals for the operations department, there is a critical need to establish both performance indexes and performance standards. This allows actual data to be compared against standards. Performance indexes should include items in the following areas:

- Cost performance, both aggregate performance and the performance for different IT services.
- Staff turnover rates.
- Average and worst 5 percent response times for different services.
- Quality of service indicators, such as amount of system downtime, by service.
- Number of user complaints, by service.
- Number of misrouted reports and incorrect outputs.
- Usage of services—such as word processing, electronic mail, and computer utilization—and peak hours.
- Surveys of user satisfaction with service.

While the data generated may be quite voluminous, the data (including trends) should be summarizable in a one- to two-page report each week or month. Such quantitative data provide a framework for making qualitative assessments of performance against the standards that reflect the department's goals.

SECURITY

One of the emotional topics related to IT operations is how much security is necessary for protecting the site and how much actually exists. This complex subject is discussed only briefly here in order to call attention to its nature and importance. Exhaustively covered in other sources, the breadth of the issue is defined by the following points:

1. Perfect security is unattainable at any price. The key need is to determine the point of diminishing returns for an organization's particular mission and geography. Different units in the organization and different systems may have distinctly different security requirements.

2. Smaller organizations for which the IT activity is critical have found it desirable to go to something like the SUNGUARD solution, in which a consortium of firms funded the construction and equipping of an empty data center. If a member firm incurs a major disaster, this site is available for use. Backing up networks, today's major challenge, has made this much more complex.

3. Large organizations for which IT activity is fundamental to their functioning and existence appropriately will think about this differently. Such firms will be strongly motivated to establish multiple remote centers (to avoid the investment bank's experience described at the beginning of the chapter). Duplicate data files, extra telecommunications expense, and duplicate staff and office space all make this an expensive (although necessary) security measure. These firms have concluded that if they do not back themselves up, no one else will. The architecture of these networks is extraordinarily complex to design in an efficient, yet responsive, fashion.

4. For organizations in which the IT operation is less critical, appropriate steps may include arranging backup with another organization, which is very hard in a networked world. Another alternative is to prepare a warehouse site with appropriate wiring, telephone lines, air conditioning, and so on. (In a real emergency, locating and installing the computer is the easiest thing to do. Locating and installing all the other items consumes much more time.) Backing up the network is much more complex than just data centers. The insurance company in the example at the beginning of the chapter now has two entirely separate networks with two carriers and carefully allocates work between them in order to reduce their operational vulnerability. Reuters news service has processing nodes around the world with multiple paths out of each node. If one path fails, the network is not impacted; if a node fails, the network degrades but does not fail in all respects.

5. Within a single site, a number of steps can be taken to improve security. Listed here are some of the most common, each of which has a different cost associated with it.

a. Limiting physical access to the computer room. Methods from simple buzzers to isolated "diving chamber" entrances can be used.

b. Complex, encrypted access codes that serve to deny file and system entry to unauthorized personnel through the network. External hackers have successfully penetrated a large number of organizations that have not paid attention to this item.

c. Surrounding the data center with chain-link fences, automatic alarms, and dogs. Monitoring access to inner areas by guards using remote TV cameras.

d. Ensuring an uninterrupted power supply, including banks of batteries and stand-alone generators.

e. Storing a significant number of files off-site and updating them with a high level of frequency.

f. Using a Halon inert gas system to protect the installation in case of fire.

g. Systematically rotating people through jobs, enforcement of mandatory vacations (with no entry to building allowed during vacation time), and physical separation of IT development and operations staff.

h. Rigorous procedures for both certifying new programs and change in the existing programs.

This is merely an illustrative list and in no sense is intended to be comprehensive. Sadly, it is extremely difficult to fully secure files in a world of PCs, viruses, and floppy disks that go home at night.

PRIVACY

An explosive issue that cuts across the IT applications world of the 1990s is IT's increasing intrusiveness into privacy. This issue transcends all aspects of the field of information technology and is included in this chapter only as a matter of organizational convenience. Consider the following examples.

A consumer foods company uses information from redeemed coupons and rebate forms to create a database for targeted marketing. It is assailed in a national consumer-advocacy publication with the headline "Smile—You're on Corporate Camera!"

An entrepreneur realizes that he can easily tie together several credit bureau databases and some other sources of information (such as motor vehicle records) about individuals. When he begins to market this service to small businesses for credit checking and preemployment screening, the state assembly passes a bill that would significantly regulate his activities.

Many credit bureaus offer services in which mailing lists are "prescreened" according to a customer's stated criteria. In addition, some credit bureaus transfer selected information from their credit files to marketing databases, from which mailing lists are sold for targeted marketing. These policies became major topics of discussion in a House of Representatives subcommittee hearing, where there were many calls for additional federal legislation.

These examples—all of which occurred in 1990—demonstrate an increasing challenge to managers for the 1990s. Societal concerns about information privacy—the belief that limits are needed on access to information about individuals—are increasing, and these concerns could erupt in the next decade with considerable force. Unless proactive steps are taken, firms will find themselves grappling with these anxieties in two forms: public-opinion backlash against various computerized processes and a tightened legal environment with additional governmental control.

The Roots of the Privacy Issue

Two forces are behind this focus on privacy in the 1990s: the new technology capabilities that allow these new applications and the vacuum surrounding the distinction between "right and wrong."

Technological Capabilities. Much more information is in computer-processable form today. Information that was previously stored in hand-written or typed paper files is now digitally encoded and electronically accessible from thousands of miles away.

Owing to less-expensive storage devices, faster processors, and the development of relational database techniques and structured query languages, it has become both more feasible and vastly more economical to cross-classify information. Likewise, passing and correlating information between organizations is now relatively inexpensive and easy to accomplish. As networks become commonplace, new strategic applications pool data from different sources.

In addition to the potential intrusiveness of this pooling is the almost unsolvable issue of correcting errors in information. In many cases, it is virtually impossible to stop the trickle of errors as data pass from firm to firm.

Not only have both the speed/cost of computing and network availability undergone phenomenal improvements in the last decade, but the trend is accelerating; thus, in the future, it will be even easier and more economical to search for information and store it. As personal computers and local area networks proliferate across organizations in the hands of nonsystems personnel, people will propagate uncontrolled databases (on personal hard disks and file servers), and the number of people accessing networks will increase.

Add to this the growing use of artificial intelligence. As more decision rules are automated in expert systems, perceptions of these problems may be amplified as mistakes are inexorably carried to their logical conclusion in a documented form.

Taken together, these technological trends could easily and inexpensively lead to applications that would create unacceptable intrusions into people's privacy.

Ethical Concerns. The technological forces operate in a large vacuum regarding right and wrong. Situations have been created for which the rules of behavior that worked well in earlier decades do not offer meaningful guidance. We are confronting a new set of policy decisions. While it is true that individuals and organizations may be inappropriately harmed by certain applications and activities, the degree of the impact is uneven. Some practices can be deeply damaging to people, while many others lie in the category of "merely inconvenient." Some inconvenient results of increased information gathering—such as mailbox clutter—are accepted by many as the "cost of progress," but society will eventually draw a line to protect against other applications that are recognized as more damaging.

For example, tenant-screening services, which allow landlords to exchange information about problems with former tenants, can lead to the unjust refusal of an individual's rental application if incorrect information is in the database or if mistaken identification occurs.[6] More often than not, however, such services protect landlords from losses incurred in renting to tenants who have already proven to be bad risks, and they thereby facilitate lower rents. Will society demand that such screening services be restrained?

The Implications

Questions for Organizations. Firms must anticipate potential privacy problems as they make decisions and take action to avoid negative public opinion and extreme legislative responses to inflammatory charges. Good planning may help your firm avoid the cost of adapting to new rules. Some critical questions regarding privacy issues are discussed here.

Storage of Information. *Is there any information in the organization's files that should not be there? If it were brought to light that such information was being collected and stored, would there be a public backlash?* For example, several insurance firms have recently struggled with this issue as it applies to AIDS test results and where and how this information should be disseminated. Some advocates became outraged when they learned that individuals' files contained notations about positive test results. Lawsuits and numerous pieces of legislation (mostly at a state level) followed quickly.

---

[6]Some of the examples used here are adapted from *The Privacy Journal,* an independent monthly newsletter based in Washington, DC.

Use of Information. *Is information being used for the purposes individuals believed it was being collected to serve?* Many individuals who provide information for what they believe is one purpose become angry when they learn it has been used for another. For example, a credit card issuer came under legal scrutiny when it installed a computer system that could evaluate cardholders' purchasing histories for the purpose of enclosing targeted advertising material with their monthly statements. In another example, a car dealership installed an interactive computer system that asked potential customers to answer questions about their personalities and attitudes. The computer printed a "recommended car profile" for each customer. It also printed—with a different printer, in a back room—suggested sales strategy for the salesperson, based on the customer's answers. Had the potential customers known about this back-room printer, they might never have entered the dealer's showroom.

Sharing of Information. *Are pieces of information about individuals being shared electronically with other organizations? If so, would individuals approve of this sharing if they knew about it?* Certainly, extraordinary opportunities for gaining strategic advantage have come through such sharing activities (micromarketing strategies). However, some people object when a company with which they do business sells their names and addresses, purchasing histories, and other demographic details to other companies. If the shared information is highly sensitive—if, for example, it concerns individuals' medical or financial histories—the reaction to having it shared—sold even—is dramatically exacerbated.

Human Judgment. *Are decisions that require human judgment being made within appropriate processes?* Individuals legitimately become upset and request governmental protection when decisions that they feel require human judgment are being made without it. For example, an insurance company's decisions on whether to accept or reject new applicants—made within prescribed formulas and without direct human involvement—caused considerable difficulties when blindly applied in extraordinary situations that had not been contemplated when the rules were formulated.

Combining Information. *Are pieces of personal information from different sources combined into larger files?* The concerns of individuals and lawmakers are heightened when disparate pieces of information—even if innocuous in themselves—are pulled together. The possibility of creating a single profile of an individual's life is, to many, a threatening prospect. The entrepreneur who tied together several databases in order to provide "one-stop shopping" for several types of information through one vehicle faced this perception.

Error Detection and Correction. *Are appropriate procedures in place for preventing and correcting errors?* At issue here are both deliberate and inadvertent errors. Deliberate errors, which include unauthorized intrusions into databases, are often subject to audit controls. Inadvertent errors, on the other hand, are much more subtle and stubborn. They include misclassifications, data-entry errors, and the sorts of errors that arise when information is not updated as circumstances in people's lives change. It is impossible to achieve 100 percent error-free operation, but observers may reasonably ask whether the trade-offs a company makes for assuring accuracy are reasonable. If your organization were examined by lawmakers or consumer advocates, would you appear to be making the "correct" trade-offs?

An example from the public sector comes from the National Crime Information Center, a nationwide computer system linked to many state criminal-justice information systems. Outstanding warrants, parole violations, and other criminal data are often entered into local systems and are later "uploaded" to the national system. Law-enforcement agencies can then query the system to learn if individuals are wanted in other areas. Unfortunately, for a long time, problems with inaccurate data and mistaken identities were not uncommon, leading to improper arrests and incarcerations, and a number of lawsuits.

Other Issues.   An audit of the questions we have enumerated often reveals several items for action in the organization. Additional issues to be considered by firms include the following:

Long Term versus Short Term.   Line management should carefully think through each new use of information before they embrace it. In some cases, a "quick hit" for short-term profitability can yield disastrous results later. For example, an insurance company sold a list of its policyholders to a direct-marketing firm, earning a healthy fee. However, many policyholders determined that the company had done this—because of unique spellings of their names and other peculiarities—and were unhappy about it. The company received an avalanche of mail complaining about this use of their names and addresses, as well as a nontrivial number of policy cancelations, which brought the CEO to vow "never again." The short-term gain was not worth the long-term fallout.

Education.   Problems can be avoided through appropriate education initiatives. An organization's clients (customers or other individuals about whom information is stored) should be informed regarding the corporation's use of information about them when it strays from the narrow purpose for which it was collected. Clients should be told (1) what type of information about them is permanently stored in the corporation's files, (2) what is done with the information they provide, and (3) whether additional information from external sources is added to their files. This education process can take place in several forums, including inserts with monthly statements, special letters, and press releases. Corporations in particularly sensitive industries might provide toll-free telephone lines for clients' questions about information use.

Organizational Mechanism.   Through both an initial audit and on a continuing basis, the internal and external uses and distribution of data should be given close scrutiny—especially if the firm is in an industry where such data sharing is likely to occur, such as consumer marketing or financial services. In very sensitive situations, a standing Data Distribution Committee can provide a forum for evaluating these issues. Such a committee should have high visibility and comprise senior executives. It could also be augmented by outside advisers (such as corporate directors) to ensure that objective viewpoints are provided and that problems are approached with sufficient breadth.

As laws and public opinion change in the next decade, it will be necessary to check current and planned applications against evolving policies and attitudes. Data files should be organized in ways that facilitate such ad hoc evaluations. For example, one might be called upon to list all data elements that are exchanged between internal organizational entities and with external entities. Could your organization construct this list in a quick and credible way?

Conclusions.   Our discussion of these issues indicates the complexity of the privacy concerns growing up around IT use. Chief information officers and other members of senior management should brace themselves for intense scrutiny of their activities by both legislators and privacy advocates. No doubt, there will be more focus on commercial IT activities than on governmental ones in the 1990s. The tension between the effective functioning of commerce and individuals' rights to privacy will certainly become more pronounced. It is far better for the business community to be taking a voluntary, proactive stance now than to have to adopt a reactive posture later.

SUMMARY

IT operations management is a complex, evolutionary field. This is partly due to a changing technology that continually makes obsolete existing IT service delivery processes and controls, partly due to the continuing questions related to in-house versus outsourcing of the service, and partly due to the changing profile of the IT workforce. Major insights for dealing with these issues come from applying the understandings gained in managing technological change and manufacturing to this very special type of high-technology endeavor. Most large firms now know how to schedule and control multiprocessing batch computer systems working on numerical data from decentralized input stations. Building upon this base to include word processing, electronic mail, CAD, image processing, links to outside customers and suppliers, and a host of more decentralized IT activities is an extraordinarily challenging task. Underlying this, the most critical need for operations success is for recruiting, training, and retaining knowledgeable people to operate, maintain, and develop IT services. Finally, of course, are the issues of privacy, what forms of data files should be kept, what forms of cross-correlation are acceptable, and who should have access to them.

Chapter

9

Information Technology Management Processes

The management processes linking IT activities to the rest of the firm's activities are extraordinarily important. IT management control systems ensure that IT activities are congruent with other organizational activities; planning systems diagnose potential operating problems; and project management systems ensure that disciplines likely to optimize success of individual pieces of work are in place. This chapter emphasizes the first two processes—the IT management control and planning systems—while Chapter 11 will focus on project management.

MANAGEMENT CONTROL

The IT management control system, which integrates IT activities into the rest of the firm's operations, ensures that IT is being managed in a cost-efficient, reliable fashion, on a year-to-year basis. The planning process, conversely, takes a multiyear view in assimilating technologies and systems to match the company's evolving needs and strategies. Finally, the project management system *guides* the life cycle of individual projects (many of which last more than a year).

The management control system builds on the output of the planning process to develop a portfolio of projects, hardware/software enhancements and additions, facilities plans, and staffing levels for the year. It then monitors their progress, raising red flags for action when necessary. The broad objectives of an effective IT management control system include:

1. Facilitate appropriate communication between the user and provider of IT services and provide motivational incentives for them to work together on

a day-to-day, month-to-month basis. The management control system must encourage users and IT to act in the best interests of the organization as a whole—to motivate users to use IT resources appropriately and help them balance investments in this area against those in other areas.

2. Encourage effective utilization of the IT department's resources and educate users in the potential of existing and evolving technologies. In so doing, the management control system must guide the transfer of technology consistent with strategic needs.

3. Provide the means for efficiently managing IT resources and provide necessary information for investment decisions. This requires developing the standards for measuring performance and the methods for evaluating performance against the standards to ensure productivity; it should also help to facilitate "make" or "buy" decisions and make sure that existing services are delivered in a reliable, timely, error-free fashion.

In the 1960s and 1970s, IT management control systems tended to be very cost focused, for example, relying heavily upon ROI (return-on-investment) evaluations of capital investments. Where the technology was installed on a cost-displacement justification basis, these systems proved workable; however, where the computer was a competitive wedge (such as CAD/CAM or industrial robotics today) or where the technology was pervasively influencing the industry's structure of operations (such as in banking and financial services), cost analysis and displacement alone did not provide appropriate measurements of performance. Thus, developing additional management control techniques has been necessary.

Several years ago, for example, a large metropolitan bank instituted an expensive, complex charge-out system for improving user awareness of costs. Poorly thought out in broad context, the system generated a surge in demand for "cheap" minicomputers and inadequate investment in integrating network services; it triggered an overall decline in quality of central IT support in comparison with leading-edge banks and ultimately created market image and sales difficulties for the bank as a whole. It also led to soaring support/maintenance costs. The system ultimately had to be completely restructured to correct these problems.

Four special inputs now appear to be critical to an IT management control system structure for an organization:

1. The control system must be adapted to very different software and operations technology in the 1990s than that existing in the 1970s. An important part of this adaptation is becoming sensitive to the mix of phases of information technologies in the company. The more mature technologies must be managed and controlled in a tighter, more efficient way than those in early phases, which need protective treatment similar to that of a research development activity.

2. Specific corporate environmental factors determine the appropriate IT management control system, influencing what is workable. They include users' IT sophistication, geographic dispersion of the organization, stability of the management team, the firm's overall size and structure, nature of the relationship between line and staff departments, and so on.
3. The architecture of the organization's overall management control system and the philosophy underlying it influence IT control systems.
4. The system is affected by the perceived strategic significance of IT, in both the thrust of its applications portfolio and the ever more-important dependence on existing automated systems in many settings.

IT EVOLUTION AND MANAGEMENT CONTROL

Software Issues

An increasing percentage of central data processing software support is for maintenance, while most desktop software is bought. Thus, the operational changes necessary for keeping the business running have become intermixed with a stream of small, long-term, service-improving capital investments whose consistency and standards are vital. Since these two streams are not easily separated in many organizations, controls designed to influence operating expense maintenance are often inappropriately applied to stimulate or choke off systems enhancements that are really capital investments.

A second software issue arises with outside sourcing. As the percentage of development money devoted to outside software acquisition grows, management control systems designed for an environment where all sourcing was internal are often inappropriate for environments dominated by software make/buy alternatives.

Operations Issues

For IT operations, management control is complex because measuring and allocating costs to encourage desired behavior is difficult. In the short term, overall operations costs are relatively fixed, yet the mix of applications running on a day-to-day basis is volatile. The operations cost control problem is further complicated by the cost behavior of IT over time. Today, a replacement computer generally has 4 to 10 times the capacity and costs less than its predecessor. This has created an interesting control issue: Should the cost per unit of IT processing be lower in the early years (to reflect the lower load factor) so that it can be held flat over the life of the unit while permitting full (but not excessive) recovery of costs? Conversely, as utilization grows over the years, should the user's cost per unit of IT processing decline?

Selecting a particular method of cost allocation varies with the firm's experience with technology. In many organizations, the current control system gives broad management of desktop support to the user and complete management of networks to IT. As we have noted, however, desktops and telecommunications are so interrelated that such a separation is highly suspect and expensive. A critical contemporary problem is to ensure that IT control systems evolve along with changes in the organization's technical environment. For example, a large industrial organization gave out free desktop technology to stimulate users, while simultaneously charging for its traditional database time-sharing decision-support system. Very quickly, users started creating their own databases on the desktop equipment, underutilized the time-sharing, and made it difficult for important data elements to be shared among multiple users. Our discussion of control structure, while recognizing these issues, does not attempt to resolve them definitively.

Growth in User Influence.   A major stimulant to growth in IT usage has been the emergence of a group of users who are familiar with problem solving using information technology—although today's users are vastly different from those of even four years ago. After 20 years, it is clear that effective user applications generate ideas for additional applications. This is desirable and healthy, provided a control system exists to encourage appropriate appraisal of the new use's potential costs and benefits (broadly defined) to the organization. The absence of such controls can result in explosive growth (often unprofitable and poorly managed), requiring inefficient cost structures—or, alternatively, in little growth, with frustrated users obtaining necessary services surreptitiously (and also more expensively). Both situations erode confidence in the IT delivery process and its management control system. Also, for many of the new generation of user demands, articulating benefits is more difficult than determining costs. In repeated situations, the control system has given the hard cost of an applications implementation undue weight against the soft, but often very strategic, management benefits.

The control of information services thus presents a paradox: while the area is technologically complex, most factors critical to its effective, efficient use are human factors. This seemingly poses very familiar management control challenges; however, since both technology and user sophistication are continually changing, the types of applications are also changing. Many individuals are sufficiently set in their ways (reinforced by a control approach) that they find change difficult to implement and thus resist it. As a by-product, these users' perceptions of the change agent (IT staff) are often unnecessarily poor. For example, these users attribute all sorts of spurious effects to the introduction of new client-server architectures, LANS, and so on.

External and Internal Factors. Forces of change also exist in external items such as patterns of external computation and in numerous internal strategic items. Internal changes include the addition of new customers and products, new office locations, and modifications in the organization. A well-designed management control system recognizes these changes and handles them appropriately.

Geographic and Organizational Structure. Other important control aspects relate to the organization's geographic dispersion and size. As the number of business sites grows and staff levels increase, substantial changes may be needed in organizational structure, corporate management control, and IT management control. Informal personnel supervision and control appropriate for a more limited setting can fall apart in the larger, more dispersed setting. Similarly, the nature of relationships between line and staff departments within the company influences expectations about the evolving IT-user relationship and thus the appropriate IT management control.

An important aspect of the IT management control architecture is the firm's organizational structure. Over time, it becomes increasingly difficult to manage with good results an IT organization whose control architecture is sharply different from that of the rest of the firm. A firm with a strong functional organization that maintains the central services function as an unallocated cost center may find it appropriate to keep IT as an unallocated cost center. Conversely, a firm that is heavily decentralized into profit or investment centers or that traditionally charges out for corporate services is propelled down the path of charging for corporate IT activities—and may go as far as setting it up as a profit or investment center.

Corporate Control Process

In concept, then, the IT management control system should be similar to that of the corporation. Ideally, as mentioned later in the chapter, there is a multiyear plan linked to the overall business strategy, which, in turn, is linked to a budget process that allows the responsible managers to negotiate their operating budgets. As such, IT budgeting should be compatible with the overall business budgeting. If business planning primarily consists of an annual budget with periodic follow-up of performance during the year, however, a very difficult environment exists for IT management control. Implementing many sizable IT changes can easily take two or more years—including as much as a year to formulate, select, and refine the appropriate design approach. Thus, an IT organization often must maintain at least a three-year view of its activities to ensure that resources are available to meet these demands. In many cases, this extends the IT planning horizon beyond the organization's planning horizon.

To be useful, IT project plans must systematically and precisely identify alternative steps for providing necessary service. For example, to upgrade reservation service in a large hotel chain, the IT department, in concert with key hotel managers, had to project the type of service the hotels would need four years hence in order to select the proper terminals and provide an orderly transition to the new system over a 30-month period. A major bottleneck in this massive, one-time, 600-terminal installation was a corporate planning and control approach that extended only one year into the future.

This combination of short corporate time horizons, long IT time horizons, and technical innovation can generate intense corporate management control conflicts. These conflicts, which can only be resolved by repeated judgments over time, raise two major clusters of managerial issues.

1. How congruent/similar should the IT management control architecture and process be with that of other parts of the organization? Where differences exist, how can the dissonance best be managed? Should it be allowed to exist long term?
2. How can the tension between sound control and timely innovation best be balanced?

Control typically depends on measuring costs against budgets—actual achievements versus predictions—and returns against investments. Innovation calls for risk taking, gaining trial experience with emerging technologies; it relies on faith and, at times, moving forward despite unclear objectives. A portfolio excessively balanced in either direction poses grave risks. (As will be discussed in Chapter 10, different companies will balance their portfolios quite differently.)

Strategic Impact of IT on the Corporation

An important consideration in determining how closely the IT control system should match the business's planning/control process is the strategic importance of IT systems developments for the next three years. If these developments are very strategic, then close linkage between corporate control and IT control is important, and any differences between the two will cause great difficulty. Additionally, IT investment decisions and key product development innovations must be subject to periodic top-management review.

The control system for these strategic environments must encourage value-based innovations, even if only one out of three will pay off. Often, the key challenge is to encourage the generation, evaluation, and management of suggestions for new services from multiple unplanned sources while maintaining adequate control. Several now-defunct brokerage houses and soon-to-be-merged banks were unable to do this.

If IT is not strategic to the business but is more a "factory" or "support" effort, congruency of links to the rest of the business planning and control activities is not as critical. IT can more appropriately develop an independent control process to deal with its need to manage changing user demand and the evolving technology. A factory environment, for example, must emphasize efficiency controls, while a "turnaround" should focus on effective utilization of new technology.

A useful way of looking at management control was developed by Ken Merchant,[1] who suggested that controls can be grouped into three categories: results controls, personnel controls, and action controls.

- *Results* controls focus on the measurement of concrete results; they include such measurements as amount of profit, percentage of variance from the budget, number of items procured/hour versus the budget, and the like.
- *Personnel* controls focus on hiring practices, types of training and testing in place, evaluation procedures, and so on.
- *Action* controls involve the establishment and monitoring of certain protocols and procedures; examples include segregation of duties, establishment of certain task sequences, control of access to certain areas, and so on.

All of these are important in the IT context and will be discussed. Because of the special managerial problems historically associated with results control issues, however, the rest of this chapter pays particular attention to them.

Looking Ahead: Other Aspects of Control

To achieve desired results, the specific approach to IT management control is tailored to an organization, based on one or more of the dimensions discussed. Further, as circumstances change, it will evolve over time. The remainder of the chapter describes additional key factors that influence selection of control architecture (financial), control process (financial and nonfinancial), and the audit function. Briefly introduced below, each aspect of control is discussed in depth later in the chapter.

Control Architecture. *Should the IT function be set up as an unallocated cost center, an allocated cost center, or a profit center?* Each alternative generates quite different behavior and motivation, and each decision is a

---

[1] Kenneth A. Merchant, *Control in Business Organizations,"* (Marshfield, MA: Pitman Publishing, 1986.)

fundamental one; once made, it is not lightly changed. Finally, what nonfinancial measurements should be designed to facilitate effective use of IT?

Control Process, Financial and Nonfinancial.   *What form of action plan is most appropriate?* Typically, this is represented by the annual budget and drives both operations and project development. What forms of periodic reporting instruments and exception (against budget targets) reporting tools are appropriate during the year? These forms change much more frequently than architectural forms.

Audit Function.   Issues here include ensuring that an IT audit function exists, that it is focused on the right problems, and that it is staffed appropriately.

RESULTS CONTROL ARCHITECTURE

Unallocated Cost Center

Establishing the IT activity as an unallocated cost center is a widely used approach offering many advantages. When IT is essentially free to users, user requests are stimulated and user experimentation is encouraged. This climate is particularly good for technologies in phase 1 or 2 of their assimilation into the firm. The lack of red tape makes it easier for the IT department to sell its services, and all the controversy and acrimony over the IT charge-out process is avoided, since no charge-out system exists. Further, expenditures for developing and operating IT accounting procedures are very low.

In aggregate, these factors make this a good alternative for situations in which the IT budget is small. Innovation is facilitated in settings where financial resource allocation is not a high-tension activity. A large bank, operating as an unallocated cost center, for example, introduced electronic mail, spreadsheets, and word processing over a two-year period. The most senior levels had resolved that this infrastructure was critical to long-term operational viability; the lack of an end-user charge-out system was seen as an important facilitator to its introduction.

On the other hand, treating IT as an unallocated cost center can pose significant problems. With no financial pressure, the user can quickly perceive IT as a free resource, and everyone wants a piece of the action. This perception can rapidly generate a series of irresponsible user requests for service that may be difficult to turn down. Further, where staff or financial resources are short, the absence of a charge-out framework may excessively politicize IT resource-allocation decisions.

The unallocated cost center also insulates the IT department from competitive pressures and external measures of performance, permitting operational inefficiencies to develop or to be hidden. Further, this approach fits the management control structure of some firms poorly (e.g., firms with a strong tradition of charging out corporate staff services to users). Finally, by blurring important revenue/cost trade-offs, an unallocated cost center poses particular problems for organizations where IT charges are perceived to be both large and strategic. In combination, these pressures explain why many firms that start with an unallocated cost center approach evolve another approach, at least for their more mature technologies and users.

One approach widely followed is to keep IT as an unallocated cost center but to inform users through memos what their development and operations charges would be if a charge-out system were in place. Without raising the frictions (described next) associated with charge-out procedures, this shows users that they are not using a free resource of the corporation and gives them an idea of the magnitude of their charges. The approach is often adopted as a transitional measure when a firm is moving IT from an unallocated cost center to some other organizational form. Unfortunately, however, a memo about a charge does not have the same bite as the actual assignment of the charge.

Allocated Cost Center and Charge-Out

From a corporate perspective, establishing the IT activity as an allocated cost center has the immediate virtue of helping to stimulate honesty in user requests. This approach fits rather well the later phases of technology assimilation, where the technology's usefulness has been widely communicated within the firm. While it may open up heated debate about costs, it avoids controversy about whether an internal IT activity should be perceived as a profit-making entity. An allocated approach particularly fits environments that have a strong tradition of corporate services charges.

Allocation Problems. The allocated cost center introduces a series of complexities and frictions, however, since such a system necessarily has arbitrary elements in it. The following paragraphs suggest some practical problems that come from allocating IT department costs to users (whether in a cost center or via some other approach).

The first problem is that the IT charges will be compared to IT charges prepared both by other companies in the same industry and by outside service organizations, raising the possibility of misleading and invidious conclusions. The words *misleading* and *invidious* are related, because the prices prepared by other organizations often have one or more of the following characteristics:

1. The service being priced out is being treated as a by-product rather than as a joint costing problem, and thus the numbers may be very misleading.

2. IT is being treated under a management control system different from that of the company making the evaluation (that is, a profit center in one organization and a cost center in the other); thus, the cost comparison is highly misleading because the charges have been developed under very different bases. Communication costs, for example, are treated very differently across organizations, with many firms literally not knowing what their full communications budget is.

3. An independent IT services firm or an in-house operation selling services to outside customers may deliberately produce an artificially low price as a way of buying short-term market share; thus, their prices may be perceived as fair market when in fact they are nothing of the sort over the long term.

Since the prices produced by other companies are not the result of an efficient market, comparing them to in-house prices may easily produce misleading data for management decisions.

Another issue of concern is innovation. Unless carefully managed, the charge-out system tends to discourage phase 1 and phase 2 research projects. These activities must be segregated and managed differently from projects utilizing the more mature technologies. In our view, nothing necessarily useful is accomplished by charging 100 percent of all IT costs to the users. Segregating as much as 15 to 25 percent as a separately managed, emerging-technology function and including it in corporate over-head (after careful analysis) can be a sound strategy.

On a more technical note, in the majority of companies charging out IT costs today, two major concepts underlie the charge-out process:

1. The charge-out system for IT operations costs uses a very complex formula (based on use of computer technology by an application) that spreads the costs in a supposedly equitable fashion to the ultimate users. Featuring terms such as *EXCP,* the concept is that users should bear computer costs in relation to their pro rata use of the underlying resource.

2. The charge-out system ensures that all costs of the activity are passed to consumers of the service. Not infrequently, this involves users' reimbursing all IT operations costs the firm incurs each month and certainly by year-end.

Rigorous application of these concepts has led to a number of unsatisfactory consequences from the user's perspective. Most important, in many cases the charges are absolutely unintelligible and unpredictable to the end user, as they are clothed in technical jargon and highly affected by whether it has been a heavy or light IT-activity month. There is no way for the user to predict or control the charges short of disengaging from the IT activity entirely. This was one reason for the explosion of stand-alone minis and desktops in the early and mid-1980s.

Not infrequently, the charges are highly unstable. The same application processing the same amount of data run at the same time of the week will cost very different amounts from week to week depending on what else happens to be running in IT operations during the week. In addition, if all unallocated costs are charged out to the users at the end of the year, they are often hit with an entirely unwelcome and unanticipated surprise, which generates considerable hostility.

The charges tend to be artificially high in relation to incremental costs. As mentioned earlier, this can cause considerable IT-user friction and encourage the user to examine alternatives that may optimize short-term cost behavior at the expense of the long-term strategic interests of the firm.

In addition, in both operations and development, this approach makes no attempt to hold IT uniquely responsible for variances in IT efficiency. Rather, all efficiency variances are directly assigned to the ultimate users, which creates additional friction and allegations of IT irresponsibility and mismanagement. Finally, administration of a charge-out system of this type frequently turns out to be very expensive.

These factors in combination have generated a number of charge-out systems that do not satisfactorily meet the needs of many organizations. We believe this is a direct result of the technical and accounting foundations of the system. For most situations, technology and accounting are the wrong disciplines to bring to the problem. The task can be better approached as a problem in applied social psychology: What type of behaviors do you want to trigger in the IT organization and the users? What incentives can be provided to help assure that as they aim for their individual goals, they are moving in a more or less congruent fashion with the overall goals of the corporation?

The design of such a system is a very complex task, requiring trade-offs along many dimensions. As the corporation's needs change, the structures of the charge-out system will also have to change. Critical questions to ask include:

1. Should the system be designed to encourage use of IT services (or components thereof), or should it set high barriers for potential investments?
2. Should the system encourage IT to focus on efficiency or on effectiveness? The answer to this question may well evolve over time.
3. Should the system favor the use of internal IT resources or outside resources?
4. What steps must be taken to ensure that the system is congruent with the organization's general control architecture, or if it is not, to ensure that the deviation is acceptable inside the firm?

Desirable Characteristics.   While the answers to these questions will dictate different solutions in different settings, some generalizations fit most settings and represent the next step in the evolution of a charge-out system. First, for an IT charge-out system to be effective, users must understand it—that is, the system needs to be simple. Again and again, evidence suggests that a chargeout system that grossly distorts the underlying electronics but that users can understand is vastly preferable to a technically accurate system that no one can comprehend. Put another way, user understanding that encourages even partial motivation and goal congruence is better than no motivation or goal congruence. In this context, systems that are based on an agreed-upon standard cost per unit of output are better than those that allocate all costs to whoever happened to use the system. Even better (and a clear trend today) is designing these standards, not in IT resource units, but in transactions that users understand (for example, so much per paycheck, so much per order line, so much per inquiry), where the prices of these transactions are established at the beginning of the budget year.

A second desirable characteristic of an IT operations charge-out system is that it should be perceived as fair and reasonable on all sides. In an absolute technical sense, it does not have to *be* fair; it is enough that all involved believe that it is fair and reasonable. In this vein, the IT operations charge-out system should produce replicable results; processing a certain level of transactions at 10 AM every Tuesday should cost the same amount week after week. If it does not, skepticism sets in and undermines the system's credibility.

A third desirable characteristic of an IT operations charge-out system is that it should distinguish IT efficiency issues from user utilization of the system. IT operations should be held responsible for its inefficiencies. Charging month-end or year-end cost-efficiency variances to the user usually accomplishes no useful purpose—it only raises the emotional temperature. After appropriate analysis of the causes for the variances, they normally should be closed directly to corporate overhead.

IT Maintenance and Development Charges.   The issues involved in charging for IT maintenance and systems development are fundamentally different from those of IT operations and must be dealt with separately. In advance of development and maintenance expenditures of any size, a professional contract should be prepared between IT and the users (as though it were a relationship with an outside software company). Elements of a good contract include:

1. A provision indicating that estimates of job costs are to be prepared by IT and that IT is to be held responsible for all costs in excess of those amounts.
2. Procedures for reestimating and, if necessary, canceling the job if job scope changes.
3. A provision that if a job is bid on a time-and-materials basis (very frequent in the software industry), a clear understanding must be

reached with the user, in advance, about what significant changes in scope would make the contract be reviewed.

For many systems (e.g., database systems), the most challenging, and sometimes impossible, task is to identify the definable user (or group thereof) with which to write the contract. Moreover, if the contract is written with one group of users but others subsequently join, are the new users charged at incremental cost, full cost, or full cost plus (because they have undertaken none of the development risks and are buying into a sure thing)? Neither easy nor general-purpose solutions to these issues are possible.

Example.   One company approached these issues in an effective way, in our judgment. It provided computer services to 14 user groups, many of which had very similar needs, spreading operations expenses as follows:

1. Every time a piece of data was inputted or extracted on a computer screen, a standard charge was levied on the user, irrespective of the type of processing system involved. This charge was understandable to the user.
2. Since all costs from the modems out (terminal, line) could be directly associated with a user in a completely understandable fashion, these charges were passed directly to the end user.
3. All report and other paper costs were charged to the user on a standard cost-per-ton basis, irrespective of the complexity of the system that generated them.
4. All over- or under-recovered variances were analyzed for indications of IT efficiency and then closed directly to a corporate overhead account, bypassing the users.

With respect to maintenance and development cost, the following procedures were used:

1. Items budgeted for less than 40 hours were charged directly to the users at a standard rate per hour.
2. Projects budgeted to take more than 40 hours were estimated by the IT organization. If the estimate was acceptable to the user, work would be done. Any variances in relation to the estimate were debited or credited to the IT organization, with the user being billed only the estimated amount.
3. A job-reestimating process handled potential changes in job specification, with the users having the option of accepting the new costs, using the old specifications, or jettisoning the job.
4. The IT organization budgeted research and development projects separately. IT was accountable to corporate for the costs of these jobs, and the users were not charged for them.

Over a several-year period, these procedures were remarkably successful in defusing tensions in user-IT relationships, enabling the groups to work together more easily.

Profit Center

A third frequently discussed and used method of management control is to establish the IT department as a profit center. Advocates of this approach note that it puts the inside service on the same footing as an outside one and brings marketplace pressures to bear; it also hastens the emergence of the IT marketing function, which, if well managed, will improve relationships with users; thus, the IT function is encouraged to hold costs down through efficiency and to market itself more aggressively inside the company. Further, IT management tends to deal promptly with excess IT capacity and is willing to run more risks on the user service side.

Excess capacity also encourages the IT department to sell services to outside firms—often a mixed blessing. When priced as incremental sales (rather than on a full-cost basis), these are unprofitable; in addition, many IT departments—excited by the volatile "hard" outside dollars as opposed to the captive "soft" inside ones—begin to give preferential treatment to outside customers, with a resulting erosion of service to inside users.

Establishing IT as a profit center may generate other problems. First, significant concern is often raised within the organization about the appropriateness of an inside "service department" establishing itself as a profit center, particularly when it does not sell any products outside the company. "Profits should come from outside sales, not service department practices" is the dominant complaint. The problem is exacerbated when, because of geography, shared data files, and privacy and security reasons, users do not have the legitimate alternative of going outside (unless the entire IT department is outsourced). Therefore, users perceive the argument that the profit center is subject to normal market forces as spurious.

At least in the short run, setting up the IT activity as a profit center leads to higher user costs, because a profit figure is added to user costs. Not only can this create user hostility, but in many settings it prevents the user from having legitimate full-cost data from the corporation for external pricing decisions.

Overall, the above issues must be addressed before an organization adopts a profit center approach. A deceptively intriguing idea on the surface, it has many pitfalls.

Summary.   Although many potential IT results control architectures are possible, none represents a perfect general-purpose solution. The challenge is to pick the one that best fits the company's general management control culture, current user-IT relationships, and current state of IT sophistication. The typical firm has approached these issues in an evolutionary fashion, rather than having selected the right one the first time.

Financial Reporting Process

Budget Objectives. A key foundation of the IT results control process is the budgeting system. Put together under a very complex set of trade-offs and interlocked with the corporate budgeting process, its first objective is to provide a mechanism for appropriately allocating financial resources. While the planning effort sets the broad framework for the IT activity, the budgeting process ensures fine-tuning in relation to staffing, hardware, and resource levels. A second objective of budgeting is to trigger a dialogue that ensures that organizational consensus is reached on the specific goals and possible short-term achievements of the IT activity; this dialogue is particularly important in organizations without a well-formed planning process. Finally, the budget establishes a framework around which an early warning system for negative deviations can be erected. In the absence of a budget, it is difficult to spot deviations in a deteriorating cost situation in time to take appropriate corrective action.

Budget Process. The budget system must involve senior management, IT management, and user groups. Its primary outputs include establishing the planned service levels and costs of central operations, the amount of internal development and maintenance support to be implemented, and the amount and form of external services to be acquired. The planned central IT department service levels and their associated costs must flow from review of existing services and the approved application development portfolio as well as user desire for new services. In addition, these planned service levels must take into account long-term systems maintenance needs. The budget must also ensure that there are appropriate controls on purchased IT services for the firm as a whole (software and hardware, such as desktop devices). The practices that organizations have assembled to understand the totality of their IT expenditures are very uneven. A dialogue between users and the IT department regarding anticipated needs and usage for the budget year helps clarify the IT department's goals and constraints and iteratively leads to generating a better IT plan and clarifying users' plans.

Example. A leading chemical company asks users and the IT department each to develop two budgets, one for the same amount of dollars and head count as the preceding year and one for 10 percent more dollars and 2 percent more headcount. In recent years, the IT department's proposals have involved an expansion of networks and desktop devices. To help ensure a dialogue, the main descriptions of key items are stated in user terms—such as the number of personnel records and types of pension planning support—with all the jargon relating to IT technical support issues being confined to appendixes. Both groups are asked to rank services of critical importance as well as to identify those that are of lower priority or that are likely to be superseded. A senior management group then spends a day reviewing a joint presentation that examines the budget in terms of probable levels of expenditure and develops a tentative ranking of the priority items. This meeting allows senior management to provide overall direction to the final budget negotiations between the two groups. The IT manager then consolidates priorities established in these discussions for final approval. This modified, zero-based budgeting approach is judged to have provided good results in this setting.

Budget Targets.   The IT budget should establish benchmark dates for project progress, clarify the type and timing of technical changeovers, and identify needed levels and mixes of personnel as well as set spending levels. A further mission is to identify important milestones and completion dates and tie them to the budget. This helps to ensure that periodic review will allow for early detection of variances from the plan. Budgeting key staff headcount and levels is a particularly important management decision: A major cause of project overruns and delays is lack of talent available to support multiple projects in a timely manner. Shortage of personnel must be dealt with realistically in fitting projects together—and should be done periodically through the year as well.

An important benefit of involving users and suppliers in the budget process is education. The IT department can understand each user department's particular needs for IT support and assess them relative to other departments'. At the same time, users become aware of what is possible with available technology and can better define their potential needs. In one financial institution, the budget process is heavily used as a stimulus for innovation. During budget preparation, both users and IT staff take many trips to other installations and receive information from their hardware/software suppliers to generate thinking on potential new banking services. This activity has significantly improved the relationship between the two groups over the past several years.

Periodic Reporting.   Effective monitoring of the department's financial performance requires a variety of tools, most of which are common to other settings. These normally include monthly reports highlighting actual performance versus the plan and exception reports as needed; design and operation of these systems are rather routine. Obvious issues to consider include: (1) Are budget targets readjusted during the year through a forecasting mechanism? (2) If so, is the key performance target actual versus budget or actual versus forecast? (3) Are budgets modified for seasonal factors, or are they prepared on a basis of one-twelfth of the annual expense each month?

The IT financial reporting task is a bit different because an IT organization requires a matrix cost reporting system as it grows in size. One side of the matrix represents the IT department structure and tracks costs and variances by IT organizational unit. The other side of the matrix tracks costs and variances by programs or projects.

Whether budget numbers and actual results should be reported in nominal dollars or in inflation-adjusted dollars is an issue of major importance for corporate management control systems today, particularly for multinational firms. It is, however, beyond the scope of this book.

Nonfinancial Reporting Process

At least in an operational sense, the nonfinancial controls are more important than the financial ones in assuring management that the IT function's day-to-day and month-to-month activities remain on target. One critical item here is regularly surveying (every six months) user attitudes toward the IT support they are receiving. Such surveys identify problems and provide a benchmark against which progress can be measured over time. Their distribution to the users for completion also clearly communicates that IT is concerned about user perception of service. Problems surfacing in surveys need to be acted on promptly if the instrument is to be an effective control.

Another category of controls relates to staff. Reports monitoring personnel turnover trends can provide critical early insight into the problems of this notoriously unstable group. These data allow timely action on such items as sensitivity of leadership, adequacy of salary levels, and workplace climate. In the same vein, formal training plans and periodic measurement of progress are important management tools for ensuring a professionally relevant group and maintaining morale.

Reports and other procedures generating absolute measures of operational service levels are very important in IT operations. These include data on such items as trends in network uptime, ability to meet schedules on batch jobs, average transaction response time by type of system, number of missends and other operational errors, and a customer complaint log. To be effective, these systems must be maintained and adhered to; when quality-control errors are allowed to creep in, performance appears better than it actually is. As noted in Chapter 8, all dimensions of service cannot be optimized simultaneously.

In relation to systems development, reports on development projects in terms of elapsed time and work-months expended (vis-à-vis budget) provide a crucial early warning system for assessing overall performance. The type of data needed and available varies widely by company. The company's maturity in dealing with information technology, the relative strategic role of IT development and operations, and the corporation's general approach to managerial control also influence both the form these issues take and the detail with which they are approached.

IT AUDIT FUNCTION

Located as a part of the office of the general auditor, the IT auditor function provides a vital check and balance on IT activity. Given "worms," interorganizational systems, and electronic fraud, it is hard to overstate the importance of this function, which forms the front line of defense in an increasingly complex networked world. There are three basic elements of the audit function mission. The first is ensuring that appropriate standards for IT development and operations have been developed and installed consistent with the control architecture. With changes in both technology and the organization's familiarity with it, developing these standards is not a onetime job but requires continuous effort.

The second element is ensuring that operating units adhere to these standards in order to help reduce operations errors and omissions and increase user confidence and satisfaction. This activity includes both regular progress reviews and surprise audits. Such audits should reduce fraud and loss; they also serve as a prod toward improving operating efficiency.

The third element is active involvement in the systems design and maintenance functions to ensure that systems can be easily audited and that maintenance changes do not create problems. Such involvement clearly compromises the supposedly independent mission of the auditor but is a necessary accommodation to the real world. It helps ensure the smooth running of the final system.

Successful execution of the above mission elements helps to reduce the amount of outside assistance needed by the firm; yet these seemingly straightforward tasks are very difficult to implement in the real world—for the following reasons.

1. Maintaining necessary auditing staff skills is difficult. Operating at the intersection of two disciplines (IT and auditing), good practice demands thorough mastery of both. Unfortunately, because IT auditing is frequently a "dead end" career path, staff members who are retained may be sufficiently deficient in both disciplines to be ineligible as practitioners in either. Higher salaries and visibly attractive career paths are essential preconditions to reversing this situation.
2. The "art" of IT auditing continually lags behind the challenges posed by new technologies. Understanding methodologies for controlling batch systems for computers, for instance, is not very relevant for a world currently dominated by complex operating systems, networks, and on-line technologies. Managing catch-up for such lags poses a significant IT auditing challenge for the future.
3. Management support for IT auditing has been uneven. Partly owing to the lack of formally defined requirements from an outside authority, support for a strong IT auditing function tends to be very episodic, with periods of strong interest following conspicuous internal or external

failure. This interest, however, tends to erode rapidly once the calamity has been corrected.

Overall, the role of the IT auditing function is poorly defined in most organizations at this time. Typically part of the internal auditing organization, and often not reporting to senior management, this function, in fact, deserves serious consideration at that management level.

SUMMARY

Although many IT management control issues resemble general management control concerns, there are several different aspects to them. The first arises from the rapid changes in the underlying technology and the long time span required for users to adapt to new technologies.

Phase 1 and phase 2 technologies require a commitment to R&D and user learning that directly conflicts with the charge-out techniques appropriate for phase 3 and phase 4 technologies. It is very easy for an organization to become too uniform in its control system, standardizing in order to use systems "efficiently" and stamping out innovation as a by-product. In most organizations today, different divisions (at varying stages of learning and using varying mixes of technologies) necessitate quite different control approaches. Further, as organizational learning occurs, other control approaches become appropriate; thus, quite apart from any breakthroughs in the general area of IT control methods, their practice in an organization undergoes continual evolution.

As IT becomes more firmly established in an operation, the penalties of uneven performance of technology may impose very severe consequences for the organization as a whole: action controls become vital. As a company, department, or system evolves from "turnaround" to "factory" to "support," very different control philosophies become appropriate.

Adding these issues to those concerning the changing corporate environment and evolving corporate control processes (in a world shifting from "make" to "buy" in software), the full complexity of the IT management control problem is apparent. Different organizations must adopt quite different control approaches, which then must evolve over time to deal with a changing corporate environment, changing strategic role of IT, and changing technologies.

PLANNING—A CONTINGENT FOCUS

Organizations launch IT planning efforts with great hope and often witness positive early results. Subsequently, however, many of these efforts run into difficulty. This section explores key managerial issues surrounding IT planning and provides guidelines to help assure success.

As information technology applications have grown in size and complexity over the past two decades, developing a strategy for assimilating these resources into firms' operations has grown steadily more important. A primary vehicle for strategy development is a sensitive architecture planning process, which, to be effective, must deal simultaneously with the realities of the firm's organizational culture, corporate planning culture, various technologies, and the importance of IT activities to the corporate goals.

Many studies have shown a positive correlation between user perception that IT activities are effective and a focused, articulated, appropriate planning process.[2] Since good standards do not exist for measuring the overall effectiveness of the IT activity, however, the evidence linking its effectiveness with planning processes is necessarily diffuse and fragmentary.

The material in this section is organized around four topics:

1. External and internal pressures generating the need for an articulated IT planning process.
2. Pressures limiting the value derived from IT planning.
3. The relationship between IT planning and corporate strategy formulation.
4. Corporate factors influencing the effectiveness of IT planning—tailoring the IT planning process to a specific firm.

PRESSURES TOWARD IT PLANNING

External (Corporate) Pressures

Although a variety of external pressures define the need for IT planning, the most important ones are discussed here.

Rapid Changes in Technology. Hardware and software continue to evolve rapidly, providing substantially different and potentially profitable IT applications from year to year. This requires continual interaction between IT staff and management groups in order to identify the technology changes significant to the company and develop appropriate plans and pilot projects. IT staff must make potential users, such as office managers and analytical staffs, aware of the implications (including the possible problems) of these new technologies so they can identify those potential new applications in their areas of responsibility that IT staff might not recognize.

---

[2] Philip Pyburn, "Information Systems Planning—A Contingency Perspective," DBA thesis, Harvard Business School, 1981.

As technology changes, planning grows increasingly important in order to avoid the problems of incompatible systems and inaccessible data files. The networked organization is becoming reality, and developing network linkages frequently requires implementation schedules of up to four years.

For example, an insurance company instituted a two- to three-year program for placing a portable PC containing expert financial counseling software into the hands of each of its 5,000 agents. A detailed plan was absolutely critical to maintaining senior management's confidence in the integrity of the program and the salesforce's effectiveness and good morale during the implementation.

Personnel Scarcity. The scarcity of trained, perceptive analysts and programmers, coupled with their long training cycles, continues to restrain IT development and to demand that planning priorities be established. As discussed, these appear to be long-term difficulties rather than cyclical problems and are forcing larger amounts of software and electronic support to be sourced from outside and necessitating tough internal resource allocation decisions.

Scarcity of Other Corporate Resources. Limited availability of financial and managerial resources is another planning pressure. IT is only one of many strategic investment opportunities for a company, and the potential financial return of investment in it must be weighed against alternatives. Most U.S. companies' financial accounting practice, which charges IT expenditure against current year's earnings, even though much of it is actually a capital expenditure, intensifies this problem. Reviewing the effectiveness and the efficiency of these expenditures is of great importance, as resource availability is a crucial limiting factor for new projects— particularly in companies under profit or cost pressures.

Trend to Database Design and Integrated Systems. An increasing and significant proportion of the applications portfolio involves the design of relational data architecture for supporting sophisticated applications that link different parts of the firm as well as its customers and suppliers. A long-term view of the evolution of applications is critical to appropriately selecting database contents, the methods for interrelating them, and the protocols for updating them.

Validation of Corporate Plan. In many organizations, new marketing programs, new-product design, and introduction and implementation of organizational strategies depend on the development of IT support programs. Understanding these points of dependency is also vital. If IT limitations render corporate strategy infeasible, corporate management must hear that message loud and clear; the problem must be faced and resolved while alternatives are still available.

In organizations where IT products and processes are integral to elements of the corporate strategy, this linkage is very important. A large paper company, for example, was forced to abandon its planned new billing discount promotions—a key part of its marketing strategy—because its IT function was unable to translate the very complex ideas into the existing computer programs with the present level of staff skills. Advance coordination between IT and marketing management would have identified the problem much earlier and permitted satisfactory solutions to be identified.

Internal (IT Process) Pressures

At various points in the evolution of an information technology, the balance between pressures shifts and planning serves substantially different purposes. Reflecting upon the advent and growth of business data processing, databases, distributed systems, fiber optics, image processing, and other new technologies (as noted in earlier chapters), one can identify four distinct phases of technology assimilation, each posing different pressures.

Phase 1: Technology Identification and Investment.   In the initial phase of a new technology, the basic planning focus is on both technology identification and the need for new human resource skills. Problems include identifying appropriate technologies for study, preparing the site, developing staff skills, identifying potential product champions, and managing initial pilot applications.

Phase 2: Technological Learning and Adaptation.   The basic thrust of planning in this second phase is making potential users aware of the new technology and communicating how it can be useful to them. Sequencing projects and ensuring good coordination between team members is also important as the company continues to master the technology's nuances. The effectiveness of this phase's planning can be measured by a series of user-supported pilot projects.

As a secondary output, the planning process in this phase identifies the number of staff and the skills to be acquired.

Since technology will continue to evolve for the foreseeable future, there will normally be a phase 2 flavor to some part of a company's IT development portfolio. Our observations of successful planning in this phase suggest clearly that:

1. A new technology is best introduced by starting with a pilot test to generate both IT staff and user learning, rather than by spending years on advance introspection and design without any practical hands-on experience.
2. Attracting the interest of potential users on their terms and stimulating their understanding about what the technology can do for them are

critical to success, and success here leads to later requests for service; pilot users become important allies.

3. Planning during this phase (and phase 1 as well) involves a program of planned technological innovations, encouraging users to build upon their past experience and organizational receptivity to change. There is a desirable "softness" in the tangible and intangible benefits specified for these projects.

Phase 3: Rationalization/Management Control. Effective planning for technologies in this phase has a strong efficiency focus; the emphasis shifts to getting the results of the successful pilot projects implemented cost-efficiently. Whereas planning for technological learning and adaptation (phase 2) has a long-range (though not terribly accurate) perspective, planning for phase 3 technologies has a short-term, one- to two-year efficiency focus. Activities include identifying and completing applications, upgrading staff to acceptable knowledge levels with the new technology, reorganizing to develop and implement further projects using the technology, and efficiently utilizing the technology. For technologies themselves, the objective in this phase is to set appropriate limits on the types of applications that make sense and to ensure they are implemented cost-efficiently. In terms of Robert Anthony's framework,[3] effective planning for phase 3 technologies has a much stronger management and operational control flavor and a weaker strategic planning thrust.

Phase 4: Maturity/Widespread Technology Transfer. The final phase is one of managed evolution, whereby the technology is transferred to a wider spectrum of applications. With organizational learning essentially complete and a technology base with appropriate controls in place, it is time to look seriously into the future and to plot longer-term trends in exploitation of the technology. If one is not careful, however, such planning—based on the business and technology as they are now understood—can be too rigid. Unexpected quirks in the business and evolution of technology alike may invalidate what has been done during phase 4 planning as the technology is superseded by a still better one.

Given the current dynamic state of information technology, technologies in all four planning phases are normally present simultaneously in a typical firm—suggesting that uniformity and consistency in IT planning protocols throughout the firm are inappropriate. Instead, the organization is dealing with a portfolio of technologies, each of which poses a different planning challenge.

For example, one manufacturing company studied was in phase 4 in terms of its ability to conceptualize and deal with enhancements to its

---

[3] Robert Anthony, *Planning and Control Systems: A Framework for Analysis* (Boston: Division of Research, Harvard University Graduate School of Business Administration, 1965).

on-line MRP-II production scheduling system. At the same time, it was in phase 3 in terms of driving its new CAD system across the entire engineering and product development functions. Finally, as it was just experimenting with several forms of client-server architecture, it was clearly in phase 1 in these technologies. The firm's plans for the MRP-II system were detailed and crisp, whereas the client-server project was essentially a research project, and no coherent view existed as to where it was going.

In summary, "planned clutter" (as opposed to consistency) is desirable in a firm's approach to IT planning. Similarly, the approach to IT planning for different organizational units within a company should vary, since each often has quite different familiarity with specific technologies.

LIMITATIONS ON IT PLANNING RESULTS

As new products appear, as the competitive environment shifts, as laws and corporate strategies change, and as mergers and spin-offs take place, the priorities a company assigns to its various applications evolve. Some previous low-priority or unconceived applications may become critically important, while others once seen as vital will diminish in significance. This volatility places a real premium on building a flexible management framework that permits orderly and consistent change to meet evolving business requirements.

In a similar vein, every IT planning process must make some very specific assumptions about the nature and role of technological evolution. If this evolution occurs at a different rate from the one forecast, then major segments of the plan may have to be reworked, both in scope and thrust. For example, the recent explosion of Internet, a potential new way of communicating with customers, has caused many firms to rethink their priorities.

Planning as a Resource Drain

Every person and every dollar assigned to IT planning represent resources diverted from such activities as new systems development; the extent to which human and financial resources should be devoted to planning is always in question. Just as the style of planning changes over time as parts of the organization pass through different phases with different technologies, so should the commitment of resources to planning also change. This phenomenon too suggests that the instability in an IT planning process relates positively to its role of stimulating a creative view of the future. If not carefully managed, IT planning can become a mind-numbing, noncreative process of routinely changing the numbers, as opposed to a sensitive focus on the company's real opportunities and problems.

Fit to Corporate Culture

An important aspect of IT planning is implementation within the realities of the corporate culture. For example, in organizations with a very formal corporate planning process actively supported by senior management, the internal user-management climate typically supports formal approaches to IT planning. Other organizations, however, have quite different cultures and approaches to corporate planning. These factors significantly alter both the form and the degree of commitment that can be expected from users of an IT planning process, as is discussed later in the chapter.

Strategic Impact of IT Activities

As we have noted, IT activities are of strategic importance in some organizations, while playing a cost-effective, useful, but distinctly support-ive role in others. The latter organizations should not expect senior managers to devote the same amount of thinking to IT items as in organizations of the former type. Moreover, the IT function that hitherto held little strategic importance may, because of its new-technology-enabled applications portfolio, assume great significance in the future. Thus, IT planning may become very important to the firm at some time, and in the process it must face and surmount the challenge of breaking the habits and molds of the past.

In an environment of management turmoil, high turnover, and reassess-ment, one is unlikely to find the intensity and commitment to IT planning possible in a stable environment, where people are emotionally attached to the organization. Although such negative factors limit the benefits of planning and make the process more complex, they do not eliminate the need for it. Rather, they increase the multidimensional complexity of the planning task and diminish reasonable expectations of the output's quality.

For other organizations, the opposite is true. While IT now plays an important operational role, future applications may not offer great payoffs or significance. If this occurs, a less intensive focus on IT strategic planning will be in order, and different people will be involved than when it was more significant.

Mismatches: Using the Strategic Grid

Selecting the appropriate planning approach is further complicated when a mismatch exists between where an organization is on the grid (see Figure 9–1) and where senior management believes it should be. In such a case, more planning is needed for energizing the firm to make appropriate adjustments, as is illustrated in Figure 9–1.

FIGURE 9–1 Information Technology Strategic Grid

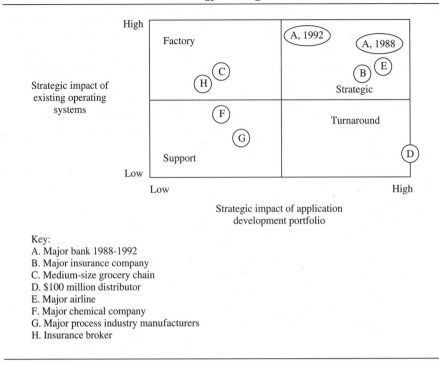

Key:
A. Major bank 1988-1992
B. Major insurance company
C. Medium-size grocery chain
D. $100 million distributor
E. Major airline
F. Major chemical company
G. Major process industry manufacturers
H. Insurance broker

A large international financial institution's senior management was very comfortable with the company's IT performance, although the issue infrequently appeared on their agenda. The IT management team, however, was deeply concerned that their senior IT managers lacked a thorough understanding of the firm's goals, what its products would be four to five years hence, and the types of organization structures and controls required. IT management knew that senior IT managers needed this input so IT could support the firm's goals.

The institution had a very sophisticated but closely held corporate planning activity. In a world of major shifts in what financial institutions can and should do, top management was greatly concerned about the confidentiality of planning information, and only a handful of individuals (four or five) knew the full scope of it. Since neither the IT manager nor his boss was among this handful, IT was substantially in the dark about the organization's direction and could only crudely assess it by trying to guess why some projects were funded and others were not.

The company's full-time IT planning manager had three assistants and reported to the IT manager. For the past two years, IT planners had worked closely with middle management users and information technologists to develop strategies and applications portfolios that both sides perceived as relevant to their needs. Because there was little formal or informal linkage between the IT planning activity and the corporate planning department (which had repeatedly communicated, "Don't call us, we'll call you"), the IT staff had two overriding concerns:

1. The plans and strategies developed for IT may be technically sound and meet the needs of user management as they understand them today, but they may be unproductive or indeed counterproductive if they do not support the corporate thrust.
2. Corporate plans are developed "at the top" by a few executives completely isolated from IT and its issues. This could unwittingly place onerous or unworkable support requests on IT in the future.

At this stage, senior management perceived IT as a factory, believed it was being staffed and managed appropriately, and had no concerns about the IT planning process. IT saw itself as strategic but could not sell the concept to anyone.

This frustration was resolved when an outside review of the institution's overall strategy (initiated by the chairman) noted in its conclusions that IT, a strategic force in similar firms, was not being so treated in this firm and was moving in an unproductive direction. Given the outside reviewer's credibility, senior management readily acknowledged they had misunderstood the role of IT and that IT should indeed be treated as strategic. Unfortunately, they perceived IT management as inadequate for this newly defined (i.e., newly recognized) challenge, and many senior IT staff did not survive the transition.

On the surface, based on the written plan, IT planning had looked good; in fact, however, it had failed to come to grips with the realities of the corporate environment. Consequently, an organization for which IT activities were of significant strategic importance had been left in a state of potential unpreparedness and risk. When IT activities were belatedly recognized as critical, the result was fatal for the IT planners—they were held accountable for this state of affairs.

The extent to which IT is strategic for the company as a whole and for individual business units and functions must be assessed. IT's impact typically varies widely by unit and function, and thus the IT planning process must be adapted to deal with these differences. Those units where IT is of high impact require much more intense IT planning than those units for which it is of low impact, of course. This makes the planning more complex, but it also makes it more useful.

Table 9–1 suggests that a firm's position on the strategic grid not only influences its IT planning needs, but has numerous other implications, including the role of the executive steering committee, the placement of IT

TABLE 9-1 Managerial Strategies for "Support" and "Strategic" Companies

Factor	"Support Company"	"Strategic" Company
Steering committee	Middle-level management membership. Existence of committee is less critical.	Active senior management involvement. Committee is key.
Planning	Less urgent. Mistakes in resource allocation not fatal.	Critical. Must link to corporate strategy. Careful attention to resource allocation is vital.
Project portfolio risk profile	Avoid high-risk projects because of constrained benefits. A poor place for corporate strategic gambles.	Some high-risk, high-potential-benefit projects are appropriate if possibility exists to gain strategic advantage.
IT capacity management	Can be managed in a looser way. Operational headaches are less severe.	Critical to manage. Must leave slack.
IT management reporting level	Can be low.	Should be very high.
Technical innovation	A conservative posture one to two years behind state of art is appropriate.	Critical to stay current and fund R&D. Competitor can gain advantage.
User involvement and control over system	Lower priority. Less heated debate.	Very high priority. Often emotional.
Charge-out system	Managed cost center is viable. Charge-out is less critical and less emotional.	Critical that it be sensitively designed.
Expense control	System modernization and development expenses are postponables in times of crisis.	Effectiveness is key. Must keep applications up to date; save money other places.
Uneven performance of IT management	Time is available to resolve it.	Serious and immediately actionable.

in the organization, the appropriate IT management control system, and so on. Further, since organizational units may be in different quadrants of the grid, the planning, organization, and control approaches suitable for one unit may be inappropriate for another. Finally, an IT planning approach that is suitable at one time may be totally wrong if the firm's position on the grid changes.

Corporate Environmental Factors That Influence Planning

Research has identified four corporate environmental factors influencing how IT planning must be structured to improve its likelihood of success.[4]

Perceived Importance and Status of the Systems Manager. The IT manager's status must align with the role that IT plays, or should play, in the overall operation and strategy-formulating process of the company. If IT has strategic or turnaround importance, a low-status IT manager (low status in reporting level and/or compensation) will have difficulty getting the necessary information from general management in the planning process. If the corporate communication culture (style) at the top is informal, this low status can be fatal, as the IT manager will be outside the key communication loop. If the corporate culture is more formal, development and management of appropriate committees and other formal processes can significantly alleviate this potential problem.

In a company where IT is and should be serving a support function, lower status is appropriate for the IT director, and less effort is needed to align IT and corporate strategy. A lower level of investment (in dollars and type of staff) in IT planning is also appropriate for such situations. These factors are apparent in the comments of a director of strategic planning for a large process-manufacturing company: "We relate to IT by giving them insight on the corporate goals and the elements and forms of a good planning system. Because of their role in the company, we do not solicit feedback from them as to 'the art of the possible.' The nature of their operation is such that they can provide no useful input to decisions of corporate strategy."

Physical Proximity of the Systems Group and the General Management Team. In an organization where many important decisions are made informally in ad hoc sessions and where IT has strategic or turnaround importance, key IT management staff should be physically close to the senior line manager; literally, their offices should be nearby. Regardless of the systems manager's status, being an active member of the team in this type of organization is difficult when one is geographically distant from the other members of the team. According to a manager in one such company, "The people who are around when a problem surfaces are the ones who solve it. We don't wait to round up the missing bodies." When the prevailing management culture is more formal, physical proximity is less important. In these situations, formal written communications and scheduled formal meetings largely replace the informal give-and-take.

In informal organizations in which IT is strategic or turnaround, it is critical that the IT managers, and preferably a small staff, be at corporate

---

[4] Pyburn, "Information Systems Planning" (see footnote 2).

headquarters, even if their systems development groups must be located many miles away. For support and factory organizations with informal cultures, location at corporate headquarters is much less critical.

Corporate Culture and Management Style. In an organization where the management culture is low key and informal and the relationship between the IT manager and senior management is informal and personal, formal IT planning procedures do not appear to be critical to effective planning. The relationship is typically fostered by geographic proximity and the IT manager's status. As an organization becomes more formal, however, disciplined IT planning becomes more significant, even in a systems environment that is not highly strategic.

Organizational Size and Complexity. As organizations increase in size and complexity and as IT applications grow larger and more complex, formal planning processes help ensure the kind of broad-based dialogue essential to creating an integrated vision of IT. This point relates to the previous comments concerning management culture and style, for greater size and complexity typically necessitate more formal practices. If the business unit size is small and relatively simple, formal planning approaches are less critical, irrespective of other factors. Similarly, for a smaller business unit where the systems environment is primarily "support," IT planning can safely be more informal. However, as the portfolio of work increases in size and integration across user areas, planning must be more disciplined and formal.

In aggregate, these corporate environmental items explain why recommendations on how to do IT planning "in general" almost always are too inflexible for a specific firm. Even within a firm, these issues often force considerable diversity of practice among organization units. The following illustrates how these issues have shaped the planning process in a billion-dollar manufacturing organization.

An Example. This company has a medium-sized corporate IT facility and stand-alone IT facilities of some significant size in its six U.S. divisions. The divisional IT facilities report "straight-line" to their respective divisions and "dotted-line" to the corporate IT function. The corporate IT group is part of a cluster of corporate staff activities, and considerable power has traditionally been located at the corporate level.

The corporate planning activity reports to the vice president of corporate IT, who has enjoyed a long personal and professional relationship with both the chairman of the board and the CEO. IT responsibility was initially given to this vice president because operational and developmental problems had reached crisis proportions. Under normal circumstances, IT has had a "support" role, but these difficulties had pushed the firm into the turnaround category.

While the company's management culture is informal, the closeness of relationships between division general managers and their IT managers varies widely. The size of the divisions' application portfolios in relation to their overall size also varies considerably, with IT activities playing a more significant role in some divisions than in others.

IT planning at the divisional level begins when the corporate IT group gives a division some rather loose guidelines concerning technological direction; it culminates in division IT plan. The planning processes and dialogues vary widely from division to division in terms of line manager involvement. In some divisions, the line managers are intimately involved in the process of developing the plan, and the division general manager invests considerable time in final review and modification. Elsewhere the relationship is less close: IT plans are developed almost entirely by the IT organization, and general management review is very limited. These differences seem to reflect IT's respective contributions to individual divisions' strategic functioning.

Critical to the IT planning process is an annual three-day meeting of the vice president of corporate IT and his key staff, in which the divisional IT managers present their plans. The vice president plays a major role in these sessions, critiquing and suggesting modifications to the plans to ensure their fit with corporate objectives. His thorough understanding of the corporation's plans, the thinking of the divisional general managers, and the thinking of the chairman and president enable him immediately to spot shortfalls in IT plans, especially in those of divisions with weak IT-line management relationships.

As a result, emerging IT plans fit the organization's real business needs, and the IT activity is well regarded. A set of planning processes that might lead to disaster in other settings has worked well here, given the vice president's special qualities and the style of communication between him and general management that is appropriate to this firm's culture.

SUMMARY

Research evidence continues to show a correlation between effective IT planning and user perception of effective IT activity. Effective execution of IT planning, however, has been found to be far more subtle and complex than envisioned by earlier authors. In addition to generating new ideas, a major role of the IT planning process is to stimulate discussion and exchange of insights between the specialists and the users. Effectively managed, this is an important element in averting potential conflicts in the firm.

In this context we conclude that:

1. Organizations in which IT activity is integral to corporate strategy implementation have a special need to build links between IT and the

corporate strategy formulation process. Complex to implement, this requires dialogue and resolution along many dimensions. Key aspects of the dialogue are:

a. Testing elements of corporate strategy to ensure they are possible within the existing IT resource constraints and capabilities. Sometimes the resources needed are obtainable; in other settings, they are unavailable and painful readjustments must be made. Conversely, formulators of corporate strategy must understand the potentials of new technologies because they may suggest new ways of operating.

b. Transfer of planning and strategy-formulation skills to the IT function.

c. Ensuring long-term availability of appropriate IT resources.

In "support" and "factory" settings such linkage is less critical. Over time, the nature of this linkage may change as the firm's strategic IT mission evolves.

2. As an organization grows in size, systems complexity, and formality, IT planning must be directly assigned to someone in order to retain focus and avoid significant pieces "dropping between the cracks." The job is subtle, not simple. The planner must possess a strong set of enabling and communication skills to relate to all individuals and units affected by this technology and cope with their differing familiarity with it. Ensuring the involvement of IT staff and users for both inputs and conclusions is key. The great danger is that planners will define the task with more of a "doing" orientation than an "enabling" one and inappropriately interpose their own priorities and understandings. To overcome this problem, many organizations define this job as a transitional one rather than a career one.

3. "Planned clutter" in the planning approach is appropriate, because the company's applications portfolio should contain technologies in different phases with different strategic payouts to different units of the firm at different times. While planning all technologies for all business units at the same level of detail and schedule may appear superficially attractive and orderly, in reality this would be inappropriate.

4. IT planning must be tailored to the realities of the organization's environment. The IT manager's importance and status, the physical placement of senior IT staff in relation to general management, the corporate culture and management style, and organization size and complexity all influence how IT planning should be carried out.

5. The planning process must incorporate and integrate a broad range of technologies—internal and external electronic communications, data processing, image processing, and personal computers.

Chapter 10

Managing the Information Technology Resource through Strategic Partnerships[1]

Companies are increasingly outsourcing the management of information technology for reasons that include concern for cost and quality, lagging IT performance, supplier pressure, plus other financial factors. The outsourcing solution is acceptable to large and small firms alike because strategic alliances are now more common and the IT environment is changing rapidly. This chapter identifies when situations for outsourcing make sense and the issues of how the resulting alliance should be structured and managed. In addition to clear successes, we have identified troublesome relationships and several that had to be terminated.

Long-term, sustained management of a strategic alliance is turning out to be the dominant challenge of effective IT outsourcing. From a relatively unusual entrepreneurial activity in the past, IT outsourcing has recently exploded across the global corporate landscape. Xerox, Delta Airlines, AMP Insurance (Australia), British Aerospace, and U.K.'s Inland Revenue Service are the latest of these mega-alliances. Several years ago, Shell Oil outsourced its Brazilian IT activities. Like marriages, however, these arrangements are much easier to enter than to sustain or dissolve. The special economic technology issues surrounding outsourcing agreements necessarily make them more complex and fluid than an ordinary contract. Both parties must make special efforts for outsourcing to be successful.

---

[1]This chapter is adapted from F. Warren McFarlan and Richard L. Nolan, "How to Manage an IT Outsourcing Alliance," *Sloan Management Review* 36, no. 2 (Winter 1995).

Our purpose in this chapter is to provide a concrete framework to help senior managers think about IT outsourcing and focus on how to manage an alliance to ensure its success.

WHY OUTSOURCING ALLIANCES ARE SO DIFFICULT

Outsourcing contracts are structured for very long periods in a world of fast-moving technical and business change. Ten years is the normal length of a contract in an environment in which computer chip performance is shifting by 20 to 30 percent per year. (This standard contract length has emerged to deal with switching cost issues and to make the economics work for the outsourcer.) Consequently, a rigid deal that made sense at the beginning may make less economic sense three years later and require adjustments to function effectively.

Exacerbating the situation is the timing of benefits. The first-year benefits are clear to the customer, who usually receives a one-time capital payment; the customer then feels relieved to shift problems and issues to another organization. Moreover, the tangible payments in the first year occur in an environment where the outputs most closely resemble those anticipated in the contract. In each subsequent year, however, the contract payment stream becomes less and less tied to the initial set of planned outputs (as the world changes) and, thus, more subject to negotiation and misunderstanding.

The situation from the outsourcer's perspective is just the reverse. The first year requires a heavy capital payment followed by the extraordinary costs for switching responsibility and executing the appropriate cost-reduction initiatives. All this is done in anticipation of a back-loaded profit flow. At precisely the time the outsourcer is finally moving into its earnings stream, the customer, perhaps feeling the need for new services, is chafing under monthly charges and anxious to move to new IT architectures. If the customer has not had experience in partnering activities before, the relationship can develop profound tensions.

A further complication is that only a few outsourcers have the critical mass and access to capital markets to undertake large contracts. Electronic Data Systems (EDS), Computer Sciences Corporation (CSC), IBM, and AT&T constitute the bulk of the current market. A much larger group of firms specializes in certain niches in the outsourcing market, fulfilling either small contracts or specific subfunctions such as network operations. If an alliance is not working out, a company has limited options for resolving the situation, particularly because outsourcing is relatively easy but insourcing again is very difficult. One international oil company, for example, transferred the relationship to another outsourcer when the original arrangement did not work out.

Finally, the evolution of technologies often changes the strategic relevance of IT service to a firm. From the customer's viewpoint, assigning a commodity service to an outsider is very attractive if the price is right. Delegating a firm's service differentiator is another matter. The customer that made the original decision based on efficiency will judge it differently if using effectiveness criteria later.

OUTSOURCING IN RETROSPECT

Outsourcing IT has been popular for a long time—in the mid-1960s, for example, computer services bureaus ran a variety of programs, whose applications focused heavily on the financial and operations support areas (general ledger, payroll, inventory control, and so on). The programs were both customized and general-purpose, and the individual firm had to accommodate its operations to the standard options in the package. Customers of the service bureaus were mostly small and medium-sized firms, although some large firms used them for specialized needs or highly confidential items like executive payroll.

A good example of a provider in this industry then and now is ADP. ADP, which began as a small punch card payroll company in 1949, grew to a $3 billion organization by specializing in large-volume, standard transaction-type activities, such as payroll and handling proxy solicitations (almost 100 percent of the industry). Software contracting companies like Andersen Consulting in the private sector and CSC in the public sector developed large turnkey applications for firms requiring either specialized staff or a large number of staff people, either of which the firm deemed inconvenient, imprudent, or impossible to retain. EDS, in the state and local government sector, provided full outsourcing for organizations whose cultures and salary scales made it impossible to attract people with the necessary skills in a competitive job market. These were the exceptions, however, to the general trend of developing IT in-house. Until 1990, the major drivers for outsourcing were primarily:

- Cost-effective access to specialized or occasionally needed computing power or systems development skills.
- Avoidance of building in-house IT skills and skill sets, primarily an issue for small and very low-technology organizations.
- Access to special functional capabilities. Outsourcing during this period was important but, in retrospect, largely peripheral to the main IT activities that took place in midsized and large organizations.

Kodak's decision in 1990 to outsource IT was the first real wake-up call. Kodak's CIO at the time, who had been a general manager rather than a computer professional, took an aggressive position in outsourcing mainframes, telecommunications, and PCs. Until then, outsourcing for medium-sized to large companies had been mostly a sideshow, and outsourcing was generally reserved for small and medium-sized companies with problematic, grossly mismanaged IS departments.

In the wake of Kodak's decision was a flurry of oversubscribed IS conferences on outsourcing, at which the Kodak CIO was often the featured speaker. The authors attended a number of these conferences and independently witnessed the hostility from many CIO participants (who perceived outsourcing as a terrifying threat to their status quo) toward the Kodak CIO as she explained her rationale. Even today, many of those very same CIOs quickly point out with some relief that only one (albeit the largest) of the three original Kodak outsourcing contracts was totally problem-free—although all three contracts are still in place.

OUTSOURCING IN THE 1990s

We have conducted more than four years of case research on Kodak, General Dynamics, and over a dozen other outsourcing situations and have concluded that IT outsourcing is not a "flash in the pan" management fad. IT outsourcing is a harbinger of traditional IT department transformation and provides a glimpse at the emerging organizational structures of the information economy. Our research indicates that more than half of midsized-to-large firms have outsourced or are considering some type of outsourcing of their IT activities. And this phenomenon is not limited to the United States; for example, in 1993, AMP Insurance Company (the largest insurance company in Australia), British Aerospace, and the Inland Revenue Service all outsourced substantial parts of their IT activities.

Two factors have affected the growth of IT outsourcing—the recognition of strategic alliances and the changes in the technological environment.

Acceptance of Strategic Alliances.   The value of strategic alliances has been widely recognized, and their creation is motivated by interrelated forces. On one level, finding a strong partner to complement an area of weakness gives an organization an island of stability in a turbulent world. It is difficult to fight simultaneously on all fronts, and alliances allow a company to simplify its management agenda safely. Alternatively, alliances allow a firm to leverage a key part of the value chain by bringing in a strong partner that complements its skills. Such a partner may create an opportunity to innovate synergistically: the whole should become greater than the sum of the parts. Also, early, successful experiences with alliances increase a firm's confidence in undertaking new alliances in other parts of the value chain as a profitable way to do business. The experience provides insight into how the likelihood of a successful alliance can be increased.

For an alliance to be successful and endure for the long term, both firms must believe that they are winners. Because of the synergistic potential of the relationships and the opportunity to specialize, both firms should legitimately feel that they are benefiting: this is not a zero-sum game.

IT's Changing Environment.   Today, firms are not focusing on internal transaction processing systems; rather, in a networked fashion, they are integrating both internal and external computers so they can change their structure to more efficient forms for competing flexibly in the global marketplace. This integration places extraordinary pressures on firms trying to keep the old services running while developing the interconnections and services demanded by the new environment. Thus, outsourcing has become a viable alternative for these firms to get access to appropriate skills and to speed up the transition reliably and cost-effectively.

In fact, as shown in Table 10–1, the development of most of the code that companies now use is already outsourced. A distinct minority of the code in operating systems, e-mail systems, word processing packages, and spreadsheet software has actually been developed within the firm (with a much smaller percentage expected in the future). This trend, which occurred for obvious reasons of economies of scale and scarcity of competent staff, will only continue. Currently, Computer Associates, Lotus, IBM, Borland, and Microsoft are the de facto software providers to most companies. The internal IT organization is already a selector of code rather than a developer.

At the same time, many firms have a residue of 15- to 30-year-old systems primarily written in COBOL and PL/1. Although this problem is particularly acute in the financial services industry and manufacturing, it is not confined to it. The cost-effective transformation of these systems to the client/server model (a key technology of the network era that separates the management of files and their integrity onto one machine, the server, from devices accessing these files, the clients) is an enormous challenge. On the one hand, firms are looking for low-cost maintenance of the old systems to ensure they operate reliably, while, on the other hand, gaining access to the new skills to permit their transformation to the new model. This shift is as significant today as the move from tabulating equipment 35 years ago in terms of providing new capabilities to the firm. A number of organizations see outsourcing as a way of bringing the appropriate specialized skills to this task.

WHAT DRIVES OUTSOURCING?

Although the mix of factors raising the possibility of outsourcing varies widely from one company to another, our research has revealed a series of themes that, in aggregate, explain most of the pressures to outsource.

TABLE 10–1   IT Markets

Location	Physical Aspects	Information
Internal	*Automating:* Computerizing physical and clerical processes. DP era (1960–1980) • Dominant use of mainframe and minicomputers. • Operational level systems automated primarily with COBOL. • Process controls automate primarily with machine language. • Standard packages for payroll and general ledger. • Applications portfolio consists of millions of lines of code with 50% typically purchased from outside.	*Informating:* Leveraging knowledge workers with computers. • User tasks leveraged through direct use of microcomputers enabled by graphical use interfaces (GU) and purchased software such as word processing, spreadsheet, graphics, and CAD/CAM. • Local area networks (LANs)—user-oriented software for e-mail, database sharing, file transfer, and groupware for work teams. • Microcomputer software consists of millions of lines of code—almost 100% purchased from other companies.
External	*Embedding:* Integrating computers into products and services. Micro era (1980–1995) • Specialized code embedded in products and services to enhance function. • Microcomputers in physical products such as automobiles and "smart cards" in services. • Thousands of lines of code developed by both specialized internal programmers and outside contract programmers.	*Networking:* "The Information Highway." Network era (1990–?) • Wide area networks (WANS) networking workers, suppliers, and customers. • Internet for commercial use. • Millions of lines of code, almost 100% purchased and maintained from outside software firms.

General Managers' Concerns about Costs and Quality.   The same questions about IT costs and response times came up repeatedly when we talked to managers: Can we get our existing services for a reduced price at acceptable quality standards? Can we get new systems developed faster? We have uncovered the following ways an outsourcer can save money for a customer:

• Tighter overhead cost control of fringe benefits. On balance, the outsourcers run much leaner overhead structures than do many of their customers.

- More aggressive use of low-cost labor pools by creatively using geography. Frequently, the outsourcer moves data centers to low-cost areas (modern telecommunications make this possible).
- Tough world-class standards applied to the company's existing staff, all of whom have to requalify for appointment at the time of outsourcing. Frequently, employees may have become lazy or are unskilled in leading-edge IT management practices.
- More effective bulk purchasing and leasing arrangements for all aspects of the hardware/software configuration through discounts and better use of capacity.
- Better management of excess hardware capacity. The outsourcer can sell or utilize underused hardware that would otherwise be idle by combining many firms' work in the same operations center. One small firm's on-line operations (a $27 million, 10-year contract) was transferred to a larger data center at no extra cost to the outsourcer. Capacity was simply better used.
- Better control over software licenses, both through negotiation and realistic examination.
- More aggressive management of service and response time to meet, but not wildly exceed, corporate standards. Tighter control over inventories of paper and other supplies.
- Hustle. Outsourcers are professionals; this is their only business, and their success is measured by satisfied customers who recommend them to others, by bottom-line profitability, and by stock market performance.
- The ability to run with a leaner management structure because of increased competence and critical mass volumes of work.
- Creative and more realistic structuring of leases.

While the cumulative impact of these items can be significant, we issue a few cautionary notes. Until several knowledgeable bidders have closely analyzed an existing operation to propose an alliance, the true picture isn't revealed. An IT efficiency study funded by the IT department and performed by a consulting company hoping to get future business is simply inadequate. Equally important is assessing whether the outsourcer can rapidly mobilize its staff for the quick-response development jobs needed to get products and services to market much faster.

Breakdown in IT Performance.   Failure to meet service standards can force general management to find other ways of achieving reliability. As we reflect on the past 30 years of computer growth in most companies, it is not atypical to find a company in which cumulative IT management neglect eventually culminated in an out-of-control situation the current IT department could not recover from. For example, Massachusetts Blue Cross and Blue Shield's decision to outsource to EDS was triggered by the failure of three major systems development projects (and losses in the tens of millions of dollars). It saw outsourcing as a way to fix a broken department.

Similarly, a midsized bank's interest in outsourcing came after a one-day total collapse of its ATM network, caused by faulty internally designed software patches.

An additional driving factor is the need to rapidly retool a backward IT structure to maintain its competitiveness. In one firm, general managers thought the internal IT culture (correctly, in our judgment) was both frozen and backward; it needed to leap forward in performance. The general managers, who lacked both the time and the inclination to undertake the task personally, found outsourcing a good choice for making the transition from the DP era to the network era.

Intense Supplier Pressures.   Kodak's decision to outsource its data center and telecommunications to IBM, DEC, and Businessland was, as we noted, a flash point. Suddenly, all general managers saw outsourcing as a highly visible, if often misunderstood, alternative. At the same time, IBM and DEC were looking for new value-added services to reach their customer bases and compensate for declining hardware margins and sales. They moved aggressively into the field with expanded and highly energetic sales forces. EDS, the largest firm in the field, used its General Motors operations center to demonstrate its expertise. CSC, strong in the federal sector, built a bridge to the commercial sector with its General Dynamics' contract. The visibility of these and other arrangements, combined with the suppliers' aggressive sales forces, enabled them to approach general managers with compelling reasons to outsource.

Simplified General Management Agenda.   A firm under intense cost or competitive pressures, which does not see IT as its core competence, may find outsourcing a way to delegate time-consuming, messy problems so it can focus scarce management time and energy on other differentiators. If managers perceive the outsourcer as competent and are able to transfer a noncore function to reliable hands, they will not hesitate to choose outsourcing. These IT activities must be done respectably, but long-term upside competitive differentiation does not come from the outsourcer executing them in an outstanding fashion.

Financial Factors.   Several financial issues can make outsourcing appealing. One is the opportunity to liquefy the firm's intangible IT asset, thus strengthening the balance sheet and avoiding a stream of sporadic capital investments in the future. An important part of many arrangements struck in the past two years has been the significant up-front capital paid for both the real value of the hardware/software assets and the intangible value of the IT systems. General Dynamics, for example, received $200 million for its IT asset. Publicly held outsourcers with access to the capital markets have pushed this; partnerships like Andersen Consulting do not have such access.

Outsourcing can turn a largely fixed-cost business into one with variable costs; this is particularly important for firms whose activities vary widely in volume from one year to another or which face significant downsizing. The outsourcer can make the change much less painfully than the firm; it can broker the slack more effectively and potentially provide greater employment stability for the company's IT employees, who are there because of their ability to handle multiple operations. In fact, in several of the firms we studied, outsourcing has been very positively received by the staffs. They saw themselves leaving a cost-constrained environment with limited potential for promotion and entering a growth company where IT was the firm's only business. In variable cost arrangements, price deescalation clauses—rather than inflation protection clauses—should be negotiated in the sections of the contract that deal with IT hardware costs because of the dramatic downward changes in the technology costs.

Finally, a third-party relationship brings an entirely different set of dynamics to a firm's view of IT expenditures. It is now dealing with a hard-dollar expenditure that all users must take seriously (it is no longer soft-dollar allocation). There is a sense of discipline and tough-mindedness that an arm's-length, fully-charged-out internal cost center has trouble achieving. Further, firms that do not see IT as a high-leverage function may perceive outside professionals as adding special value and, hence, as quite influential.

For a firm considering divestiture or outright sale of one or more of its divisions, outsourcing has special advantages. It liquefies and gets value for an asset unlikely to be recognized in the divestiture. It gives the acquirer fewer problems to deal with in assimilating the firm. And the outsourcing contract may provide the acquirer a very nice dowry, particularly if the firm is small in relation to the acquirer. The contract can be phased out neatly, and the IT transaction volume can be added to the firm's internal IT activities with little or no additional expense. This was the guiding rationale for outsourcing in several midsized banks we studied. It gave them access to reliable IT support while making their eventual sale (which they saw as inevitable) more attractive from the acquirers' viewpoint.

Corporate Culture. A company's values can make it very hard for managers to take appropriate action, however. One firm we studied had several internal data centers, and there were obvious and compelling advantages to consolidating them. The internal IT department, however, simply lacked the clout to pull off the centralized strategy in what was a highly decentralized firm, built up over the years by acquisitions. The firm saw the decentralized culture as a major strength, not subject to reconsideration. Outsourcing, driven by very senior management, provided the fulcrum for overcoming this impasse, since it was not directly associated with any division or corporate staff. Similarly, an internal IT organization may fall behind the state of the art without being immediately attacked, while an outsourcer is forced to keep up with the latest technology to be successful.

Eliminating an Internal Irritant.   No matter how competent and adaptive existing IT management and staff are (and usually they are very good), there is usually tension between the end users of the resources and the IT staff. Often, this is exacerbated by the different language IT professionals use, lack of career paths for users and IT staff across the organization, perceived high IT costs, perceived unresponsiveness to urgent requests, and perceived technical obsolescence. In this context, the notion of a remote, efficient, experienced outsourcer is particularly compelling, even though the internal perceptions are not necessarily realistic.

Other Factors.   We found a variety of other drivers for outsourcing in specific situations. Some companies with a low-technology culture appeared to have trouble attracting and retaining high-technology IT staff. Outsourcing offered a way to gain these skills without getting involved in complex management issues.

A midsized high-tech firm needed to develop and run a series of critically important applications, for instance. Outsourcing gave it access to skills it could not attract to its organization. Managers felt that outsourcing had substantially reduced their corporate risk while providing needed access to specialized knowledge.

One large organization felt it was getting a level of commitment and energy difficult to gain from an in-house unit. For the rapidly growing outsourcer, good performance on the contract would provide a reference that was critical to achieving the kind of market growth it wanted.

Still another firm was frustrated by its inability to get its products to market faster. Its in-house resources, limited in size and training, were simply not moving quickly enough. Outsourcing gave it an adrenaline boost for building the IT infrastructure to achieve a two-thirds improvement in time to market.

WHEN TO OUTSOURCE IT

When do the benefits of outsourcing outweigh the risks? Our research suggests that there are five factors that tip the scale one way or the other. Each factor is fundamentally linked to the basic research models in the IT field.

Position on the Strategic Grid

Outsourcing operational activities is generically attractive, particularly as the budget grows and the contract becomes more important to the outsourcer. The more the firm is operationally dependent on IT, the more sense outsourcing makes. The bigger the firm's IT budget, however, the higher in the customer organization the decisions will be made, and thus the more careful the analysis must become. At the super-large scale, the burden falls on the outsourcer, who must show it can bring more intellectual firepower to the task.

When the application's development portfolio is filled with maintenance work or projects, which are valuable but not vitally important to the firm, transferring these tasks to a partner holds few strategic risks. However, as the new systems and processes increasingly come to deliver potentially significant differentiation and/or massive cost reduction, the outsourcing decision comes under greater scrutiny, particularly when the firm possesses a large, technically innovative, well-run IT organization. The potential loss of control and of flexibility and inherent delays in dealing with a project management structure that cuts across two organizations become much more binding and of greater concern. There are examples, like General Dynamics, where outsourcing was successful, but it was more the exception than the rule.

As shown in Figure 10–1, for companies in the support quadrant, the outsourcing presumption is yes, particularly for the large firms. For companies in the factory quadrant, the presumption is yes, unless they are huge and perceived as exceptionally well managed. For firms in the turnaround quadrant, the presumption is no; it represents an unnecessary, unacceptable delegation of competitiveness. For companies in the strategic and turnaround quadrants, the presumption is no; not facing a crisis of IT competence, companies in the strategic quadrant will find it hard to justify outsourcing under most circumstances. Having a subcritical mass in potentially core differentiating skills for the firm, however, is one important driver that might move such a company to consider outsourcing.

For larger multidivision firms, this analysis suggests that various divisions and clusters of application systems can legitimately be treated differently (i.e., strategic differentiated outsourcing). For example, an international oil company outsourced its operationally troublesome Brazilian subsidiary's IT activities while keeping the other items in-house. Similarly, because of the dynamic nature of the grid, firms under profit pressures after a period of sustained strategic innovation (in either the transforming or strategic quadrants) are good candidates for outsourcing as a means to clean up their shop and procedures. This was true for one large high-technology organization, which saved over $100 million by outsourcing.

Development Portfolio

The higher the percentage of the systems development portfolio in maintenance or high-structured projects, the more the portfolio is a candidate for

FIGURE 10–1 Strategic Grid for Information Resource Management

High

Factory—uninterrupted service-oriented information resource management.	*Strategic information resource management.*
Outsourcing Presumption: Yes, unless company is huge and well managed.	*Outsourcing Presumption:* No.
Reasons to consider outsourcing: • Possibilities of economies of scale for small and midsized firms. • Higher-quality service and backup. • Management focus facilitated. • Fiber optic and extended channel technologies facilitate international IT solutions.	Reasons to consider outsourcing: • Rescue an out-of-control internal IT unit. • Tap a source of cash. • Facilitate management of divestiture.
Support-oriented information resource management.	*Turnaround information resource management.*
Outsourcing Presumption: Yes.	*Outsourcing Presumption:* No.
Reasons to consider outsourcing: • Access to higher IT professionalism. • Possibility of laying off is of low priority and problematic. • Access to current IT technologies. • Risk of inappropriate IT architecture reduced.	Reasons to consider outsourcing: • Internal IT unit not capable in required technologies. • Internal IT unit not capable in required project management skills.

Current Dependence on Information *(row label, left of grid)*

Low   **High**

**Importance of Sustained, Innovative
Information Resource Development**

outsourcing. (High-structured projects are those in which the end outputs are clearly defined, there is little opportunity to redefine them, and little or no organizational change is involved in implementing them.) Outsourcers with access to high-quality, cheap labor pools (in, for example, Russia, India, or Ireland) and good project management skills can consistently outperform, on both cost and quality, a local unit that is caught in a high-cost geographic area and lacks the contacts, skills, and confidence to manage extended relationships. The growth of global fiber optic networks has made all conventional thinking on where work should be done obsolete. For example, Citibank does much of its processing work in South Dakota, and more than 100,000 programmers are working in India on software development for U.S. and European firms.

High-technology, highly structured work (e.g., building a vehicle tracking system) is also a strong candidate for outsourcing, because the customer needs staff people with specialized, leading-edge technical skills. These technical skills are widely available in countries such as Ireland, India, and the Philippines.

Conversely, large, low-structured projects pose very difficult coordination problems for outsourcing. (In low-structured projects the end outputs and processes are susceptible to significant evolution as the project unfolds.) Design is iterative, as users discover what they really want by trial and error. This work requires that the design team be physically much closer to consumers, thus eliminating significant additional savings. It can, of course, be outsourced, but that requires more coordination to be effective than the projects described above. One firm outsourced a large section of such work to a very standards-oriented outsourcer as a way of bringing discipline to an undisciplined organization.

Organizational Learning

The sophistication of a firm's organizational learning substantially facilitates its ability to effectively manage an outsourcing arrangement in the systems development area. A significant component of many firms' applications development portfolios comprises projects related to business process reengineering or organization transformation. Process reengineering seeks to install very different procedures for handling transactions and doing the firm's work. Organization transformation tries to redesign where decisions in the firm are made and what controls are used. The success of both types of projects depends on having internal staff people radically change the way they work and often involves significant downsizing as well. While much of this restructuring relies on new IT capabilities, at its heart, it is an exercise in applied human psychology, where 70 percent of the work falls disappointingly short of target.

Responsibility for such development work (low structure by its very nature) is the hardest to outsource, although an extraordinary consulting industry assists its facilitation. A firm with substantial experience in restructuring will have less difficulty in defining the dividing line between the outsourcer and the company in terms of responsibility for success. Firms that have not yet worked on these projects will find that outsourcing significantly complicates an already difficult task. The more experience the firm has had in implementing these projects, the easier the outsourcing will be.

A Firm's Position in the Market

The farther a company is from the network era in its internal use of IT, the more useful outsourcing can be to close the gap. Firms still in the DP era and early micro era often do not have the IT leadership, staff skills, or architecture to quickly move ahead. The outsourcer, by contrast, cannot just keep its old systems running, but must drive forward with contemporary practice and technology. The advanced micro era firms are more likely to have internal staff skills and perspectives to leap to the next stage by themselves. The world of client/server architecture, the networked organization, and process redesign is so different from the large COBOL systems and stand-alone PCs of 1985 that it is often prohibitively challenging for a firm to easily bridge the 10-year gap by itself. For those in this situation, it is not worth dwelling on how the firm got where it is but, rather, how to extricate itself.

Current IT Organization

The more IT development and operations are already segregated, in the organization and in accounting, the easier it is to negotiate an enduring outsourcing contract. A stand-alone differentiated IT unit has already developed the integrating organizational and control mechanisms that are the foundation for an outsourcing contract. Separate functions and their ways of integrating with the rest of the organization already exist. Cost accounting processes have been hammered out. While both sets of protocols may require significant modification, a framework is in place to deal with them.

When there are no protocols, developing an enduring contract is much more complex because the firm must establish both the framework for resolving the issue and the specific technical approaches. This structure facilitated the General Dynamics implementation effort tremendously; the lack of this structure in another high-technology firm extended the resulting outsourcing process over a period of years, with a diminution of savings and a complex conversion.

STRUCTURING THE ALLIANCE

Establishing the parameters of the outsourcing arrangement at the beginning is crucial. The right structure is not a guarantee of success, but the wrong structure will make the governance process almost impossible. Several factors are vital to a successful alliance.

Contract Flexibility

From the customer's viewpoint, a 10-year contract simply cannot be written in an iron-clad, inflexible way. The arrangements we have examined have altered over time—often radically. Evolving technology, changing business economic conditions, and emerging new competitive services make this inevitable. The necessary evolutionary features of the contract make the alliance's cognitive and strategic fit absolutely crucial. If there is mutual interest in the relationship and if there are shared approaches to problem solving, the alliance is more likely to be successful. If these do not exist, a troublesome relationship may emerge.

No matter how much detail and thought go into drafting the contract, the resulting clauses will provide imperfect protection if things go wrong. Indeed, the process of contract drafting (which often takes six to eight months) is likely to be more important than the contract. At this phase, one side gains insights into the other's values and the ability to redirect emphasis as the world changes. Kodak has already altered its outsourcing arrangement as both business circumstances and technologies changed. General Dynamics had eight contracts to provide for different divisions evolving in separate ways.

Standards and Control

One concern for customers is that they are handing control over an important part of the firm's operations to a third party—particularly if IT innovation is vital to the firm's success or if the firm is very dependent on IT for smooth daily operations. A company must carefully address such concerns in the outsourcing agreement.

Control, in some ways, is just a state of mind. Most organizations accustom themselves to loss of control in various settings, as long as the arrangement is working out well and the supplier is fully accountable. Moreover, vital parts of a firm's day-to-day operations have *always* been controlled by others. Electricity, telephone, and water are normally provided by third parties; and interruption in their support can severely cripple any organization in a very short time. Providing sustained internal backup is often impractical or impossible. For example, if a hotel's electricity or water fails for more than 24 hours, it will probably have to close until the situation is rectified. The managers at a major chemical company who were particularly concerned about loss of control were brought up short by one of us who asked to see its power-generating facilities and water wells (of course, they had neither).

Nevertheless, disruption of operations support has immediate and dramatic implications for many firms. It is also a short-term area where firms are likely to feel comfortable about their protection, if carefully structured. Conversely, putting innovation and responsibility for new services and products in the hands of a third party is correctly seen as a risky, high-stakes game. As we discuss later, in outsourcing, these issues are much more capable of being resolved for the firms in the factory and support quadrants, where innovation is much less important, than for firms in the turnaround and strategic quadrants (unless they are midsized and looking for access to critical innovation skills they cannot command on their own). A company must carefully develop detailed performance standards for systems response time, availability of service, responsiveness to systems requests, and so on. Only with these standards in place can the company discuss the quality of support and new trends.

Areas to Outsource

A company can outsource a wide selection of IT functions and activities. Data center operations, telecommunications, PC acquisition/maintenance, and systems development are all examples of pieces that can be outsourced individually. Continental Illinois outsourced everything, while Kodak kept systems development but outsourced, in separate contracts, data center operations, communication, and acquisition management of PCs. At its core, *outsourcing is more an approach than a technique.* As we noted earlier, significant portions of a firm's IT software development activities have been routinely outsourced for years. What is at stake here is a discontinuous major shift to move additional portions of a firm's IT activities outside the firm. Between the current situation and total outsourcing lie a variety of different scenarios. When assessing partial outsourcing, managers frequently ask the following questions:

- Can the proposed outsourced piece be separated easily from the rest of the firm, or will the complexities of disentanglement absorb most of the savings?
- Does the piece require particular specialized competencies that we either do not possess or lack the time and energy to build?
- How central are the proposed outsourced pieces to our firm? Are they either more or less significant to the firm's value chain than the other IT activities and, thus, deserve different treatment?

Total outsourcing is not necessary for attracting a supplier, but the portion to be outsourced must be sufficiently meaningful that the vendor will pay attention to it. Several organizations we studied had spun off bits and pieces of their activities to various organizations in a way that engendered enormous coordination costs among multiple organizations. These contracts were also very small in relation to the outsourcers' other work, and we had significant concerns about their long-term viability (in one case, the firm has already insourced again).

Cost Savings

Some CIOs believe that the firm's IT activities are so well managed or so unique that there is no way to achieve savings through outsourcing or for the vendor to profit. This may be true. But two caveats are important. First, only if several outsiders study outsourcing with senior management sponsorship is an honest, realistic viewpoint ensured. Having a study done objectively under the sponsorship of the local IT organization can be very difficult. The IT operation may see an outsourcing recommendation as so deeply disruptive that the study may be negatively biased from the start. Additionally, since consultants whom the IT organization retains are often dependent on it for future billing, either consciously or unconsciously, they may skew the results. One firm's internally initiated IT study, done by a consultant, purported to show that the firm was 40 percent more efficient than the average in its industry. Needless to say, IT's control of the evaluation process led to general management skepticism; the study is being redone under different sponsorship.

Disinterested professionals can make a real contribution in evaluating cost savings. A major aerospace firm recently retained a consulting firm to help it design and manage the outsourcing review process. Doing an audit in this area is difficult. Because situations change rapidly and new priorities emerge, it is usually impossible to determine what the results would have been if the alternative had been selected. Thus, the IT organization may be tempted to anticipate internal efficiencies so that IT outsourcing does not appear to be viable.

Supplier Stability and Quality

How a supplier will perform over a decade is an unanswerable question, yet one of the most critical a customer must ask. In 10 years, technologies will change beyond recognition, and the supplier without a culture that encourages relentless modernization and staff retraining will rapidly become a liability as a strategic partner. The stability of the outsourcer's financial structure is also critical. Cash crunches and/or Subchapter 11, or worse, are genuine nightmares for customers. This issue is complicated by the reality that once a firm outsources, it is very hard to insource again, as the firm's technical and managerial competence may have evaporated. While it is difficult to move quickly from one outsourcer to another (the only practical alternative), if a firm considers the possibility in advance, the risks can be mitigated. Some of the best bids come from newcomers trying to crack the market.

Problems are intensified if the way a firm uses technology becomes incompatible with the outsourcer's skill base. For example, a firm in the factory quadrant that selects an operationally strong outsourcer may be in trouble if it suddenly moves toward the strategic quadrant and its partner lacks the necessary project management and innovation skills to operate there.

Finally, there is a potential, built-in conflict of interest between the firm and the outsourcer that must be carefully managed so that it does not become disabling. The outsourcer makes its money by lengthening leases, driving down operational costs, and charging premium prices for new value-added services. By contrast, the customer has no empathy for the joys of harvesting old technology benefits (one of the reasons it got out of the business in the first place) and also wants rapid access to cheap, high-quality, project-development skills on demand. Managing this tension is complex, imperfect, and very delicate and must be covered in the contract. Both firms must make a profit. The more the customer moves to the strategic quadrant, however, the harder it is to ensure a good fit with an outsourcer.

Management Fit

Putting together a 10-year, flexible, evolving relationship requires more than just technical skill and making the numbers work. A shared approach to problem solving, similar values, and good personal chemistry among key staff people are critical determinants of long-term success. Various out-sourcers have very different management cultures and styles. It is worth giving up something on the initial price to ensure that you find a partner with which you can work productively over a long term. The information gained in the tortuous six- to eight-month process of putting an alliance together is crucial for identifying the likelihood of a successful partnership. Of course, this chemistry is a necessary, but insufficient, condition for ultimate success. Realistically, it is corporate cultural fit that is most important, since, after several years, the key people in the initial relationship will have moved to other assignments.

Conversion Problems

The period of time for an outsourcing study and conversion is one of great stress for a company's IT staff. Uncertainties about career trajectories and job security offer the possibility of things going awry. All the expertise a firm gains when acquiring another is vital during conversion. The sooner plans and processes for dealing with staff career issues, outplacement processes, and separation pay are dealt with, the more effective the results will be. Almost invariably, paralyzing fears of the unknown are worse than any reality.

MANAGING THE ALLIANCE

The ongoing management of an alliance is the single most important aspect of outsourcing's success. We have identified four critical areas that require close attention.

The CIO Function

The customer must retain a strong, active CIO function. The heart of the CIO's job is planning—ensuring IT resources are at the right level and appropriately distributed. This role has always been distinctly separate from the active line management of networks, data centers, and systems development, although it has not always been recognized as such. As noted, these line activities have been successfully outsourced in a variety of companies. In a fully outsourced firm, however, sustained internal CIO responsibility for certain critical areas must be maintained.

- *Partnership/contract management.* Outsourcing does not take place in a static environment. The nature of the technologies, external competitive situations, and so on, are all in a state of evolution. An informed CIO who actively plans and deals with the broad issues is critical to ensuring that this input is part of the alliance so it can continuously adapt to change. The evolving Kodak contract gives ample evidence of this.
- *Architecture planning.* A CIO's staff must visualize and coordinate the long-term approach to interconnectivity. Networks, standard hardware/software conventions, and database accessibility all need customer planning. The firm can delegate execution of these areas—but not its viewpoint of what it needs to support the firm in the long term. The wide range of management practice in firms that do not outsource complicates this. One insurance company we studied supported a network of 15,000 PCs, 18 e-mail systems, and literally hundreds of support staff to maintain its networks. Its CIO stated succinctly, "Even if technology costs 'zero,' we cannot continue in this way."
- *Emerging technologies.* A company must develop a clear grasp of emerging technologies and their potential applications. To understand new technology, managers must attend vendor briefings and peer group seminars and visit firms currently using the new technology. Assessing the hardware/software network alternatives and their capabilities requires knowing what is in the market and where it is going. This knowledge cannot be delegated to a third party or assessed by sitting in one's office.

  Similarly, identifying discontinuous applications and the opportunities and problems they pose is critical. At one large pharmaceutical organization, the CIO's staff was vindicated when it became clear that they had first spotted business process redesign as an emerging area, funded appropriate pilot projects (which were skillfully transferred to line management), and finally repositioned the firm's entire IT effort. (Users and an outside systems house executed the project, with the CIO playing the crucial initiator role.) Clearly, an outsourcer has an incentive to suggest new ideas that lead to additional work, but delegating responsibility for IT-enabled innovation in strategic and turnaround firms is risky because it is such an important part of the value chain.

• *Continuous learning.* A firm should create an internal IT learning environment to bring users up to speed so they are comfortable in a climate of continuous IT change. An aerospace firm felt this was so important that, when outsourcing, it kept this piece in-house.

Performance Measurements

Realistic measurement of success is generally very hard, so a company must make an effort to develop performance standards, measure results, and then interpret them continuously. Individual firms bring entirely different motivations and expectations to the table. In addition, many of the most important measures of success are intangible and play out over a long period of time. Hard, immediate cost savings, for example, may be measurable (at least in the short run), but simplification of the general management agenda is impossible to assess.

The most celebrated cases of outsourcing have evolved in interesting ways. Of Kodak's three selected vendors, while the major one remains intact, another has gone through several organizational transformations, triggered by financial distress. General Dynamics, in the first 18 months, has spun off three of its divisions, along with their contracts. It is too early to determine the outcomes. EDS and GM took years to work out an acceptable agreement; ultimately, several very senior EDS managers resigned.

A major power company recently postponed an outsourcing study for a year. Its general managers believed their internal IT staff and processes to be so bloated that, while outsourcing IT would clearly produce major savings, they would still be leaving money on the table. Consequently, in 1993, they reduced their IT staff from 450 to 250 and reduced the total IT expenditure level by 30 percent. With the "easy" things now done, they are now entertaining several outsourcing proposals to examine more closely what additional savings and changes in their method of operation would be appropriate.

Mix and Coordination of Tasks

As we noted earlier, the larger the percentage of a firm's systems development portfolio devoted to maintaining legacy systems, the lower the risk of outsourcing the portfolio. The question becomes: Can we get these tasks done significantly faster and less expensively? The larger the percentage of large, low-structured projects in the systems development portfolio, the more difficult it becomes to execute a prudent outsourcing arrangement and the more intense the coordination work to be done. Large systems development projects using advanced technology play directly to the outsourcers' strengths. Conversely, issues relating to structure (and thus close, sustained give-and-take by users) require so much extra coordination that many outsourcing benefits tend to evaporate.

On the one hand, the costing systems, implicit in outsourcing contracts using hard dollars, force users to be more precise in their systems specifications early on (albeit a bit resentfully) and thus cut costs. On the other hand, evolving a sensible final design requires trial-and-error and discussion. Both the contract and the various geographic locations of the outsourcer's development staff can inhibit discussion and lead to additional costs if not carefully managed. Managing the dialogue across two organizations with very different financial structures and motivations is both challenging and, at the core, critical to the alliance's success. Concerns in this area led Kodak not to outsource development. Other firms, such as British Aerospace, did, after careful analysis.

Customer-Outsourcer Interface

The importance of the sensitive interface between the company and the outsourcer cannot be overestimated. First, outsourcing can imply delegation of final responsibility to the outsourcer. The reality is that oversight simply is not delegatable, and, as we mentioned, a CIO and supporting staff need to manage the agreement and relationships. Additionally, the interfaces between customer and outsourcer are very complex and should occur at multiple levels, as noted in both sidebars. At the most senior levels, there must be links to deal with major issues of policy and relationship restructuring, while at lower levels, there must be mechanisms for identifying and handling more operational and tactical issues. For firms in the strategic quadrant, these policy discussions occur at the CEO level and occasionally involve the board of directors.

Both the customer and outsourcer need regular, full-time relationship managers and coordinating groups lower in the organization to deal with narrow operational issues and potential difficulties. These integrators are crucial for managing different economic motivations and friction. The smaller the firm in relationship to the outsourcer's total business, the more important it is that these arrangements be specified in advance before they get lost in other priorities.

During the past five years, an entirely different way of gaining IT support for outsourcing has emerged. While outsourcing is not for everyone, some very large and sophisticated organizations have successfully made the transition. What determines success or failure is managing the relationship less as a contract and more as a strategic alliance.

A Portfolio Approach to Information Technology Development

In December 1994, Microsoft announced its third major delay in Windows 95, intimating that the program's introduction might be as late as 1996, thereby failing to live up to its name. At the same time, Intel painfully admitted that flaws in its Pentium chip were more significant than planned and promised to replace all installed ones. Such highly visible failures of two major players in the IT industry give pause to other smaller, less-professional IT shops.

One of the largest suppliers in North America discovers major bugs in its vendor-supplied software controlling the hospital's entire operations. As the customer was located 3,000 miles from its vendor, communications gaps between the two reached crisis proportion levels. Lawsuits, the easiest outcome, may ensue, yet the real danger is in lives being lost as a result of software failure.

A major pharmaceutical company notes that while three of its software projects developed in India are great successes, one is a major fiasco: a complex marketing information systems turns out to be an elegant solution to a nonexistent problem, and 600,000 lines of codes have to be written off as valueless.

Two major insurance companies attempt to install the same software package to solve the same problem with their field sales force. In one company, all the money expended turned out to be totally wasted, and $600 million was written off with no benefit. The other company, using a different installation process, uses the new technology to generate a 46 percent increase in sales from one year to the next.

Horror stories from the stage 1 and stage 2 days of the late 1960s and early 1970s? Hardly! These examples come from the mid-1990s. Although it is disturbing to admit, the day of the big disaster on a major information technology (IT) project has not passed—and given business's more than 30 years of IT experience, the question becomes, Why? An analysis of these cases (all of them domestic companies, although we could have selected equally dramatic tales from overseas) and firsthand acquaintance with a number of IT projects in the past 10 years suggest three serious deficiencies that involve both general management and IT management: (1) failure to assess the implementation risk of a project at the time it is funded; (2) failure to consider the aggregate implementation risk of the portfolio of projects; (3) failure to recognize that different projects require different managerial approaches.

These aspects of the IT project management and development process are so important that we address them in this separate chapter. Chapter 7 discussed the influences of corporate culture and the technology's perceived strategic relevance on the balance of control between IT and the user over the various stages of the project management life cycle. Since many projects have multiyear life cycles, these project management issues must be dealt with separately from those of the management control system with its calendar-year focus, as discussed in Chapter 9.

PROJECT RISK

Elements of Project Implementation Risk

In discussing risk, we assume that the IT manager has brought appropriate methods and approaches to bear on the project—mismanagement is obviously another element of risk. Implementation risk, by definition here, is what remains after application of proper tools. Also, we are not implying that risk itself is bad. Rather, higher-risk projects must have potential for greater benefits to offset the risk.

The typical project feasibility study exhaustively covers such topics as financial benefits, qualitative benefits, implementation costs, target milestone and completion dates, and necessary staffing levels. Developers of these estimates provide voluminous supporting documentation, conveyed in clear-cut terms. Only rarely, however, do they deal frankly with the risks of slippage in time, cost overrun, technical shortfall, or outright failure: more usually, they deny the existence of such possibilities by ignoring them. They assume the appropriate human skills, controls, and other critical factors are in place to ensure success.

Consequences of Risk. Risk, we suggest, implies exposure to such consequences as:

1. Failure to obtain all, or any, of the anticipated benefits because of implementation difficulties.

2. Much higher-than-expected implementation costs.
3. Much longer-than-expected implementation time.
4. Resulting systems whose technical performance is significantly below estimate.
5. System incompatibility with selected hardware and software.

In the real world. of course, these risks are closely related, not independent of each other.

Project Dimensions Influencing Inherent Risk. Three important project dimensions (among others) influence *inherent* implementation risk:

Project Size. The larger the project in monetary terms, staffing levels, elapsed time, and number of departments affected, the greater the risk. Multimilliondollar projects obviously carry more risk than $50,000 efforts and tend to affect the company more if the risk is realized. Project size relative to the normal size of an IT development group's projects is also important: a $1 million project in a department whose average undertaking costs $2 to $3 million usually has lower implicit risk than a $250,000 project in a department whose projects have never cost more than $50,000.

Experience with the Technology. Because unexpected technical problems are more likely, project risk increases as the project team's and organization's familiarity with the hardware, operating systems, database handler, and project application language decreases. Phase 1 and phase 2 technology projects are intrinsically more risky for a company than phase 3 and phase 4 technology efforts. A project posing a slight risk for a leading-edge, large-systems development group may be highly risky for a smaller, less technically advanced group. (The latter could reduce its risk by purchasing outside skills for an undertaking involving technology in general commercial use. This rapidly growing market for outside skills is served by the major systems integrators such as Arthur Andersen, Computer Science Corporation, Electronic Data Services, and IBM.

Project Structure. In some projects, from the moment of their conceptualization, the nature of the task completely defines the outputs; these are fixed, not subject to change during the project's lifetime. Such "highly structured" efforts carry much less risk than do those whose outputs, being subject to user-manager's judgment and learning, are more vulnerable to modification.

An insurance company's automating the preparation of its agents' rate book for use on a laptop exemplifies a highly structured project. At the project's beginning, planners reached agreement on the product lines to be included, the layout of each page screen, the process of generating each number, and the type of client illustration that would be possible. Throughout the life of the project, there was no need to alter these decisions. Consequently, the team organized to reach a stable, fixed output rather than to cope with a potentially mobile target.

Project Categories and Degree of Risk

Figure 11–1, which combines in a matrix the various dimensions influencing risk, identifies eight distinct project categories with varying degrees of implementation risk. (Figure 11–2 gives examples of projects that fit this categorization.) Even at this grossly intuitive level, such a classification is useful to separate projects for different types of management review. IT organizations have used the matrix successfully for understanding relative implementation risk and for communicating that risk to users and senior executives. The matrix helps to address the legitimate concern that all people viewing a project will have the same understanding of its risks.

FIGURE 11–1   Effect of Degree of Structure, Company-Relative Technology, and Project Size on Project Implementation Risk

		Low Structure	High Structure
Low Technology	Large Project	Low risk (very susceptible to mismanagement)	Low risk
	Small Project	Very Low risk (very susceptible to mismanagement)	Very low risk
High Technology	Large Project	Very high risk	Medium risk
	Small Project	High risk	Medium-low risk

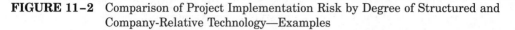

FIGURE 11-2   Comparison of Project Implementation Risk by Degree of Structured and Company-Relative Technology—Examples

	Low Structure	High Structure
Low Technology	Spreadsheet support for budgeting	Inventory control of oil tank farms
High Technology	On-line graphic support for advertising copy	Al-driven bond trading

Assessing Risk of Individual Projects

Figure 11–3 displays excerpts from a questionnaire a company developed for assessing project implementation risk: a list of 42 questions the project manager[1] answers about a project prior to senior management's approval and then several times during implementation. The company drew up the questions after analyzing its experience with successful and unsuccessful projects. Although no analytic framework underlies the questions and they may not be appropriate for all companies, they provide a good starting point—and a number of other companies have used them in developing their own instruments for measuring implementation risk.

These questions not only highlight the sources of implementation risk but also suggest alternative routes to conceiving the project and managing it to reduce risk. If the initial aggregate risk score seems high, analysis of the answers may suggest ways of lessening the risk through reduced scope, lower-level technology, multiple phases, and so on. Thus, managers should not consider risk as a static descriptor; rather, its presence should encourage better approaches to project management. Questions 5 and 6 in the "Structured Risk Assessment" section are particularly good examples of questions that could trigger changes.

The higher the assessment score, the greater the need for corporate approval. Only the executive committee in this company approves very risky projects. Such an approach ensures that top managers are aware of

---

[1] Actually, both the project leader and the key user answer these questions, and then they reconcile differences in their answers; of course, the questionnaire data are no better than the quality of thinking that goes into the answers.

FIGURE 11–3 Project Implementation Risk Assessment Questionnaire (sample from a total of 42 questions)

Size Risk Assessment

Risk Factor			Weight
1. Total development work-hours for system[a]			5
100 to 3,000	Low	1	
3,000 to 15,000	Medium	2	
15,000 to 30,000	Medium	3	
More than 30,000	High	4	
2. Estimated project implementation time			4
12 months or less	Low	1	
13 months to 24 months	Medium	2	
More than 24 months	High	3	
3. Number of departments (other than IT) involved with system)			4
One	Low	1	
Two	Medium	2	
Three or more	High	3	

Structure Risk Assessment

Risk Factor			Weight
1. If replacement system is proposed, what percentage of existing functions are replaced on a one-to-one basis?			5
0% to 25%	High	3	
25% to 50%	Medium	2	
50% to 100%	Low	1	
2. What is severity of user-department procedural changes caused by proposed system?			5
Low		1	
Medium		2	
High		3	
3. What is degree of needed user-organization structural change to meet requirements of new system?			5
None		0	
Minimal	Low	1	
Somewhat	Medium	2	
Major	High	3	
4. What is general attidue of user?			5
Poor; against IT solution	High	3	
Fair; sometimes reluctant	Medium	2	
Good; understands value of IT solution		0	
5. How committed is upper-level user management to system?			5
Somewhat reluctant, or unknown	High	3	
Adequate	Medium	2	
Extremely enthusiastic	Low	1	
6. Has a joint IT-user team been established?			5
No	High	3	
Part-time user representative appointed	Low	1	
Full-time user representative appointed		0	

FIGURE 11–3   *(continued)*

Technology Risk Assessment

Risk Factor			Weight
1. Which of the hardware is new to the company?[b]			5
None		0	
CPU	High	3	
Peripheral and/or additional storage	High	3	
Terminals	High	3	
Mini or micro	High	3	
2. Is the system software (nonoperating system) new to IT project team?[a]			5
No		0	
Programming language	High	3	
Database	High	3	
Data communications	High	3	
Other (Please specify)	High	3	
3. How knowledgeable is user in area of IT?			5
First exposure	High	3	
Previous exposure but limited knowledge	Medium	2	
High degree of capability	Low	1	
4. How knowledgeable is user representative in proposed application area?			5
Limited	High	3	
Understands concept but has no experience	Medium	2	
Has been involved in prior implementation efforts	Low	1	
5. How knowledgeable is IT team in proposed application area?			5
Limited	High	3	
Understands concept but has no experience	Medium	2	
Has been involved in prior implementation efforts	Low	1	

[a]Time to develop includes systems design, programming, testing, and installation.
[b]This question is scored by multiplying the sum of the numbers attached to the positive responses by the weight.

Source: This questionnaire is adapted from the "Dallas Tire" case, No. 180-006 (Boston: Harvard Business School Case Services, 1980).

Note: Since the questions vary in importance, the company assigned weights to them subjectively. The numerical answer to the questions is multiplied by the question weight to calculate the question's contribution to the project's risk. The numbers are then added to produce a risk score for the project. Projects with risk scores within 10 points of each other are indistinguishable in their relative risk but those separated by 100 points or more are very different in their implementation risk to even the casual observer.

significant hazards and are making appropriate trade offs between risk and strategic benefits. Managers should ask themselves:

1. Are the benefits great enough to offset the risks?
2. Can the affected parts of the organization survive if the project fails?
3. Have the planners considered appropriate alternatives?

Periodically, the questionnaire is used again to reveal any major changes as the project unfolds. If assessments are positive, the risk continually declines during implementation as the number and size of remaining tasks dwindle and familiarity with the technology increases.

When senior managers believe a project has low implementation risk, yet IT managers know it has high implementation risk, "horror stories" typically result. IT managers may not admit their assessment because they fear that senior executives will not tolerate such uncertainty in information systems projects and will cancel a project of potential benefit to the organization. The questionnaire data, however, encourage a common understanding among senior management, IT, and user managers about a project's relative implementation risk.

PORTFOLIO RISK

In addition to determining relative risk for single projects, a company should develop a profile of aggregate implementation risk for its portfolio of systems and programming projects. Although a universally appropriate implementation risk profile for all firms does not exist, different types of companies and strategies offer different appropriate risk profiles.

For example, in an industry where IT is strategic (such as retailing and catalogs), managers should be concerned if no high-risk projects are in evidence. Such a cautious stance may open a product or service gap for competition to step into. On the other hand, a portfolio loaded with high-risk projects suggests that the company may be vulnerable to operational disruptions if projects are not completed as planned. In "support" companies, heavy investment in high-risk projects may not be appropriate; they should not be taking strategic gambles. Yet even these companies should have some technologically challenging ventures to ensure familiarity with leading-edge technology and maintain staff morale and interest.

These examples suggest that the aggregate implementation risk profiles of the portfolios of any two companies could legitimately differ. Table 11–1 lists the issues that influence toward or away from high-risk efforts. (The risk profile should include projects executed by outside systems integrators as well as those of the internal systems development group.) As the table shows, IT's aggregate impact on corporate strategy is an important determinant of the appropriate amount of implementation risk to undertake.

Summary

It is both possible and useful to assess a project's implementation risk at the feasibility study stage. Discussing risk is important to those working on the project and to the user departments as a whole. Not only can this systematic

TABLE 11-1   Factors That Influence Implementation Risk Profile of Project Portfolio

	Portfolio Risk Focus	
Factor	*Low*	*High*
Stability of IT development group.	High	Low
Perceived quality of IT development group by insiders.	High	Low
IT critical to delivery of current corporate services.	No	Yes
IT important decision support aid.	No	Yes
Experienced IT systems development group.	Yes	No
Major IT fiascoes in last two years.	No	Yes
New IT management team.	No	Yes
IT perceived critical to delivery of future corporate services.	No	Yes
IT perceived critical to future decision support aids.	No	Yes
Company perceived as backward in use of IT.	No	Yes

analysis reduce the number of failures, its power as a communication link helps IT managers and senior executives reach agreement on the risks to be taken in relation to corporate goals.

PROJECT MANAGEMENT: A CONTINGENCY APPROACH

Much of the literature and conventional wisdom suggest that there is a single right approach to project management. A similar bias holds that managers should apply a cluster of tools, project management methods, and organizational linkages uniformly to all such ventures.

While there may indeed be a set of general-purpose tools (and we describe some later), the contribution each device makes to project planning and control varies widely according to the project's characteristics. Further, the means of involving the user—through steering committees, representation on the team, or as leader—should also vary by project type; in short, there is no universally correct way to run all projects.

Management Tools

The general methods (tools) for managing projects are of four principal types:

- *External integration* tools include organizational and other communication devices that link the project team's work to users at both the managerial and the lower levels.
- *Internal integration* devices, which include various personnel controls, ensure that the team operates as an integrated unit.

- *Formal planning* tools help structure the sequence of tasks in advance and estimate the time, money, and technical resources the team will need for executing them.
- *Formal results-control* mechanisms help managers evaluate progress and spot potential discrepancies so that corrective action can be taken.

Results controls have been particularly effective in the following settings:[2]

1. Clear knowledge of the desired results exists.
2. The desired result can be controlled (at least to some extent by the individuals whose actions are being influenced).
3. The controllable result areas can be measured effectively.

Highly structured projects involving a low degree of technology satisfy these conditions very well; formal results-control mechanisms are very effective in these settings. For low-structured projects involving a high degree of technology, none of the above conditions applies; consequently, results control can make only a limited contribution. In those settings, major contributions are derived from internal integration devices (personnel controls).

Table 11–2 gives examples of commonly used types of integration and control tools. The following paragraphs suggest how the degree of structure and the company-relative technology influence the selection of tools.

Influences on Tool Selection

High-Structure–Low-Technology Projects. Highly structured projects that present familiar technical problems are not only lower-risk endeavors but also are the easiest to manage (see Figure 11–1). They are the least common as well. High structure implies that the nature of the task clearly defines its outputs and that the possibility of users changing their minds about the desired outputs is essentially nonexistent. Project leaders, therefore, do not have to create extensive administrative processes to get a diverse group of users to agree to a design structure and then stick to their decision. Such external integration devices as assigning IT systems analysts to user departments, heavy representation of users on the design team, and formal user approval of design specifications are cumbersome and unnecessary for this type of project. Other integrating devices, however, such as training users how to operate the system, remain important.

Since the system's concept and design are stable in this environment, and since the technology involved is familiar to the company, the project can

---

[2] Kenneth A. Merchant, *Control in Business Organizations* (Marshfield, MA: Pitman Publishing, 1985).

TABLE 11-2 Tools of Project Management

Integration Tools, External	*Integration Tools, Internal*
Selection of user as project manager.	Selection of experienced IT professional to lead team.
Creation of user steering committee.	Frequent team meetings.
Frequent in-depth meetings of user steering committee.	Regular preparation and distribution of minutes within team on key design evolution decisions.
User-managed change control process.	
Frequent and detailed distribution of project team minutes to key users.	Regular technical status reviews.
Selection of users as team members.	Managed low turnover of team members.
Formal user specification approval process.	Selection of high percentage of team members with significant previous work relationships.
Progress reports prepared for corporate steering committee.	Participation of team members in goal setting and deadline establishment.
User responsibility for education and installation of system.	Outside technical assistance.
User management decision on key action dates.	

Formal Planning Tools	*Formal Control Tools*
PERT, "critical path," etc.; networking.	Periodic formal status reports versus plan.
Milestone phases selection.	Change control disciplines.
Systems specification standards.	Regular milestone presentation meetings.
Feasibility study specifications.	Deviations from plan, reports.
Project approval processs.	
Project postaudit procedures.	

proceed with a high percentage of people having only average technical backgrounds and experience. The project leader does not need extraordinary IT skills. This type of project readily provides opportunities to the department's junior managers, who can gain experience applicable to more ambitious tasks in the future.

With their focus on defining tasks and budgeting resources against them, project life-cycle planning concepts—such as PERT (Program Evaluation and Review Technique) and "critical path"—force the team to develop a thorough and detailed plan (exposing areas of "soft" thinking in the process). Such projects are likely to meet the resulting milestone dates and adhere to the target budget. Moreover, the usual results-control techniques for measuring progress against dates and budgets provide very reliable data for spotting discrepancies and building a desirable tension within the design team to work harder to avoid slippage.

An example of this type of highly structured project is the insurance agents' rate-book project mentioned earlier. A portfolio in which 90 percent of the projects are of this type should produce little unplanned excitement for senior and user managers. It also requires a much more limited set of skills for the IT organization than would be needed for portfolios with a different mixture of project types.

High-Structure–High-Technology Projects. Vastly more complex than high-structure–low-technology projects, high-structure–high-technology projects involve significant modifications of practices outlined in project management handbooks. A good example is converting one computer manufacturer's systems to another's, all the code being rewritten with no enhancements. Another example is converting a set of mainframe procedures into a client-server architecture with the main objective being performing the same functions more quickly and cheaply.

The normal mechanisms for liaison with users are not crucial here; the outputs are so well defined by the nature of the undertaking that both the development of specifications with user inputs and the need to deal with systems changes that users request are unimportant aspects. However, liaison with users is nevertheless important in two respects: (1) to ensure coordination on any changes in input/output or any other manual procedure changes necessary for project success and (2) to deal with any systems restructuring that must follow from unexpected shortcomings in the project's technology.

In this kind of project, it is common to discover during implementation that the selected technology is inadequate for the task, which forces a long postponement while either new technology is chosen or vital features of the system are modified to make the task fit the available technology. For instance, an industrial products company had to convert some computerized order-entry procedures back to a manual basis so the rest of an integrated materials management system could be shifted to already purchased hardware.

Such technological shortcomings were also the main difficulty the insurance company described at the beginning of the chapter faced. In cases in which system performance is much poorer than expected, user involvement is important both to prevent demoralization and to help implement either an alternative approach (less ambitious in selection of technology) or to attain a mutual agreement to end the project.

The skills leading to success in this type of project, however, are identical to those that effectively administer projects involving any technical complexity. The leader needs a strong background in high-technology projects (preferably, but not necessarily, in an IT environment) plus administrative experience. The leader must also "connect" to technicians. By talking individually and collectively with the project team members at various times, the ideal manager will anticipate difficulties before the technicians understand they have a problem. In dealing with larger projects in this category, the effective manager must establish and maintain teamwork through meetings, develop a record of all key design decisions, and facilitate subproject conferences as needed.

Project life-cycle planning methods identify tasks and suitable completion dates. Their predictive value is much less in high-structure–high-technology projects than in high-structure–low-technology projects. The team will not understand key elements of the technology in advance; thus, seemingly minor bugs will have a curious way of becoming major financial drains of consequence.

Roughly once an hour, an online banking system in one company, for example, generated "garbage" (Os and Xs) across all computer screens. Although simply hitting a release key erased this "ghost," four months and more than $200,000 were dedicated to actually eliminating it. That involved uncovering a complex interaction of hardware features, operating system functions, and application traffic patterns; indeed, the vendor ultimately had to redesign several chips. Formal results-control mechanisms have limits in monitoring the progress of such projects, and personnel controls become more important.

In summary, technical leadership and internal integration are the keys in this type of project, and external integration plays a distinctly secondary role. Formal planning and control tools give projections that intrinsically may contain major inaccuracies, and the great danger is that neither IT managers nor high-level executives will recognize this. They may believe they have precise planning and close control, when in fact they have neither.

Low-Structure–Low-Technology Projects.   When low-structure–low-technology projects are intelligently managed, they present low risk. Again and again, however, such projects fail because of inadequate direction. (In this respect they differ from the high-structure–low-technology project, where more ordinary managerial skills could ensure success.) The key to operating this kind of project lies in effective efforts to involve the users.

Developing substantial user support for only one of the thousands of design options and keeping the users committed to that design are critical. Essential aspects of this process include:

1. A user as either project leader or the number two person on the team.
2. A user steering committee to evaluate the evolving design periodically.
3. Breaking the project into a sequence of very small, discrete subprojects.
4. Formal user review and approval on all key project specifications.
5. Distributing minutes of all key design meetings to users.
6. Adhering, when possible, to all key subproject time schedules. Low managerial and staff turnover in the user areas is vital in this respect, since a consensus on approach with a user manager's predecessor is of dubious value.

The hospital debacle described in the beginning of the chapter illustrates what can happen when the above process does not take place. From the beginning, in a highly fluid world where end-user systems specifications were not clear, the project manager and his staff, located thousands of miles from end users, paid little attention to the need for user communications. A third of the way through the project, the two key users in the hospital suddenly left the organization and were replaced by people with limited technical background and no familiarity with major parts of the hospital's operations being impacted by this system. The change in priorities and lack of communications resulted in the project team's continuing on a course at variance from the real needs of the hospital. Much of the programming and systems work done was obsolete before it was completed. Tough, pragmatic leadership throughout the design stages, combined with close interaction with the technological staff of the software house, would have made a major difference in the outcome.

The importance of user leadership increases once the design is finalized. At that stage, users almost inevitably will state some version of "I have been thinking . . ." Unless the alternatives they suggest imply critical strategic significance (a judgment best made by a responsible, user-oriented project manager), the requests must be postponed for consideration in some formal change process. Unless this control is rigorous (a problem intensified by the near impossibility of distinguishing between the economies of a proposed alternative and those implicit in the original design), users will make change after change, with the project evolving rapidly to a state of permanent deferral, its completion forever six months in the future.

If the project has been well integrated with users, the formal planning tools will be very helpful in structuring tasks and in removing remaining uncertainties. Target completion dates will be quite firm as long as the system's target remains fixed. Similarly, the formal results-control devices afford clear insight into progress to date, flagging both advances and slippages (as long as the systems target remains fixed). Personnel controls also are vital here. If integration with user departments is weak, for example, excessive reliance on results controls will produce an entirely unwarranted feeling of confidence in the project team. By definition, however, the problems of technology management are usually less difficult in this type of project than in the high-technology ventures, and a staff with a normal mixture of technical backgrounds should be adequate.

In almost every respect, in fact, effective management of a low-structure–low-technology type of project differs from that of the previous two. The key to success is close, aggressive management of external integration, supplemented by formal planning and control tools. Leadership must flow from the user rather than from the technical side.

Low-Structure–High-Technology Projects. Because these projects' outputs are not clear at the start and they also carry high technical complexity, their leaders require technical experience along with the ability to communicate with users. The same intensive effort toward external integration needed for low-structure–low-technology projects is necessary here. Total user commitment to a particular set of design specifications is critical; and again, they must agree to one out of the many thousands of options.

Unfortunately, however, an option desirable from the user's perspective may turn out to be not feasible in the selected hardware/software system. In the past several years, such situations have occurred, particularly with network designs, and they commonly lead either to significant restructuring of the project or to its elimination. This makes it critical that users be well represented at both the policy and the operations levels.

At the same time, technical considerations make strong technical leadership and internal project integration vital. This kind of effort requires the most experienced project leaders, and they need wholehearted support from the users. Before undertaking such a project, managers must intensely explore the possibility of dividing it into a series of much smaller subprojects and/or employing less innovative technology.

While formal planning and results-control tools can be useful here, at the early stages they contribute little either to reducing overall uncertainty or to highlighting overall problems.In addition, while planning tools do allow the manager to structure the sequence of tasks, unfortunately, in this type of project, new tasks crop up with monotonous regularity, and those that appear simple and small can suddenly become complex and protracted. Further, unsuspected interdependencies between tasks often become apparent. Time, cost, and resulting technical performance are almost impossible to predict simultaneously. In NASA's Apollo moon project, for example, technical performance achievement was key, and cost and time were secondary, which in the private sector is usually unacceptable.

Relative Contribution of Management Tools

Table 11–3 shows the relative contribution each of the four groups of project management tools makes to maximizing potential project success. It reveals that quite different management styles and approaches are needed for managing the different types of projects effectively. Although the framework could be made more complex by including more dimensions, it would only confirm this primary conclusion.

SUMMARY

The usual corporate handbook on project management, with its single-minded prescriptive approach, fails to deal with the realities of the tasks facing today's managers, particularly those dealing with information technology. The right approach for managing a project flows from the specific characteristics of the project.

TABLE 11–3 Relative Contribution of Tools to Ensuring Project Success by Project Type

Project Type	Project Description	*Contribution*			
		External Integration	*Internal Integration*	*Formal Planning*	*Formal Results Control*
I	High structure–low technology, large	Low	Medium	High	High
II	High structure–low technology, small	Low	Low	Medium	High
III	High structure–high technology, large	Low	High	Medium	Medium
IV	High structure–high technology, small	Low	High	Low	Low
V	Low structure–low technology, large	High	Medium	High	High
VI	Low structure–low technology, small	High	Low	Medium	High
VII	Low structure–high technology, large	High	High	Low+	Low+
VIII	Low structure–high technology, small	High	High	Low	Low

Additionally, the need to deal with the corporate culture within which both IT and the project team operate further complicates the project management problem. Formal project planning and results-control tools are much more likely to produce successful results in highly formal environments than in ones where the prevailing culture is more personal and informal. Similarly, the selection and effective use of integrating mechanisms is very much a function of the corporate culture. (Too many former IT managers have made the fatal assumption that they were in an ideal position to reform corporate culture!)

The past decade has brought new challenges to IT project management and new insights into the management process. Our conclusion is threefold:

1. Firms will continue to experience major disappointments as they push into new application areas and technologies. Today, however, the dimensions of implementation risk can be identified in advance, and this information can be included in the decision process. Inevitably, if a firm only implements high-risk projects, it will sometimes fail.
2. A firm's IT development projects in aggregate represent a portfolio. Just as financial fund managers calculate and manage the risks within their portfolios, general management must make critical strategic decisions on the aggregate implementation risk profile of the IT portfolio.
3. Project management in the IT field is complex and multidimensional; to succeed, different types of projects require different clusters of management tools.

Chapter 12

Transnational IT Issues

In a major chemical company, the executive vice president of administrative services recently received a proposal to shut down their European data center and, using channel extender technology, to run the entire network of 1,000 European terminals out of the U.S. center. According to the proposal, this would save $3 million a year in operating costs plus provide better backup and faster response time to the *European* operations. Several other organizations had recently made a similar move, he was told.

A large pharmaceutical company was reviewing its software development experiences in India. Five projects had been developed there in the previous year; three had been outstanding successes, with the software being delivered for roughly 50 percent of its cost domestically; the other two were conspicuous disasters, with all money invested wasted. Apparently, specification changes and the distance of the India development group were the major causes of these disasters. The IT manager was uncertain how to proceed, given this information.

Asea Brown Boveri developed, in the early 1990s, a worldwide personal computer-based network that allowed it to close all books around the world in 10 working days and have all financial and operating data available both to corporate and country management. In a major article, ABB's chairman noted that his firm was a massive, information-intensive organization that could not operate without such support.

These stories illustrate two major shifts in the 1990s: (1) the management of a transnational organization has been dramatically impacted by new technologies, which allows new controls and the placement of work in very different locations; (2) the development of IT support for organizations has likewise changed dramatically.

In the past, investigating transnational IT issues has been neglected; it seemed too specialized and technical to the scholars of international business, and, for their part, scholars of IT management have been highly national (i.e., United States) in their orientation. However, new work is being done in the field, exemplified by Peter Hagstrom's *The 'Wired' MNC*[1] and the two-year-old *Journal of Global Information Management.*

Not only is transnational IT management evolving dramatically, but its issues will become even more significant in the coming years. Managing the forces (described as six trends in Chapter 2) driving transition in IT is complicated in the international arena by the wide diversity in cost, quality, and maturity of national IT infrastructures (e.g., those of Germany versus those of Hungary), local manufacturing and distribution technologies, and the scope and sophistication of IT applications. Building on the concepts of strategic relevance, culture, contingent planning, and managing diffusion of technology, this chapter focuses on aspects of transnational business influenced by IT and the new ways of delivering IT service internationally.

IT coordination issues for international operations are vastly more complex than purely domestic ones because they involve all the issues of domestic operations plus many additional difficulties. During the coming decade, IT will continue to be challenged by the opening of Eastern Europe and Asia to private enterprise, the need to share technologies within a firm for common problems around the world, and the continued evolution of transnational firms in both products and structure. The cross-border flows of research, goods, and materials are accelerating, requiring new and complex information infrastructures.

Financial and human resources for global operations require extremely coordinated management. Many firms have growing pools of staff needing extensive global coordination and development, including the underlying electronic support. Finally, technology skills, expertise, and intelligence all require much tighter coordination in the multinational realm. Information technology is central to accomplishing this.

Additional complexity comes from wide differences in cultures, labor and technology costs, products, and the need for and viability of IT support in different areas of the world. India, for example, with its cheap labor and good telecommunications gateways, is a highly cost-effective location to do certain kinds of software development. Its marginal in-country telecommunications, however, realistically pose fundamentally different integration issues for in-country operations than those faced by firms in Singapore, with its high-cost labor, high-quality telecommunications, and small geography. Likewise, technology advances have significantly affected firms' overall organization structures, permitting tasks to be moved cost-effectively around the globe while maintaining tighter control and facilitating new ways of defining and doing work.

---

[1] Peter Hagstrom, *The 'Wired' MNC: The Role of Information Systems for Structural Change in Complex Organizations,* Stockholm School of Economics, Institute of International Business, Stockholm, Sweden: 1991.

The first section of this chapter reviews IT's impact on the operations of transnational firms. The second section examines national characteristics determining what type of IT support is both possible and appropriate for a firm's operations within a country. Environmental issues that influence how a firm can develop IT support in another country are explained in the third section, while company-specific issues helping corporations develop and coordinate IT activity internationally are discussed in the fourth section. The final part reviews some IT policies firms have adopted and discusses their appropriateness in particular settings.

INFORMATION TECHNOLOGY IMPACT ON TRANSNATIONAL FIRMS

The new technologies of the past decade have affected the ways and places where firms do work in many ways, and their impact will be even greater in the coming decade as the technologies evolve and firms gain experience in implementing the changes enabled by them. Organization structures, control procedures, and tasks are being altered, albeit with great effort and expense.

Geographic Transfer of Work

The new technologies have facilitated the physical movement of work from areas with high-cost labor pools to areas where labor pools are both high quality and low cost. A domestic U.S. example is Citibank's moving its credit card operation from high-cost New York City to Sioux Falls, South Dakota. (Citibank achieved enormous savings.) In the same vein, American Airlines has moved a significant amount of its data entry work out of Dallas, where the company is headquartered. Documents are now keyed in Barbados, and the resulting outputs are transmitted electronically back to Dallas. Opportunities to source engineering and design activities internationally have also emerged. Several years ago a U.S. insurance company developed a significant systems development and programming unit in Ireland. This allowed the company to access the much less-expensive, high-quality Irish labor pool, effecting important savings. An added bonus was the firm's ability to use the third shift of domestic computer operations for debugging because of the five-hour time difference between Ireland and the United States. Similarly, a number of software organizations with more than 100,000 employees have developed in India; these compete aggressively for Western Europe and American systems development activities, particularly for highly structured tasks and ones with medium to high technology. In a world where the economy is increasingly service oriented and where telecommunications costs continue to drop, such trends will accelerate.

Global Networking and Expertise Sharing

Firms like IBM and Price Waterhouse have developed very sophisticated international electronic mail, groupware, and conferencing technology and procedures. Tens of thousands of professional support staff around the world now have direct electronic access to each other. Global sources of knowledge can be quickly tapped, the barriers of time zones swept away, and the overall response time to problems sharply altered. (Recall our earlier example of a marketing representative assembling documentation from around the world and preparing a 200-page, multimillion-dollar project proposal in 48 hours.) As overseas markets, manufacturing facilities, and research facilities proliferate, these coordinating mechanisms become vitally important in a world where competition is time-based. Inexpensive, broad-band, fiber-based global communication provides important opportunities for sharing and managing designs, manufacturing schedules, and text. Identifying expertise and then sharing it globally are allowing some transnational firms to differentiate themselves in the late 1990s. The new capabilities and costs made possible by optical fiber are only accelerating this.

Global Service Levels

The standards constituting world-class service are sharply increasing. Several years ago, for example, a major U.S. trucking company could tell you where each of its trucks was and what was on it (e.g., a truck had just left the Kansas City depot carrying a certain load and should arrive in San Francisco in 36 hours). The truck's location at a precise moment was unknown, however, and there was no way to direct the driver to cities in between for emergency pickups. (This was as good as any of its competitors could do.) Today, on top of each of the company's trucks is a small satellite dish containing a computer. The firm now knows exactly where each truck is (within a city) and at any time can send instructions to drivers to alter their routes as customer needs emerge and change.

In the overseas transportation business, global information links have allowed U.S. carriers such as American President Lines to survive in a world dominated by low-cost competitors. Since the 1970s, this firm has used IT to provide a highly customized and differentiated electronic-based service for its customers around the world. It has thereby neutralized its competitors' significant labor cost advantage by providing a highly valuable customer service, which includes up-to-the-minute cargo locations, reliable delivery promises, and flexibility in handling emergencies. Such advantages, of course, do not endure forever, and the pressure to innovate to maintain this edge is constant.

Time-Based Competition

The required response time in the global community is dramatically shrinking. Automobile manufacturers and large construction firms, for example, have been able to shave months—even years—off the design cycle as local computer-aided design equipment is linked internationally to CAD equipment owned by them, their suppliers, and their customers. In financial services, the question repeatedly arises, "Is two-second response time enough, or are we at a significant competitive disadvantage?" A speaker at a telecommunication conference recently noted that within a week after the opening of the new London stock exchange, which allows automatic electronic tracking, firms using satellites had shifted to optical fiber because the 50-*millisecond* delay put them at a distinct competitive disadvantage.

In between these extremes, of course, are situations where taking weeks off order entry, order confirmation, and manufacturing cycles is the issue. A UK chemical company's $30 million investment in manufacturing and information technology transformed what had been a 10-week order entry and manufacturing cycle to one or two days. Needless to say, this changed the rules of industry competition and put unbearable pressure on some competitors. In the words of one of our colleagues, "Competing on the basis of time is done not just by speeding up the mess, but by enabling the construction of very different infrastructures that challenge every aspect of the firm's procedures." Global time-based competition will be a major item for world business in the next decade.

Cost Reduction

Much tighter information links between overseas operations, customers, and suppliers allow a firm to eliminate significant slack from its manufacturing systems, resulting in significant reductions in buffer inventories and staffing levels and a general acceleration in asset utilization. At the extreme, these links enable the creation of "hollow" global corporations such as Benetton, which owns virtually nothing but a sophisticated global information system that connects the activities of its franchises with its suppliers.

In sum, IT has transformed the very structures of transnational organizations, the type of work they do, and where they do the work; it has also meant massive disruptions in existing patterns of work. More important, the new technologies assure that this impact shall evolve. The dark side of this trend, of course, is a huge increase in operational dependence on networks, central processors, and so on. In consequence, firms have built high levels of redundancy into their networks, creating alternative paths for information flow to back up their computing centers and so on. Reuters, as we have seen, provides more than a dozen electronic information paths from one part of the world to others. For many organizations, these issues are so fundamental and of such potential impact that the IT activity is positioned near the top of the firm and is intimately involved in all strategic planning activities to ensure it can fully support the firm's plans.

COUNTRY DIVERSITY

A number of factors inherent in a culture, government, and economy determine which IT applications are feasible within the country, how they should be implemented, and how (if at all) they should be directed by a corporate IT function located in another country. The most important factors are discussed here.

Sociopolitical

A country's industrial maturity and form of government are particularly important factors when considering the use of information technology. Developing countries with high birth rates and low labor cost structures have views and opportunities far different from those of mature industrialized nations with their shrinking labor populations and well-established bureaucracies that provide the necessary stability for developing communication systems. In some countries, investments in technical infrastructure are made at the expense of such other national priorities as food and medical care. This was a driving force for Malaysia, for example, to privatize their telecommunications so they could gain access to the capital markets. In countries like Hungary, investments in land lines are so inadequate (and time will be needed to rectify this) that cellular networks have taken over the dominant role.

Language

A common spoken language facilitates technical communication and the sharing of relevant documentation. When that is lacking, the potential for errors, mishaps, or worse is greatly increased. Frequently, senior managers of international subsidiaries are fluent in the language of the parent company, but lower-level managers and staff technicians are not. Ciba-Geigy, the large Swiss pharmaceutical/chemical company, for example, has made a major effort to establish English as the companywide language, but, realistically, full fluency lies only at the senior management and staff levels.

Local Constraints

A multitude of local cultural traditions can inhibit the development of coordinated systems and orderly technology transfer between countries. Differing union agreements, holidays, tax regulations, and customs procedures all force major modifications of software for applications like accounting and personnel. Further, differences in holidays, working hours, and so on, complicate coordination of reporting and data gathering.

Also important are issues relating to geography and demographics. For example, a large music company centralized its order-entry and warehouse management functions for France in Paris, because doing so fit the structure of that country's distribution system. In Germany, however, the company had to establish multiple factories and distribution points and a quite different order-entry system for serving the German market, because that structure reflects the realities of German geography and prevailing distribution patterns. Unfortunately, the software and procedures used in the French subsidiary are inappropriate for German operations.

Economics

Serving the interests of different national cultures in a transnational IT organization often means building country-specific solutions. A mature industrial economy, for instance, normally has an available pool of well-trained, procedurally oriented individuals who are well paid relative to world standards. Further, the economic incentive to replace clerical people with IT systems is complemented by a limited availability of well-trained clerical staff. In countries with low wage rates, however, perhaps dependent on one or two main raw material exports for currency, both human talent and economic incentive toward IT are lacking. (In the microchip world, however, this is changing quickly.) Organizations operating in such countries need to develop, within these countries, both reliable sources of information and more conducive environments for IT use.

Currency Issues

Currency restrictions and exchange-rate volatility also complicate the operation of international information service activities. A sharp change in exchange rates may make the supposed cost-effective location for providing service to neighboring countries suddenly cost-ineffective. The late 1994 devaluation of the Mexican peso and the steady appreciation of the Japanese yen during the 1990s are examples of moves that caused major rethinking of the location of software development activities.

Autonomy

The drive for autonomy and feelings of nationalism also represent important issues. The normal drive for autonomy in units within a country is intensified by differences in language and culture as one deals with international subsidiaries. In general, more integration effort is needed to coordinate foreign subsidiaries than domestic ones. Coordination difficulties increase with the subsidiary's distance from corporate headquarters as its relative economic importance to the corporation decreases and if different spoken languages are the norm.

National Infrastructure

The cost and availability of utilities (particularly telecommunications utilities), reliable electric power, and a transportation system can place important constraints on feasible alternatives. On the other hand, their absence may provide an opportunity to experiment with certain emerging technologies. For example, to overcome one country's unpredictable transportation and communication systems, a South American distributor developed a private microwave tower network to link the records of a remote satellite depot with the central warehouses. Direct ground links to satellites and cells can by-pass the need for expensive ground line installation.

Summary

These factors in aggregate make coordinating international IT activities more complicated than domestic IT activities; indeed, the complications are so deep-rooted as to provide enduring challenges. Consequently, most multinationals have had to develop special staff and organizational approaches for these issues.

NATIONAL IT ENVIRONMENT ISSUES

In addition to the many differences among countries, some specific IT issues make coordinating and transferring information technology from one country to another particularly challenging. These are due in part to the long lead times necessary for building effective systems and in part to the changing nature of the technology. The most important of these issues are discussed in this section.

Availability of IT Professional Staff

Inadequate availability of systems and programming resources, a worldwide problem, is more severe in some settings than others. Further, as soon as people in some English-speaking countries develop these skills, they become targets for recruiters from more industrialized countries where salaries are higher—a particular problem in the Philippines, for example.

If local IT staff are supplemented by people from corporate headquarters, the results are often not totally satisfactory. The expatriates can provide an initial outburst of productivity and an effective transfer of new technology and skills. This may result in local staff resentment. It can also lead to broken career paths for the expatriates who find they have become both technically and managerially obsolete when they return to corporate headquarters. Management of IT expatriates' reentry to their home offices has generally been quite inadequate.

This personnel shortage has led to the growth of India-based software companies such as Tata and HCL (Hindustani Computers Limited), which take advantage of India's high skill levels and very low wage rates to bid effectively on overseas programming jobs. Obviously, geographic distances limit the types of work these companies can bid on. Highly structured applications are much easier to develop remotely than those with less structure requiring much closer interaction between end user and developer during the systems development phase.

Central Telecommunications

The price, quality, and availability of telecommunications support vary widely from one country to another. On all three dimensions, the United States sets the standard. In many European countries, the tariffs on these services are an order-of-magnitude higher than those in the United States (although with the trend toward deregulation, this is beginning to change rapidly). Also, lead times to get extra land lines, terminals, and so forth, can stretch to years instead of weeks in many countries—if they are available at any price (thus, the move to cellular and satellite links). Conversely, the service may be outstanding to international gateways and terrible inside the country. Finally, communication quality, availability, and cost differ widely among countries. As a consequence of varying line capacity, costs, and uptime performance, profitable home-country on-line applications can become cost-ineffective, inadequate, or unreliable in some other countries.

National IT Strategy

In some countries, development of a local computer manufacturing and software industry is a key national priority. This has been true of France, Germany, Singapore, and the United Kingdom in the past and more recently for India and the Philippines. In these situations, subsidiaries of foreign companies can view buying the products of the local manufacturer as both evidence of good citizenship and as an opportunity to build credit for later dealings with the government. This motivation creates a legitimate need for local deviation from corporate hardware/software standards.

General Level of IT Sophistication

The speed and ease with which companies can implement or develop an IT activity are linked to the general level of IT activity in the country. A firm located in a country with a substantial base of installed state-of-the-art electronic-based information systems and well-trained, mobile labor can develop its IT capabilities more rapidly and effectively than if these conditions did not exist. Countries with limited installed electronic-based information systems require substantially more expatriate labor to implement IT work, as well as great effort and time to educate users in the idiosyncrasies of IT and how best to interface with it. Careful investigation of the staff mobility factor is particularly important, because bonding arrangements and cultural norms may place considerable rigidity on what appears to be a potentially satisfactory labor supply. In all but the most backward of countries, however, the past decade has seen a surge of IT skills and expertise.

Size of Local Market

The size of the local market influences the number of vendors who compete for service in it. Thus, in small markets, a company's preferred international supplier for particular hardware and for software may not have a presence, thereby complicating service. Further, the quality of service support varies widely from one setting to another; vendors who provide good support in one country may give inadequate support in another. Also important is the availability and quality of local software and consulting companies (or subsidiaries of large international ones). A thriving, competent local IT industry can offset other differences in local support and staff availability.

Data Export Control

Since the mid-1980s, significant publicity has been given to the issue of how much information about people and finances may be transmitted electronically across national boundaries. It has been driven both by concerns about individual privacy and the often weak security and low-quality controls over these data.

A relatively benign point of discussion in the 1980s, it is rearing its head much more vigorously in the 1990s. The use of personal data generates a wide range of sensitivities in different societies. In general, it is of most concern in Western Europe today, particularly in the Scandinavian countries, and is of less concern in the United States, although this is changing. Existing legislation and practice vary widely among countries, as do criteria for evaluating and resolving these issues. The business community should not misread current apparent lack of interest in these issues; they are deep and emotional and the spotlight will eventually make this a burning topic. What is seen in one environment as a sharp consumer micromarketing implementation may be seen as deeply intrusive and immoral in another. Increasingly, the word *Orwellian* has become a label for some new IT applications that use personal data.

Technological Awareness

Awareness of contemporary technology spreads very rapidly around the globe because IT magazines, journals, and consultants are distributed internationally. This awareness poses problems for effective applications development in less IT-sophisticated countries because it leads subsidiaries to promote technologies that they neither understand, need, nor are capable of managing. Conversely, late starters with a high degree of IT awareness have advantages because they can pioneer distinctly different and faster paths for exploiting information technology in the subsidiaries than are used in home offices.

Summary

For a transnational firm, the factors described above severely constrain the way in which policies and controls can be implemented in its international activities. Rigid policy cannot be dictated effectively from corporate headquarters, often located a vast distance from the subsidiary's operating management. Because there are many legitimate reasons for diversity, local know-how must be brought to decisions.

CORPORATE FACTORS AFFECTING IT REQUIREMENTS

Within the context of the different national cultures and the current state of the IT profession in different countries, numerous factors inside a company influence how fast information technology can be transferred internationally and how centralized its control of international IT activity should be. As we have stressed, more control must be delegated in an international environment than in a domestic one. Important opportunities exist for technology transfer, however, but important limitations in service and cost performance can arise if these opportunities are not managed. The more important company-specific factors are discussed here.

Nature of the Firm's Business

Some firms' businesses demand that key data files be managed centrally so that they are accessible, immediately or on a short delayed-access basis, to all units around the world. Airline reservation files for international air carriers require such access. A United Airlines agent in Boston confirming a flight segment from Tokyo to Hong Kong needs up-to-the-minute access to the flight's loading to make a valid commitment, while other agents around the globe need to know that seat is no longer available for sale. Failure to have this information poses risks of significant loss of market share, as customers perceive the firm to be both unreliable and uncompetitive.

American President Lines, an international shipping company, maintains a file, updated every 24 hours, comprising the location of each of its containers, its status, and its availability for future commitment by regional officers in 20 countries. Without this information, the firm would most likely make unfulfillable commitments, which would present an unreliable image to present and potential customers. In another example, the standards of international banking have evolved to where the leaders provide customers with an instantaneous worldwide picture of clearances, and so on, thus opening the door for more sophisticated cash management—for which the banks charge significant fees. Those firms not providing such services find themselves increasingly at a competitive disadvantage.

Other firms require integration and on-line updating of only some of their files. A European electronics firm attempts to provide its European managers with up-to-date, on-line access to various key operational files on such items as production schedules, order status, and so forth. This is done for its network of 20-plus factories in order to manage an integrated logistics system. International client/server architecture is up and running. No such integration, however, is attempted for key marketing or accounting data, which essentially are processed on a batch basis and organized by country. While developing such integration is technically possible, at present the firm sees no operational or marketing advantage in doing so.

Still other firms require essentially no integration of data, and each country can be managed on a stand-alone basis. A U.S. conglomerate, for example, manages each division this way. Eight of its divisions have operations in the United Kingdom, and by corporate policy they have no formal interaction with each other in IT or any other operational matters. (A single tax specialist who files a joint tax return for them is the sole linking specialist.) The company's staff generally perceives this to be an appropriate way to operate, with nothing of significance being lost. Such examples suggest the impossibility of generalizing about how transnational IT activities should be organized.

Strategic Impact of IT

If IT activity is strategic to the company, tighter corporate overview is needed to ensure that new technology (with its accompanying new ways of operating) is rapidly and efficiently introduced to outlying areas. One of the United States' largest international banks, for example, has a staff of more than 100 at corporate headquarters to develop software for their international branches and to coordinate its orderly dissemination to them. The bank feels the successful use of IT is too critical to the firm's ultimate success to be managed without technical coordination and senior management perspective. At the other extreme is a reasonably large manufacturer of chemicals that sees IT as playing an important but clearly a support role. At least twice a year, the head of the European IT unit and the head of corporate IT exchange visits and share perceptions. The general consensus is that there is not enough potential payoff to warrant further coordination.

Corporate Organization

As its international activity grows, a firm adopts different structures, each requiring quite different levels of international IT support and coordination. The earliest phase of an export division generally requires only limited numbers of overseas staff, who need little if any local IT processing and support. As the activity grows in size, it tends to be reorganized as an international division with a larger number of marketing, accounting, and manufacturing staff located abroad. At this stage, an increasing need for local IT support may arise. A full-blown level of international activity may involve regional headquarters (in Europe, the Far East, and Latin America, for example) to coordinate the activities of the diverse countries.

Coordinating such a structure is very complex. Not only are there vertical relationships between corporate IT and the national IT activities, but cross-border marketing and manufacturing integration requirements create the need for relationships between individual countries' IT units. Appropriate forms of this coordination, of course, vary widely. A multibillion dollar pharmaceutical firm was discovered to have very close links between corporate IT and its major national IT units (defined by the firm as those with budgets in excess of $5 million). None of the IT unit managers, however, knew the names of their contemporaries nor had visited any of the other units. Since little cross-border product flow existed and none was planned for the near future, this did not appear to present a significant problem.

At the most complex level are firms organized in a matrix fashion—with corporate IT activity, divisional IT activities (which may or may not be located at corporate headquarters), and national IT activities. Here, balancing relationships is a major challenge. Divisions having substantial vertical supplier relationships with each other and substantial integration of activities across national borders possess even more complicated relationships. In such cases, the policies that work for the international divisions are too simplistic.

Company Technical and Control Characteristics

Level of Functional Control.   An important factor in effective IT control structures is the corporation's general level of functional control. Companies with a strong tradition of central control find it both appropriate and relatively easy to implement line IT control worldwide. A major manufacturer of farm equipment, for example, has for years implemented very strong management and operational control over its worldwide manufacturing and marketing functions. Consequently, it found considerable acceptance of similar controls for the IT organization. Most of the software that runs the overseas plants has been developed and is maintained by the corporate IT headquarters group.

At the other extreme is a 30-division, multibillion dollar conglomerate with a 100-person corporate staff involved mostly in financial and legal work associated with acquisitions and divestitures. This company has totally decentralized operating decisions to the divisions, and the number of corporate staff is deliberately controlled as a means of preventing "meddling." At present, a two-person corporate IT "group" works on only very broad policy and consulting issues. Effective execution of even this limited role is very challenging, and its expansion is very difficult to visualize.

Technology Base.   A company's technology base is another important factor. High-technology companies with traditions of spearheading technical change from a central research and engineering laboratory and disseminating it around the world have successfully used a similar approach with IT. Their transnational managers are used to corporately initiated technical change. Firms without this experience have had more difficulty assimilating information technology in general, as well as more problems in transplanting IT developed in one location to other settings.

Corporate Size.   Finally, corporate size is also relevant. Smaller organizations, because of the limited and specialized nature of their application, find transferring IT packages and expertise to be particularly complex. As the scope of the operation increases, however, it becomes easier to discover common applications and facilitate transfer of technology—perhaps because the stakes are higher.

Other Considerations

Other factors also influence IT coordination policies. Is there substantial rotation of staff between international locations? If so, is it desirable to have common reporting systems and operating procedures in place in each subsidiary to ease the assimilation of the transfers? Do the firm's operating and financial requirements essentially demand up-to-the-week reporting of overseas financial results? If not, consolidating smaller overseas operations on a one-month, delayed-time basis is attractive.

TRANSNATIONAL IT POLICY ISSUES

As the preceding sections explain, great diversity exists in the policies for coordinating and managing international IT activities. This section identifies the most common types of policies and relationships and briefly addresses key issues associated with the selection and implementation of each. The scope of these policies and the amount of effort needed to implement them are influenced by the degree of needed central control, corporate culture and policies, strategic importance of information technologies, and other factors.

Guidance on Architecture

The most important central IT role is to facilitate the development and implementation of a view on appropriate telecommunications architecture, operating systems, and database standards. The firm must pragmatically move to ensure that these standards are installed in all of its operations. There are no substitutes in this task for pragmatism and the ability to listen. Ideas that make perfect sense in Detroit may need selective fine tuning in Thailand—if indeed they are even viable there at all.

The opportunity to transmit data electronically between countries for file updating and processing purposes has created the need for a corporate international data dictionary. Too often, this need is not addressed, leading to clumsy systems designs and incorrect outputs. Where data should be stored, the form in which they should be stored, and how they should be updated are all considerations requiring a centrally managed policy—operating, of course, within the framework of what is legally permissible.

Similarly, central guidance and coordination in the acquisition of communication technology are important. At present, communication flexibility and cost not only vary widely from country to country, but they are shifting rapidly.

Effectively anticipating these cost and flexibility changes requires a corporate view and broad design of telecommunications needs for meeting the demands of growth and changing business needs over the coming decade. The service levels and the technologies to be utilized must be specified. Such a plan requires capable technical inputs and careful management review. An important by-product of the plan is guidance for corporate negotiation and lobbying efforts on relevant items of national legislation and policies regarding the form, availability, and cost of telecommunication.

Central Hardware/Software Concurrence or Approval

The objectives of a central policy for acquiring hardware and software are to ensure that cost-effective global networking is acquired, that obvious mistakes in vendor viability are avoided, and that purchasing decisions achieve economies of scale. Other benefits include the bargaining leverage a company gains by being perceived as an important customer, the reduction of potential interface problems between national systems, and the enhancement of applications software transferability between countries. Practical factors demanding sensitive interpretation and execution of central policy include:

- Corporate headquarters' awareness of the vendor's support and servicing problems in the local country.
- The local subsidiary's desire to exercise its autonomy and control its operations in a timely way. The Korean subsidiary of a large bank, for example, wanted to buy a $25,000 word processing system. Its request for approval took six months to pass through three locations and involved one senior vice president and two executive vice presidents. Whatever benefits standardization might have achieved for the bank in this situation seemed to be more than offset by the cost and time of the approval process.
- Need to maintain good relationships with local governments. This may involve patronizing local vendors, agreeing not to eliminate certain types of staff, and using the government-controlled IT network.
- Level and skill of corporate headquarters people who set the technical and managerial policies. A technically weak corporate staff dealing with large, well-managed foreign subsidiaries must operate quite differently from a technically gifted central staff working with small, unsophisticated subsidiaries.

Central Approval of Software Standards and Feasibility Studies

Central control of software standards can ensure that software is written or sourced in a maintainable, secure way so that the company's long-term operational position is not jeopardized. Control of feasibility studies can ensure that potential applications are evaluated in a consistent and professional fashion. Practical problems with this policy of central approval revolve around both the level of effort required and the potential erosion of corporate culture.

Implementing such standards can be expensive and time-consuming in relation to the potential benefits. The art is to be flexible with small investments and to review more closely the investments that involve real operational exposure. Unfortunately, this approach requires more sensitivity than many staffs possess.

Further, a decentralized company's prevailing management control system and the location of other operating decisions may directly conflict with central control. The significance of this conflict depends on the size and strategic importance of the investment. Relatively small distinctly "support" investments in decentralized organizations should clearly be resolved in the local country. Large strategic investments, however, should be subject to central review in these organizations, even if time delays and cost overruns result.

Central Software Development

In the name of efficiency, reduced costs, and standard operating procedures worldwide, some firms have attempted to develop software centrally, or at a designated subsidiary, for installation in subsidiaries in other countries. The success of this approach has definitely been mixed. Most companies that have succeeded have well-established patterns of technology transfer, strong functional control over their subsidiaries, substantial numbers of expatriates working in the overseas subsidiaries, and some homogeneity in their manufacturing, accounting, and distribution practices. Success has also resulted when the IT unit responsible for the package's development and installation has carried out very intensive marketing and liaison activities.

When these preconditions have not been present, however, installation has often been troubled. The reasons most commonly cited by IT managers for the failure include:

- The developers of the system did not understand local needs well enough. Major functions were left out, and the package required extensive and expensive enhancements.
- The package was adequate, but the efforts needed to train people to input data and handle outputs properly were significantly underestimated (or mishandled). This was complicated by extensive language difficulties and insensitivity to existing local procedures.
- The system evolution and maintenance involved a dependence on central staff that was not sustainable in the long run. Flexibility and timeliness of response were problems.

- Costs were significantly underestimated. The overrun on the basic package was bad enough, but the fat was really in the fire when the installation costs were added.

Such statements seem to reflect the importance of organizational and cultural factors. In reality, an outside software house, with its marketing orientation and its existence beyond the corporate family, often does a better job of selling standard software than an in-house IT unit in a decentralized transnational environment. Finally, in many settings, the sheer desire on both sides for success is the best guarantee of success.

IT Communications

Although they are expensive, investments in improving communications between the various national IT units often pay big dividends. Several devices have proven useful:

1. *Regular interunit meetings*—An annual or biannual conference of the IT directors and the key staff of the major international subsidiaries. For organizations in the "turnaround" or "strategic" categories, these meetings should occur at least as frequently as do meetings of international controllers. Small subsidiaries (IT budgets under $1 million) probably do not generate enough profitable opportunities to warrant inclusion in this conference or to have a separate one.

The conference agenda should combine planned formal activities (e.g., technical briefings, application briefings, and company directives) with substantial blocks of unplanned time. The informal exchange of ideas, initiation of joint projects, and sharing of mutual problems are among the most important activities of a successful conference.

2. *Corporate-subsidiary exchange visits*—Regular visits of corporate IT personnel to the national organizations, as well as of national IT personnel to corporate IT headquarters. These visits should occur at planned intervals, rather than only when an operational crisis or technical problem arises. Less contact is needed with the smaller units than with the larger ones.

3. *Newsletters*—A monthly or bimonthly newsletter to communicate staffing shifts, new technical insights, major project completions, experience with software packages and vendors, and so forth.

4. *Education*—Organizing joint education programs where possible. This may involve the creation and/or acquisition of audiovisual materials to be distributed around the world. A large oil company recently supplemented written communications about a radically different IT organization structure with a special film, complete with sound track in five languages.

One of the largest UK chemical companies has literally a one-person corporate IT "department," who continuously travels the world, helping to facilitate education and training sessions and identifying appropriate topics and sources of expertise for IT staff in far-flung places. The individual is a member of the firm's most senior general management and clearly adds substantial value. General management and middle management staff awareness programs remain a central challenge for this leader.

Developing stronger psychological links between the national IT units is fundamental. These links can be as important as the formal ties between the national IT units and the parent company's IT unit.

Facilitating the development of centers of systems expertise in many parts of the world is another important need. A single-system unit in the parent company's home country is not necessarily the best way to operate. Many jobs can usefully be split over three or four development centers. One of the large entertainment companies recently assigned large portions of its financial systems, marketing systems, and production systems to its UK, German, and French development units, respectively. While each unit was enthusiastic about leading their part of the effort, they also knew that if they did not cooperate, they in turn would not receive the cooperation necessary to assure the success of their unit's output. This approach tapped new sources of expertise and was successful because of the shared interdependencies of leadership and innovation.

Staff Rotation

Rotating staff between national IT units and corporate IT is an important way of encouraging communication; at the same time, the practice can generate problems. Both advantages and disadvantages are addressed below.

Advantages

- Better corporate IT awareness of the problems and issues in the overseas IT units. As a corollary, the local IT units have a much better perspective on the goals and thinking at corporate headquarters because one of their members has spent a tour of duty there.
- More flexibility in managing career paths and matching positions with individual development needs. Particularly to someone working in a crowded corporate IT department, an overseas assignment could seem very attractive.
- Efficient dispersion of technical know-how throughout the organization.

Disadvantages

- People can jeopardize their career paths by moving from corporate headquarters to less IT-developed parts of the world. The individuals bring leading-edge expertise to the overseas installation and have a major positive impact for several years. When they return to corporate headquarters they may find themselves completely out of touch with the contemporary technologies being used. Also, some of these people have been dropped out of the normal progression stream through oversight.

- Assigning people overseas not only involves expensive moving allowances and cost-of-living differentials, but it also raises a myriad of potential personal problems. These problems, normally of a family nature, make the success of an international transfer more speculative than a domestic one.
- Transfers from corporate to smaller overseas locations may cause substantial resentment and feelings of nationalism in the overseas location: "Why aren't our people good enough?" Such problems can be tempered with appropriate language skills and efforts on the part of the transferred executive, corporate control over the number of transfers, local promotions, and clearly visible opportunities for local staff to be transferred to corporate.

Appropriately managed within reasonable limits, the advantages far outweigh the disadvantages.

Consulting Services

Major benefits can come from a central IT group's providing foreign subsidiaries with consulting services on both technical and managerial matters. In many cases, corporate headquarters is not only located in a technically sophisticated country, but its IT activities are bigger in scope than those of individual foreign installations. Among other things, this means that:

1. Corporate IT is more aware of leading-edge hardware/software technology and has had firsthand experience with its potential strengths and weaknesses.
2. Corporate IT is more likely to have experience with large project-management systems and other management methods.

In both cases, the communication must be done with sensitivity in order to move the company forward at an appropriate pace. All too often, the corporate group pushes too fast in a culturally insensitive fashion, creating substantial problems. Movement through the phases of technology assimilation can be speeded up and smoothed, but no phase should be skipped.

As an organization becomes more IT intensive, effective IT auditing becomes increasingly important for shielding the organization from excessive and unnecessary risks. IT auditing is a rapidly evolving profession that faces a serious staff shortage. The shortage is more severe outside the United States and Europe. Thus, the corporate audit group of a transnational frequently must take responsibility for conducting international IT audits and for helping to develop national IT audit staffs and capabilities.

Central IT Processing Support

The extent to which IT should be pushed toward a central hub or a linked international network depends on the firm's industry and the dimensions along which it chooses to compete. At one extreme is the airline industry, where being unable, on a global basis, to confirm seats is a significant competitive disadvantage. Originally, international airlines were driven to centralize as an offensive weapon; now it is a defensive one. At the other extreme is a company with a network of operations for converting paper (a commodity). Transportation costs severely limit how far away from a plant orders can profitably be shipped. Thus, the company handles order entry and factory management on a strictly national basis, with a modest interchange of data between countries. Even here, however, substantial economies have come from international standardization of packages and corporate purchasing agreements.

Technology Appraisal Program—An Example

An international appraisal can provide perspective, allowing greater coordination of overseas IT efforts. A U.S.-based transnational company with a long history of European operations discovered that its operations in the Far East and South America were posing increasingly complicated information problems. General management initiated a three-year program for bringing the overseas operation under control. The first step was to appraise the condition of each national IT unit and its potential business, which was conducted by a three-person IT team with multilingual abilities. It was followed by a formulation of policies and appropriate action programs at the annual meeting of company executives.

Originally planned as a one-time assessment of only 11 national IT units, the effort was considered so successful that it was reorganized as an established audit function. The team learned to appraise locally available technology and to guide local management in judging its potential. This required at least one week and often two weeks in the field, typically in two trips. The first visit appraised existing services and raised general concerns that local management could effectively pursue. The second visit assessed problems of:

1. Government restrictions.
2. Quality and quantity of available human skills.
3. Present and planned communications services.

Alternatives to the present means of service were examined further, and economic analyses of at least three standard alternatives were prepared. The three standard alternatives were:

1. Expansion of present system.
2. Transfer of all or portions of IT work to a neighboring country.
3. Transfer of all or portions of IT work to regional headquarters.

Local managers' enthusiasm for this review was not universal, and, in several countries, long delays occurred between the first and second visits.

However, in 7 of the original 11 units, the appraisals succeeded in generating appropriate change by bringing better understanding of the potential impact of uncertainties—such as changing import duties, planned market introduction of new technologies by U.S. suppliers, and a new satellite communications alternative. This organized appraisal significantly increased senior management's awareness and comfort concerning IT. The activity became an ongoing effort for the company, and several persons were added to the appraisal team.

SUMMARY

Coordinating international IT is extraordinarily complex. Corporate IT management may have maximum responsibility for, but only limited authority over, distant staff and technologies. Leadership demands persuasion and cajoling, plus being well informed on new technologies, the corporate culture, and the wide diversity of cultures existing in the world. The job requires very high visibility and an appropriate reporting structure inside the firm. The latter is particularly important, given the need to lead through *relationships*.

If IT is globally strategic, the IT leadership must be represented at the very top of the firm, where acquisition, divestiture, and other components of corporate strategy are developed. The IT department's effectiveness crucially depends on its being heard in this forum. However, the interpretation of the function varies widely by industry, global reach, and size of firm. For example, the international airline business requires a large central hub to manage a global database. The IT leadership role in this industry consequently has a very strong global line management component. The earlier described chemical company's operations, on the other hand, are contained within individual, autonomous national units; hence, an entirely different structure of central IT is appropriate for that company, and IT corporate leadership involves more limited line responsibility but high-placed coordination.

International IT development must be managed actively to avert major long-term difficulties within and between national IT activities. Doing so is complicated because assimilation of information technology in countries is often more heavily influenced by local conditions such as infrastructure and service availability. Overcoming obstacles presented by the local conditions demands much more than simply keeping abreast of technology: a long view is required to succeed.

Chapter

13

The IT Business

The previous chapters in this book have presented frameworks for viewing the information technology activity and the functions of IT management; taken together, they specify how to conduct an IT management audit. This final chapter highlights the impact of the book's six major themes:

1. The strategic importance of information technology both evolves over time and is different for different organizations.
2. Computing, telecommunication, and desktop technologies are merging into a single whole.
3. Organization learning is important to technology assimilation.
4. Make-or-buy decisions are shifting toward much greater reliance on external sources of software and computing support.
5. The systems life-cycle concept continues to be valid, although the timing and process of executing the pieces have changed dramatically.
6. The pressures of the three constituencies—IT management, user management, and general management—must be continuously balanced.

"THE IT BUSINESS" ANALOGY

We view an organization's IT activity as a stand-alone "business within a business" and, in particular, choose to apply the concepts of marketing-mix analysis. This permits us to synthesize the concepts of organization, planning, control, and strategy formulation for IT. Using this analogy, we will speak of the business's strategy formulation as its marketing mix, its steering committee as the board of directors, and its IT director as the chief executive officer. These items are particularly relevant to the interface between the IT business and its host, or parent, organization—the firm.[1] We will not explain the details of operating strategy, since the general aspects of IT operations management are covered in Chapter 8; nor do we discuss here the issues of internal accounting and control within the IT organization, as they do not impact directly on the interface between the two businesses. For similar reasons, we discuss only those IT organizational issues dealing with external relations of the IT business.

IT is a high-technology, fast-changing industry. A particular "IT business" in this industry may be growing rapidly, remain more or less steady, or decline. Its territory encompasses the development, maintenance, and operation of all information technologies supporting a firm, regardless of where they are located and to whom they report.

The scope of IT technologies to be coordinated has expanded tremendously as computers, telecommunications, external databases, and desktop devices have merged, and its product offerings are exploding into such new consumer areas as electronic mail, groupware, editing, and computer-aided design/computer-aided manufacturing. The complexity of implementing projects, the magnitude of work to be done, and the scarcity of human resources have forced the IT business to change from a business that primarily produced things to one that identifies and distributes things; a significant percentage of its work now involves coordinating the acquisition of outside services for its customers to use. This shift has forced major changes in its approach to planning and controls in order to deal effectively with these new products and new sources of supply.

Implicit in this view of the IT business is that, at least at a policy level, the overwhelming majority of firms require an integrated perspective and approach to IT. The IT activities include not just the corporate IT center and its client-server networks, but also desktop devices, distributed systems development activities, outside software company contracts, computer service bureaus, and so on. Many users of IT services—its customers—possess options to buy services from providers other than the central IT organization—the business within the business.

We believe this analogy is useful for applying management principles and theories to the IT business in a way that generates important insights. Similarly, we believe that the analogy we draw between general management and a board of directors is useful in conceptualizing a realistic role for an executive steering committee.

Like all analogies, this one can be pushed too far and some caution is in order. For example, the financing of the IT business is not analogous to the corporate capital markets, since its capital support comes directly from the

---

[1]Throughout this chapter, the term *firm* refers to the parent holding company of the IT business.

firm (with no debt analogy), and its revenues—exclusively, in many cases—also come directly from the firm. In many respects, the customer bases of the IT business and the firm are dependent on common files, and so on, so that customers cannot be treated as entirely independent. Similarly, the IT business is free from many of the legal and governmental constraints on the firm. Other legal and governmental constraints—such as the Equal Employment Opportunity Commission (EEOC), for instance—are placed on it in the context of the firm's total corporate posture, and there is little possibility or need for the IT business to strike an independent posture.

The rest of this chapter is devoted to three topics related to managing the IT business:

- The IT marketing mix.
- The role of the IT board of directors.
- The role of the IT chief executive officer.

THE IT MARKETING MIX

The Products

The IT product line is continuously evolving. Table 13–1 summarizes the key aspects of change. Some of the dynamism of the product line is due to the enormous proliferation of opportunities afforded by the economics of new technology. Other dynamic elements include changing customer needs as a result of ordinary shifts in business and new insights (phase 2 learning) into how technology can be applied to specific operations.

In terms of development time and complexity to operate, IT products range in size from very small to enormous. A large product's development period can be so lengthy that it may not even meet the current customers' needs when it is completed. (Four years—for truly megaprojects—is not uncommon.) The introduction of some products can be delayed with only limited damage to the firm; however, if delays of any magnitude occur in the development of other products, the damage to consumers (users) may be severe. In terms of day-to-day operations, the importance of tight cost control, good response time, quality control, and so on, varies widely from one firm to another, as well as within different parts of the firm.

Product Obsolescence.   Product obsolescence is a major headache in the IT business. Products rapidly become clumsy, and introducing the necessary enhancements—styling changes—to keep them relevant can be very expensive. Eventually, major factory retooling is necessary. Emerging consumer needs (which can only be satisfied by new technologies) and those new manufacturing technologies combine to put sustained pressure on the IT business.

TABLE 13-1   Changes in IT Product Line

Factor	Focus	
	The Past	*The Future*
Product obsolescence.	Developing new products.	Heavy maintenance of old products to meet challenges of obsolescence.
Source.	Most products manufactured inside.	Significant percent sourced from outside.
Dominant economic constraint.	Capital intensive (hardware; economy of scale).	Personnel intensive (economy of skill).
Product mix.	Many large, few medium, many small products.	Some large, many medium, thousands of small products.
Profits/benefits.	Good return on investment.	Many projects have intangible benefits.
New-product technologies.	New technologies.	New technologies and regroupings of old ones.
Services.	Structured, such as automated accounting and inventory control.	Unstructured, such as executive decision support systems and query systems.

Sources, Marketplace Climate.   The method of delivering IT products is shifting as the IT customer makes many more of the sourcing decisions. An increasing percentage of IT development expenditures is going to software houses and database vendors, while production expenditures are being devoted to networks of server minicomputers and client personal computers. Formerly, IT was primarily a developer and manufacturer of products; now it is becoming a significant distributor of products manufactured by others, including being a complete distributor in outsourcing situations (e.g., at Eastman Kodak and General Dynamics). The distributor role involves identifying and evaluating products and professionally evaluating those that customers identify, with a view to ensuring that the costs and services of the firm as a whole are fully competitive.

IT products run the gamut from those whose need customers clearly and correctly understand (such as point-of-sale terminals) to those for which there is no perceived need and considerable, extended sales efforts must precede a sale. Products range from those that are absolutely essential and critical to the customer (inventory control systems, for instance) to those that are desirable but whose purchase can essentially be postponed (e.g., standard industry databases for spreadsheet files). Obviously, products at the two extremes require quite different sales approaches.

Sourcing decisions are complicated by differences in the maturity of IT suppliers. A relatively stable competitive pattern exists among suppliers of large mainframe computers, for instance, but the personal computer and middleware software markets are far more turbulent; in fact, it is not clear which companies will survive and what form their products will take five years from now. Although a competitive pattern is emerging, the Microsoft lawsuits, cellular innovations, new object-oriented database firms—among other factors—will confound the nature of competition for the foreseeable future.

In the past, monopoly control over product delivery gave IT businesses considerable discretion in timing their new-product introductions. The changed climate of competition and nature of products among IT suppliers imply that IT has lost control over the marketing of new products in many organizations.

Profits/Benefits. IT products range from those whose benefits can be crisply summarized in a return-on-investment (ROI) framework for the customer to those whose benefits are more qualitative and intangible and, thus, extremely hard to justify analytically. Again, products at the ends of the spectrum require different marketing approaches. Some products are absolutely structured (e.g., certain types of accounting data), while others are tailored to individual tastes and preferences. Further, in many instances, purchasers may not easily comprehend a product's complexity and the inherent factors influencing its quality. Finally, some products require tailoring during installation and thus need specific field support and distribution staffs whose costs are not easily estimated in advance.

Implications for Marketing. The above description of evolving IT product characteristics highlights the complexity of the IT marketing task. Other businesses attempt to streamline the product line in order to facilitate economy and efficiency in manufacturing and distribution; many IT businesses' inability to do this has contributed to turbulence in their management. Too often, they are trying to deliver too many products from their traditional monopoly-supplier position with weak promotion, surly sales, and fixation on manufacturing—as opposed to focusing on service and distribution. What works for one set of products may not work for another. Recognizing the need for and implementing a differentiated marketing approach is very difficult, particularly for a medium-sized IT business.

The IT Consumer

Description of the Consumer. The IT consumer's needs and sophistication are changing, as Table 13–2 summarizes. After 20 years of working with mature technologies, older consumers have become sensitive to the

TABLE 13–2 Changes in IT Consumer Profile

Factor	Consumers	
	Older	*Younger*
Experience with older technologies.	Experienced.	Inexperienced.
Attitude toward newer technologies.	Leery.	Enthusiastic and unsophisticated (but they do not recognize their lack of sophistication).
Visibility.	Identifiable as consumers.	Often unidentifiable as consumers; numerous at all levels in organizations.
Attitude toward IT unit.	Willing to accept IT staff as experts.	Many are hostile because they want to develop their own solutions.
Self-confidence.	Low confidence in their own abilities (often cautious because of cost).	High confidence in their abilities and judgment (often unwarranted).
Turnover rate.	High.	High.

problems of working within constraints; at the same time, many of them are quite unaware of the newer technologies and the enormous personal and organization behavioral modifications they must make in order to use them properly. These older consumers often bring their old purchasing habits to the new environment without understanding that it is new. Younger consumers, on the other hand, have close familiarity with GUI, personal computing, and surfing the Internet and tend to be intolerant when they are unable to get immediate access to whatever they need. They also, however, tend to be naive about the problems of designing and maintaining IT systems that must run on a regular basis. In general, both classes of consumers have major educational needs if they are to become responsible consumers.

The new user-friendly technologies have made the problem more complicated because many consumers see the opportunity to set up their own businesses, withdrawing from reliance on the IT business. Propelling them in this direction are their own entrepreneurs or purchasing agents (i.e., decentralized systems analysts), who are long on optimism and short on practical, firsthand expertise and realistic risk assessment. This go-it-alone, no-standards approach has turned out to be very expensive.

In such an environment, the IT marketing force particularly needs to target potential new consumers and reach them before they make independent sourcing decisions. New application clusters and groups of consumers keep surfacing. This ever-changing composition of consumer groups sustains the need for a field sales force. An effective job of educating people does no good if they move on to other assignments and are replaced by people unaware of current technologies and the sequence of decisions that led to the present status of the organization.

Firsthand personal computing experience and a barrage of advertising have substantially raised consumers' expectations and their general level of self-confidence in making IT decisions. Unfortunately, this confidence is often misplaced; there seems to be a lack of appreciation for subtle but important nuances and for the IT control practices necessary to ensure a significant probability of success. This also increases the need for sustained direct sales and follow-up.

In today's environment, the number of service alternatives for customers, some of which appear to have very low prices, has exploded. It is confusing to consumers when products essentially similar to those available in-house appear to be available at much lower prices out-of-house (by conveniently forgetting the long-term costs of maintenance and interchangability). Great consumer sophistication is needed to identify a *real* IT bargain.

Implications for Marketing.   The above factors have substantially complicated the IT marketing effort. An unstable group of consumers with diversified, rapidly changing needs (often linked among customers in ways they don't understand) requires a far higher level of direct-selling effort than do consumers without this cluster of characteristics. Intensifying the need to spend promotion money on these customers is the low regard for IT business's management in many settings. Consumers who are hostile about the perceived quality of IT support welcome solutions that will carry them as far away as possible from reliance on the IT business management. Trained to respond correctly to many of yesterday's technologies, they are inappropriately trained for today's. Underinvestment in the marketing necessary for dealing with these realities has been a major cause of dissatisfaction among users.

Costs

Cost Factors.   From a marketing viewpoint, significant changes are occurring in the costs of producing and delivering systems, as summarized in Table 13–3. On the one hand, the cost of many IT hardware elements has decreased dramatically and is likely to continue to drop significantly. On the other hand, reducing the cost of software development is likely to progress slowly for some time (although object-oriented technology offers the potential to change this). Moreover, the ability to accurately estimate the development, production, and maintenance costs for large, high-technology, low-structure systems continues to be disappointing.

TABLE 13–3   Changes in Consumer Costs

Cost Factor	Cost to the Consumer	
	The Past	*The Future*
Hardware.	Very expensive.	Very expensive.
Economies of scale.	Major in large systems; user stand-alones not feasible in most cases.	Limited in large systems; user stand-alones very attractive.
Software systems development.	Expensive.	Less expensive in some cases.
Software acquisitions.	Limited cost-effective outside opportunities.	Attractive cost-effective opportunities.
Development and production.	Hard to estimate.	Hard to estimate.
Maintenance.	Underestimated.	Soaring.

The steady increase in the cost of maintaining installed software (either self-developed or purchased) is a critical component of cost explosion. These expenses are usually not factored in carefully at the time of purchase, and they tend to grow as the business grows and changes over the years. In the short term, these costs can be deferred with apparently little damage. In the long term, however, neglecting them can cause a virtual collapse of the product. Similarly, a purchased or rented package generates a never-ending stream of upgrades to be handled, which can generate considerable costs and time delays.

The proliferation of software houses and packages and the overall cost reductions have accelerated the movement of the IT business into the distributor role. It is now cost-effective to purchase specialized databases and software useful to many users that would be utterly uneconomic if developed and maintained by single users for their own purposes. Not all efforts in developing shared software have been successful, however. For example, a consortium of 25 regional banks funded a joint $13 million software development project (in areas such as demand deposit accounting and savings accounts). The consortium's inability to manage the project doomed it to failure. Additionally, the failure rate of fledgling software package companies is quite high. Another change is the growing number of users who have their own computer capacity. At some business schools, for instance, 100 percent of the students and nearly all of the faculty own personal computers. The schools may or may not own this equipment, but facilitate its acquisition by the students and faculty and identify the standards it must conform to if it is to be attached to the school's networks.

As will be discussed in the section on pricing, identifying potential or actual total costs for a particular product or service is difficult—in part because data clusters or software modules often support multiple products and consumers. This raises the issue of whether costs should be treated as joint costs or by-product costs. Another complicating factor is the extent to which previously spent R&D costs (to get to today's skill levels) should be treated as part of a product's cost.

While cost management and control are a critical component of the IT business strategy, how they are executed varies significantly among IT settings. High-growth, product-competitive environments place more emphasis on new services and products with less emphasis on IT efficiency and cost control than do environments where the firm's products are more stable and competition is cost-based; in these settings, IT efficiency and cost control can be paramount.

Implications for Marketing.   In summary, the changing cost structure of IT products has forced the IT business to reconsider its sourcing decisions and has pushed it to assume a much stronger distribution role. The relative emphasis an IT business places on cost control, product-line growth, quality, and service depends on its business strategy; thus, wide variances exist.

Channels of Distribution

As described in Chapters 2, 4, 5, and 6, the number of channels of distribution (to users) and their relative importance have been shifting rapidly. Table 13–4 shows some of the important changes in this domain. Historically, the major channel for both manufacturing and delivering the IT product has been the IT business itself; in most firms it has had a complete monopoly. Changing cost factors and shifts in user preferences have placed great pressure on this channel, causing deep concern inside the IT business as it has adapted to the new challenges of a competitive market—which it cannot totally serve in a cost-effective fashion from its manufacturing facility. Adapting to a new mission, the IT business is now not the sole channel for service and manufacturing but, rather, one of many sources of manufacturing. It has assumed the major new role of identifying products in other channels and assessing their cost, quality, and so on, bringing them to their customer's attention. Adapting to this new role has made many IT businesses very uncomfortable psychologically as they have struggled with such incorrect notions as loss of power.

Risks in Using New Channels.   Successful, rapid adaptation by the IT business is critical to the health of its present and future consumers. The new channels, while offering very attractive products and cost structures, introduce sizable risks in many cases. The most important of these risks include:

1. Misassessment of the real development and operations costs of the products in the channel. Important short-term and more important long-term cost factors may be completely overlooked. The earlier men-

TABLE 13–4 Changes in the IT Channels of Distribution

Distribution Factor	The Past	The Future
Development by central IT.	Heavy.	Significant but smaller percent of total.
Direct purchase of hardware/ software by user.	Limited.	Major.
Service source for individual user.	Limited to service from large, shared system.	Can obtain powerful independent system.
Service bureaus.	Sell time.	Sell products and time bundled together.
Use of external databases via time-sharing.	Limited.	Major.
Number of software and processing services.	A few; crude.	Many.
Software development by users.	Limited.	Major (facilitated by packages and user-friendly languages).
Reliance on external contract analysts/programmers.	Very significant.	More significant; full outsourcing is a real alternative.

tioned 1994 report by the Gartner Group on the annual cost of supporting a networked PC came as a shock to many IT customers.

2. Consumer vulnerability to abuse of data by failure to control access, install documentation procedures, and implement data updating and management disciplines.
3. Financial vulnerability of the supplier. If the possibility of failure exists, the consumer's fundamental interests need to be protected through identifying an appropriate exit path.
4. Obsolescence of products. If the supplier is not likely to keep the products modernized (at some suitable cost) for the consumer over the years, alternatives (if modern products are important) should be available. (Obviously, a financial-transaction processing system may be more vulnerable to obsolescence than a decision support model.)

The IT business must employ considerable marketing efforts and adjust its internal perspectives if its consumers are to feel they can rely on staff to evaluate alternate channels objectively—instead of pushing their own manufacturing facility at every opportunity. A long-term flexible solution will develop knowledgeable and supportive consumers. Failure to think through and execute these issues will ultimately cripple the IT business's effectiveness in servicing its customers' needs. The results will be fragmentation of data needed by many consumers, redundant development efforts, and an increase in poorly conceived and managed local factories.

Competition

The IT marketing-mix analogy is weakest in describing administrative practice and problems in the area of competition. The IT business faces two principal competitive obstacles:

1. Potential consumers independently seeking solutions without engaging the IT business in either its manufacturing or its distribution capacity.
2. Potential consumers failing to recognize they have problems or opportunities that IT can address.

In the first case, competition arises because of the IT business' poor performance. An inability to formulate and implement sensible, useful guidelines to assist consumers in their purchase decisions represents IT's failure to adapt its product line to meet the needs of the changing times. For the broad purposes of the firm, it may be useful to run this aspect of the IT business as a loss leader. Loss of manufacturing business to other channels in a planned or managed way should not be seen as a competitive loss to the IT business, but simply as a restructuring of its product line to meet changing consumer needs.

With regard to the second case, competition—really the cost of delayed market opportunity—arises as a result of ineffective management of price, product, or distribution policies; the result is consumers, in an imperfect market, allocating funds to projects that may have less payoff than IT products. The IT business has a monopoly responsibility: sometimes it produces a product; other times it stimulates consumer awareness of appropriate external sources of supply. The notion of aggressive external competition hurting the IT business through pricing, product innovation, and creative distribution is not appropriate.

Promotion

The rapid changes in information technology and consumer turnover make promotion one of the most important elements of the marketing mix to manage: unlike the previously discussed elements, promotion is largely within the control of IT management. Phase 2 learning by consumers is at the core of a successful IT business; thus, even as today's consumers take delivery of mature technologies, tomorrow's consumers must be cultivated by exposing them to tomorrow's products. Price discounts (introductory offers), branch offices (decentralized analysts), and a central IT sales force are key to making this happen.

A multinational electronics company, for example, has a 400-person central IT manufacturing facility near its corporate headquarters. Included in this staff are five international marketing representatives who constantly promote new IT products and services. They prepare promotional material, organize educational seminars, and frequently visit overseas units to build and maintain close professional relationships with IT consumers. These relationships permit them to effectively disseminate services and to acquire insight into the performance of the existing products and the need for new ones. This level of effort is regarded as absolutely essential to the IT business.

In large part, the need to adapt is due to the recent shift in the industry. From the industry's beginning to the late 1970s, large information systems suppliers sold primarily to IT managers. Most vendors that initially had a strong industrial marketing approach have now added a retail marketing one. Desktop hardware and software suppliers have not only opened retail stores, but they also now sell directly to end users. This has forced the IT business to promote the validity of its guidelines within the firm to protect its firm's users from disasters.

A number of IT businesses have organized both their development and production control activities around market structure, as opposed to manufacturing technology. In other words, rather than having a traditional development group, a programming group, and a maintenance group, they assign development staffs to specific clusters of customers. This structure promotes close, long-term relationships and better understanding and action on operation problems as they arise.

An example of this approach is Air Products and Chemicals' 1991 decision to move, physically and organizationally, nearly 80 percent of their development staff from the IT business into the divisional structure of the firm. This move fundamentally and positively changed the communications environment between consumers and IT specialists.

IT newsletters containing announcements of new services and products—that is, advertising and promotional material—should be sent to key present and potential business consumers regularly. Similarly, the IT business can conduct consumer educational seminars or classes and publicize appropriate external educational programs to assist the marketing effort. Complemented by appropriate sales calls, this can accelerate phase 2 learning.

The ideal mix of these promotional tools varies widely by organizational setting. Just as industrial and consumer companies have very different promotion programs, so also should different IT businesses. The strategic relevance of products to consumers, customer sophistication level, and geographic location are some factors that affect appropriate promotion.

Price

The setting of IT prices—an emotional and rapidly changing process—is a very important element in establishing a businesslike, professional relationship between the IT business and its customers. Aggressive, marketing-oriented pricing policies legitimize the concept of the stand-alone IT business. Issues that influence pricing are discussed here.

Inefficient Market. Establishing rational, competitive criteria is complicated by several factors:

1. Product quality is largely hidden and is very elusive to all but the most sophisticated and meticulous customer. Prices that on the surface appear widely disparate may actually be quite comparable analyzed carefully.
2. Hardware/software vendors differ in their goals, product mixes, and stability. A small vendor trying to buy into a market may offer a very attractive price to defuse questions about its financial viability or to gain what it considers a strategic customer relationship.
3. Vendors may price a service as a by-product of some other necessary business—resulting in a more attractive price than a pricing system that attempts to charge each user a proportionate share of the full cost of the manufacturing operation. This practice explains the bargains available when organizations try to dispose of excess capacity in return for some "financial contribution." Long-term stability should be a concern to the customer. (What if my output became the main product and the other consumer's output the by-product?)
4. Excess-capacity considerations may allow attractive short-term marginal prices (a variant is a bargain entry-level price). Once captured, however, the customer is subjected to significantly higher prices. This pricing practice is particularly prevalent for large, internally developed telecommunications systems.

Introductory Offers. To stimulate phase 2 learning and long-term demand, deep discounts on early business are often appropriate. This can generate access to long-term profits at quite different price or cost structures as volumes build.

Monopoly Issues. Senior management review and regulation of pricing decisions are sometimes needed, given the IT business's de facto monopoly. Highly confidential data and databases needed by multiple users in geographically remote locations exemplify IT products that normally cannot be supplied by providers other than the firm's IT business. The prices of these services should be appropriately regulated to prevent abuses.

"Unbundling." The pricing strategy should incorporate two practices that are not widely used. The first is "unbundling" development, maintenance, operations, and special turnaround requirements into separate packages, each with its own price. Establishing these prices "at arm's length" in advance is critical to maintaining a professional relationship with the customers. The IT business must negotiate the prices with as much care as outside software companies exercise in their negotiations with these customers. This negotiation can be useful in educating users on the true costs of service.

Making prices understandable to the customers is the second desirable practice, which is accomplished by stating prices in *customer* units such as price per number of report pages, per number of customer records, per invoice, and so on, rather than as utilization of such IT resource units as CPU cycles and MIPS. The added risk (if any) of shocking a potential customer with the facts of economic life tends to be more than offset by much better communication between the IT business and the customer.

Profit.   A final pricing issue, which also strains the independent-business analogy, is how much emphasis should be placed on showing a profit. In the short term (in some cases, even for the long term), should an IT business make a profit or even break even in some settings? IT businesses in firms where consumers require significant education and where much phase 1 and 2 experimentation occurs may appropriately run at a deficit for a long time. This issue must be resolved before the pricing policy is established.

Establishing an IT pricing policy is one of the most complex pricing decisions made in industry. An appropriate resolution, critical to a healthy relationship with the IT consumer, weaves a course between monopolistic and genuine competitive issues, deals with imperfect markets, and resolves ambiguities concerning the role of profits.

THE ROLE OF THE BOARD OF DIRECTORS

The appropriate relationship of the firm's general management to the IT business, a topic first raised in Chapter 1, can be usefully compared to the role of a board of directors in any business. (Many firms give this de facto recognition by creating an executive steering committee.) Viewed this way, the key tasks of general management can be summarized as follows:

1. Appoint and continually assess the performance of the IT chief executive officer (normally a function of the nominating committee).
2. Assure that appropriate standards are in place and being adhered to. This includes receiving and reviewing detailed reports on the subject from the IT auditor and a more cursory review by the firm's external auditors (normally a function of the audit committee).
3. Ensure that the board is constructed to provide overall guidance to the IT business from its various constituencies. Unlike the board of a publicly held firm, the IT board does not need a representation of lawyers, bankers, investment bankers, and so forth. However, it does need senior user managers who can and are willing to provide user perspective. (As the strategic importance of the IT business to the firm decreases, the level of these managers should also decrease.) At the same

time, people from R&D and technology planning and production (people who have IT development and operations backgrounds) need to be present to ensure that suggestions are feasible.

4. Provide broad guidance for the strategic direction of the IT business, ensuring that comprehensive planning processes within the IT business are present and that the outputs of the planning processes fit the firm's strategic direction. In practice, the board will carry out this surveillance through a combination of:

   a. IT management presentations on market development, product planning, and financial plans.
   b. Review of summary documentation of overall direction.
   c. Formal and informal briefings by selected board members on how the IT business is supporting the firm's business needs.
   d. Request for and receipt of internal and external reviews of these issues as appropriate.

The above description of the board's role addresses the realities of the members' backgrounds and available time for this kind of work. Focusing on operational or technical detail is unlikely to be suitable or effective. In many settings, periodic (every one to two years) education sessions for the board members have been useful for making them more comfortable in their responsibilities and for bringing them up-to-date on trends within the particular IT business and the IT industry in general.

THE ROLE OF THE IT CHIEF EXECUTIVE OFFICER

Historically a high-turnover job, the IT chief executive position is difficult and demanding, requiring a steadily shifting mix of skills over time. It is critical that the IT CEO:

1. Maintain board relationships personally. This includes keeping the board appropriately informed about major policy issues and problems and being fully responsive to their needs and concerns. A strong link between the board and the customers, not present in many other settings, is critical.
2. Ensure that the strategy-formulation process evolves adequately and that appropriate detailed action programs are developed. As in any high-technology business, high-quality technical review of potential new technologies and new channels of distribution is absolutely essential. Its interpretation is crucial and may well lead to major changes in organization, product mix, and marketing strategy. Without aggressive CEO leadership, the forces of cultural inertia may cause the IT business to delay far too long, with the parent firm's general management eventually taking corrective initiatives as a result.

3. Pay close attention to salary, personnel practices, and employee quality-of-life issues. In many firms, the IT workforce is far more mobile and difficult to replace than many of the firm's other employees.

4. Give high priority to manufacturing security, which is more important in an IT business than in many other businesses. A single disgruntled employee can do a vast amount of damage that may go undetected for a long time. Similarly, an external hacker can reach across the switched network and do damage to the firm's files.

5. Assure an appropriate management balance between the marketing, manufacturing, and control parts of the IT business. Of the three, marketing—in its broadest sense—is the one most often neglected. CEOs who have begun their careers in manufacturing and dealt with operating difficulties tend to be most sensitive to manufacturing issues. However, since their manufacturing experience was at a particular time with a particular mix of technology assimilation problems and a particular set of control responses, even their perspectives in these areas may not be very appropriate for today's manufacturing challenges.

6. Develop an IT esprit de corps. A key factor of success in the IT business is the belief in IT's value to the firm. Senior IT managers must develop team spirit and lead their organizations into new ventures with enthusiasm. At the same time, they must earn the confidence of the board by exhibiting good judgment—not only taking risks, but also making wise decisions on how to limit the market and when to forgo a useful technology. They must balance keeping abreast by accurately reading the market's receptiveness.

SUMMARY

This chapter has discussed several important complicating aspects of the IT business. Complex and shifting products, changing customers, new channels of distribution, and evolving cost structures have forced a major reanalysis and redirection of IT's product offerings and marketing efforts. The changed marketing environment has forced significant changes in IT manufacturing, organization, control systems, and, most fundamentally, in its perception of its strategic mission.

Ted Levitt's classic article, "Marketing Myopia,"[2] best captures this idea. Levitt noted that the great growth industry of the 19th century—the railroads—languished because the owners and managers saw themselves in the railroad business, rather than the *transportation* business. Similarly, IT is not in the electronic-based computer, telecommunications, and desktop support business. Rather, it is in *the business of bringing a sustained*

---

[2]Theodore Levitt, "Marketing Myopia," *Harvard Business Review,* September–October 1975.

*relevant stream of innovation in information technology to companies'
operations* and, in many cases, *products*. Far too many people in the IT
business myopically believe they are running a computer center! Failure to
perceive and act on their broader role can lead to a collapse of their
operations, loss of jobs, and great disservice to the customer base.

When IT is defined in this way, the dynamic, successful marketing mix for
the 1990s suddenly snaps into focus. To rely on an existing product
structure and attempt to devise more efficient ways to deliver the old
technology within old organizational structures or even new technologies
within the old organizational structure will certainly lead to dissolution of
the IT business. The IT organization has been an agent of change for its
customers for 30 years. The change agent itself also must change if it is to
remain relevant.

ANNOTATED BIBLIOGRAPHY
GENERAL MANAGEMENT LIBRARY
FOR THE IT MANAGER

Ackoff, Russell L. *Creating the Corporate Future: Plan or Be Planned For.* New York: John Wiley & Sons, 1981. An important book that provides a broad context for IT planning.

Anthony, Robert N. *The Management Control Function.* Boston: Harvard Business School Press, 1988. This book introduces the framework of operational control, management control, and strategic planning and has been a major contributor to thinking about the different areas of IT application and their different management problems.

Argyris, Chris. *On Organizational Learning.* Cambridge, MA: Blackwell Business, 1993. How to achieve organizational effectiveness by managing through improved communication processes.

Badaracco, Joseph L., Jr. *The Knowledge Link.* Boston: Harvard Business School Press, 1991. How firms cooperate to exchange information to capitalize on each other's knowledge.

Barabba, Vincent P., and Gerald Zaltman. *Hearing the Voice of the Market.* Boston: Harvard Business School Press, 1991. How to develop an inquisitive market program that develops competence in utilizing information.

Bartlett, Christopher A., and Sumantra Ghoshal. *Managing across Borders: The Transnational Solution.* Boston: Harvard Business School Press, 1991. A succinct and mind-expanding discussion of the impact, true costs, and strategic value of computer systems and their notable future influence.

Bower, Joseph L. *Managing the Resource Allocation Process: A Study of Corporate Planning and Investment.* Boston: Division of Research, Harvard Business School Classics, 1986. This in-depth analysis of corporate planning and capital budgeting provides critical insights relevant to both the role of steering committees and how IT planning can be done effectively.

Bower, Joseph L.; C. A. Bartlett; H. Unterhoven; and R. E. Walton. *Managing Strategic Processes.* Irwin, 1995. A comprehensive review of the essentials of creating and implementing a global strategy.

Burgleman, Robert A., and Modesto A. Maidique. *Strategic Management of Technology & Innovation, 1992.* An effective lens in establishing an overall view of managing technology for the long run.

Buzzell, Robert D., ed. *Marketing in an Electronic Age.* Boston: Harvard Business School Press, 1985. A series of essays on how information technology will impact the marketing function.

Cash, James I., Jr.; Robert G. Eccles; Nitin Nohria. *Building the Information-Age Organization: Structure, Control, and Information Technologies,* 3rd ed. Harvard University Graduate School of Business Administration, The Irwin Case Book Series in Information Systems Management, July 1993. A case-oriented text that provides an integrated approach to understanding the management implications of the trade-offs between IT systems and the organization, and approaches to exploiting the potential of the technology.

Champy, James, and Michael Hammer. *Reengineering the Corporation.* New York: Harper Collins, 1993. This book discusses the practical barriers and problems to achieving reengineering successes.

Chandler, Alfred D. Jr. *Scale and Scope: The Dynamics of Industrial Capitalism.* Cambridge, MA: The Belknap Press of Harvard University Press, 1990. The synthesis of a lifetime of work in articulating how management, structure, strategy, and industry evolve.

Clark, Kim B., and Takahiro Fujimoto. *Product Development Performance.* Boston: Harvard Business School Press, 1991. A descriptive analysis of European, Japanese, and U.S. automobile manufacturing to demonstrate the salient aspects of quality and timely manufacturing management.

Foulkes, Fred K. *Executive Compensation.* Boston: Harvard Business School Press, 1991. Thirty leading compensation consultants advise on effective programs.

Graham, Pauline. *Mary Parker Follett: Prophet of Management: A Celebration of Writings from the 1920s.* Boston: Harvard Business School Press, 1994. A reprint of a management classic that provides real perspective on the beginning of systematic analysis of the management process.

Hamel, Gary, and C. K. Prahalad. *Competing for the Future.* Boston: Harvard Business School Press, 1994. How to develop core competencies to implement a future oriented strategy.

Heskett, James L. *Managing in the Service Economy.* Boston: Harvard Business School Press, 1986. Practical advice on the issues in managing a service organization. Much of this advice translates directly to the IT resource.

Itami, Hiroyuki, with Thomas W. Roehl. *Mobilizing Invisible Assets.* Cambridge, MA: Harvard University Press, 1987. A description of how the Japanese organization brings experience and analysis to bear in developing and implementing strategy.

Kaplan, Robert S. *Measures for Manufacturing Excellence.* Boston: Harvard Business School Press, 1990. A selection of articles on control systems for manufacturing.

Kimberly Miles and Associates. *The Organizational Life Cycle.* San Francisco: Jossey-Bass, 1981. Reports, findings, and analyses of key issues concerning the creation, transformation, and decline of organizations.

Lawrence, Paul R., and Jay W. Lorsch. *Organization and Environment: Managing Integration and Differentiation.* Boston: Harvard Business School Classics, 1986. This classic presents the underlying thinking of the need for specialized departments and how they should interface with the rest of the organization. It is relevant for all IT organizational decisions.

Lax, David A., and James K. Sebenius. *The Manager as Negotiator: Bargaining for Cooperation and Competitive Gain.* New York: Free Press, 1986. A thoughtful set of insights on the issues and means of negotiation.

McKenney, James L. *Waves of Change: Business Evolution through Information Technology.* Boston: Harvard Business School Press, 1995. This book captures the long-term dynamics of an evolving information architecture as it traces more than 30 years of the history of information technology in four organizations.

Merchant, Kenneth A. *Control in Business Organizations.* Marshfield, MA: Pitman Publishing, 1986. An excellent framework for thinking about contemporary management control issues.

Nohria, Nitin, and Robert G. Eccles. *Network and Organizations: Structure, Form, and Action.* Boston: Harvard Business School Press, 1992. A comprehensive set of 19 papers from a conference on how present theoretical concepts can help influence the functioning of networks to better shape structure and influence actions.

Nolan, Richard L., and David C. Croson. *Creative Destruction: A Six-Step Process for Transforming the Organization.* Boston: Harvard Business School Press, 1995. This book analyzes the very different organization structures that are made possible by new information technology and the problems involved in implementing these structures.

Porter, Michael E., ed. *Competition in Global Industries.* Boston: Harvard Business School Press, 1986. A series of articles relating to competitive issues in the international environment.

Revolution in Real Time: Managing Information Technology in the 1990s, Boston: Harvard Business School Publications, 1991, The *Harvard Business Review Book Series.* A compendium of 17 recent *Harvard Business Review* articles on the art and science of designing, implementing, and managing the evolution of information technology as a competitive means.

Rosenberg, Nathan. *Inside the Black Box: Technology, Economics and History.* Cambridge University Press, 1982. A useful conceptual analysis of technological change as the driver in economic shifts. Frames the issues within the Schumpeterian model to substantiate the shifts and nature of activities in technology that change the competitive basis of industries.

Schein, Edgar H. *Organizational Psychology,* 3rd ed. Englewood Cliffs, NJ: Prentice Hall, 1980. This classic book focuses on how to manage the tension between the individual and the organization.

Simons, Robert. *Levers of Control.* Boston: Harvard Business School Press, 1995. This book provides a refreshing and new way to think about management control.

Smith, H. Jeff. *Managing Privacy Information Technology and Corporate America.* North Carolina: University of North Carolina Press, 1994. This is a very practical book that talks about information technology privacy, current practices, and issues for the future.

Treacy, Michael, and Fred Wiersema. *Disciplines of Market Leaders: Choose Your Customers, Narrow Your Focus, Dominate Your Market.* Reading, MA: Addison-Wesley Publishing Co., 1994. This book presents a view of what needs to be done for firms to be successful in the market.

Utterback, James. *Mastering the Dynamics of Innovation: How Companies Can Seize Opportunities in the Face of Technological Change.* Boston: Harvard Business School Press, 1994. An analysis of the forces to manage in developing new products and processes as a strategic force.

Wheelwright, Steven C., and Kim B. Clark. *Leading Product Development.* New York: Free Press, 1995. A focused view on senior management's role in shaping strategy based on continuous product development as a competitive means. Time from concept to market is the critical success factor.

Yates, Joanne. *Control through Communication: The Rise of System in American Management.* Baltimore, MD: Johns Hopkins University Press, 1993. Traces the evolution of internal communication systems through the late 19th century into the 20th century through a focus on innovative companies such as DuPont.

IT LIBRARY FOR THE GENERAL MANAGER

Anderla, Georges, and Anthony Dunning. *Computer Strategies: 1990–1999: Technologies, Costs, Markets.* New York: John Wiley & Sons, 1987. A description of the Japanese chip-maker strategy and the economic implications of chip development, and the true "costs" of computing in the 1990s.

Bradley, Stephen P., and Jerry A. Hausman, eds. *Future Competition in Telecommunications.* Boston: Harvard Business School Press, 1989. A symposium of industry suppliers, customers, and regulators discussing the future impacts of deregulation.

Bradley, Stephen P.; Jerry A. Hausman; and Richard L. Nolan. *Globalization, Technology, and Competition: The Fusion of Computers and Telecommunications in the 1990s.* Boston: Harvard Business School Press, 1993. This book is a series of essays on how the new telecommunications technologies change the patterns of global business competition.

Forcht, Karen A. *Computer Security Management.* Danvers, MA: Boyd & Fraser Publishing Company, 1994. This is a practical book that describes the multiple aspects of computer security and the steps to be taken to gain good results.

Keen, Peter G. W. *Every Manager's Guide to Information Technology.* Boston: Harvard Business School Press, 1991. A glossary of key terms and concepts of computer and planning procedures.

Keen, Peter G. W. *Shaping the Future: Business Design through Information Technology.* Boston: Harvard Business School Press, 1991. A succinct and mind-expanding discussion of the impact, true costs, and strategic value of computer systems and their notable future influence.

Leebaert, Derek, ed. *Technology 2001: The Future of Computing and Communications.* Cambridge, MIT Press, 1991. A set of articles by research scientists from every major player in the business (e.g., IBM, DEC, Cray, Apple, etc). A sound view of the future.

Rochester, Jack B., and John Gantz. *The Naked Computer.* New York: William Morrow and Company, Inc., 1983. An interesting and broad compendium of computer lore that has shaped the myths and realities of developing and using computer systems.

Walton, Richard E. *Up and Running: Integrating Information Technology and the Organization.* Boston: Harvard Business School Press, 1989. A thoughtful perspective on how to develop and maintain congruence between the organization and systems in the implementation of an IT-based strategy by a leading organizational scholar/consultant.

Whinston, Patrick H. *Artificial Intelligence,* 3rd ed. Reading, MA: Addison-Wesley, 1992. A comprehensive review of the essentials of artificial intelligence and examples of useful implementations.

Zuboff, Shoshana. *In the Age of the Smart Machine.* New York: Basic Books, 1988. An insightful integration of the dual nature of the influence of computer-based systems on work.

Index